W9-BSS-875

The Double Eagle Guide to

CAMPING *in*

WESTERN

PARKS *and* FORESTS

VOLUME II
ROCKY MOUNTAINS

COLORADO
MONTANA
WYOMING

A **DOUBLE EAGLE GUIDE**™

DISCOVERY PUBLISHING
BILLINGS, YELLOWSTONE COUNTY, MONTANA USA

The Double Eagle Guide to Camping in Western Parks and Forests
Volume II Rocky Mountains

PUBLISHED BY
Discovery Publishing
Editorial Offices
Post Office Box 50545
Billings, Montana 59105 USA

Discovery Publishing is an independent, private enterprise. The information contained herein should not be construed as reflecting the publisher's approval of the policies or practices of the public agencies listed.

Information in this book is subject to change without notice.

Cover Photos (clockwise from the top)
Humboldt National Forest, Nevada
Lake Owyhee State Park, Oregon
Memphis Lake State Recreation Area, Nebraska
Big Bend National Park, Texas

Frontispiece: Glacier National Park, Montana

10 9 8 7 6 5 4 3 2 1

August 4, 1994   2:36 PM Mountain Time

Produced, printed, and bound in the United States of America.

ISBN 0-929760-22-0

TABLE OF CONTENTS

(Continued on the following page)

INTRODUCTION TO THE *Double Eagle*™ SERIES

Whether you're a veteran of many Western camps or are planning your first visit, this series is for you.

In the six volumes of *The Double Eagle Guide to Camping in Western Parks and Forests*, we've described most public campgrounds along or conveniently near the highways and byways of the 17 contiguous Western United States. Also included is basic information about jackcamping and backpacking on the millions of acres of undeveloped public lands in the West. Our goal is to provide you with accurate, detailed, and yet concise, *first-hand* information about literally thousands of camping areas you're most likely to want to know about.

The volumes which comprise the *Double Eagle*™ series constitute a significant departure from the sketchy, plain vanilla approach to campground information provided by other guidebooks. Here, for the first time, is the most *useful* information about the West's most *useable* public camping areas. We've included a broad assortment of campgrounds from which you can choose: From simple, free camps, to sites in deluxe, landscaped surroundings.

The name for this critically acclaimed series was suggested by the celebrated United States twenty-dollar gold piece--most often called the "*Double Eagle*"--the largest and finest denomination of coinage ever issued by the U.S. Mint. The *Double Eagle* has long been associated with the history of the West, as a symbol of traditional Western values, prosperity, and excellence.

So, too, the *Double Eagle*™ series seeks to provide you with information about what are perhaps the finest of all the West's treasures--its public recreational lands owned, operated, and overseen by the citizens of the Western United States.

We hope you'll enjoy reading these pages, and come to use the information in the volumes to enhance your own appreciation for the outstanding camping opportunities available in the West.

Live long and prosper.

Thomas and *Elizabeth Preston*
Publishers

CONVENTIONS USED IN THIS SERIES

The following conventions or standards are used throughout the *Double Eagle*™ series as a means of providing a sense of continuity between one park or forest and other public lands, and between one campground and the next.

State Identifier: The state name and number combination in the upper left corner of each campground description provides an easy means of cross-referencing the written information to the numbered locations on the maps in the Appendix.

Whenever possible, the campgrounds have been arranged in what we have determined to be a reasonable progression, and based on *typical travel patterns* within a region. Generally speaking, a north to south, west to east pattern has been followed. In certain cases, particularly those involving one-way-in, same-way-out roads, we have arranged the camps in the order in which they would be encountered on the way into the area, so the standard plan occasionally may be reversed.

Campground Name: The officially designated name for the campground is listed, followed by the park, forest, or other public recreation area in which it is located.

Location: This section allows you to obtain a quick approximation of a campground's location in relation to nearby major communities.

Access: Our *Accurate Access* system makes extensive use of highway mileposts in order to pinpoint the location of access roads, intersections, and other major terminal points. (Mileposts are about 98 percent reliable--but occasionally they are mowed by a snowplow or an errant motorist, and may be missing; or, worse yet, the mileposts were replaced in the wrong spot!) In some instances, locations are noted primarily utilizing mileages between two or more nearby locations--usually communities, but occasionally key junctions or prominent structures or landmarks.

Since everyone won't be approaching a campground from the same direction, we've provided access information from two, sometimes three, points. In all cases, we've chosen the access points for their likelihood of use. Distances from communities are listed from the approximate **midtown** point, unless otherwise specified. Mileages from Interstate highways and other freeway exits are usually given from the approximate center of the interchange. Mileages from access points have been rounded to the nearest mile, unless the exact mileage is critical. All instructions are given using the current official highway map available free from each state.

Directions are given using a combination of compass and hand headings, i.e., "turn north (left)" or "swing west (right)". This isn't a bonehead navigation system, by any means. When the sun is shining or you're in a region where moss grows on tree trunks, it's easy enough to figure out which way is north. But anyone can become temporarily disoriented on an overcast day or a moonless night while looking for an inconspicuous campground turnoff, or while being buzzed by heavy traffic at a key intersection, so we built this redundancy into the system.

Facilities: The items in this section have been listed in the approximate order in which a visitor might observe them during a typical swing through a campground. Following the total number of individual camp units, items pertinent to the campsites themselves are listed, then information related to 'community' facilities. It has been assumed that each campsite has a picnic table.

Site types: (1) Standard--no hookup; (2) Partial hookup--water, electricity; (3) Full hookup--water, electricity, sewer.

We have extensively employed the use of *general* and *relative* terms in describing the size, separation, and levelness of the campsites ("medium to large", "fairly well separated", "basically level", etc.). Please note that "separation" is a measure of relative privacy and is a composite of both natural visual screens and spacing between campsites. The information is presented as an *estimate* by highly experienced observers. Please allow for variations in perception between yourself and the reporters.

Parking Pads: (1) Straight-ins, (sometimes called "back-ins")-- the most common type, are just that--straight strips angled off the driveway; (2) Pull-throughs--usually the most convenient type for large rv's, they provide an in-one-end-and-out-the-other parking space; pull-throughs may be either arc-shaped and separated from the main driveway by some sort of barrier or 'island' (usually vegetation), or arranged in parallel rows; (3) Pull-offs--essentially just wide spots adjacent to the driveway. Pad lengths have been categorized as: (1) Short-- a single, large vehicle up to about the size of a standard pickup truck; (2) Medium--a single vehicle or combination up to the length of a pickup towing a single-axle trailer; Long--a single vehicle or combo as long as a crew cab pickup towing a double-axle trailer. Normally, any overhang out the back of the pad has been ignored in the estimate, so it might be possible to slip a crew cab pickup hauling a fifth-wheel trailer in tandem with a ski boat into some pads, but we'll leave that to your discretion.

Fire appliances have been categorized in three basic forms: (1) Fireplaces--angular, steel or concrete, ground-level; (2) Fire rings--circular, steel or concrete, ground-level or below ground-level; (3) Barbecue grills--angular steel box, supported by a steel post about 36 inches high. (The trend is toward installing steel fire rings, since they're durable, relatively inexpensive--50 to 80 dollars apiece--and easy to install and maintain. Barbecue grills are often used in areas where ground fires are a problem, as when charcoal-only fires are permitted.)

Toilet facilities have been listed thusly: (1) Restrooms--"modern", i.e., flush toilets and usually a wash basin; (2) Vault facilities--"simple", i.e., outhouses, pit toilets, call them what you like, (a rose by any other name.....).

Campers' supply points have been described at five levels: (1) Camper Supplies--buns, beans and beverages; (2) Gas and Groceries--a 'convenience' stop; (3) Limited--at least one store which approximates a small supermarket, more than one fuel station, a general merchandise store, hardware store, and other basic services; (4) Adequate--more than one supermarket, (including something that resembles an IGA or a Safeway), a choice of fuel brands, and several general and specialty stores and services; (5) Complete--they have a major discount store.

Campground managers, attendants and hosts are not specifically listed since their presence can be expected during the regular camping season in more than 85 percent of the campgrounds listed in this volume.

Activities & Attractions: As is mentioned a number of times throughout this series, the local scenery may be the principal attraction of the campground (and, indeed, may be the *only* one you'll need). Other nearby attractions/activities have been listed if they are low-cost or free, and are available to the general public. An important item: *Swimming and boating areas usually do not have lifeguards.*

Natural Features: Here we've drawn a word picture of the natural environment in and around each campground. Please remember that seasonal, even daily, conditions will affect the appearance of the area. A normally "sparkling stream" can be a muddy torrent for a couple of weeks in late spring; a "deep blue lake" might be a nearly empty hole in a drought year; "lush vegetation" may have lost all its greenery by the time you arrive in late October. Elevations above 500' are rounded to the nearest 100'; lower elevations are rounded to the nearest 50'. (Some elevations are estimated, but no one should develop a nosebleed or a headache because of a 100' difference in altitude.)

Season, Fees & Phone: Seasons listed are approximate, since weather conditions, particularly in mountainous/hilly regions, may require adjustments in opening/closing dates. Campground gates are usually unlocked from 6:00 a.m. to 10:00 p.m. Fee information listed here was obtained directly from the responsible agencies just a few hours before press time. Fees should be considered **minimum** fees *per camping vehicle*, since they are always subject to adjustment by agencies or legislatures. Discounts and special passes are usually available for seniors and disabled persons. The listed telephone number can be called to obtain information about current conditions in or near that campground.

Camp Notes: Consider this section to be somewhat more subjective in nature than the others. In order to provide our readers with a well-rounded report, we have listed personal comments related to our field observations. (Our enthusiasm for the West is, at times, unabashedly proclaimed. So if the prose sometimes sounds like a tourist promotion booklet, please bear with us--there's a lot to be enthusiastic about!)

Editorial remarks (Ed.) occasionally have been included.

A Word About Style...

Throughout the *Double Eagle*™ series, we've utilized a free-form writing concept which we call "Notation Format". Complete sentences, phrases, and single words have been incorporated into the camp descriptions as appropriate under the circumstances. We've adopted this style in order to provide our readers with detailed information about each item, while maintaining conciseness, clarity, and conversationality.

A Word About Print...

Another departure from the norm is our use of print sizes which are 10 to 20 percent larger (or more) than ordinary guides. (We also use narrower margins for less paper waste.) It's one thing to read a guidebook in the convenience and comfort of your well-lit living room. It's another matter to peruse the pages while you're bounding and bouncing along in your car or camper as the sun is setting; or by a flickering flashlight inside a breeze-buffeted dome tent. We hope *this* works for you, too.

A Word About Maps...

After extensive tests of the state maps by seasoned campers, both at home and in the field, we decided to localize all of the maps in one place in the book. Campers felt that, since pages must be flipped regardless of where the maps are located, it would be more desirable to have them all in one place. We're confident that you'll also find this to be a convenient feature.

A Word About 'Regs'...

Although this series is about public campgrounds, you'll find comparatively few mentions of rules, regulations, policies, ordinances, statutes, decrees or dictates. Our editorial policy is this: (1) It's the duty of a citizen or a visitor to know his legal responsibilities (and, of course, his corresponding *rights*); (2) Virtually every campground has the appropriate regulations publicly posted for all to study; and (3) If you're reading this *Double Eagle*™ Guide, chances are you're in the upper ten percent of the conscientious citizens of the United States or some other civilized country and you probably don't need to be constantly reminded of these matters.

And a Final Word...

We've tried very, very hard to provide you with accurate information about the West's great camping opportunities But occasionally, things aren't as they're supposed to be .....

If a campground's access, facilities or fees have been recently changed, please let us know. We'll try to pass along the news to other campers.

If the persons in the next campsite keep their generator poppety-popping past midnight so they can cook a turkey in the microwave, blame the bozos, not the book.

If the beasties are a bit bothersome in that beautiful spot down by the bog, note the day's delights and not the difficulties.

Thank you for buying our book. We hope that you'll have many terrific camping trips!

Colorado

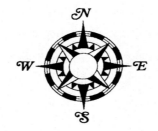

Public Campgrounds

The Colorado map is located in the Appendix on page 197.

Colorado
West
Please refer to the Colorado map in the Appendix

Colorado 1

RIFLE GAP
Rifle Gap State Recreation Area

Location: Western Colorado north of Rifle.

Access: From the junction of Colorado State Highways 13 & 325 (at milepost 4 +.1 on Highway 13, 4 miles north of Rifle, 37 miles south of Meeker), head north and northeast on Highway 325, across Rifle Gap Dam and around to the east side of the reservoir, to milepost 5 +.8; turn west (left) onto a gravel park road and proceed 0.1 mile to the park entrance station; continue past the entrance for 0.5 mile to 1.3 miles to the *Cottonwood*, *Cedar*, *Piñon* and *Sage Flats* camp areas; (listed below in order of closest to farthest from the entrance.)

Facilities: *Cottonwood*: 12 campsites with short to medium-length straight-in or long pull-through parking pads; *Cedar*: 10 campsites with mostly medium to long straight-ins pads; *Piñon*: 5 campsites with medium-length straight-ins; *Sage Flats*: 11 campsites with long, pull-off pads and small ramadas; *all areas*: medium to large areas for tents; fire rings or barbecue grills; b-y-o firewood; water at central faucets; vault facilities; gravel driveways; holding tank disposal station near Cottonwood; adequate supplies and services are available in Rifle.

Activities & Attractions: Boating; large boat launch; fishing; designated swimming area; day use areas.

Natural Features: Located along the shore and on a sage-covered hillside on the north side of Rifle Gap Reservoir, an impoundment on Rifle Creek; some scattered hardwoods and evergreens grow around the reservoir, but otherwise the terrain is quite open; elevation 6000'.

Season, Fees & Phone: Open all year; principal season is April to November, with limited services in winter; please see Appendix for reservation information and standard Colorado state park fees; park office (303) 625-1607.

Camp Notes: Cottonwood is named for a few large specimens of that species that shade the shore. Otherwise, big sage provides the shelter for most campsites in all four camp loops. However, there are quite a few evergreens (piñon pines and junipers/cedars) on the slope above the camps. Each area has its strong points in terms of levelness, vegetation and proximity to the water's edge.

Colorado 2

RIFLE FALLS
Rifle Falls State Park

Location: Western Colorado north of Rifle.

Access: From the junction of Colorado State Highways 13 & 325 (at milepost 4 +.1 on Highway 13, 4 miles north of Rifle, 37 miles south of Meeker), turn northeast onto Colorado State Highway 325; travel northeast on Highway 325 (across Rifle Gap Dam, around the east side of the reservoir and past Rifle Gap SRA) for a total of 10 miles to the campground.

Facilities: 16 campsites in 2 sections; 11 sites are located in a standard arrangement at the north end of the campground; standard units are medium-sized, basically level, with a mixture of straight-in and pull-through parking pads; medium to large, grassy tent areas; the remaining 7 campsites are walk-in units located along the Squirrel Trail at the south end of the campground; fire rings; b-y-o firewood; water at central faucets; vault facilities; gravel driveway; nearest supplies and services (adequate) are in Rifle.

Activities & Attractions: Rifle Falls; 2 miles of hiking and nature trails; fishing for rainbow and brown trout; day use area.

Natural Features: Located on a flat along East Rifle Creek in a red rock box canyon; standard campsites are in an open section surrounded by hardwoods; the walk-in sites are situated among the trees next to, or within a stone's throw of, the creek; bordered by forested hills and mountains; elevation 6600'.

Season, Fees & Phone: Open all year, with limited services November to April; 14 day limit; please see Appendix for reservation information and standard Colorado state park fees; park office (303) 625-1607.

Camp Notes: This little park, tucked away up in the hills, is a really neat spot. Be advised, though, that it is also a very *popular* spot. Try to arrange to camp here on a weekday in the off-season, if at all possible. September and October are terrific times.

Colorado 3

HIGHLINE
Highline State Recreation Area

Location: Western Colorado west of Grand Junction.

Access: From Colorado State Highway 139 a few yards north of milepost 5 (5 miles north of Interstate 70 Exit 15 for Loma/Rangely west of Grand Junction), turn west onto Q Road, and proceed 1.3 miles to 11.8 Road; turn north onto 11.8 Road, and continue for 1 mile to the park entrance, then west for a final 0.2 mile to the campground.

Facilities: 25 campsites; sites are medium to large, level, with nominal separation; parking pads are gravel, medium to long, pull-offs or pull-throughs; large, grassy tent areas; barbecue grills; b-y-o firewood; water at faucets throughout; restrooms in the day use area; holding tank disposal station; gravel driveway; gas and groceries in Loma, 2 miles south, and at a truck stop at the Interstate; complete supplies and services are available in Grand Junction, 14 miles east, off Interstate 70 Exit 15.

Activities & Attractions: Designated swimming area on Highline Lake; boating and boat launches on Highline Lake; limited boating (manual or electric power) on Mack Mesa Lake; fishing for crappie and catfish on Highline Lake; trout fishing (early in the season) on Mack Mesa Lake; day use area.

Natural Features: Located on the shore of Highline Lake, a dry-rimmed reservoir in the semi-arid reclaimed land of the Grand Valley of the Colorado River; tall hardwoods and evergreens on a surface of watered, mown grass provide a light to moderate amount of shelter/shade in the campground; small Mack Mesa Lake (a large pond) lies just northwest of the main lake; dry, rugged mountains rise to the north, high mesas lie to the south; elevation 4700'.

Season, Fees & Phone: Open all year, with limited services November to April; 14 day limit; please see Appendix for reservation information and standard Colorado state park fees; park office (303) 858-7208.

Camp Notes: The campground's landscaping stands in distinct contrast to the surrounding countryside. This is one of only a half-dozen green and wet overnight stops within a few miles of I-70 in Colorado or Utah.

Colorado 4

SADDLEHORN
Colorado National Monument

Location: Western Colorado west of Grand Junction.

Access: From Interstate 70 Exit 19 for Fruita (10 miles west of Grand Junction, 19 miles east of the Colorado-Utah border), turn south onto Colorado State Highway 340 and proceed 2.4 miles to the national monument entrance; continue up a narrow, winding, steep road for 4.2 miles to the campground entrance, near the visitor center.

Facilities: 80 campsites in 3 loops; most sites are small to medium in size, with fair separation; parking pads are gravel, pull-offs or pull-throughs in many sites, other sites have straight-ins; a little additional leveling will probably be needed on most pads; some sites have framed tent pads; barbecue grills; charcoal fires only; water at several faucets; restrooms; paved driveways; limited supplies in Fruita; complete supplies and services are available in Grand Junction.

Activities & Attractions: Scenic drives; visitor center; amphitheater for scheduled ranger-naturalist programs.

Natural Features: Located on the north edge of a mesa overlooking the Colorado River Valley; some sites have views of the chimney and spire rock formations of the Monument Canyon area of the national monument; vegetation consists primarily of short juniper and other evergreens; elevation 5700'.

Season, Fees & Phone: Open all year, subject to weather conditions, with limited services October to April; $7.00 for a site, $3.00 for the park entrance fee; 14 day limit; park headquarters (303) 858-3617.

Camp Notes: Incredible! The vast, sweeping, color-packed views from this campground are absolutely astounding. (And in many visitors' opinions, *that's* an understatement.)

ISLAND ACRES
Island Acres State Recreation Area

Location: West-central Colorado east of Grand Junction.

Access: From Interstate 70 Exit 47 (16 miles east of Grand Junction, 43 miles west of Rifle), proceed to the north side of the freeway, then go easterly (right) on a frontage road for 0.5 mile to the park entrance; bear right to the campground.

Facilities: 32 campsites; sites are small+ to medium-sized, quite level, with minimal to nominal separation; parking pads are gravel, long straight-ins; large, grassy tent areas; several units have ramadas (sun/partial wind shelters); fire rings or barbecue grills; b-y-o firewood; water at several faucets; vault facilities; holding tank disposal station; gravel driveway; camper supplies on the south side of the Interstate near the interchange; complete supplies and services are available in Grand Junction.

Activities & Attractions: Fishing; limited boating (no gas motors); x-c skiing; day use area.

Natural Features: Located in a narrow canyon on a large open flat on the bank of the Colorado River; vegetation consists of watered, mown grass dotted by planted hardwoods and evergreens; a buffalo herd is pastured adjacent to the park; typically breezy; elevation 4800'.

Season, Fees & Phone: Principal season is April to November, plus limited availability in winter; 14 day limit; please see Appendix for reservation information and standard Colorado state park fees; park office (303) 464-0548.

Camp Notes: Even though it's not without some disadvantages, Island Acres provides a really convenient stop for Interstate 70 travelers. Some highway noise does reach the campsites; and there's a power plant less than a mile west. The campground seems to have been planned primarily with rv campers in mind, but the tenting opportunities are excellent also.

VEGA
Vega State Recreation Area

Location: Western Colorado northeast of Grand Junction.

Access: From the junction of Colorado State Highways 65 & 330 near the hamlet of Mesa (10 miles east of Interstate 70 Exit 49), cruise easterly on Highway 330 for 11 miles into midtown Collbran and the corner of East High & Main Streets; turn north (left) onto Main Street, go 0.2 mile across a bridge to a "T" intersection, then turn east (right) and continue easterly on a paved county road for 6.5 miles to a fork; angle onto the right fork and keep heading east for another 3.5 miles to the park entrance at the north side of the dam on the northwest corner of the lake; travel clockwise on the lake road (continuing easterly along the north shore from the entrance) around the lake to the following camp areas, all just off the right side of the road (mileages are between camp areas, not cumulative from the entrance): *Vega Cove*, 0.9 mile; *Oak Point*, 1.1 miles; *Aspen Grove*, 3.2 miles; (Note: The road is paved to just beyond Oak Point, then it becomes gravel.)

Facilities: *Vega Cove*: 20 rv campsites; sites are situated around the perimeter of a gravel parking lot, with medium-length, level, straight-in parking slots; no tents; water at a central faucet; *Oak Point*: 40 campsites; sites are smallish, sloped, with nominal separation; parking surfaces are gravel, medium-length pull-offs or straight-ins; medium to large areas for tents; fire rings; b-y-o firewood; water at several faucets; *Aspen Grove*: 40 campsites; sites are small+, essentially level, with very good separation; parking pads are gravel, medium-length straight-ins; medium-sized tent areas; *all areas*: fire rings; b-y-o firewood; vault facilities; gravel driveways; (a group camp is also available at Marmot Flat, south of the dam); gas and groceries+ in Collbran.

Activities & Attractions: Boating; boat launches with docks at Island and Oak Point; windsurfing; fishing for stocked rainbow trout, also some cutthroats, brookies and browns; hiking trails; cross-country skiing; ice fishing.

Natural Features: Located around the shore of Vega Reservoir; Island and Oak Point are situated on the middle-north shore, Aspen Grove is on the southeast shore; campsites are unshaded to lightly shaded by aspens and oaks; surrounded by high, forested mountains; elevation 8000'.

Season, Fees & Phone: Open all year, subject to weather and road conditions, with limited services October to May; 14 day limit; please see Appendix for reservation information and standard Colorado state park fees; park office (303) 487-3407.

Camp Notes: Mountain views from just about anywhere on the lake are very good. Most Vega Cove and Oak Point campsites are out in the open. However, there are several nice sites right along the lake shore at Oak Point. (You could almost catch and cook your fish dinner and never leave your seat at the camp table.) For privacy and shelter, you can't beat the Aspen Grove thicket with its dense, low foliage.

Colorado 7

JUMBO
Grand Mesa National Forest

Location: Western Colorado southeast of Grand Junction.

Access: From Colorado State Highway 65 at milepost 36 +.6 (19 miles south of Interstate 70 Exit 49, 13 miles south of Mesa, 42 miles north of Delta), turn southwesterly (i.e., right if approaching from I-70) onto a paved access road and proceed 0.2 mile to the campground.

Facilities: 23 campsites; sites are medium-sized, with fair to good separation; parking pads are gravel, medium-length straight-ins; some pads may require minor additional leveling; small to medium-sized tent spots, may be a bit sloped; fire rings; firewood is available for gathering in the area; water at several faucets; vault facilities; paved driveways; gas and groceries in Mesa; adequate+ supplies and services are available in Delta.

Activities & Attractions: Boating; trout fishing; hiking; superscenic drive across Grand Mesa on Highway 65.

Natural Features: Located on a forested slope on Grand Mesa between Sunset Lake and Jumbo Reservoir; campground vegetation consists of very tall conifers, aspens, and moderate underbrush; a small creek and a pond are within the campground; most sites are lakeside or have a view of at least one of the lakes; Grand Mesa is an expansive plateau with countless small lakes, fantastic scenery and nearby views of the Colorado River Valley to the north; elevation 9800'.

Season, Fees & Phone: May to September; $6.00; 14 day limit; Collbran Ranger District (303) 487-3249.

Camp Notes: The 9800' altitude at Jumbo Campground makes for a fairly short camping season here. Each spring there is a profusion of wildflowers on the slopes which makes this a really special place to visit.

Colorado 8

SPRUCE GROVE
Grand Mesa National Forest

Location: Western Colorado southeast of Grand Junction.

Access: From Colorado State Highway 65 at milepost 35 +.8 (40 miles north of Delta, 21 miles south of Interstate 70 Exit 49), turn southwesterly (i.e., right if approaching from I-70) onto a gravel access road and proceed 0.1 mile to the campground.

Facilities: 16 campsites; sites are basically medium-sized, level, with good separation; parking pads are gravel, mostly medium length straight-ins, plus some pull-throughs; some sites may be a bit snug for larger tents; barbecue grills; firewood is available for gathering; water at several faucets; vault facilities; gravel driveway; camper supplies at a lodge, 0.7 mile north; gas and groceries in Mesa, 15 miles north; nearest source of complete supplies and services is Delta.

Activities & Attractions: Tremendous views of the lakes, mountains and mesas of the northern Grand Mesa area from highway overlook points just south of the campground; fishing; boating; several hiking trails and four-wheel drive roads lead to numerous small lakes and reservoirs.

Natural Features: Located in a grove of very tall spruce; some low-level underbrush helps provide additional visual separation between sites; steep, timbered hillsides surround the campground; Mesa Lakes are just west of here; elevation 9900'.

Season, Fees & Phone: June to September; $6.00; 14 day limit; Collbran Ranger District (303) 487-3249.

Camp Notes: The name chosen for this campground is certainly appropriate. The mature timber provides most campsites with a substantial amount of shelter.

ISLAND LAKE
Grand Mesa National Forest

Location: Western Colorado north of Delta.

Access: From Colorado State Highway 65 at milepost 27 (31 miles north of Delta, 34 miles south of Interstate 70 Exit 49), turn southwest (i.e., right, if coming from I-70) and proceed 0.9 mile to the campground. (This campground, as well as nearby Little Bear Campground, can also be reached from milepost 28 +.2 on the north side of Island Lake, but the access isn't quite as straightforward as this one.)

Facilities: 42 campsites in 1 large loop; most sites are fairly good-sized and reasonably well separated; parking pads are gravel, medium to long straight-ins, which may require additional leveling; adequate tent space in most sites; fire rings; firewood is available for gathering; water at faucets; restrooms plus auxiliary vaults; gravel driveway; camper supplies at a lodge on the highway on the north side of the lake; limited supplies in Cedaredge, 17 miles south.

Activities & Attractions: Commanding views of the Grand Mesa region and of the great valley to the south; fishing; boating; Crag Crest Trailhead at the northeast corner of Island Lake.

Natural Features: Located near the southwest end of Island Lake, on a partially forested hillside which faces west and south; the lake isn't visible from the campground; about one third of the campsites are in the open, the others are situated among conifers; another small lake is south of the camp area; elevation 10,400'.

Season, Fees & Phone: June to September; $6.00; 14 day limit; Grand Junction Ranger District (303) 242-8211.

Camp Notes: If you don't have to have waterfront property, this might be a good choice. In exchange for a lakeside setting, the campground provides unrestricted panoramas of seemingly hundreds of square miles of varying terrain.

LITTLE BEAR
Grand Mesa National Forest

Location: Western Colorado north of Delta.

Access: From Colorado State Highway 65 at milepost 27 (31 miles north of Delta, 34 miles south of Interstate 70 exit 49), turn southwest (i.e., right, if approaching from I-70) and go 0.6 mile on a gravel road to the campground. (See Camp Notes, below.)

Facilities: 36 campsites in 2 loops; most sites are small to medium-sized, with matching straight-in gravel parking pads and tent spaces; some additional leveling may be needed; fireplaces; firewood is available for gathering; water at several faucets; vault facilities; gravel driveways (the loop driveways are a little snug); camper supplies at a lodge on the highway, 1 mile north; limited supplies in Cedaredge, 17 miles south; gas and groceries in Mesa, 23 miles north.

Activities & Attractions: Fishing; boating; Crag Crest Trailhead at the northeast corner of the Lake.

Natural Features: Located midway along the south shore of Island Lake on a forested bluff; boulder strewn, slightly rolling terrain within the campground; high ridges in the surrounding area; elev. 10,300'.

Season, Fees & Phone: June to September; $6.00; 14 day limit; Grand Junction Ranger District (303) 242-8211.

Camp Notes: Most campsites have a view of Island Lake through the trees. Just a short, easy walk down the hill will get you to the water's edge. Note that the highway meanders considerably as it traverses Grand Mesa, and curves around to the northeast end of Island Lake at this point. Maintaining a sense of direction through here can be slightly difficult, particularly in cloudy weather. It might help to visualize that the long thin lake lies in a northeast-to-southwest line.

CARP LAKE
Grand Mesa National Forest

Location: Western Colorado north of Delta.

Access: From Colorado State Highway 65 at milepost 27, (31 miles north of Delta, 34 miles south of Interstate 70 Exit 49), turn east (i.e., left, if coming from I-70) onto a paved access road; proceed 0.1 mile to the campground.

Facilities: 21 campsites; sites are average or better in size, with fair to good separation; parking pads are gravel, mostly level, medium-length straight-ins; some really nice tent areas, but a few are a bit rocky; fire rings; firewood is available for gathering in the area; water at faucets; vault facilities; paved driveways; camper supplies at a lodge, 1 mile north; limited supplies in Cedaredge, 16 miles south; gas and groceries in Mesa, 23 miles north; adequate+ supplies and services are available in Delta.

Activities & Attractions: Fishing; boating; hiking; Crag Crest Trailhead nearby; great scenic views of the lakes, and, from a short walk away, of the expansive valley to the southwest.

Natural Features: Located on Grand Mesa, on gently rolling forested hills between Carp Lake on the south and a pair of small lakes to the northeast; most sites are within a few yards of one lake or another; campground vegetation varies from grassy, open areas, to tall conifers and light underbrush; elevation 10,300'.

Season, Fees & Phone: June to September; $6.00; 14 day limit; Grand Junction Ranger District (303) 242-8211.

Camp Notes: Because of the high altitude, this campground may not be snow-free until late in June; but it's so close to Highway 65 that, if you're passing by, it's worth a pre-season or post-season hike in, just to put yourself in this really neat setting surrounded by picturesque subalpine lakes.

Colorado 12

WARD LAKE
Grand Mesa National Forest

Location: Western Colorado north of Delta.

Access: From Colorado State Highway 65 at milepost 26 +.9 (31 miles north of Delta, 34 miles south of Interstate 70 Exit 49), turn east (i.e., left, if approaching from I-70) onto a paved access road signed for "Ward Lake Recreation Area"; proceed 0.4 mile east and south on a fairly curvy, steep road; turn southwest (right) into the campground.

Facilities: 13 campsites; sites are medium or better in size, with fair to good separation; parking pads are gravel, medium to long straight-ins; many pads may require additional leveling; some nice, large tent spots, though most are a bit sloped; fire rings; firewood is available for gathering in the area; water at faucets; vault facilities; paved driveways; limited supplies in Cedaredge, 16 miles south; gas and groceries in Mesa, 23 miles north; adequate+ supplies and services are available in Delta.

Activities & Attractions: Fishing; boating; hiking; Crag Crest Trailhead nearby; spectacular views of beautiful Ward Lake and the surrounding forested ridges; access road leads beyond Ward Lake Campground toward the east and south through some beautifully scenic country.

Natural Features: Located on the north shore of Ward Lake on a lightly forested hillside between the lake and a more densely forested ridge to the north; about half the sites are lakeside; campground vegetation consists of tall timber, a few aspens, light underbrush and a pine needle forest floor; elevation 10,300'.

Season, Fees & Phone: June to September; $6.00; 14 day limit; Grand Junction Ranger District (303) 242-8211.

Camp Notes: Continuing on the paved access road past Ward Lake for another mile will take you to Kiser Campground. Kiser is a pleasant, though not exceptional, 12-site camp with drinking water and vaults. In contrast, yet another nearby campground, Valley View, is very close to Highway 65 just off the Ward Lake access road. It has seven sites with similar facilities rather near the roadway, and a breathtaking valley view.

Colorado 13

SUNSHINE
Uncompahgre National Forest

Location: Southwest Colorado north of Durango.

Access: From Colorado State Highway 145 at milepost 66 +.5 (5 miles south of the junction of Highway 145 with the Highway 145 Spur into Telluride, 8 miles southwest of Telluride, 70 miles northeast of Cortez), turn west onto a gravel access road and proceed 0.1 mile to the campground.

Facilities: 15 campsites; sites are small to medium-sized, with fair to good separation; parking pads are gravel, mostly smaller straight-ins, which may require some additional leveling; some very nice, though small, tent spots in about half the sites; fire rings; some firewood is available for gathering in the area; water at central faucets; vault facilities; gravel driveway; limited supplies and services are available in Telluride.

Activities & Attractions: The scenery along the highway from Telluride and up through Lizard Head Pass is fantastic; hiking trail to an overlook; fishing on Lake Cushman.

Natural Features: Located on a grassy, lightly forested hillside in the Rocky Mountains; views across the vast valleys to the rugged 14,000' peaks of the San Miguel Mountains and the Wilson Mountains Primitive Area to the south and southwest are particularly impressive; the South Fork of the San Miguel River meanders through the valley below; small Lake Cushman is just across the highway; elevation 9500'.

Season, Fees & Phone: June to September; $7.00; 14 day limit; Norwood Ranger District (303) 327-4261.

Camp Notes: The campsites may be a bit small, but the views from the sites are really immense! The superb panoramas here just might make you feel like singing a John Denver song.

Colorado 14

MATTERHORN
Uncompahgre National Forest

Location: Southwest Colorado north of Durango.

Access: From Colorado State Highway 145 at milepost 62 +.4 (10 miles south of the junction of Highway 145 with the Highway 145 Spur into Telluride, 13 miles south of Telluride and 65 miles northeast of Cortez), turn east onto a gravel access road, and proceed 0.1 mile to the campground.

Facilities: 24 campsites in 2 loops; sites are medium-sized, with fair to good separation; parking pads are gravel, basically level, straight-ins or pull-throughs, long enough to accommodate medium or large vehicles; many sites have good tent spots; fire rings; some firewood is available for gathering in the area; water at central faucets; vault facilities; gravel driveways; limited supplies and services are available in Telluride.

Activities & Attractions: Trout Lake, less than 2 miles south on Highway 145, has fishing; the drive south across Lizard Head Pass and north toward Telluride offers spectacular scenery.

Natural Features: Located on a forested flat in a narrow valley east of the San Miguel Mountains, 3 miles north of the summit of Lizard Head Pass; timbered, rugged peaks surround the valley; a few sites at the south end are on a slight slope; most sites are in a moderately dense stand of pines, aspens and willows; a little creek flows through the campground; elevation 9500'.

Season, Fees & Phone: June to September; $7.00; 14 day limit; Norwood Ranger District (303) 327-4261.

Camp Notes: The nearby community of Telluride has received a considerable amount of attention in recent years, and is becoming somewhat of a mountain hideaway. The town is in a truly stunning location.

Colorado 15

CAYTON
San Juan National Forest

Location: Southwest Colorado north of Durango.

Access: From Colorado State Highway 145 at milepost 53 +.4 (20 miles southwest of Telluride, 55 miles northeast of Cortez), turn east onto a gravel access road; proceed across the bridge and continue for another 0.6 mile to the campground.

Facilities: 27 campsites in 2 loops; sites are medium-sized, with fair to good separation; parking pads are gravel, mostly short to medium-length straight-ins, plus some medium-length pull-throughs; additional leveling may be required; some nice tent spots in among the trees; assorted fire appliances; firewood is available for gathering in the vicinity; water at several faucets; vault facilities; gravel driveways; minimal camper supplies are available in Rico, 6 miles south.

Activities & Attractions: Fishing on the Dolores River and in nearby Trout Lake; a number of trails lead up into the mountains; popular hunters' camp.

Natural Features: Located in a fairly narrow canyon along the Dolores River, where it is joined by waters of Barlow Creek; a heavily timbered ridge lies behind the campground to the east; a sparsely forested ridge flanks the canyon on the west; sites in the lower loop are right along the river; some sites in the upper loop are built into the hillside; elevation 9400'.

Season, Fees & Phone: June to October; $8.00; 14 day limit; Dolores Ranger District (303) 882-7296.

Camp Notes: The campground is in a narrow canyon, so the views are not as 'commanding' as they are from campgrounds to the north. But the close-in scenery is very nice, and the sites themselves are in a very pleasant, forested setting. There are also two, small, rustic, forest campgrounds, Priest Gulch and Forks, 18 and 30 miles south of here, on the west side of the highway.

Colorado 16

McPhee
San Juan National Forest

Location: Southwest Colorado north of Cortez.

Access: From Colorado State Highway 184 at milepost 4 (4 miles west of the junction of Highway 184 & State Highway 145 near Dolores, 4 miles east of the junction of Highway 184 & U.S. Highway 666 south of Lewis), turn north onto Road 25 (paved) and proceed northerly for 2.1 miles to the campground.

Facilities: 66 campsites, including several with electrical hookups, in 2 loops, plus a dozen walk-in sites; sites are medium to large, essentially level, with fair to fairly good separation; parking pads are paved, short to medium-length straight-ins or long pull-throughs or pull-offs; tent space in standard units varies from small to large; tent space is generally small in walk-in sites; fire rings; limited firewood is available for gathering in the area, b-y-o to be sure; water at several faucets; restrooms; holding tank disposal station; paved driveways; limited supplies and services are available in Dolores.

Activities & Attractions: Foot trail; viewpoint; fishing and boating on McPhee Reservoir.

Natural Features: Located near the edge of a mesa above the southwest side of McPhee Reservoir; sites are lightly shaded by piñon pines and junipers; elevation 7100'.

Season, Fees & Phone: Open all year, subject to snow closures, with limited services October to May; $6.00-$8.00 for a walk-in site, $10.00-$12.00 for a standard site, $12.00 for a hookup site; 14 day limit; Dolores Ranger District (303) 882-7296.

Camp Notes: The walk-in sites here are really neat. Some are along the rim of the mesa and look out over the reservoir. (This has also been locally known as Mesa Campground.) There's another campground on McPhee Reservoir, House Creek. It's on a virtually treeless, windswept point near the reservoir's high-water mark, and is accessible via a paved road (County Road AA/Forest Road 528) from downtown Dolores. House Creek has 45 individual campsites, a pair of group camp areas, drinking water and vaults and is priced similarly to McPhee Campground.

Colorado 17

Morefield
Mesa Verde National Park

Location: Southwest Colorado west of Durango.

Access: From U.S. Highway 160 at milepost 48 +.5 (8 miles east of Cortez, 35 miles west of Durango), turn south onto the Mesa Verde National Park paved access road and travel 4 miles (steep and curvy) to the campground.

Facilities: 477 campsites in 10 loops; (a group camp is also available); sites are relatively small, most are tolerably level, with fair to very good separation, depending upon the individual loops; parking pads are gravel, mostly short to medium-length straight-ins, plus some pull-offs; adequate space for a medium to large tent in most units; fireplaces or barbecue grills; firewood is usually for sale, b-y-o is recommended; water at central faucets; restrooms; holding tank disposal station; paved driveways; showers, laundry and camper supplies near the campground; complete supplies and services are available in Cortez.

Activities & Attractions: The park's major attractions are the ruins of Indian cliff dwellings dating back nearly a millennium; self-guided interpretive trails; ranger-guided tours; museum; campground amphitheater for summer evening programs.

Natural Features: Located on a forested mesa (hence the name "Mesa Verde" or "green table") above the rest of southwest Colorado; vegetation varies from fairly open grassy spots to sites closely surrounded by evergreens, small hardwoods and shrubs; deer are frequent visitors to the campground; elevation 7600'.

Season, Fees & Phone: Mid-April to mid-October; $7.00 for a site, $5.00 for the park entrance fee; 14 day limit; (may be operated by concessionaire); park headquarters (303) 539-4465.

Camp Notes: Incredible panoramic views from the edge of the mesa, just a short walk from the campsites, and from along the park road. (Important note: Trailers are not permitted on the park roads beyond the campground.)

Colorado 18

MANCOS
Mancos State Recreation Area

Location: Southwest corner of Colorado east of Cortez.

Access: From the junction of U.S. Highway 160 & Colorado State Highway 184 in the town of Mancos (at milepost 56 on U.S. 160, 17 miles east of Cortez, 27 miles west of Durango), go north on Highway 184 for 0.3 mile; turn northeast (right) onto Montezuma County Road 42/Forest Road 561 (paved for the first 1.2 miles, then gravel) and travel northerly for 4.2 miles; turn west (left) onto a gravel park access road for 0.2 mile to the park entrance; the East Shore (main) campground is just south (left) of the entrance; or continue westerly across the dam for 1 mile and another 1 mile along the west shore to the West Shore areas.

Facilities: *East Shore*: 24 campsites; sites are medium to large, with fairly good to very good separation; parking pads are gravel, medium to long straight-ins; a little additional leveling may be needed in some sites; large tent areas; water at a central faucet; *West Shore*: 9 campsites in several clusters scattered along the shore; sites are small, a bit sloped, with nominal to good separation; parking surfaces are dirt/gravel, short straight-ins; generally medium to large tent areas; no drinking water on the west shore; *both areas*: fire rings and/or barbecue grills; some firewood may be available for gathering on national forest lands within 3 miles north of the park, b-y-o to be sure; vault facilities; gravel driveways; gas and groceries+ in Mancos; complete supplies and services are available in Cortez and Durango.

Activities & Attractions: Fishing for stocked trout; limited boating (wakeless); hiking trail; x-c skiing; ice fishing.

Natural Features: Located around the shoreline of Mancos Reservoir; campsites are lightly to moderately shaded/sheltered by tall conifers, plus some hardwoods; the San Juan Mountains rise above 12,000' a few miles east; elevation 7800'.

Season, Fees & Phone: Open all year, subject to weather and road conditions; principal season is May to October; 14 day limit; please see Appendix for reservation information and standard Colorado state park fees; phone c/o Navajo State Recreation Area.

Camp Notes: Southwest Colorado has that special look and feel of a place apart. You can *sense* the great distances from the country's population centers. From the recreation area you can look southwest out across the great valley toward Mesa Verde, or east to the San Juans. It's the kind of simple spot where you'll be glad you brought enough supplies to take you through an extra day of gazing across the lake to the classic peaks beyond.

Colorado 19

TARGET TREE
San Juan National Forest

Location: Southwest Colorado west of Durango.

Access: From U.S. Highway 160 at milepost 63 (22 miles west of Durango, 25 miles east of Cortez), turn north onto a gravel access road and proceed 0.2 mile to the campground.

Facilities: 52 campsites in a main loop and 2 smaller loops; sites are medium to large, with good to excellent separation; most parking pads are gravel, spacious straight-ins; pads may require additional leveling; some sites have large tent areas; fire rings or fireplaces; some firewood is available for gathering in the area; water at several faucets; vault facilities; gravel driveways; gas and groceries+ in Mancos, 6 miles west; complete supplies and services are available in Cortez and Durango.

Activities & Attractions: Trails into the La Plata Mountains; terrific views of the valley and hills to the south and west.

Natural Features: Located on a forested hilltop and hillside above a long valley in the La Plata Mountains; some of the sites surround a large, grassy infield, and some are tucked in among tall conifers and leafy underbrush; tall peaks of the La Plata Mountains rise to 12,000' to the north; elevation 7800'.

Season, Fees & Phone: May to September; $6.00; 14 day limit; Mancos Ranger District (303) 533-7716.

Camp Notes: Formerly named Thompson Park Campground, Target Tree was re-christened for a large local arbor that was used for marksmanship practice by the Indians. There are some really expansive views from a number of the sites here. This is the closest public campground outside of nearby Mesa Verde National Park. If the park's huge campground is just a little too populated, or if you just prefer a large, secluded campsite somewhat closer to the main highway, Target Tree would make an excellent choice.

Colorado 20

KROEGER
San Juan National Forest

Location: Southwest Colorado west of Durango.

Access: From U.S. Highway 160 at milepost 72 +.7 (0.4 mile west of the junction of U.S. 50 and Colorado State Highway 140, 11.5 miles west of Durango, 35 miles east of Cortez), turn north onto a paved access road (Forest Road 571) and travel 4.5 miles to the town of Mayday; continue for another 1.6 miles on a gravel road; turn west (left) into the campground.

Facilities: 12 campsites; sites are medium to large, basically level, with nominal to good separation; parking pads are gravel, medium to long, straight-ins or pull-throughs; some sites have nice tent spots along a stream; fire rings; some firewood is available for gathering in the vicinity; water at a hand pump; vault facilities; gravel driveway; complete supplies and services are available in Durango.

Activities & Attractions: Trout fishing on the La Plata River; Snowslide Gulch Picnic Area, 0.3 mile south, along the access road; several active and inactive mines are in the area.

Natural Features: Located on a streamside flat in La Plata Canyon in the La Plata Mountains; campground vegetation consists primarily of tall conifers, plus aspens and some light underbrush, that provide ample shelter/shade in most sites; timbered ridges and peaks flank the canyon; a rivulet flows through the campground on its way to the La Plata River, just on the east side of the road; elevation 9000'.

Season, Fees & Phone: June to September; $6.00; 14 day limit; Mancos Ranger District (303) 533-7716.

Camp Notes: A pole fence surrounds the campground to separate it from private land, and it also adds a finishing touch. Some sites are right next to the road, but there is limited traffic, since the road turns into a 4wd trail a few miles north.

Colorado 21

DAKOTA TERRACES
Ridgway State Recreation Area

Location: Western Colorado south of Montrose.

Access: From U.S. Highway 550 at milepost 108 +.3 (5 miles north of the town of Ridgway, 21 miles south of Montrose), turn west onto the paved park access road and proceed 0.4 mile to the entrance station; 0.1 mile beyond the entrance station is a 3-way fork; swing right to the campground.

Facilities: 72 campsites with electrical hookups; sites are small+ to medium-sized, with minimal separation; parking pads are paved, medium to long straight-ins or long pull-throughs; additional leveling will be required in many sites; small tent areas; small ramadas (sun shelters) for a few sites; fire rings and barbecue grills; b-y-o firewood; water at several faucets; restrooms with showers; coin-op laundry; holding tank disposal station; paved driveways; gas and groceries+ in Ridgway; complete supplies and services are available in Montrose.

Activities & Attractions: Large visitor center; sandy swimming beach; boating; multi-lane boat launch and courtesy docks; marina; small playground; nice day use area a short distance down the hill from the campground.

Natural Features: Located on a slope a few hundred yards above the end of a long, slender bay on the east shore of Ridgway Reservoir; campground vegetation consists of tall grass, small brush and some small hardwoods and evergreens; bordered by high mountains; elevation 7000'.

Season, Fees & Phone: Principal season is May to October, with limited services in winter; 14 day limit; please see Appendix for reservation information and standard Colorado state park fees; park office (303) 626-5822.

Camp Notes: Dakota Terraces and nearby Elk Ridge (info below) are within the recreation area's Dutch Charlie complex, the principal developed unit on the reservoir. If you're planning to make reservations for a holiday weekend at Ridgway, the main items to remember when requesting a site are: (a) Dakota Terraces is essentially unshaded but not far from the lake; and (b) Elk Ridge has lots of trees but is a long walk (or a short drive) from the shoreline.

Colorado 22

ELK RIDGE
Ridgway State Recreation Area

Location: Western Colorado south of Montrose.

Access: From U.S. Highway 550 at milepost 108 +.3 (5 miles north of the town of Ridgway, 21 miles south of Montrose), turn west onto the paved park access road and proceed 0.4 mile to the entrance station; 0.1 mile beyond the entrance station is a 3-way fork; bear left and go up the hill for 0.5 mile to the campground.

Facilities: 108 campsites, including 98 with electrical hookups and 10 walk-in tent sites; sites are small+ to medium+, with fair to good separation; parking pads are paved, medium to long straight-ins or long pull-throughs; a little additional leveling may be needed in some sites; small to medium-sized areas for tents in the hookup section; tent sites have large, framed tent pads; water at several faucets; restrooms with showers; paved driveways; gas and groceries+ in Ridgway; complete supplies and services are available in Montrose.

Activities & Attractions: Visitor center; sandy swimming beach nearby; boating; multi-lane boat launch and courtesy docks; marina; small playground.

Natural Features: Located on a ridgetop high above Ridgway Reservoir; sites are lightly to moderately sheltered by conifers; the lake is bordered by high mountains; elevation 7300'.

Season, Fees & Phone: Principal season is May to October, with limited services in winter; 14 day limit; please see Appendix for reservation information and standard Colorado state park fees; park office (303) 626-5822.

Camp Notes: Perhaps the best campsites in the recreation area (and top contenders for 'Best in All of Colorado') go to tent campers at Elk Ridge willing to haul their vittles and trappings a few yards down a trail. Most of the nicely sheltered tent units are along the edge of the ridge and look south across the lake to the 14,000' peaks in the Uncompahgre Primitive Area. If you're an rv'er, it might tempt you to swap that slab-sided rollin' home for a good piece of canvas and a goose down slumber bag.

Colorado 23

AMPHITHEATER
Uncompahgre National Forest

Location: Southwest Colorado south of Montrose.

Access: From U.S Highway 550 near milepost 92 (1.2 miles south of midtown Ouray, 21 miles north of Silverton), turn east onto a paved access road; climb 0.7 mile on a steep and twisty road to the campground. (Note: Approaching from either north or south, the access road comes up rather quickly as you round a series of curves on the highway.)

Facilities: 30 campsites in several small loops built in tiers on a steep mountainside; sites are small, with good to excellent separation, and quite level, considering the terrain; parking pads are gravel, mostly short to medium-length straight-ins; several sites are park 'n walks; fireplaces or fire rings; some firewood is available for gathering in the area, b-y-o to be sure; water at several faucets; vault facilities; paved driveways; gas and groceries+ are available in Ouray.

Activities & Attractions: Several trails lead from the campground into the surrounding Uncompahgre Primitive Area, including Portage Trail and Cascade Falls Trail.

Natural Features: Located on a mountainside high above the Uncompahgre River, in a heavily forested 'pocket'; ample shelter/shade is provided by tall conifers and aspens; nearby peaks rise to over 13,000'; rain and snow squalls can be expected anytime; elevation 8400'.

Season, Fees & Phone: June to mid-September; $10.00; 14 day limit; Ouray Ranger District (303) 249-3711.

Camp Notes: Larger vehicles may have a little trouble making it up the access road and maneuvering in the tighter corners of the campground. But, wow! It's worth it. The views across the valley/canyon, and of the small town of Ouray nestled at the foot of the mountains, are positively astonishing.

SOUTH MINERAL
San Juan National Forest

Location: Southwest Colorado north of Durango.

Access: From U.S. Highway 550 near milepost 72 +.5 (2 miles northwest of Silverton, 18 miles south of Ouray), turn west onto Forest Road 585 (gravel) and travel 4.3 miles to the campground.

Facilities: 27 campsites; sites are large, level, with good to very good separation; parking pads are gravel, mostly medium to long straight-ins, plus a few large pull-offs; plenty of space for tents; fire rings; some firewood is available for gathering in the area; water at several faucets; vault facilities; gravel driveways; limited supplies and services are available in Silverton.

Activities & Attractions: Trout fishing; 4wd trail to Clear Lake (4 miles off Road 585).

Natural Features: Located in a narrow valley on a large, grassy flat along the South Fork of Mineral Creek; campsites are lightly to moderately shaded/sheltered by tall conifers; surrounded by lofty forested or barren peaks; elevation 9800'.

Season, Fees & Phone: June to September; $7.00; 14 day limit; Animas Ranger District, Durango, (303) 247-4874.

Camp Notes: Shortly after you turn off the highway you'll readily realize why this is a popular place to camp: Classic Rocky Mountain scenery all over the place. It's no wonder why the camp is populated by flatlanders throughout much of the summer. If the campground is full, or you're a mite short of spare change for a night's rent, alternately you can take refuge in one of the many large jackcamping spots on streamside flats in this area.

PURGATORY
San Juan National Forest

Location: Southwest Colorado north of Durango.

Access: From U.S. Highway 550 at milepost 49 (almost directly opposite the entrance to Purgatory ski area, 28 miles north of the junction of U.S. Highways 550 and 160 in Durango, 21 miles south of Silverton) turn east into the campground.

Facilities: 14 campsites; sites are small, with good separation; parking pads are gravel, mostly short straight-ins; additional leveling may be required in some sites; enough room for small to medium-sized tents in most sites; fire rings; gathering firewood on forest lands prior to arrival is suggested; water at central faucets; vault facilities; gravel driveway; limited supplies in Silverton; complete supplies and services are available in Durango.

Activities & Attractions: Rocky Mountain scenery; possible fishing.

Natural Features: Located on a densely forested hill surrounded by the high, rugged peaks of the Rockies; most sites are very well sheltered by towering conifers and tall aspens; the campground is bordered by a small lake to the north; Engineer Mountain, at 12,972', rises prominently in the north; elevation 8800'.

Season, Fees & Phone: June to September, subject to weather conditions; $7.00; 14 day limit; Animas Ranger District, Durango, (303) 247-4874.

Camp Notes: The surrounding mountain peaks offer excellent photographic opportunities. This roadside campground is probably more suitable for smaller vehicles and smaller tents. However, the other public camp along this highway, Haviland Lake (see separate info) is, overall, probably a better choice. (It's too bad that Purgatory Campground is snowed-in by the time ski season rolls around. It would be a handy spot for *après-ski*. Ed.)

HAVILAND LAKE
San Juan National Forest

Location: Southwest Colorado north of Durango.

Access: From U.S. Highway 550 at milepost 41 +.9 (21 miles north of the junction of U.S. Highways 550 and 160 in Durango, 28 miles south of Silverton), turn east onto a gravel access road; after 0.3 mile, turn north (left) at a "T" intersection; continue north for 0.7 mile to the campground.

Facilities: 47 campsites in several loops; sites are medium-sized, with nominal to fair separation; parking pads are gravel, short to medium-length straight-ins, plus a few pull-throughs; additional leveling may be necessary in some sites; some good tenting possibilities in about half of the sites; fire rings; limited firewood is available for gathering in the area; gathering firewood prior to arrival, or b-y-o, is suggested; water at several faucets; vault facilities; gravel driveways; camper supplies at a small store on the highway, 4.5 miles north; complete supplies and services are available in Durango.

Activities & Attractions: Trout fishing; motorless boating.

Natural Features: Located on a hillside on the east shore of Haviland Lake; some sites are just above the shore and the rest extend up the hill; most sites are sheltered/shaded by tall pines and aspens in an open forest; a small creek crossed by a wooden footbridge flows through the campground and into Haviland Lake; elevation 8100'.

Season, Fees & Phone: May to September, but may be available a bit earlier or later, with reduced services and no fee, subject to weather conditions; $7.00; 14 day limit; Animas Ranger District, Durango, (303) 247-4874.

Camp Notes: A half-dozen sites have really excellent views of the lake and the surrounding snow-capped peaks. (Don't forget to pack your camera and an extra roll of film.)

Colorado 27

MILLER CREEK
San Juan National Forest

Location: Southwest Colorado northeast of Durango.

Access: From U.S. Highway 160 at milepost 102 +.8 in Bayfield (14 miles east of Durango), turn north onto Vallecito Lake Road (paved) and travel 9 miles to a "Y" intersection; bear northwest (left) onto La Plata County Road 240 and continue for 2.9 miles; turn north (right) onto La Plata County Road 243 (gravel) and proceed 3.5 miles; turn west (left) into the campground. (Alternate Access Note: This area, as well as the campgrounds on nearby Vallecito Lake, are also accessible from U.S. 550; from 15th St. on the north end of Durango, take the Florida River Road (paved) east to the reservoirs.)

Facilities: 17 campsites in 2 sections; sites are average-sized, with fair to good separation; parking surfaces are paved or gravel, pull-offs or straight-ins, which will probably require a little additional leveling; tent areas vary from small to large; fire rings and/or barbecue grills; firewood is available for gathering in the area; water at several faucets; vault facilities; paved driveways; nearest reliable sources of supply are near Vallecito Lake, 9 miles east.

Activities & Attractions: Lake and stream fishing; boating; paved boat launch.

Natural Features: Located on the east shore of Lemon Reservoir on the Florida River; sites receive light to medium shelter from tall conifers and hardwoods; bordered by heavily timbered, red rock hills and mountains; elevation 8,000'.

Season, Fees & Phone: June to September; $7.00; 14 day limit; Pine Ranger District, Bayfield, (303) 884-2512.

Camp Notes: Actually, there are two types of campsites here: standard, stand-alone units, and a group of what might be called "park-along" sites just above the lake shore, around the perimeter of a large parking lot. And if you need more serenity than that which is provided here, there's more camping a half-dozen miles north at Transfer Park Campground.

Colorado 28

VALLECITO
San Juan National Forest

Location: Southwest Colorado northeast of Durango.

Access: From U.S. Highway 160 at milepost 102 +.8 in Bayfield (14 miles east of Durango), turn north onto Vallecito Lake Road and travel 9 miles to a "Y" intersection; bear northeast (right) onto La Plata County Road 501 for 3 miles to the southwest corner of the lake, then continue along the west shore for another 5.5 miles; at a point where the road turns sharply east (right), turn north onto La Plata County Road 500 (paved) for a final 2.6 miles to the campground.

Facilities: 88 campsites in 3 loops; (a group camp loop is also available); sites are medium to large, essentially level, with fairly good to excellent separation; parking pads are gravel, medium to long straight-ins or pull-throughs; adequate level space for medium to large tents in most units; fire rings; some firewood is available for gathering in the area, b-y-o to be sure; water at a hand pump; vault facilities; gravel driveways; camper limited groceries at several small stores along the west shore road.

Activities & Attractions: Trails into Weminuche Wilderness; fishing, boating and boat launch on Vallecito Lake.

Natural Features: Located on a flat on the west bank of Vallecito Creek in a moderately dense forest of conifers and aspens; bordered by high mountains; elevation 8000'.

Season, Fees & Phone: June to September; $8.00; 14 day limit; Pine Ranger District, Bayfield, (303) 884-2512.

Camp Notes: Nice-looking campground. Very nice streamside environment here (although only a relatively few sites are actually near the water's edge). In many places in the West, Vallecito Creek would be considered large enough to be called a river. All in all, this might be the most desirable campground in the Vallecito Lake area.

Colorado 29

MIDDLE MOUNTAIN
San Juan National Forest

Location: Southwest Colorado northeast of Durango.

Access: From U.S. Highway 160 at milepost 102 +.8 in Bayfield (14 miles east of Durango), turn north onto Vallecito Lake Road and travel 9 miles to a "Y" intersection; bear northeast (right) onto La Plata County Road 501 for 3 miles to the southwest corner of the lake, then proceed along the west and north shores for another 7 miles around to the northeast side of the lake and the end of the pavement; continue (south now) on gravel for 1.9 miles, then angle southwest (right) down off the road for 0.1 mile to the campground.

Facilities: 24 campsites; sites are medium-sized, with fair to fairly good separation; parking pads are gravel straight-ins or long pull-throughs which will require additional leveling; adequate, though quite sloped, space for large tents; fire rings; limited firewood is available for gathering in the general vicinity, b-y-o is suggested; water at several faucets; vault facilities; gravel driveway; camper supplies are available along the west shore.

Activities & Attractions: Fishing; boating.

Natural Features: Located on the steeply sloping northeast shore of Vallecito Lake; campground vegetation consists of tall grass, and tall conifers and short aspens which provide fairly good shade/shelter for most sites; well-timbered mountains surround the lake; elevation 7900'.

Season, Fees & Phone: June to September; $8.00; 14 day limit; Pine Ranger District, Bayfield, (303) 884-2512.

Camp Notes: They gave it the good old college try when it came down to leveling the parking spaces and tables on this steeeeep slope. (Better fill your coffee mug no more than half way, 'cause if you set it down, the java might spill out over the west rim.) But forget the tilt. The sites here have some of the nicest lake views of all the camps in the area.

Colorado 30

GRAHAM CREEK & NORTH CANYON
San Juan National Forest

Location: Southwest Colorado northeast of Durango.

Access: From U.S. Highway 160 at milepost 102 +.8 in Bayfield (14 miles east of Durango), turn north onto Vallecito Lake Road (paved) and travel 9 miles to a "Y" intersection; bear northeast (right) onto La Plata County Road 501 for 3 miles to the southwest corner of the lake; turn southeast (right) onto a paved road and proceed 1 mile across the dam to the southeast corner of the lake; continue northeasterly (on gravel) along the east shore of the lake for 2.2 miles to *Graham Creek* or 2.6 miles to *North Canyon*.

Facilities: *Graham Creek*: 25 campsites; *North Canyon*: 22 campsites; sites are medium+ in size, with fairly good to very good separation; parking pads are gravel, generally medium-length straight-ins, plus some pull-throughs and pull-offs; most pads will require at least a little additional leveling; fire rings; some firewood is available for gathering in the area; water at central faucets; vault facilities; gravel driveways; camper supplies are available at several points on the west shore.

Activities & Attractions: Fishing; boating; small boat launch.

Natural Features: Located on the east shore of Vallecito Lake; some sites are located several yards from the lakeshore, others are on a slope above the lake; a variety of tall conifers provide light to medium shelter/shade for the campsites; small streams flow through both camps; the lake is bordered by forested mountains; elevation 7900'.

Season, Fees & Phone: June to September; $8.00; 14 day limit; Pine Ranger District, Bayfield, (303) 884-2512.

Camp Notes: The characteristics of this pair of adjacent camps are understandably quite similar. Lake access is a tad limited because of dense brush along the shore. On the way to this duo you'll pass a small forest camp called Old Timers. It has 11 smallish, tilted sites (4 are lakeside), tap water, vaults, and day-tripper traffic. Super views from here.

Colorado 31

PINE POINT
San Juan National Forest

Location: Southwest Colorado northeast of Durango.

Access: From U.S. Highway 160 at milepost 102 +.8 in Bayfield (14 miles east of Durango), turn north onto Vallecito Lake Road and travel 9 miles to a "Y" intersection; bear northeast (right) onto La Plata County Road 501 for 3 miles to the southwest corner of the lake; turn southeast (right) onto a paved road and proceed 1 mile across the dam to the southeast corner of the lake; continue northeasterly (on gravel) along the east shore of the lake for 3.2 miles to the campground.

Facilities: 31 campsites; sites are medium-sized, with fair to good separation; parking pads are gravel, short to medium-length straight-ins or medium-length pull-throughs; most pads will require a little additional leveling; small to large, sloped spaces for tents; fire rings; some firewood is available for gathering in the vicinity; water at several faucets; vault facilities; gravel driveway; camper supplies are available at several points on the west shore.

Activities & Attractions: Fishing; boating.

Natural Features: Located on the east shore of Vallecito Lake on the south side of a bay at the outlet of the Los Pinos River; tall conifers provide quite ample shade/shelter for most sites; small, grassy beach; timbered mountains surround the lake; elevation 7900'.

Season, Fees & Phone: June to September; $8.00; 14 day limit; Pine Ranger District, Bayfield, (303) 884-2512.

Camp Notes: If you plan to camp on Vallecito's shore, this is the 'end of the line' insofar as access from the east shore road goes. (Some maps vaguely depict the road continuing north across the Los Pinos River to the northeast shore. There is a one-lane bridge, but the passage is through private land. Sorry.) If you want to take a look at Middle Mountain Campground on the northeast shore (see info), you'll have to get there via the west shore road.

Colorado 32

LOWER PIEDRA
San Juan National Forest

Location: Southwest Colorado east of Durango.

Access: From U.S. Highway 160 just west of milepost 121 (35 miles east of Durango, 22 miles west of Pagosa Springs), turn north onto a gravel, single-lane road with pull-outs (First Fork Road/Forest Road 622); proceed along the west bank of the river for 1.2 miles to the campground.

Facilities: 18 campsites; sites are medium to large, level, and quite well separated; parking pads are gravel, medium to long straight-ins or pull-throughs; most sites have large tent areas; fireplaces and barbecue grills; firewood is available for gathering; no drinking water; vault facilities; gravel driveways; gas and groceries+ in Bayfield, 18 miles west; adequate supplies and services are available in Pagosa Springs.

Activities & Attractions: Trout fishing (flies and lures only).

Natural Features: Located on the west bank of the Piedra River; campground vegetation consists of patches of tall grass, moderately dense, tall conifers, and some low-level brush, and a forest floor thickly carpeted with pine needles; about half the campsites are right along the river, the remainder are several yards from the water's edge; timbered hills and mountains are in the surrounding area; elevation 7200'.

Season, Fees & Phone: May to October; no fee (subject to change); 14 day limit; Pine Ranger District, Bayfield, (303) 884-2512

Camp Notes: This is a very nice little campground. Don't let the lack of potable water discourage you from considering stopping here. There are also some jack camping spots along the river, north and south of the campground proper. Another national forest campground, Ute, is located just off the north side of U.S. 160 at milepost 126 +.5. However, it's usually only open during big game hunting season.

Colorado 33

NAVAJO
Navajo State Recreation Area

Location: Southwest Colorado southeast of Durango.

Access: From Colorado State Highway 151 at the north edge of the hamlet of Arboles (17 miles southwest of the junction of Highway 151 & U.S. Highway 160 near Chimney Rock, 18 miles southeast of Ignacio), turn east onto Archuleta County Road 982 (paved) and travel 1.6 miles to the park entrance station; proceed ahead for 0.35 mile to a fork; bear right and continue for another 0.5 mile to a second fork, then angle left into the campground.

Facilities: 71 campsites, including a few with electrical hookups, in 2 loops; sites are small to medium-sized, level, with very little separation; parking pads are gravel, short to scant medium-length straight-ins, or long pull-throughs; many straight-ins are snug extra-wides; spacious tent areas on a grassy or earthen surface; barbecue grills in most sites, some fireplaces and fire rings; b-y-o firewood; water at several faucets; restrooms with showers; holding tank disposal station; paved or gravel driveways; gas and camper supplies at the marina and in Arboles.

Activities & Attractions: Boating; huge, multi-lane boat launch; marina; fishing for largemouth bass, catfish, crappie in the shallows, kokanee and assorted trout in cooler water; small playground; airfield next to the campground; x-c skiing, shoreline ice fishing, open-water fishing and boating, in winter.

Natural Features: Located on a grassy bluff above the northwest shore of Navajo Lake on the San Juan River; vegetation consists of large tracts of watered and mown grass dotted with hardwoods, small pines and junipers; moderately forested hills, mountains and mesas surround the lake; elevation 6100'.

Season, Fees & Phone: Open all year; principal season is March to November; 14 day limit; please see Appendix for reservation information and standard Colorado state park fees; park office (303) 883-2208.

Camp Notes: There isn't much natural shade here, but on the other hand, there isn't much to intercept your view of the terrific vistas either. The majority of campsites look out across the lake. Overall, this excellent campground and its facilities are a cut above the park's counterparts on the New Mexico end of Navajo Lake. An out-of-the-way region worth going out of your way for.

Colorado 34

REDSTONE
White River National Forest

Location: West-central Colorado south of Glenwood Springs.

Access: From Colorado State Highway 133 at milepost 53 (1.5 miles north of the community of Redstone, 16 miles south of Carbondale), turn east, cross a bridge, then turn south (right) and continue for 0.1 mile to the campground.

Facilities: 24 campsites in 2 loops; majority of the sites are a little on the small side, with good separation; parking pads are gravel, most are short to medium length straight-ins parking pads; several sites have pull-through pads; some sites may require additional leveling; limited tent space; fire rings; some firewood is available for gathering; water at several faucets; vault facilities; gravel driveways; very limited supplies in Redstone; adequate supplies and services are available in Carbondale.

Activities & Attractions: Fishing.

Natural Features: Located on a tiered slope in a red rock canyon just above the Crystal River; campground vegetation consists of short aspens mixed with conifers, plus a substantial quantity of low-level vegetation between campsites; one loop has a large, open grass infield; views of rugged peaks to the south; elevation 7200'.

Season, Fees & Phone: May to mid-September, but may be available as late as October; $8.00; 14 day limit; Sopris Ranger District, Carbondale, (303) 963-2266.

Camp Notes: The brilliant red rock canyon walls stand out in remarkable contrast to the rich green vegetation here. Another local national forest campground, Janeway, is located 0.6 mile east of the highway, on a gravel road which begins near milepost 56 + .8. It's a cozy little 10-site campground along Avalanche Creek, but it has no drinking water.

Colorado 35

BOGAN FLATS
White River National Forest

Location: West-central Colorado south of Glenwood Springs.

Access: From Colorado State Highway 133 at milepost 46 + .4 (23 miles south of Carbondale, 46 miles east of Hotchkiss), turn east onto Gunnison County Road 3 (paved somewhat narrow), and proceed 1.5 miles to the campground. (Note that you must continue on Road 3 past the campground to reach the entrance driveway at the far east end.)

Facilities: 37 campsites in 1 large loop; sites are medium-sized, quite level, with little or no separation between most sites, except those on the east end; parking pads are gravel, mostly medium to long straight-ins, plus some pull-throughs; large, level tent areas; fire rings; firewood is available for collecting in the vicinity; water at several faucets; vault facilities; gravel driveway with a large turnaround loop at the west end; very limited supplies in Redstone, 5 miles north; adequate supplies and services are available in Carbondale.

Activities & Attractions: Fishing; rockhounding; numerous hiking trails east of here lead to the Maroon Bells.

Natural Features: Located on a flat in a narrow valley along the south bank of the Crystal River; most sites are on the open flat, a few are in a wooded area at the east end of the campground; elev. 7600'.

Season, Fees & Phone: May to September; $9.00; 14 day limit; Sopris Ranger District, Carbondale, (303) 963-2266.

Camp Notes: During most of the year, the Crystal River runs true to its name. Since the sites on the open flat are in full view of the county road, the sheltered units on the east end may be more desirable to some campers. For a camp spot with a little more privacy, you might want to check out nearby Redstone Campground, just north of the community of the same name.

Colorado 36

McCLURE
White River National Forest

Location: West-central Colorado south of Glenwood Springs.

Access: From Colorado State Highway 133 at milepost 41 + .8 (27 miles south of Carbondale, 42 miles east of Hotchkiss), turn south into the campground.

Facilities: 19 campsites; sites are medium sized, with fairly good separation; parking pads are gravel, medium-length straight-ins, plus some pull-throughs; fireplaces or fire rings; firewood is available for gathering; water at a hand pump; vault facilities; paved driveway; very limited supplies in Redstone, 12 miles north; adequate supplies and services are available in Carbondale.

Activities & Attractions: Principally the majestic mountain scenery; some fishing in nearby streams; a few back roads and jeep trails are in the area.

Natural Features: Located in an aspen grove on a hill overlooking Lee Creek, 1 mile west of McClure Pass; high, aspen-covered ridges lie north and south; campground tends to be quite cool and breezy; elevation 8200'.

Season, Fees & Phone: June to September, but may be available earlier and/or later, with reduced services, depending upon weather conditions; $8.00; 14 day limit; Sopris Ranger District, Carbondale, (303) 963-2266.

Camp Notes: The local mountains seem to be about 99 percent aspen-clothed, so a visit here in mid to late September, when the leaves turn to iridescent yellow, is an unforgettable treat. Although the campground is located right next to the highway, the road is not heavily traveled at night.

Colorado 37

CRAWFORD
Crawford State Recreation Area

Location: Western Colorado east of Delta.

Access: From Colorado State Highway 92 at the following mileposts (beginning 1.5 miles south of the town of Crawford, 4 miles north of Maher, listed north to south), turn west into the camp units: *Peninsula* (Area #3), mile 33; *Clear Fork* (Area #4), mile 33 +.6; *Iron Creek*, mile 34 +.1.

Facilities: *Peninsula*: 22 campsites in a parking lot arrangement, plus several park 'n walk tent sites; most sites are very small, level, with zero separation; parking surfaces are short+ to medium-length; enough space for small or medium-sized tents on the grass bordering the parking lot; water at several faucets; vault facilities; *Clear Fork*: 26 campsites; most sites are small to medium-sized, tolerably level, with minimal to nominal separation; parking pads are gravel, short to medium-length pull-offs; large, grassy tent areas; several sites have small ramadas (sun shelters); water at faucets throughout; restrooms; holding tank disposal station; *Iron Creek*: 6 campsites; sites are small, with nominal separation; parking surfaces are gravel/dirt; enough space for large tents; vault facilities; *all areas*: fire rings or barbecue grills; b-y-o firewood; gravel driveways; gas and groceries in Crawford; adequate supplies and services are available in Hotchkiss, 13 miles north.

Activities & Attractions: Boating; boat launches; windsurfing; small swimming beach; fishing for stocked trout and perch, also bass and catfish; arboretum; x-c skiing and other winter sports.

Natural Features: Located in a valley along the shore of Crawford Reservoir; each camp area is on a separate point of land on the east shore; a few hardwoods and evergreens offer very light shelter, but otherwise the camping areas are quite open; semi-arid low hills and ridges and rolling agricultural land lie in the vicinity; to the east, lofty peaks rise sharply from the valley floor; elevation 6600'.

Season, Fees & Phone: Open all year, with limited services October to April; 14 day limit; please see Appendix for reservation information and standard Colorado state park fees; park office (303) 921-5721.

Camp Notes: Next to having a campsite on an island, probably most campers would choose one on a point of land, thus maximizing the locally available lakefront property. The simple camps here offer plenty of that. (But be careful not to mistake the small, steeply sloped swim beach in the Peninsula area for the boat ramp). Knowledgeable fishermen make a special effort to come here for the excellent perch fishing. Another state park area in this region that also offers camping is Paonia SRA, located at the north end of Paonia Reservoir off Colorado State Highway 133 near milepost 28, 17 miles northeast of the town of Paonia. There are a dozen primitive sites, vaults, but no drinking water at Paonia. However, the mountain views are excellent.

Colorado 38

SOUTH RIM
Black Canyon of the Gunnison National Monument

Location: West-Central Colorado east of Montrose.

Access: From U.S. Highway 50 at milepost 100 +.5 (15 miles east of Montrose, 57 miles west of Gunnison), turn north onto Colorado State Highway 347; travel 6 miles on a steep and twisty road to the park entrance; the campground is 1 mile farther.

Facilities: 102 campsites in 3 loops; sites are small, with good separation; most parking pads are gravel, short to medium-length straight-ins or pull-throughs; some nice, small tent sites are snuggled in among the dense vegetation; fireplaces; b-y-o firewood; water is limited, and available at central faucets; restrooms, supplemented by vault facilities; paved driveways; ranger station; complete supplies and services are available in Montrose.

Activities & Attractions: Scenic drive along the South Rim; several nature trails lead from the roadway to the rim and some spectacular views; the river is accessible from the rim, but the trek isn't advised for the inexperienced hiker/climber; visitor center; campfire circle for nature programs.

Natural Features: Located on the edge of Vernal Mesa, near the South Rim of Black Canyon of the Gunnison River; the 2000-feet-deep canyon was named for the long shadows which linger for most of the day in the steep and narrow gorge; campground vegetation consists of short hardwoods, evergreens and shrubbery that provide privacy and shelter from the wind, but only limited shade; elevation 8300'.

Season, Fees & Phone: May to September; may be available with limited services before and after the season, depending upon snow conditions; $8.00 for a site, $5.00 for the park entrance fee; 14 day limit; Black Canyon of the Gunnison National Monument Headquarters (303) 249-7036.

Camp Notes: It's not uncommon for mule deer to visit the campground. Eagles and falcons can often be seen soaring above the canyon, taking advantage of the updrafts. Some grand views are just a short walk from this campground. There's also a small campground on the canyon's north rim. North Rim Campground has a dozen sites, drinking water and vaults on the brink of a narrow chasm. North Rim is accessible via a 14-mile gravel road from Crawford State Recreation Area.

CIMARRON
Curecanti National Recreation Area

Location: West-central Colorado east of Montrose.

Access: From U.S. Highway 50 at milepost 112 +.4 in Cimarron (20 miles east of Montrose, 45 miles west of Gunnison), turn north onto a paved access road and proceed across the bridge to the campground.

Facilities: 25 campsites; sites are medium to large, level, with minimal separation; parking pads are paved, medium to long straight-ins or pull-offs; most sites have large tent areas; fireplaces; b-y-o firewood; water at several faucets; restrooms; holding tank disposal station; paved driveway; gas and groceries in Cimarron.

Activities & Attractions: Visitor center; narrow gauge railroad exhibit; amphitheater for evening campfire programs; day use area; fishing; self-guided tour at Morrow Point.

Natural Features: Located along the Little Cimarron River, which flows into the Gunnison River 2 miles to the north; sites are on a grassy flat in a narrow canyon ringed by sage and evergreen-dotted hills; hardwoods provide light shelter/shade within the campground, although most sites are quite out in the open; Black Canyon of the Gunnison and Morrow Point Reservoir are just a few miles to the north; elevation 6900'.

Season, Fees & Phone: May to October; $8.00; 14 day limit; Curecanti NRA Headquarters (303) 641-2337.

Camp Notes: The campground is located conveniently close to the small town of Cimarron, and just across a pleasant stream from the highway. Extraordinary scenery in this national recreation area. The railroad display is neat.

LAKE FORK
Curecanti National Recreation Area

Location: West-central Colorado west of Gunnison.

Access: From U.S. Highway 50 at milepost 131 +.1 (near the junction of Highway 50 and Colorado State Highway 92, 26 miles west of Gunnison, 40 miles east of Montrose), turn north onto a paved access road and go 0.3 mile to the campground.

Facilities: 90 campsites, including 5 walk-ins, in somewhat of a paved parking lot arrangement; sites are small and very close together; most parking spaces are medium to large pull-offs; additional leveling may be required; many sites have windbreaks; fireplaces; b-y-o firewood; water at several faucets; restrooms; holding tank disposal station; gas and groceries in Sapinero, 2 miles east; complete supplies and services are available in Montrose and Gunnison.

Activities & Attractions: Small visitor center and ranger station in the campground; amphitheater for evening programs; large marina with launch facilities and docks; West Elk Wilderness Area is accessible by gravel road or boat to Ponderosa Campground and the Coal Creek Trailhead.

Natural Features: Located on a bench near the bottom of a steep hillside at the west tip of Blue Mesa Reservoir, where the Gunnison River is dammed to form the reservoir; vegetation consists of patches of grass and sage on the adjacent slope; great views across the lake to the mountains beyond; elevation 7600'.

Season, Fees & Phone: May to November; $8.00; 14 day limit; Curecanti NRA Headquarters (303) 641-2337.

Camp Notes: Twenty-mile-long Blue Mesa Reservoir is the largest body of water in Colorado. The campground provides comfortable accommodations for campers who enjoy the boating opportunities and the stiff breeze from the west that incessantly funnels through the narrow Black Canyon of the Gunnison here at the dam where it all begins.

DRY GULCH
Curecanti National Recreation Area

Location: West-central Colorado west of Gunnison.

Access: From U.S. Highway 50 at milepost 140 +.4 (17 miles west of Gunnison, 48 miles east of Montrose), turn north onto a gravel access road and proceed 0.2 mile to the campground.

Facilities: 10 campsites; sites are fairly good-sized, basically level, with some separation; parking pads are gravel, short straight-ins; some good tent-pitching opportunities; fireplaces; b-y-o firewood; water at a hand pump; vault facilities; gravel driveway; complete supplies and services are available in Gunnison.

Activities & Attractions: Boating, boat launch, fishing on Blue Mesa Reservoir; designated windsurfing area just east of here; the lake is within walking distance; a little footbridge crosses the creekbed; 4wd trail leads off to the north along Red Creek from about milepost 138 on Highway 50.

Natural Features: Located along a seasonal creek which flows into Blue Mesa Reservoir; unlike the lakeshore campgrounds, large hardwoods here provide shelter/shade for most campsites; interesting rock spires and fluted formations tower along both sides of this small canyon; the foliage and shrubbery turn into a burst of color in autumn; though there is no view of the lake from the campsites, the mountains to the south of the reservoir are visible through the draw; elevation 7600'.

Season, Fees & Phone: May to October; $8.00; 14 day limit; Curecanti NRA Headquarters (303) 641-2337.

Camp Notes: This is a little winner of a campground. The setting would particularly appeal to campers who prefer something a bit away from the mainstream. Another nice little campground, called Red Creek, with 7 sites, is located just off the highway at milepost 138, and has similar facilities. It is located between a pair of rocky ridges along gurgling little Red Creek.

Colorado 42

ELK CREEK
Curecanti National Recreation Area

Location: West-central Colorado west of Gunnison.

Access: From U.S. Highway 50 at milepost 142 (15 miles west of Gunnison, 50 miles east of Montrose), turn south onto a paved access road and proceed 0.5 mile to the campground.

Facilities: 180 campsites in 4 loops; sites are small to medium-sized, with adequate spacing, but with minimal visual separation; most parking pads are paved, basically level, short to medium-length straight-ins or pull-offs; a half-dozen nice, hike/bike sites are on a grassy lakeshore area; fireplaces and barbecue grills; b-y-o firewood; water at central faucets; restrooms; coin-op showers nearby; paved driveways; complete supplies and services are available in Gunnison.

Activities & Attractions: Boating; windsurfing; boat launch; marina; fishing for rainbow, brown and lake trout, kokanee salmon; amphitheater for ranger-naturalist programs; guided nature walks; visitor center.

Natural Features: Located midway between the east and west ends of Blue Mesa Reservoir on a point of land on the north shore; the peaks of the Continental Divide are visible to the east; the setting for the campsites is a sage flat surrounded by rolling, sage-covered hills dotted with only a few colorful shrubs or small stands of aspen; a few small trees have been planted in the campground; elevation 7600'.

Season, Fees & Phone: May to October; $8.00; 14 day limit; Curecanti NRA Headquarters (303) 641-2337.

Camp Notes: All sites have views of the extensive valley and hills surrounding the campground. The landscape in the near-distance is interesting to view as the morning and evening shadows change. This is a winter range for deer and elk. Curecanti NRA was named for the Ute Chief Curicata, who used this area as his tribal hunting ground.

Colorado 43

STEVENS CREEK
Curecanti National Recreation Area

Location: West-central Colorado west of Gunnison.

Access: From U.S. Highway 50 near milepost 146 (11 miles west of Gunnison, 55 miles east of Montrose), turn south onto a paved access road into the campground.

Facilities: 55 campsites in 3 loops; sites are generally small, level, fairly well spaced, but with zero visual separation; parking pads are paved, short to medium-length straight-ins; large, level tent spots; fireplaces; b-y-o firewood; water at several faucets; vault facilities; paved driveways; complete supplies and services are available in Gunnison.

Activities & Attractions: Boating; boat launch; windsurfing; fishing; amphitheater for ranger-naturalist programs; visitor center, 4 miles west near Elk Creek Campground.

Natural Features: Located at the east end of Blue Mesa Reservoir; the setting for the campsites is a starkly treeless sage flat surrounded by rolling, sage-covered hills dotted with a few colorful shrubs or small stands of aspen; the Gunnison River has been dammed at a point nearly 20 miles to the west to form the lake; high peaks of The Rockies are visible to the east; typically breezy; elevation 7600'.

Season, Fees & Phone: May to September; $8.00; 14 day limit; Curecanti NRA Headquarters, Gunnison, (303) 641-2337.

Camp Notes: Though the campground is located in very dry country with predominantly sage for vegetation, the scenery is really different and thus a source of diversion. A fairly constant wind blows across the lake. This area appeals particularly to individuals who prefer a sunny, dry climate. Water-related recreational activities are the main drawing card. Remember to bring sunglasses, sunscreen, and something to batten down the hatches.

Colorado 44

ALMONT
Gunnison National Forest

Location: Central Colorado northeast of Gunnison.

Access: From Colorado State Highway 135 at milepost 9 +.3 (9 miles north of Gunnison, 1 mile south of Almont) turn east onto a paved access road and proceed 0.1 mile; turn north or south into the camp areas.

Facilities: 10 campsites in 2 sections; sites are very small to small+, with nominal to fair separation; parking pads are gravel, most are short straight-ins; small tent spots; fire rings; b-y-o firewood; water at a hand pump; vault facilities; narrow, surfaced driveways; nearest reliable sources of supplies and services (complete) are in Gunnison.

Activities & Attractions: Trout fishing (flies and lures only).

Natural Features: Located in a canyon along the west bank of the Taylor River; sites receive light to medium shade/shelter from large hardwoods and a few scattered conifers; bordered by a sage flat; flanking hillsides are dotted with junipers, plus lots of sage and rocks; elevation 8000'.

Season, Fees & Phone: May to October; $7.00; 7 day limit; Taylor River Ranger District, Gunnison, (303) 641-0471.

Camp Notes: The Taylor River corridor is a very popular trout fishing and rafting region, and its public beginnings are here in the Almont area. This camp is useful principally to fishermen who enjoy good angling with a lot of company. Most of the camps farther up the river surpass this simple, streamside spot.

Colorado 45

SPRING CREEK
Gunnison National Forest

Location: Central Colorado northeast of Gunnison.

Access: From the junction of Colorado State Highway 135 & Gunnison County Road 742 in Almont (10 miles northeast of Gunnison), travel northeast on County Road 742 (paved) for 7 miles to a major fork (by a resort); take the left fork onto County Road 744 (paved) and proceed northerly for 1.9 miles; turn east (right) into the campground.

Facilities: 12 campsites; sites are medium-sized, reasonably level, with nominal to fair separation; parking pads are gravel, medium-length straight-ins, or long pull-offs or pull-throughs; adequate space for tents in most sites; fire rings; a limited amount of firewood is available for gathering in the area, b-y-o might be a good idea; water at a hand pump; vault facilities; gravel driveway; complete supplies and services are available in Gunnison.

Activities & Attractions: Trout fishing on the Taylor River; possible fishing on Spring Creek in spring and early summer.

Natural Features: Located in a rocky canyon on a shelftop flat just above the west bank of Spring Creek, a major tributary of the region's principal stream, the Taylor River; sites are minimally to lightly shaded/sheltered by tall conifers and some aspens on a surface of tall grass and sage; elevation 8600'.

Season, Fees & Phone: May to October; $7.00; 14 day limit; Taylor River Ranger District, Gunnison, (303) 641-0471.

Camp Notes: Good views out there, both up and down this canyon. If you prefer a somewhat more 'open' atmosphere than might be found elsewhere in the Taylor River country, Spring Creek may be the one for you.

Colorado 46

NORTH BANK
Gunnison National Forest

Location: Central Colorado northeast of Gunnison.

Access: From the junction of Colorado State Highway 135 & Gunnison County Road 742 in Almont (10 miles northeast of Gunnison), travel northeast on Road 742 (paved) for 8 miles; turn north onto a gravel road for 0.2 mile to the campground.

Special Access Note: Total mileages from Colorado 135 for this and the other campgrounds northeast of here in the Taylor River region have been rounded to the nearest half-mile. With all the stops and zigzags a typical traveler is bound to make along the way, it would be unlikely that odometer mileage would reflect actual mileage with any higher degree of accuracy than that.

Facilities: 16 campsites; sites are medium to large, with fair separation; parking pads are gravel, long pull-throughs or medium-length straight-ins; additional leveling will be needed in most sites; medium to large spots for tents; fire rings; limited firewood is available for gathering in the area; water at a hand pump; vault facilities; gravel driveway; complete supplies and services are available in Gunnison.

Activities & Attractions: Trout fishing.

Natural Features: Located above the north bank of the Taylor River in Taylor Canyon; many of the longer pads are out in the open, but table areas for most sites, as well as the straight-in sites in a side loop, are well-sheltered; elevation 8600'.

Season, Fees & Phone: May to October; $7.00; 14 day limit; Taylor River Ranger District, Gunnison, (303) 641-0471.

Camp Notes: This camp is a peculiarity, of sorts, among the many Taylor Canyon campgrounds: it's the only one on the north bank of the river. Whoever named the place must also have considered that singular trait to be noteworthy as well. (However, take a look at a detailed map. You might agree that, based on the overall direction of the river's flow, the campground is actually on the *west* bank of this fine stream.)

Colorado 47

ONEMILE
Gunnison National Forest

Location: Central Colorado northeast of Gunnison.

Access: From the junction of Colorado State Highway 135 & Gunnison County Road 742 in Almont (10 miles northeast of Gunnison), travel northeast on Road 742 for 8 miles; turn south (right) into the south-west section; or continue for another 0.7 mile, then turn south into the north-east section.

Facilities: 25 campsites with electrical hookups; sites are medium-sized, with fair separation; parking pads are paved, medium to long straight-ins; medium to large areas for tents; fire rings; firewood is available for gathering in the area; water at faucets; vault facilities; paved driveways; complete supplies and services are available in Gunnison.

Activities & Attractions: Trout fishing; rafting; rafter's parking nearby.

Natural Features: Located on a rolling flat at the base of a slope a hundred yards above the Taylor River; sites are sheltered by medium-dense conifers and aspens above a ground cover of sage and grass; closely bordered by densely forested slopes; elevation 8600'.

Season, Fees & Phone: May to October; $12.00; 14 day limit; Taylor River Ranger District, Gunnison, (303) 641-0471.

Camp Notes: From this point southwest, the river becomes floatable during periods of springtime high water. From here northeast, the canyon narrows markedly, and in many places has a wall-to-wall width of little more than 100 yards. If you're a tent camper there's a small camp designated for your purposes about a quarter mile southwest of Onemile on the southeast side of the highway (right, as you approach Onemile Cg. from Almont). The tent unit has a few sites, rings and grills, on a sage flat bordered by conifers; It is often used as a bivouac camp by rock climbers who scale the roadside cliffs.

ROSY LANE
Gunnison National Forest

Location: Central Colorado northeast of Gunnison.

Access: From the junction of Colorado State Highway 135 & Gunnison County Road 742 in Almont (10 miles northeast of Gunnison), travel northeast on Road 742 for 8 miles; turn north (left) into the campground.

Facilities: 19 campsites; sites are medium to large, with fair to fairly good separation; parking pads are paved, super-long pull-throughs plus several medium-length straight-ins; a bit of additional leveling may be needed on some pads; adequate tent spaces; fire rings; some firewood is available for gathering in the area; water at a central faucet; vault facilities; paved driveway; complete supplies and services in Gunnison.

Activities & Attractions: Trout fishing.

Natural Features: Located on a gentle slope a dozen feet above the south-east bank of the Taylor River in Taylor Canyon; most campsites have light or light-medium shade/shelter provided by conifers and some aspens; elevation 8600'.

Season, Fees & Phone: May to October; $8.00; 14 day limit; Taylor River Ranger District, Gunnison, (303) 641-0471.

Camp Notes: Rosy Lane is one of the more scenic camps in uncommonly scenic Taylor Canyon. High, colorful palisades sharply rise from the opposite riverbank to several hundred feet above the campground on the canyon floor.

LODGEPOLE
Gunnison National Forest

Location: Central Colorado northeast of Gunnison.

Access: From the junction of Colorado State Highway 135 & Gunnison County Road 742 in Almont (10 miles northeast of Gunnison), travel northeast on Road 742 for 13.5 miles; turn southeast (right) into the campground's south section; or continue for another 0.1 mile, then turn southeast into the north section.

Facilities: 16 campsites in 2 sections; sites are medium-sized, with fair to fairly good separation; parking pads are gravel, mostly short or medium-length straight-ins in the south section, primarily long pull-throughs on the north side; small to medium-sized tent areas; fire rings; some firewood is available for gathering in the area; water at a hand pump; vault facilities; gravel driveway; nearest reliable sources of supplies are in Gunnison.

Activities & Attractions: Trout fishing; major trailhead with parking for Summerville Trail, 1.5 miles southwest.

Natural Features: Located in Taylor Canyon on moderately sloping terrain above the Taylor River; sites receive light-medium to medium shelter from conifers and a few aspens; elev. 8800'.

Season, Fees & Phone: May to October; $7.00; 14 day limit; Taylor River Ranger District, Gunnison, (303) 641-0471.

Camp Notes: Good river/canyon views toward the south and good river access, too. The Taylor River is known for it's good trout fishing, and this is one of the better camps from which to try your luck. However, if you haven't yet found anything to your liking at Lodgepole or the other camps you've passed to this point, try the next camp upstream from here, Cold Springs. The compact campground has six, snug, sheltered, somewhat sloped sites with small pads, minimal maneuvering room, vaults, and no potable water. A good roadside stop for small outfits. Contributions to the donation box are appreciated in lieu of a standard fee at Cold Springs.

LOTTIS CREEK
Gunnison National Forest

Location: Central Colorado northeast of Gunnison.

Access: From the junction of Colorado State Highway 135 & Gunnison County Road 742 in Almont (10 miles northeast of Gunnison), travel northeast on Road 742 for 16 miles; turn east (right) into the south section; or continue for another 0.1 mile, then swing east into the north section.

Facilities: 28 campsites in 2 sections; sites are medium to large, with fair separation; most parking pads are gravel, medium-length straight-ins or long pull-throughs; several pads are paved; additional leveling will be needed on some pads; fire rings; firewood is available for gathering in the area; water at central faucets; vault facilities; paved driveways; complete supplies and services in Gunnison.

Activities & Attractions: Stream fishing for trout; boating, boat launch and fishing on Taylor Park Reservoir, 5 miles north.

Natural Features: Located on gentle slopes flanking Lottis Creek, at the side stream's confluence with the Taylor River in Taylor Canyon; sites receive light to light-medium shade/shelter from tall conifers above light ground cover; bare-rock or forested cliffs closely border the river; elevation 9000'.

Season, Fees & Phone: May to October; $8.00; 14 day limit; Taylor River Ranger District, Gunnison, (303) 641-0471.

Camp Notes: Although the canyon walls press the river rather closely behind the campground, you can still see a mile or two upriver in this section. Nice camp; very nice surroundings.

Colorado 51

LAKEVIEW
Gunnison National Forest

Location: Central Colorado northeast of Gunnison.

Access: From the junction of Colorado State Highway 135 & Gunnison County Road 742 in Almont (10 miles northeast of Gunnison), travel northeast on Road 742 for 21.5 miles (through Taylor Canyon and past Taylor Dam); at a point 1.5 miles northeast of the dam, turn south (right) onto the paved campground access road and proceed 0.2 mile to the campground.

Facilities: 46 campsites in 3 loops; sites are medium to large, with nominal to fair separation; parking pads are gravel, medium to long straight-ins or very long pull-throughs; additional leveling will be needed in most sites; enough space for large tents; fire rings; a small amount of firewood is available locally, b-y-o might be a good idea; water at central faucets; vault facilities; paved driveways; complete supplies and services in Gunnison.

Activities & Attractions: Boating; boat launch nearby; fishing.

Natural Features: Located on a steepish slope above the south shore of Taylor Park Reservoir, formed by a dam across the very narrow Taylor River Canyon; the campground is situated along the edge of the timber above sage-covered lower slopes; sites are lightly to moderately sheltered/shaded by conifers; elev. 9400'.

Season, Fees & Phone: May to October; $8.00; 14 day limit; Taylor River Ranger District, Gunnison, (303) 641-0471.

Camp Notes: The lower sites are a little less-sheltered than the others higher up on the slope and deeper into the timber. But fewer trees also mean a broader view of the great, treeless valley known as Taylor Park. The campground is about 300 feet above lake level (or maybe 400 feet in a dry year), so the panoramas are excellent. The nearby dam which spans the slim gap at the head of Taylor Canyon and creates the four-square-mile reservoir is barely 50 yards long.

Colorado 52

RIVERS END
Gunnison National Forest

Location: Central Colorado northeast of Gunnison.

Access: From the junction of Colorado State Highway 135 & Gunnison County Road 742 in Almont (10 miles northeast of Gunnison), travel northeast on Road 742 for 25 miles (through Taylor Canyon and past Taylor Dam, and around the east side of Taylor Park Reservoir) to the end of the pavement; continue on Forest Road 742 (gravel) for a final 1.7 miles, then turn west (left) into the campground.

Facilities: 18 campsites in 2 loops, plus an overflow area; sites are medium to large, level, with reasonable spacing but no visual separation; parking pads are gravel, short+ to medium-length straight-ins or super-duper long pull-throughs; plenty of space for tents; fire rings; b-y-o firewood; water at a hand pump; vault facilities; gravel driveways; nearest reliable sources of supplies and services (complete) are in Gunnison.

Activities & Attractions: Boating; fishing.

Natural Features: Located on sage flats at the north shore of Taylor Park Reservoir in a large valley in the Rocky Mountains; the lower loop is streamside, near the Taylor River's entrance into the reservoir; the upper loop is a couple-dozen feet above the inlet; all sites are unsheltered; the valley's expansive sage plain ("park") is encircled by high mountains; elevation 9100'.

Season, Fees & Phone: May to October; $7.00; 14 day limit; Taylor River Ranger District, Gunnison, (303) 641-0471.

Camp Notes: No shade here whatsoever. But the vast *views*--you can't beat 'em! The upper sites have lake vistas with mountains; the lower units have river views with mountains. Another public riverside campground in this vicinity is also readily available, for the nominal cost of a few more miles of gravel travel. Dinner Station Campground is four miles north of here and has about 20 campsites and similar facilities to those at Rivers End.

Colorado 53

WILLIAMS CREEK
Gunnison National Forest

Location: South-central Colorado west of Lake City.

Access: From Colorado State Highway 149 at milepost 69 +.1 (2 miles southeast of Lake City, 7 miles northwest of Slumgullion Pass, 52 miles northwest of Creede), turn south/southwest onto Hinsdale County Road 30 (paved) and travel 7 miles (first 4 miles are paved) along the west shore of Lake San Cristobal; turn west (right) into the campground.

Facilities: 23 campsites; sites are small to quite large, with fair to very good separation; parking pads are gravel, mostly short to medium-length straight-ins or long pull-throughs, which probably will require additional leveling; medium to large tent areas, though generally sloped; fireplaces or fire rings; some firewood is available for gathering in the area; water at several faucets; vault facilities; gravel driveways; limited supplies and services are available in Lake City.

Activities & Attractions: Stream fishing; fishing and boating on Lake San Cristobal; boat launch, 4.5 miles north.

Natural Features: Located on a rocky slope along Williams Creek, near the stream's confluence with Lake Fork of the Gunnison River; sites receive light to medium shelter/shade from a mixture of tall conifers, short to medium-height aspens and light brush; Lake Fork enters Lake San Cristobal 3 miles north; the Continental Divide lies 2 miles southeast; elevation 9200'.

Season, Fees & Phone: June to September; $7.00; 14 day limit; Cebolla Ranger District, Gunnison, (303) 641-0471.

Camp Notes: A county park near here also offers camping. Wupperman Park has about two-dozen units in several clusters above the east shore of Lake San Cristobal. Easiest access is to take County Road 30 to the end of the pavement at the south end of the lake, then a gravel road back north to the east side of the lake. The park has water at faucets, vaults, a dump station, and a competitive fee.

Colorado 54

MILL CREEK
Public Lands/BLM Recreation Site

Location: South-central Colorado west of Lake City.

Access: From Colorado State Highway 149 at milepost 69 +.1 (2 miles southeast of Lake City, 7 miles northwest of Slumgullion Pass, 52 miles northwest of Creede), turn south/southwest onto Hinsdale County Road 30 and travel 11 miles south, then west; turn south (left), cross the bridge, and proceed a final 0.1 mile to the campground. (Note: the road is paved for the first 4 miles, then it becomes gravel.)

Facilities: 22 campsites; sites are small to medium-sized, with fair to good separation; parking pads are gravel, mostly short straight-ins which probably will require a little additional leveling; tent areas vary from small to large, but are mostly sloped; firewood is available for gathering in the area; fireplaces or fire rings; water at hand pumps; vault facilities; gravel driveways; limited supplies and services are available in Lake City.

Activities & Attractions: Fishing; foot trails, backroads, and 4wd trails in the area.

Natural Features: Located on a rocky slope in a canyon just above the south bank of Lake Fork of the Gunnison River at its confluence with Mill Creek; (the generally north-south Lake Fork runs east-west in this section); sites are lightly sheltered by small to medium-height aspens and conifers, plus short grass and a few bushes; bordered by timbered slopes and lofty, barren peaks; elevation 9400'.

Season, Fees & Phone: June to September; $5.00; 14 day limit; Bureau of Land Management, Gunnison, (303) 641-0471.

Camp Notes: Granted, this camp's 'appliances' are pretty basic, and the road up to here can be rough at times. But the views from some sites and from the general campground area are terrific. And the clear (usually), swift, brush-lined stream is very inviting. Another BLM camp off Highway 149 that merits a mention is Red Bridge. It's also along Lake Fork, two miles north up a gravel road from milepost 93, 7 miles west of the hamlet of Powderhorn. Red Bridge has five streamside sites, well water and vaults. Continuing northward from Red Bridge for another four miles along the same gravel road will get you to Gateview Campground, a small primitive camp in Curecanti NRA. Gateview is on Lake Fork Inlet of Blue Mesa Reservoir.

Colorado 55

SLUMGULLION
Gunnison National Forest

Location: South-central Colorado southeast of Lake City.

Access: From Colorado State Highway 149 at milepost 62 +.9 (9 miles southeast of Lake City, 0.6 mile west/northwest of Slumgullion Pass, 42 miles northeast of Creede), turn north (i.e., left if approaching from Lake City) onto Hinsdale County Road 50/Forest Road 788 (gravel) and proceed 0.1 mile; turn right or left into either of the campground's sections.

Facilities: 18 campsites in 2 sections; sites are average-sized, quite sloped, with fairly good separation; parking pads are gravel, short to medium-length straight-ins, plus several long pull-throughs; adequate space for small to medium-sized tents on a grassy/rocky surface; fireplaces or fire rings; some firewood is available for gathering in the area; water at a hand pump; vault facilities; paved driveways; limited supplies and services are available in Lake City.

Activities & Attractions: Access to La Garita Wilderness, a few miles east; scenic overlook points on the highway, within 1 mile east and west.

Natural Features: Located on a timbered slope high in the Rocky Mountains; overall, sites are fairly well sheltered by moderately dense, tall conifers; elevation 11,200'.

Season, Fees & Phone: June to September; $6.00; 14 day limit; Cebolla Ranger District, Gunnison, (303) 641-0471.

Camp Notes: Now who could pass up an opportunity to camp in a place with a salty name like Slumgullion? (Just for grins, look up the origin of "slumgullion" in *Webster's Collegiate*. Ed.) The name befits the region, though, which is rich in tall tales, mining lore and solid history. There are some fantastic views of the Rockies from in and around the campground. At over 11,000 feet, it's a great spot to really get away from the summer sizzle in Denver, Dallas, D.C., or Duluth.

Colorado 56

NORTH & SOUTH CLEAR CREEK
Rio Grande National Forest

Location: South-central Colorado west of Creede.

Access: From Colorado State Highway 149 at milepost 48 +.5 (6.5 miles south of Spring Creek Pass, 20 miles northwest of Creede), turn southeast onto a gravel road and proceed 2.4 miles to North Clear Creek; or at milepost 44, turn northeast onto a gravel road and proceed 0.3 mile to South Clear Creek. (Access to both areas is also available via a 2-mile connecting road between the camps.)

Facilities: *North Clear Creek*: 25 campsites; sites in the North unit are medium to medium+, level, with fair to good separation; parking pads are gravel, short to medium-length straight-ins or medium to long pull-throughs; medium+ to large tent areas; *South Clear Creek*: 16 campsites; sites in the South unit are medium+, with nominal to fair separation; parking pads are mostly medium to long pull-throughs, plus a few straight-ins; large tent areas; *both camps*: fire rings; firewood is available for gathering; water at hand pumps; vault facilities; gravel driveways; nearest reliable sources of supplies (limited) are in Lake City and Creede.

Activities & Attractions: Possibly small-stream fishing; North & South Clear Creek Falls; foot trail to the South Falls.

Natural Features: Located on grassy flats along their respective namesake creeks; sites in the North unit are lightly sheltered by a few conifers and aspens; sites in the South unit are along the edge of a rock-dotted, open flat, set against a low, aspen-and-conifer-covered slope; good mountain views; elevations 9800' & 9500'.

Season, Fees & Phone: June to September; $8.00; 14 day limit; Creede Ranger District (719) 658-2556.

Camp Notes: In addition to this pair of off-highway camps, South Clear Creek Falls Campground is available. It's on an open flat on the inside of a long curve at milepost 45 +.5 on Highway 149. It's OK for a quick stop (if you can find a spot that's vacant). But the off-asphalt camps generally are better options.

Colorado 57

MARSHALL PARK
Rio Grande National Forest

Location: South-central Colorado southwest of Creede.

Access: From Colorado State Highway 149 at milepost 27 +.8 (on the northeast side of the large Rio Grande highway bridge, 6 miles southwest of Creede, 34 miles southeast of Spring Creek Pass), turn south onto Middle Creek Road and proceed 0.3 mile (across the small bridge) to the campground.

Facilities: 15 campsites in a loop and a string; sites are average-sized, level, with not much separation; parking pads are gravel, medium to long straight-ins or paved pull-throughs; adequate space for large tents; fire rings and barbecue grills; b-y-o firewood is recommended; water at a hand pump; vault facilities; paved driveway; limited supplies are available in Creede.

Activities & Attractions: Fishing.

Natural Features: Located on an open flat just above the Rio Grande and a couple-hundred yards below the highway; a few conifers dot the main part of the campground and the riverbank, but otherwise most sites are unsheltered; bordered by steep canyon walls across the river, and more distant high mountains; elevation 8900'.

Season, Fees & Phone: June to September; $8.00; 14 day limit; Creede Ranger District (719) 658-2556.

Camp Notes: The local scenery is quite good and the river is wide and swift and deep here. This appears to be a popular fishing camp. (Incidentally, some currently distributed maps depict a national forest campground called "Rio Grande" 3 miles southwest of Marshall Park, but it has been turned into what amounts to a fishing access site.)

Colorado 58

PALISADE
Rio Grande National Forest

Location: South-central Colorado southeast of Creede.

Access: From Colorado State Highway 149 at milepost 9 +.5 (11 miles southeast of Creede, 10 miles northwest of South Fork), turn west into the campground.

Facilities: 13 campsites; sites are medium+ in size, basically level, with fair to midlin' separation; parking pads are gravel, mainly medium to long pull-offs or pull-throughs, plus a few short straight-ins; adequate space for large tents in most sites; fire rings and barbecue grills; some firewood is available for gathering in the vicinity, gathering wood on forest lands prior to arrival, or b-y-o, is suggested; water at a hand pump; vault facilities; gravel driveway; limited supplies in Creede, limited supplies and services are available in South Fork.

Activities & Attractions: Fishing; rafting.

Natural Features: Located on a flat along the bank of the Rio Grande; most sites receive light to moderate shelter/shade from tall conifers, hardwoods and some brush; steep, rocky, well-timbered canyon walls border the river in this area; elevation 8300'.

Season, Fees & Phone: June to September; $8.00; 14 day limit; Creede Ranger District (719) 658-2556.

Camp Notes: Most sites have some sort of a river view, and there are good views up and down the canyon from the campground area. "Palisade" refers to the rocky outcroppings along the canyon walls.

This section of the Rio Grande is classified as "Gold Medal" trout habitat. In addition to the river and the highway, the campground is also flanked by a (hopefully inactive when you stay here) railroad track.

Colorado 59

BEAVER CREEK
Rio Grande National Forest

Location: South-central Colorado west of Del Norte.

Access: From U.S. Highway 160 at milepost 184 +.8 (1 mile southwest of South Fork, 18 miles east of the summit of Wolf Creek Pass), turn south onto Beaver Creek Road (paved); proceed south/southwest for 3.1 miles, then turn west (right) into the campground.

Facilities: 21 campsites; sites are small to medium in size, most are reasonably level, with fair separation; parking pads are gravel, medium-length straight-ins; most sites have adequate space for tents; fireplaces; some firewood may be available for gathering in the vicinity; water at a hand pump; vault facilities; gravel driveway; limited supplies and services are available in South Fork.

Activities & Attractions: Stream fishing; fishing and boating on Beaver Creek Reservoir, 2 miles south.

Natural Features: Located on a boulder-strewn, rolling, grassy flat along Beaver Creek, a tributary of the South Fork of the Rio Grande; campsites are sheltered/shaded by light timber and a few hardwoods; the campground is on the edge of a small, narrow gorge, through which flows Beaver Creek; rocky, timbered hillsides in the immediate vicinity, forested mountains in the distance; elevation 8800'.

Season, Fees & Phone: May to October; $7.00; 14 day limit; Del Norte Ranger District (719) 657-3321.

Camp Notes: Many of Beaver Creek's sites provide some fine views of the valley. A second campground along this road is Upper Beaver Creek, 0.8 mile further south. It has 13 sites in 2 adjoining sections on a partially forested, streamside flat, a hand pump and vault facilities. Upper Beaver Creek's sites are just a few yards from, and parallel to, the road.

Colorado 60

CROSS CREEK
Rio Grande National Forest

Location: South-central Colorado west of Del Norte.

Access: From U.S. Highway 160 at milepost 184 +.8 (1 mile southwest of South Fork, 18 miles east of the summit of Wolf Creek Pass), turn south onto Beaver Creek Road; travel south/southwest for 4 miles on pavement, and continue for 2.3 miles on gravel (past Beaver Creek Dam and Reservoir); turn east into the campground.

Facilities: 12 campsites in 2 adjoining sections, including 3 walk-in sites; sites are average in size, with nominal separation; parking pads are gravel straight-ins, generally short to medium in length, and most will require some additional leveling; good-sized tent areas in most sites; fire rings; some firewood is available for gathering in the area; water at faucets; vault facilities; gravel driveway; limited supplies and services are available in South Fork.

Activities & Attractions: Fishing and boating on the reservoir; stream fishing on Beaver Creek; several foot trails and 4-wheel drive roads in the vicinity.

Natural Features: Located on a grassy, moderately timbered hillside at the southeast corner of Beaver Creek Reservoir; conifers and aspens provide some shelter/shade; Cross Creek rushes down through the center of the campground; densely forested slopes surround the reservoir; the dam at the north end of the reservoir impounds Beaver Creek, which joins the South Fork of the Rio Grande, 4 miles north; elevation 8900'.

Season, Fees & Phone: May to October; $7.00; 14 day limit; Del Norte Ranger Dist. (719) 657-3321.

Camp Notes: There are several really nice creekside tent spots here. Several campsites have good views of the reservoir. This campground is, however, quite heavily used in midsummer.

Colorado 61

PARK CREEK
Rio Grande National Forest

Location: South-central Colorado west of Del Norte.

Access: From U.S. Highway 160 at milepost 178 +.4 (8 miles southwest of South Fork, 12 miles east of the summit of Wolf Creek Pass), turn south onto a gravel access road and proceed 0.1 mile to the campground.

Facilities: 15 campsites; sites are small to medium-sized, level, with fair to excellent separation; parking pads are gravel, extra wide, short to medium-length straight-ins; good-sized tent areas; fireplaces; some firewood may be available for gathering; water at a hand pump; vault facilities; gravel driveway; limited supplies and services are available in South Fork.

Activities & Attractions: Fishing.

Natural Features: Located on a grassy flat at the confluence of Park Creek and the South Fork of the Rio Grande; campground vegetation consists of a variety of hardwoods and tall conifers which provide a moderate amount of shelter/shade; many of the campsites are streamside; low, timbered ridges are in the vicinity, heavily timbered peaks in the distance; elevation 8500'.

Season, Fees & Phone: May to September; $7.00; 14 day limit; Del Norte Ranger District (719) 657-3321.

Camp Notes: You might have to overlook the fact that the highway is rather close by to appreciate this camping area. It's really kind of nice. Another nearby roadside campground is Highway Springs, a national forest camping area on the south side of Highway 160 at milepost 182. Highway Springs has about 10 sites in two sections, vault facilities, but no drinking water. The campsites are simple, but the valley views are spectacular.

Colorado 62

BIG MEADOWS
Rio Grande National Forest

Location: South-central Colorado west of Del Norte.

Access: From U.S Highway 160 at milepost 174 +.7 (9 miles east of the summit of Wolf Creek Pass, 28 miles northeast of Pagosa Springs, 14 miles southwest of South Fork), turn west (the highway runs north and south through this stretch); proceed southwest on a gravel access road for 1.4 miles to a fork; take the left fork and continue for 0.4 mile to the campground.

Facilities: 50 campsites in 4 loops; sites are average or better in size, with fair to very good separation; parking pads are gravel, medium to long, mainly straight-ins; many pads may require additional leveling; mostly large tent spots, though some may be sloped; fire rings; firewood is available for gathering in the area; water at several faucets; vault facilities; gravel driveways; limited supplies and services are available in South Fork.

Activities & Attractions: Boating; boat launch; fishing; hiking trail leads up to Lobo Overlook on the Continental Divide.

Natural Features: Located on the south-east shore of Big Meadows Reservoir near the headwaters of the South Fork of the Rio Grande; campground vegetation consists of tall pines, aspens, light underbrush, and some more open, grassy meadow areas; some sites are lakeside and some are situated near the base of a steep forested hillside behind the campground; elevation 9300'.

Season, Fees & Phone: June to September; $8.00; 14 day limit; Del Norte Ranger District (719) 657-3321.

Camp Notes: Big Meadows is the preeminent recreation area along the South Fork and its tributaries. Its high elevation and the accompanying snow cover during most of the years results in a renewed freshness summer after summer.

Colorado 63

TUCKER PONDS
Rio Grande National Forest

Location: South-central Colorado west of Del Norte.

Access: From U.S. Highway 160 at milepost 172 +.9 (6 miles east of the summit of Wolf Creek Pass, 30 miles east of Pagosa Springs, 12 miles southwest of South Fork), turn southeast (i.e., right, if approaching from the pass and Pagosa Springs) onto Forest Road 390 (gravel) and proceed 2.7 miles; turn west (right) into the campground.

Facilities: 17 campsites; sites are medium-sized, with typically good visual separation; parking pads are gravel, medium to very long pull-throughs or pull-offs, plus a few medium-length straight-ins; most pads will require some additional leveling; generally smallish, sloped tent areas; fireplaces or fire rings;

firewood is available for gathering in the area; water at a hand pump; vault facilities; gravel driveways; nearest reliable sources of supplies and services are in Pagosa Springs (adequate) or South Fork (limited).

Activities & Attractions: Fishing for stocked trout; hiking.

Natural Features: Located on a heavily forested, rolling, rocky slope in the Rocky Mountains just east of the Continental Divide; tall conifers provide quite ample shelter for all sites; Tucker Ponds, a pair of impoundments on Pass Creek, are a few minutes' walk east of the campground; elevation 9700'.

Season, Fees & Phone: June to September; $7.00; 14 day limit; Del Norte Ranger District (719) 657-3321.

Camp Notes: The access road is quite rocky and rough and is very narrow in several spots. The deep, steep drop-off along the edge of the track adds garnish to the adventure. Worth the trip up the side of the mountain? You bet!

Colorado 64

WOLF CREEK
San Juan National Forest

Location: Southwest Colorado east of Pagosa Springs.

Access: From U.S. Highway 160 at milepost 158 +.1 (15 miles east of Pagosa Springs, 9 miles west of the summit of Wolf Creek Pass), turn west/northwest onto West Fork Road (gravel) and proceed 0.5 mile to the campground. (Note that U.S. 160 basically follows a north-south line in this section.)

Facilities: 26 campsites in 2 sections on both sides of the stream; sites are generally quite large and level, with good to excellent separation; parking pads are gravel, mostly long straight-ins, some are long pull-thoughs; tent areas are large; fire rings; firewood is available for gathering; water at hand pumps; vault facilities; gravel driveways; adequate supplies and services are available in Pagosa Springs.

Activities & Attractions: Fishing; excellent viewpoint of the valley in which the campground is located, on the main highway, about 2.5 miles east.

Natural Features: Located on a densely forested flat along Wolf Creek; campground vegetation consists primarily of tall conifers, a few aspens and some low-level brush; the campground lies at the northernmost section of what is essentially the Upper San Juan River Valley; spire-shaped rock formations, a mile or two distant, are visible from near the campground; elevation 8000'.

Season, Fees & Phone: May to October; $7.00; 14 day limit; Pagosa Ranger District (303) 264-2268.

Camp Notes: Well, this is definitely an excellent campground. If this area is full, or if you prefer a camp spot that is a little less forested, you might check out West Fork Campground, 1.1 miles further up West Fork Road. Access to the West Fork of the San Juan River is near there.

Colorado 65

WEST FORK
San Juan National Forest

Location: Southwest Colorado east of Pagosa Springs.

Access: From U.S. Highway 160 at milepost 158 +.1 (15 miles east of Pagosa Springs, 9 miles west of the summit of Wolf Creek Pass), turn west/northwest onto a West Fork Road (gravel) and proceed 1.6 miles to the campground. (Note that U.S. 160 basically follows a north-south line in this section.)

Facilities: 28 campsites in a single large loop; sites are very large, level and well spaced, with fair to good visual separation; parking pads are gravel, very long pull-throughs, or are good-sized straight-ins; spacious tent spots; fire rings; firewood is available for gathering; water at a hand pump; vault facilities; gravel driveway; adequate supplies and services are available in Pagosa Springs.

Activities & Attractions: Fishing (the West Fork is about a half-mile drive further on up the road, or a short, possibly brush-busting, walk to the west).

Natural Features: Located on a moderately timbered flat near the West Fork of the San Juan River; campground vegetation consists of tall conifers, aspens and willows, tall grass and a thick carpet of evergreen needles; the north end of the loop is in slightly more open forest than the south half; the campground lies at the northernmost section of what is essentially the Upper San Juan River Valley; spire-shaped rock formations, a mile or two distant, are visible from near the campground; elevation 8000'.

Season, Fees & Phone: May to October; $7.00; 14 day limit; Pagosa Ranger District (303) 264-2268.

Camp Notes: There's a good selection of campsites here--from open-air to more sheltered/shaded. Some sites provide excellent views of the mountains. And the parking pads are big enough to drive an 18-wheeler through them (if your taste in camping vehicles runs just a mite on the eccentric side).

Colorado 66

EAST FORK
San Juan National Forest

Location: Southwest Colorado east of Pagosa Springs.

Access: From U.S. Highway 160 at milepost 154 +.1 (11 miles east of Pagosa Springs, 13 miles west of the summit of Wolf Creek Pass) turn east onto East Fork Road (gravel) and proceed 0.8 mile to the campground. (Note that the highway basically lies in a north-south line in this section.)

Facilities: 26 campsites in a main loop, plus 2 small side loops; most sites are spacious, level, and well separated; parking pads are gravel, mostly medium to long, wide straight-ins, plus a couple of long pull-throughs; virtually every site can accommodate a good-sized tent; fireplaces; firewood is available for gathering; water at a hand pump; vault facilities; gravel driveways; adequate supplies and services are available in Pagosa Springs.

Activities & Attractions: Fishing; several foot trails lead down to the river.

Natural Features: Located on a moderately to heavily forested hill above the East Fork of the San Juan River; campground vegetation consists of medium-tall conifers, some aspens, and a considerable quantity of underbrush; high, timbered mountains rise throughout the surrounding area; interesting, high, fluted cliffs are nearby, though they are not visible from the campground; elevation 7600'.

Season, Fees & Phone: May to October; $7.00; 14 day limit; Pagosa Ranger District (303) 264-2268.

Camp Notes: This is an excellent spot for a forest campground. There are a couple of really nice campsites on the edge of a bluff overlooking the densely forested river valley. East Fork Road continues east/northeast from here to provide access to a half-dozen foot trails and jeep roads, some of which cross the Continental Divide.

Colorado
North Central
Please refer to the Colorado map in the Appendix

Colorado 67

PEARL LAKE
Pearl Lake State Park

Location: North-central Colorado north of Steamboat Springs.

Access: From U.S. Highway 40 at the northwest edge of Steamboat Springs, turn north onto Elk River Road (Routt County Road 129, paved) and travel 23 miles (6 miles past the hamlet of Clark); turn east/northeast onto a gravel road and proceed 2.1 miles to the campground.

Facilities: 39 campsites in 2 sections; sites are medium-sized, somewhat closely spaced, but with generally good visual separation; parking pads are gravel, mostly long pull-throughs, plus some short to medium-length straight-ins; additional leveling will probably be needed; small, somewhat sloped tent spots; fire rings; firewood is available for gathering on national forest lands in the vicinity; water at several faucets; vault facilities; gravel driveways; holding tank disposal station, 2 miles north; gas and camper supplies on Elk River Road; virtually complete supplies and services are available in Steamboat Springs.

Activities & Attractions: Fishing for cutthroat trout (artificial flies and lures only); limited boating (wakeless); small boat launch; designated swimming area; day use area.

Natural Features: Located on densely forested slopes on the west shore of Pearl Lake in the shadow of prominent Hahns Peak; tall conifers and some aspens provide adequate shelter for all sites; a few campsites are lakeside; elevation 8000'.

Season, Fees & Phone: May to October; 14 day limit; please see Appendix for reservation information and standard Colorado state park fees; phone c/o Steamboat Lake State Recreation Area.

Camp Notes: Pearl Lake is "cozy"--it has the look and 'feel' of a national forest camp. In planning your trip up to the campgrounds in the Hahns Peak area allow an average of roughly 35 mph or so on narrow, winding, Elk River Road. Your vehicle, your passengers, your fellow roadsmen and your nerves will thank you. Besides, the super scenery in the Elk River Valley warrants a roadside stop or three.

Colorado 68

SUNRISE VISTA
Steamboat Lake State Recreation Area

Location: North-central Colorado north of Steamboat Springs.

Access: From U.S. Highway 40 at the northwest edge of Steamboat Springs, turn north onto Elk River Road/Routt County Road 129 (paved); travel 26 miles to a point 0.2 mile beyond the state park office (0.9 mile past the Placer Cove turnoff); turn west (left) onto Routt County Road 62 (gravel) and proceed 0.5 mile; turn south (left) onto a gravel access road and continue for 0.2 mile to the campground.

Facilities: 103 campsites in a complex group of loops; sites are medium-sized, basically level, with fair to good separation; parking pads are gravel, medium-length straight-ins or long (or very long) pull-throughs; adequate space for large tents; fire rings; firewood is available for gathering on adjacent national forest lands; water at several faucets; vault facilities; gravel driveways; disposal station in the park's Sage Flats area; gas and camper supplies on Elk River Road; virtually complete supplies and services are available in Steamboat Springs.

Activities & Attractions: Boating; fishing; short foot trails to the lake; amphitheater for scheduled nature programs.

Natural Features: Located on a slightly rolling, forested flat near the north shore of Steamboat Lake; campground vegetation consists of tracts of tall grass, and light to medium-dense aspens and tall conifers; surrounded by wooded hills and distant mountains; elevation 8000'.

Season, Fees & Phone: Principal season is May to September, with limited availability at other times, subject to weather conditions; 14 day limit; please see Appendix for reservation information and standard Colorado state park fees; park office (303) 879-3922.

Camp Notes: Although only a few campsites have any sort of a lake view, a number of sites have terrific mountain views. (As a general guideline, the lower-numbered campsites are a little more open, with better distant views; the upper-numbered units are a bit more forested--and in some respects, a little nicer.) 10,800' Hahns Peak, the local lofty location, is three miles northeast.

Colorado 69

DUTCH HILL
Steamboat Lake State Recreation Area

Location: North-central Colorado north of Steamboat Springs.

Access: From U.S. Highway 40 at the northwest edge of Steamboat Springs, turn north onto Elk River Road/Routt County Road 129, paved); travel 26 miles to a point 0.2 mile beyond the state park office; turn west (left) onto Routt County Road 62 (gravel) and proceed 1 mile; turn south (left) onto a gravel access road and continue for 0.1 mile to the campground.

Facilities: 91 campsites in several loops and subloops; sites vary from small to medium+, with fair to reasonably good separation; parking pads are gravel, most are straight-ins; large, basically level tent areas; fire rings; firewood is available for gathering on adjacent national forest lands; water at several faucets; vault facilities; gravel driveways; disposal station at Sage Flats; gas and camper supplies on Elk River Road; virtually complete supplies and services are available in Steamboat Springs.

Activities & Attractions: Designated swimming area; boating; boat launches; marina; fishing for trout; foot trails; amphitheater for nature programs; day use area.

Natural Features: Located on a forested flat near the northwest shore of Steamboat Lake; tall conifers provide light to medium shelter/shade for most sites; bordered by hills and encircled by distant mountains; solitary Hahns Peak rises in the near distance; elevation 8000'.

Season, Fees & Phone: May to September; 14 day limit; please see Appendix for reservation information and standard Colorado state park fees; park office (303) 879-3922.

Camp Notes: Dutch Hill seems to be a bit more popular than its sister camp, Sunrise Vista (see separate info). Perhaps that's due to its slightly-closer-to-the-water's-edge position. Reservations for both campgrounds are "definitely recommended" for holiday weekends, and "just to be sure" for other midsummer weekends.

HAHNS PEAK LAKE
Routt National Forest

Location: North-central Colorado north of Steamboat Springs.

Access: From U.S. Highway 40 at the northwest edge of Steamboat Springs, turn north onto Elk River Road/Routt County Road 129, paved); travel 28 miles to a point 2 miles past the end of the pavement at the Steamboat State Park Office; turn southwest (left) onto Forest Road 486 (Hahns Peak Lake Road, gravel) and continue southwest then northwest for 1.8 miles; turn south (left), cross the bridge, and go 0.7 mile to the campground.

Facilities: 26 campsites in 2 loops; sites are medium to large, with fair to good separation; parking pads are gravel, short to medium-length straight-ins or long pull-throughs; about half of the pads will require additional leveling; tent areas vary from small to large, and about half are basically level; fire rings; firewood is available for gathering; water at several faucets; vault facilities; holding tank disposal station at Sage Flats, near the state park office; gravel driveways; gas and camper supplies at Steamboat Lake.

Activities & Attractions: Fishing; boating; boat launch.

Natural Features: Located near the shore at the northwest tip of long, slender, curved Hahns Peak Lake, 3 miles west of prominent Hahns Peak, and a dozen miles west of the Continental Divide; sites are moderately sheltered by tall conifers; flanked by steep, conifer-and-aspen-clad slopes; elevation 8500'.

Season, Fees & Phone: June to September; $7.00; 14 day limit; Hahns Peak Ranger District, Steamboat Springs, (303) 879-1870.

Camp Notes: This is the type of camp for which you'd plan to stay for a couple of days. It's not just a quick n' easy jaunt off the main drag at Steamboat Springs. Still, the trip is definitely worth it.

MEADOWS
Routt National Forest

Location: North-central Colorado east of Steamboat Springs.

Access: From U.S. Highway 40 at milepost 147+.8 (in Rabbit Ears Pass, 10 miles west of the junction of U.S. 40 & Colorado State Highway 14 at Muddy Pass, 15 miles southeast of Steamboat Springs), turn south onto the campground access road and proceed 0.3 mile to the campground.

Facilities: 33 campsites, including a few park n' walk sites, in 3 loops; sites are small to medium-sized, with fair to good separation; parking pads are gravel, short to medium+ straight-ins which probably will require additional leveling; adequate space for medium to large tents, but space may be sloped; fire rings; firewood is available for gathering in the area; water at several faucets; vault facilities; gravel driveways; nearest supplies and services (virtually complete) are in Steamboat Springs.

Activities & Attractions: Meadow walking; great scenic views at an overlook of the Yampa River Valley, 3 miles west of here.

Natural Features: Located on a forested knoll in the Park Range of the Rocky Mountains; campground vegetation consists of moderately dense, tall conifers; bordered by a large meadow; elevation 9300'.

Season, Fees & Phone: July to September; $7.00; 14 day limit; Hahns Peak Ranger District, Steamboat Springs, (303) 879-1870.

Camp Notes: Meadows *probably* wouldn't be one of those places where you'd specifically plan to spend a weekend. There just isn't a lot to do around here. But for an overnighter, it would serve very well. Most of the campsites are visibly and audibly isolated from U.S 40. As an option, you could check Walton Creek Campground at milepost 149 +.8, two miles east of Meadows off the south side of the highway. Walton Creek has 14 campsites, water and vaults, but the camp's availability at a given time is subject to the level of campsite demand in the district.

DUMONT LAKE
Routt National Forest

Location: North-central Colorado east of Steamboat Springs.

Access: From U.S. Highway 40 at milepost 152 +.7 (in Rabbit Ears Pass, 4.6 miles west of the junction of U.S. 40 Colorado State Highway 14 at Muddy Pass, 20 miles southeast of Steamboat Springs), turn north onto Forest Road 315 (paved); proceed northeast for 1.25 miles (just past the turnoff to the picnic area); turn north (left) into the campground.

Facilities: 22 campsites in 2 loops; sites are large, with good to excellent spacing and fair to very good visual separation; parking pads are gravel, mostly long straight-ins, plus a couple of pull-throughs; additional leveling may be required in many units; adequate, level space for medium to large tents on gravel tent pads or cleared earth; fire rings, plus a few barbecue grills; some firewood is available for gathering in the area; water at a hand pump; vault facilities; gravel driveways; nearest supplies and services (virtually complete) are in Steamboat Springs.

Activities & Attractions: Fishing; limited boating (hand-propelled or electric motors); foot trails.

Natural Features: Located on somewhat sloping, subalpine terrain atop the Rocky Mountains, a few yards west of the Continental Divide; campground vegetation consists of grass, wildflowers and stands of tall conifers; Dumont Lake is a few minutes' walk west of the campground; Rabbit Ears Peak lies 2 miles northeast; elevation 9500'.

Season, Fees & Phone: Late-June to September; $7.00; 14 day limit; Hahns Peak Ranger District, Steamboat Springs, (303) 879-1870.

Camp Notes: Too bad that the season up here is so short. There are some really fabulous views from some of the campsites. This looks like great country for high mountain meadow-walking. Only *22* campsites on this large piece of Rocky Mountain public real estate? Yep.

Colorado 73

STAGECOACH
Stagecoach State Park

Location: North-central Colorado southeast of Steamboat Springs.

Access: From Colorado State Highway 131 at milepost 50 (2 miles north of Phippsburg, 2 miles south of Oak Creek, 52 miles north of Interstate 70 Exit 157 at Wolcott), turn east onto Routt County Road 14 (begins as gravel, becomes paved); head northeasterly for 5.5 miles; turn southeast (right) onto Routt County Road 18 and go 200 yards to a fork; take the right fork for 0.1 mile to the park entrance station; go past the entrance for 0.1 mile to the *McKindley* Campground parking area (on the right); continue down the hill for another 0.3 mile to a major "T" intersection; turn south (right) to *Junction City* Campground. 0.4 mile; or turn north (left) to *Pinnacle* Campground and *Harding Spur* Campground, both within 0.4 mile.

Alternate Access: From Colorado State Highway 131 at milepost 62 +.3 (12 miles south of the junction of State Highways 131 & 14 southeast of Steamboat Springs, 9 miles north of Oak Creek), turn southeast onto Routt County Road 14 (paved) and proceed 5.4 miles; turn east (left) onto County Road 18 and continue as above.

(**Special Note**: Routt County Road 14 is a half-loop that connects to Highway 131 at two points; the first access works well if you're northbound from the Interstate; the Alternate Access is a good one if you're southbound from Steamboat Springs.)

Facilities: *Junction City*: 27 slightly sloped campsites with electrical hookups; parking pads are short to medium-length straight-ins or medium+ pull-throughs; *Pinnacle*: 37 reasonably level campsites with medium+ pull-through parking pads; *Harding Spur*: 18 slightly sloped campsites with short straight-in parking pads; *McKindley*: 9 level walk-in (actually walk-*up*) tent sites with gravel tent/table pads, vault facilities, and parking in a small lot below the campground; *all camps*: site size is small or small+, with nil to nominal separation; large tent pads in McKindley, enough room for only small or medium-sized tents in most other sites, (or plant your canvas on the parking pad); gravel parking pads; fire rings; b-y-o firewood; water at central faucets; restrooms; gravel driveways; holding tank disposal station; gas and groceries in Oak Creek; virtually complete supplies and services are available in Steamboat Springs, 17 miles north.

Activities & Attractions: Boating; boat launch and courtesy dock; marina; windsurfing; sandy swimming beach; fishing mostly for rainbow trout, also brook and brown trout; cross-country skiing; ice fishing; day use areas.

Natural Features: Located on open slopes and hilltops above the middle west shore of Stagecoach Reservoir in the Yampa Valley; vegetation consists mostly of shin-high brush and grass, plus small, scattered, planted trees; several prominent, forested peaks encircle the valley; elevation 7200'.

Season, Fees & Phone: Principal season is May to October; Keystone area may be open for limited parking/rv camping in winter; 14 day limit; please see Appendix for reservation information and standard Colorado state park fees; park office (303) 736-2436.

Camp Notes: The monikers of the camp loops come from old mines and mining camps. Although all areas are very much out in the open, each has slightly different characteristics which might influence you to pre-choose one over the others. Keystone and Junction City are on hillsides just above the shore; Pinnacle sits on a bench above the swim beach and marina; Harding is up a small draw, with views of the lake only if there are no large rigs parked east of your campsite; and McKindley's walk-up tent sites are on a high, windswept hilltop overlooking the entire place.

Colorado 74

LYNX PASS
Routt National Forest

Location: North-central Colorado west of Kremmling.

Access: From Colorado State Highway 134 at milepost 8 + .8, (9 miles east of Toponas, 7 miles west of Gore Pass, 18 miles west of the junction of Highway 134 & U.S. 40 north of Kremmling), turn north onto a Routt County Road 16/Forest Road 270 (gravel); proceed 2.8 miles, (after the first 0.4 mile, bear right at the intersection) to a point just beyond small Lynx Lake; turn south/southwest (left) into the campground.

Facilities: 12 campsites; sites are small to medium-sized, with nominal to good visual separation; parking pads are gravel, short straight-ins or long pull-throughs/pull-offs; additional leveling will be required; smallish, sloped areas for tents; fireplaces and barbecue grills; firewood is available for gathering in the area; water at a hand pump; vault facilities; gravel driveway; gas and groceries are available in Toponas.

Activities & Attractions: Fishing and very limited boating on Lynx Lake.

Natural Features: Located on a timbered hillside; campground vegetation consists of light to medium dense, lofty conifers and aspens on a carpet of grass and small plants and flowers; surrounded by forested mountains; elevation 8900'.

Season, Fees & Phone: June to September; $6.00; 14 day limit; Yampa Ranger District (303) 638-4516.

Camp Notes: Tiny Lynx Lake is just a short walk down the hill from the campground, but there are no lake views from the camp itself. Distant views are somewhat restricted from within the camp area, but are quite excellent from near the campground. Of the three campgrounds in the Gore Pass corridor, Lynx Pass is most likely the spot of choice. Within this region is another string of forest camps which may merit your attention. From Yampa, head southwest on County Road 7 for seven miles, then another six to nine miles southwest on Forest Road 900 to the trio of small camps, named Bear Lake, Horseshoe and Cold Springs. Bear Lake, with 29 campsites, piped water, vaults and a fee, is by far the largest and most popular of the three.

Colorado 75

GORE PASS & BLACKTAIL
Routt National Forest

Location: North-central Colorado west of Kremmling.

Access: From Colorado State Highway 134 at milepost 16 + .1, (at the summit of Gore Pass, 16 miles east of Toponas, 11 miles west of the junction of Highway 134 & U.S. 40 north of Kremmling), turn south/southeast into *Gore Pass* Campground; or at milepost 14 + .6, (1.5 miles west of Gore Pass), turn south and proceed 0.2 mile to *Blacktail* Campground. (Note: access to Blacktail is at the inside of a horseshoe turn on a steep section of highway.)

Facilities: *Gore Pass*: 12 campsites; *Blacktail*: 8 campsites; sites in both camps are small to medium-sized, with fair separation; parking pads in Gore Pass are gravel, short to medium-length straight-ins, plus a few pull-throughs; pads in Blacktail are long pull-throughs or straight-ins; additional leveling will probably be needed in most sites; small to medium-sized, sloped tent areas; fire rings; some firewood is available for gathering in the area; water at several faucets in Gore Pass, and at a hand pump in Blacktail; vault facilities; sandy gravel driveways; gas and groceries are available in Toponas.

Activities & Attractions: Mountain vistas.

Natural Features: Located on timbered slopes at, or just west of, the summit of Gore Pass; vegetation consists of light to medium dense conifers and aspens; a brushy meadow is adjacent to Blacktail; bordered by timbered mountains; elevation 9500'.

Season, Fees & Phone: June to September; $6.00; 14 day limit; Yampa Ranger District (303) 638-4516.

Camp Notes: Unless you're just passing by and need a roadside rest for the night, this pair of simple camps could probably be passed-up for better 'accommodations' in the Rockies. Although most of Blacktail's sites are in view of the highway, subjectively it might have a slight edge over Gore Pass' *closeness* to the highway. Still, they are cool and reasonably quiet camps at night.

Colorado 76

McDonald Flats
Arapahoe National Forest

Location: Central Colorado north of Silverthorne.

Access: From Colorado State Highway 9 at milepost 118 +.1 (16 miles north of Silverthorne, 21 miles south of Kremmling), turn northwest onto a gravel road and proceed 2.2 miles; turn northeast (right) onto the campground access road and continue for 0.1 mile to the campground.

Facilities: 18 campsites; sites are small to small+, level, with little or no separation; parking pads are gravel, short to medium-length; some sites, particularly the lakeside sites, may be suitable for tents; fire rings; a limited amount of firewood may be available for gathering locally, but b-y-o is recommended; water at a hand pump; vault facilities; gravel driveways; nearest reliable source of adequate supplies is the Silverthorne-Dillon area.

Activities & Attractions: Fishing; boating; boat launch.

Natural Features: Located on a completely open sage and grass covered flat at the south end of Green Mountain Reservoir; high and dry mountains surround the area; elevation 8000'.

Season, Fees & Phone: May to October; $6.00; 14 day limit; Dillon Ranger District (303) 468-5400 (office) or (303) 468-5435 (recorded recreation message).

Camp Notes: This may be a case of "best available in the vicinity". The facilities here are minimal, but since the main attraction is excellent fishing, many campers might be quite willing to forego some of the usual amenities. Other national forest campgrounds in the area include Davis Spring, a very small campground with some shelter, about 0.5 mile south of McDonald Flats; and Prairie Point, almost directly across from McDonald Flats on the highway side of the reservoir. Prairie Point, although roughly similar in size and facilities to McDonald Flat, is less level and usually somewhat more populated.

Colorado 77

Blue River
Arapahoe National Forest

Location: Central Colorado north of Silverthorne.

Access: From Colorado State Highway 9 at milepost 109 +.7 (8 miles north of Silverthorne, 31 miles south of Kremmling), turn east into the campground.

Facilities: 20 campsites in 2 sections; sites are medium to large, with adequate separation; parking pads are gravel, short to medium-length straight-ins; some additional leveling may be needed, mainly in the upper units; medium to large tent areas; fire rings; firewood is available for gathering in the vicinity; water at hand pumps; vault facilities; gravel driveways; adequate supplies and services are available in the Silverthone-Dillon area.

Activities & Attractions: Fishing is the principal pastime--usually restricted to the use of flies or lures.

Natural Features: Located in a moderately forested area along the west bank of the deep, cold Blue River; several sites are situated on the hilltop near the campground entrance; the majority of the units are located below the first set, along the river; many of the sites are located right at the river's edge; very little low-level vegetation; views of high, timbered mountains to the east and south; elevation 8400'.

Season, Fees & Phone: May to September; $6.00; 14 day limit; Dillon Ranger District (303) 468-5400 (office) or (303) 468-5435 (recorded recreation message).

Camp Notes: This is a popular spot for fishing, since several side streams enter the river near this point. The majority of the campsites are, at most, just a lure's cast away from the water.

RANGER LAKES
Colorado State Forest/State Park

Location: North-central Colorado east of Walden.

Access: From Colorado State Highway 14 at milepost 59 +100 yards (4 miles east of Gould, 25 miles east of Walden, 73 miles west of Fort Collins), turn south into the campground.

Facilities: 25 campsites; sites are medium-sized, with fair to good separation; parking pads are gravel, medium to long, mostly straight-ins; some pads may require minor additional leveling; many large tent spots, on an evergreen needle forest floor; fire rings; firewood is available for gathering in the area; water at a central hand pump; vault facilities; holding tank disposal station; gravel driveways; gas and camper supplies in Gould, 4 miles west; limited supplies in Walden; complete supplies and services are available in Fort Collins.

Activities & Attractions: Trail to Ranger Lakes (200 yards); nearby trails to Lake Agnes and American Lakes; amphitheater for evening programs; trout fishing; miles of trails designated for hiker, horse, and certain orv use; day use area.

Natural Features: Located on a slightly sloping, moderately forested flat near the north shores of Ranger Lakes; vegetation consists of medium-dense, tall conifers and light undergrowth; elevation 9300'.

Season, Fees & Phone: Principal season is May to October; limited availability in winter; 14 day limit; please see Appendix for standard Colorado state park fees; park office (303) 723-8366.

Camp Notes: Ranger Lakes is probably the best all-around campground in the state forest. In addition to Ranger Lakes and The Crags (below), there's a third campground in the state forest. North Michigan Reservoir Campground is located two miles up a gravel road from milepost 53 +.3. About 20 primitive campsites are scattered around the shore of North Michigan Reservoir.

THE CRAGS
Colorado State Forest/State Park

Location: North-central Colorado east of Walden.

Access: From Colorado State Highway 14 at milepost 62 +.2 (7 miles east of Gould, 28 miles east of Walden, 70 miles west of Fort Collins), turn south onto a steep, gravel access road and go down 1 mile to the campground. (Note: Trailers are not permitted on the access road.)

Facilities: 26 campsites; sites are small to medium-sized, with fair to good separation; parking pads are gravel, short to medium-length, straight-ins or pull-throughs; (no trailers, see *Access*); large tent pads; fire rings; firewood is available for gathering in the area; water at a hand pump; vault facilities; gravel driveway; gas and camper supplies in Gould, 7 miles west.

Activities & Attractions: Hiking trails; trout fishing.

Natural Features: Located on a hillside in a canyon along the west slope of the Medicine Bow Divide; sites are nicely shaded/sheltered by tall spruce and fir; the North Fork of Michigan Creek flows below the campground; The Crags are lofty, pinnacled peaks that rise sharply from the canyon floor and tower above the campground; elevation 9300'.

Season, Fees & Phone: Principal season is May to September; limited access during mildly inclement weather (4wd is suggested); 14 day limit; please see Appendix for standard Colorado state park fees; park office (303) 723-8366.

Camp Notes: Elevation along the length of the Medicine Bow Divide averages about 10,000'. Highest peaks are several in the Summer Mountains here in the southeast corner of the forest, topped by 12,265' Iron Mountain and The Crags at 12,400'.

CHAMBERS LAKE
Roosevelt National Forest

Location: North-central Colorado west of Fort Collins.

Access: From Colorado State Highway 14 at milepost 70 +.7 (61 miles west of Fort Collins, 37 miles east of Walden), turn north onto a paved road and proceed 0.6 mile to the campground.

Facilities: 52 campsites in two sections; one section, spread out over several little hills along the lake shore, has medium to large sites with short to medium-length, gravel parking pads; a second group of larger sites, with long pull-through pads or wide, deep straight-ins, is on more level terrain; most sites have a fair amount of spacing between them; fireplaces; firewood is available for gathering; water at central faucets; vault facilities; paved driveways; gas and groceries in Gould, 15 miles west; limited supplies in Walden; complete supplies and services are available in Fort Collins.

Activities & Attractions: Limited boating; boat ramp; fishing.

Natural Features: Located along the south shore of Chambers Lake, an impoundment on the Laramie River; campground vegetation consists of a moderately dense conifer forest, with some underbrush in the section with the larger sites; the summit of 10,276' Cameron Pass is 5 miles west; Neota Wilderness and the Never Summer Mountains are to the south; elevation 9200'.

Season, Fees & Phone: May to October; $8.00; 14 day limit; Redfeather Ranger District, Fort Collins, (303) 498-1375.

Camp Notes: The lake is subject to some extreme variations in water levels. If you arrive late in the season in a dry year, the lake may be only a puddle of its former self. Most of the pads in the lakeshore section really won't comfortably take much more than a pickup, but some of the pads in the larger sites are huge.

Colorado 81

SLEEPING ELEPHANT
Roosevelt National Forest

Location: North-central Colorado west of Fort Collins.

Access: From Colorado State Highway 14 at milepost 79 (53 miles west of Fort Collins, 45 miles east of Walden), turn north into the campground.

Facilities: 15 campsites; sites are of average size, with good separation; parking pads are gravel, short to medium-length straight-ins; some pads may require a little additional leveling; fire rings, plus some barbecue grills; some firewood is available for gathering in the area; water at a hand pump; vault facilities; gravel driveways; gas and camper supplies in resort areas along the highway east of here; limited supplies in Walden; complete supplies and services are available in Fort Collins.

Activities & Attractions: Trout fishing.

Natural Features: Located in a narrow valley on the opposite side of the highway from Cache la Poudre River; campground vegetation consists of tall grass and sage partly covered with aspens and conifers; rocky, timbered ridges flank the valley north and south; 9600' Sleeping Elephant Mountain lies to the near southeast; elevation 7900'.

Season, Fees & Phone: May to October; $8.00; 14 day limit; Estes-Poudre Ranger District, Fort Collins, (303) 482-3822.

Camp Notes: This is the largest of three national forest campgrounds along this section of Highway 14. Two other forest camps are within a half-dozen miles of Sleeping Elephant. Aspen Glen is located on a streamside flat at milepost 73. It has 8 sites pretty much in the open, a pump and vault facilities. Big Bend, east of here at milepost 82 +.8, has 9 sites, a hand pump and vault facilities. Of the two, Big Bend may be the campground of choice, since it's a tad farther from the road, and has several nice, somewhat secluded, walk-in sites down by the river.

Colorado 82

KELLY FLATS
Roosevelt National Forest

Location: North-central Colorado west of Fort Collins.

Access: From Colorado State Highway 14 at milepost 97 (35 miles west of Fort Collins, 63 miles east of Walden), turn south onto a gravel road and proceed 0.2 mile to the campground.

Facilities: 23 campsites in 2 loops; sites are generally large, level, and nicely spaced; parking pads are gravel, mostly medium to long straight-ins, plus a couple of long pull-throughs; virtually every site could handle a large tent; fire rings and barbecue grills; a limited amount of firewood is available for gathering in the vicinity; water at several faucets; vault facilities; gravel driveways; gas and camper supplies in resort areas along the highway several miles west of here; complete supplies and services are available in Fort Collins.

Activities & Attractions: Fishing; good scenery.

Natural Features: Located on a grassy flat along the banks of the Cache la Poudre River; a string of medium-tall conifers and aspens provides a nominal amount of shelter/shade; campsites are positioned along both sides of the river; almost all sites are along the riverbank or have a river view; partially timbered hills and ridges flank the narrow valley; elevation 6800'.

Season, Fees & Phone: May to October; $8.00; 14 day limit; Estes-Poudre Ranger District, Fort Collins, (303) 482-3822.

Camp Notes: *Cache la Poudre* (freely translated as "Stash the Powder"), dates back to November 1836. A band of trappers from the Hudson Bay Company concealed a supply of gunpowder along the riverbank after a fierce snowstorm impeded their heavily laden supply wagons. The mountain men retrieved their goods the following spring, and the name of the river took root.

Colorado 83

MOUNTAIN PARK
Roosevelt National Forest

Location: North-central Colorado west of Fort Collins.

Access: From Colorado State Highway 14 at milepost 98+.9 (33 miles west of Fort Collins, 65 miles east of Walden), turn south and cross a narrow bridge over the river; turn west (right), and drive parallel to the highway for 0.4 mile to the campground.

Facilities: 45 campsites, including several park 'n walk sites; sites and gravel parking pads vary in size from small to very large, but most are in the small to medium category, level, with some separation between sites; adequate space for tents in most sites; fire rings or barbecue grills; some firewood is available for gathering in the vicinity; water at faucets; vault facilities; paved driveway; gas and limited groceries in Poudre Park, 13 miles east; complete supplies and services are available in Fort Collins.

Activities & Attractions: Fishing; superscenic drive on '14'.

Natural Features: Located on the south bank of the Cache la Poudre River on a shelf just above the river; the park 'n walk units are located right along the river's edge; timbered hills and ridges border the campground; this segment of the highway and the river passes through a very narrow canyon where rock walls tower several hundred feet above either side of the canyon floor; elevation 6700'.

Season, Fees & Phone: May to October; $8.00; 14 day limit; Estes-Poudre Ranger District, Fort Collins, (303) 482-3822.

Camp Notes: Mountain Park has a little bit more of an evergreen woodsy-ness about it than many of the other campgrounds along this segment of Highway 14. Most sites also have some sort of a river view. There are a couple of other very small forest campgrounds with minimal facilities and fees a short distance to the east, on the north side of the highway: Stevens Gulch, at milepost 104 +.6; and another camp area less than a mile east of Stevens Gulch, Stove Prairie Landing.

Colorado 84

ANSEL WATROUS
Roosevelt National Forest

Location: North-central Colorado west of Fort Collins.

Access: From Colorado State Highway 14 at milepost 109 +.1 (23 miles west of Fort Collins, 75 miles east of Walden), turn north into the main section of the campground.

Facilities: 26 campsites in 3 sections; the primary area has 16 large, level units with medium to long, gravel parking pads; about half the pads are pull-throughs, the balance are straight-ins; an "annex", 0.25 mile east of the main section, has 7 sites with similar arrangements; a 3-unit, walk-in section is situated a few yards west of the main area; good to excellent tent-pitching opportunities in virtually all sites; fire rings and barbecue grills; a limited amount of firewood is available for gathering in the vicinity; water at several faucets; vault facilities; gravel driveways; gas and limited groceries in Poudre Park, at milepost 112; complete supplies and services are available in Fort Collins.

Activities & Attractions: Spectacular 15 mile drive through Cache la Poudre Canyon along this stretch of '14'; fishing.

Natural Features: Located on a grassy flat, in a grove of short to medium-height, large-needled conifers, along the bank of the Cache la Poudre River; the river flows through a very narrow, sheer-walled rocky canyon in this area; the main camping section and the 'annex' are rather tightly squeezed between the highway and the river; the walk-in's are in a *cul de sac*, slightly farther from the roadway, and closer to the river; elevation 5800'.

Season, Fees & Phone: May to October, but may be open until later in the year with limited services; $8.00; 14 day limit; Estes-Poudre Ranger District, Fort Collins, (303) 482-3822.

Camp Notes: This is the first (or last) forest campground on wonderfully scenic Colorado 14. Hope you have (or had) a terrific trip!

Colorado 85

DENVER CREEK
Arapahoe National Forest

Location: North-central Colorado northwest of Granby.

Access: From Colorado State Highway 125 near milepost 12 +.5 (16 miles north of Granby, 40 miles south of Walden), turn east into the upper loop, or west into the lower loop; the access driveways to the 2 sections are approximately 0.2 mile apart.

Facilities: 22 campsites in 2 loops; sites are generally quite spacious and well spaced, with the edge going to those in the upper loop; parking pads are gravel, medium to long straight-ins or pull-offs; pads in the upper loop may require additional leveling, but the lower loop's parking pads are fine; ditto for tent areas in the two loops; fire rings; some firewood is available for gathering in the vicinity; water at several faucets; vault facilities; gravel driveways; limited supplies and services are available in Granby and Walden.

Activities & Attractions: Fishing for small trout; nice views.

Natural Features: Located along and near Willow Creek in a small valley; the lower loop, with several streamside campsites, is situated on a flat dotted with willows, on the opposite side of Willow Creek from a steep, rocky ridge; the upper loop is on a light to moderately forested hillside above, and on the opposite side of the highway from, the creek; small Denver Creek tumbles down through the campground to join the main stream; Willow Creek Pass, at 9683', is 9 miles north; elevation 8800'.

Season, Fees & Phone: May to mid-September; $7.00; 14 day limit; Sulphur Ranger District, Granby, (303) 887-3331 (live voice) or (303) 887-3165 (recorded message).

Camp Notes: This is a large campground for the relatively small number of sites which it has. There are some really dandy campsites here. Check out both loops before you decide on a spot. Another nearby forest campground, Sawmill Gulch, is located on Highway 125 at milepost 10 +.6. It's on a creekside/roadside flat, has a half dozen good-sized sites, a hand pump and vault facilities.

Colorado 86

WILLOW CREEK
Arapahoe National Recreation Area

Location: North-central Colorado north of Granby.

Access: From U.S. Highway 34 at milepost 5 +.2 (6 miles north of Granby, 10 miles south of Rocky Mountain National Park) turn west onto Granby County Road 40 (gravel), and proceed 3.8 miles; turn north (right) into the campground.

Facilities: 35 campsites, including about a dozen walk-in units; sites vary in size from small to large, with nominal to adequate separation; parking pads are gravel and quite sloped; small to medium-sized tent areas; fire rings; some firewood is available for gathering in the area, b-y-o is suggested; water at faucets in a day use area, 1.3 miles east; vault facilities; gravel driveways; limited supplies and services are available in Granby.

Activities & Attractions: Boating; boat launch at the day use area, 1.3 miles east; fishing.

Natural Features: Located on a sage-covered hillside overlooking Willow Creek Reservoir; some aspens and tall pines provide a moderate amount of shelter/shade within the campground; south shore of the reservoir is just below the campground, a short walk away; sage-covered hills and distant mountains encircle the area; elevation 8300'.

Season, Fees & Phone: May to September, but may be open later, subject to weather conditions; $7.00; 7 day limit; Sulphur Ranger District, Granby, (303) 887-3331 (voice) or (303) 887-3165 (recorded message).

Camp Notes: Willow Creek is a somewhat more rustic campground than most of the other Arapahoe National Recreation Area camps. However, it's one of the nicest in midsummer. This would be a good spot for campers who prefer a place that isn't usually as overrun as the large camping areas along the highway.

Colorado 87

STILLWATER
Arapahoe National Recreation Area

Location: North-central Colorado north of Granby.

Access: From U.S. Highway 34 at milepost 8 +.6 (10 miles north of Granby, 6 miles south of Rocky Mountain National Park), turn east onto the campground access road and proceed 0.1 mile to the campground.

Facilities: 148 campsites in a major section, plus an extension; most sites are of average size, with nominal separation; parking pads are gravel, short to medium-length straight-ins; some additional leveling may be required; designated tent sites--tents permitted on tent pads only; fireplaces or fire rings; although a small quantity of firewood may be available for gathering in the general vicinity, b-y-o is recommended; water at faucets; restrooms; holding tank disposal station; paved driveways; nearest supplies at several small stores in the area; limited supplies and services are available in Granby.

Activities & Attractions: Boating; boat launch; fishing; Rocky Mountain Park, with its spectacular Trail Ridge Road, is just north of here.

Natural Features: Located on a point of land on the northwest corner of Lake Granby; most of the sites are situated in moderately dense conifers on a dome-shaped hill; the lake, which is dotted with several islands, covers a half-dozen square miles; classic Rocky Mountain scenery; elevation 8300'.

Season, Fees & Phone: May to September, but may be partially open until later in the season; $9.00; 7 day limit; Sulphur Ranger District, Granby, (303) 887-3331 (voice) or (303) 887-3165 (recorded message).

Camp Notes: This is a very heavily used campground during the peak summer season. A mid-week stay with an early stop is suggested. For a campground farther from the mainstream, you might check Arapahoe Bay, accessible from Highway 34 near milepost 6, then east on a gravel road for 9 miles. Arapahoe Bay is at the southeast tip of Lake Granby. A horrendous windstorm destroyed thousands of trees there, but it's worth considering.

Colorado 88

GREEN RIDGE
Arapahoe National Recreation Area

Location: North-central Colorado north of Granby.

Access: From U.S. Highway 34 at milepost 11 +.9 (13 miles north of Granby, 3 miles south of Rocky Mountain National Park), turn east/southeast onto a paved access road and proceed 1.3 miles to the campground.

Facilities: 81 campsites in two loops; sites are of average size, with fair separation; parking pads are gravel, short to medium-length straight-ins, plus some pull-offs; the majority of the pads are acceptably level; tents permitted in designated sites; fire rings; b-y-o firewood is suggested, but some may be available for gathering in the general vicinity; water at central faucets; restrooms; paved driveways; holding tank disposal station west of the campground; gas and groceries at several nearby stores; limited supplies and services are available in Granby.

Activities & Attractions: Boating; boat launch; fishing; Rocky Mountain National Park, with its own remarkable scenery, is only a few minutes' drive from here.

Natural Features: Located in a stand of light to medium-dense conifers near the dam at the southern tip of Shadow Mountain Lake; several islands dot the lake; classic Central Rockies scenery; elevation 8300'.

Season, Fees & Phone: May to September; $9.00; 7 day limit; Sulphur Ranger District, Granby, (303) 887-3331 (real-time communication) or (303) 887-3165 (recorded message).

Camp Notes: Each of the trio of sizeable lakes in the national recreation area (Granby, Shadow Mountain and Willow Creek) are endowed with a major, easily accessible campground. Green Ridge performs the honors for scenic Shadow Mountain Lake. This camp seems to see a little less activity than the other major campground in this area, Stillwater (see info above), and thus may be a slightly better bet during the peak season.

TIMBER CREEK
Rocky Mountain National Park

Location: North-central Colorado on the west side of Rocky Mountain National Park.

Access: From U.S. Highway 34, at a point 8.6 miles north of the west entrance station to the park and 40 miles from the city of Estes Park, turn west into the campground.

Facilities: 101 campsites in 4 loops; several walk-in sites at "Beaver Pond", south of the main camping area are also available; sites are average in size for a national park campground, essentially level, with nominal to fair separation; parking pads are paved, short to medium-length straight-ins; pads in some sites nearest the entrance may require a little additional leveling; large, framed-and-gravelled tent pads; fireplaces and/or fire rings; firewood is usually for sale, or b-y-o from outside the park; water at several faucets; restrooms; holding tank disposal station; paved driveways; ranger station; limited supplies and services are available in Grand Lake, 10 miles south.

Activities & Attractions: Hiking trails; visitor center at the west entrance station; Trail Ridge Road, scenic drive along U.S. 34, east of here; fishing and boating at Arapahoe National Recreation Area, a dozen miles south.

Natural Features: Located on a moderately forested flat bordered on the west by Timber Creek and its attendant meadow; timbered mountains rise just west of the campground, then lofty, barren, sharply defined peaks farther west; elevation 9200'.

Season, Fees & Phone: Open all year, subject to weather conditions, with limited services in winter; $9.00 for a site, $5.00 for the park entrance fee; 7 day limit; Rocky Mountain National Park Headquarters, Estes Park, (303) 586-2371.

Camp Notes: Timber Creek is near the western terminus of Trail Ridge Road, one of the truly magnificent alpine highways on the continent. You won't soon forget the Trail Ridge trip!

ASPENGLEN
Rocky Mountain National Park

Location: North-central Colorado in northeast Rocky Mountain National Park.

Access: From U.S. Highway 34/Fall River Road at a point 5 miles west of Estes Park, 0.1 mile west of the Fall River Entrance Station for Rocky Mountain National Park, 4 miles northeast of Dear Ridge Junction, turn south onto a paved access road; proceed 0.5 mile south to the campground.

Facilities: 50 standard campsites in 3 loops, plus 5 walk-in sites; sites are small to medium-sized, with minimal to nominal separation; parking pads are paved, short to medium-length straight-ins, plus some medium-length pull-offs; a little additional leveling will be needed on most pads; small parking area for walk-in units; majority of sites have large framed-and-gravelled tent pads; fire rings; firewood is usually for sale, or b-y-o; water at central faucets; restrooms; paved driveways; complete supplies and services are available in Estes Park.

Activities & Attractions: Hiking; amphitheater for evening programs; superscenic drive to the west across Trail Ridge Road to Alpine Visitor Center, at 11,786' Fall River Pass.

Natural Features: Located on hilly terrain in a valley near the south bank of the Fall River; some sites are unsheltered, most have light-medium shelter/shade courtesy of tall conifers and small aspens; adjacent to a large meadow and bordered by forested hills and mountains; elevation 8300'.

Season, Fees & Phone: June to September; $9.00 for a site, $5.00 for the park entrance fee; 7 day limit; Rocky Mountain National Park Headquarters, Estes Park, (303) 586-2371.

Camp Notes: Aspenglen is a particularly good campground for tent campers with small vehicles. The several walk-in sites are on a small, well-sheltered shelf along a streambank, while the standard units are several yards above the rocky stream. Good mountain views, especially off to the north, from many sites.

MORAINE PARK
Rocky Mountain National Park

Location: North-central Colorado in northeast Rocky Mountain National Park.

Access: From U.S. Highway 36 at a point 4 miles west of Estes Park, 0.2 mile west of the Beaver Meadows Entrance Station for Rocky Mountain National Park, and 2.8 miles southeast of Deer Ridge Junction, turn south onto Bear Lake Road; proceed south for 1.2 miles, then turn west (right) onto the paved campground access road and continue for 1.2 miles to the campground.

Facilities: 250 campsites, designated for either tents or rv's, in 4 loops; many tent sites are park 'n walk units; sites are small to small+, with minimal to fair separation; all parking pads are gravel; pads for tent sites are generally short straight-ins; rv pads are either short extra-wide straight-ins, or medium-length pull-offs; most pads will require additional leveling; tent space varies from small to large, though it may be off-level; fireplaces; firewood is usually for sale, or b-y-o; water at central faucets; restrooms; holding tank disposal station; paved driveways; complete supplies and services are available in Estes Park.

Activities & Attractions: Hiking trails to Cub Lake (1 mile) and Fern Lake (2 miles); nature trails; amphitheater for evening programs; visitor center, 2 miles east; Moraine Park Museum, 1 mile east.

Natural Features: Located at the north edge of a large mountain meadow, surrounded by timbered ridges and distant, rugged, mountain peaks; the campground is built on slopes and gently rolling hills; medium-sized conifers and aspens above a surface of tall grass provide very light to light shade/shelter for many sites; elevation 8200'.

Season, Fees & Phone: Open all year, with limited services from October to May; $9.00 for a site, $5.00 for the park entrance fee; reservations are mandatory during the summer; please see Appendix for reservation information; 7 day limit in summer; Rocky Mountain National Park Headquarters (303) 586-2371.

Camp Notes: Stupendous views west, south and east! Quite a few sites have an unrestricted view of Moraine Park, the grand, miles-long, miles-square valley below the campground. Best campsites? You might try for sites 141 to 162 in Loop D if you're a tent camper; or sites 190 to 215 in Loop B or 226 to 247 in Loop C if you're in an rv.

Colorado 92

GLACIER BASIN
Rocky Mountain National Park

Location: North-central Colorado in northeast Rocky Mountain National Park.

Access: From U.S. Highway 36 at a point 4 miles west of Estes Park, 0.2 mile west of the Beaver Meadows Entrance Station for Rocky Mountain National Park, and 2.8 miles southeast of Deer Ridge Junction, turn south onto Bear Lake Road; travel southerly for 3.9 miles; turn east (left) onto the paved campground access road and proceed 0.4 mile to the campground.

Facilities: 152 campsites in 4 loops, designated for tents or rv's; (group camp areas are also available); sites are small to small+, generally level, with nominal to fairly good separation; parking pads are packed sandy gravel, short straight-ins, or medium to medium+ pull-offs or pull-throughs; adequate space for at least a small tent in all sites, some sites have large, framed tent pads; fireplaces; firewood is usually for sale, or b-y-o; water at central faucets; restrooms; holding tank disposal station; paved driveways; complete supplies and services are available in Estes Park.

Activities & Attractions: Hiking; Sprague Lake 5 Senses Nature Trail; Bear Lake shuttle bus parking lot is across the main roadway from the campground turnoff; amphitheater for scheduled evening programs.

Natural Features: Located on an expansive flat amid stands of conifers in a forested basin/valley; campground vegetation consists of light to medium-dense conifers and very light undercover; the campground lies along the north edge of a very large clearing; Glacier Creek flows by within a couple-hundred yards of the campground; lofty peaks, including 14,255' Longs Peak, rise sharply from the valley floor; elevation 8600'.

Season, Fees & Phone: June to September; $9.00 for a site, $5.00 for the park entrance fee; 7 day limit; reservations mandatory; please see Appendix for reservation information; Rocky Mountain National Park Headquarters (303) 586-2371.

Camp Notes: Being within walking distance of the 'terminal' for the Bear Lake Shuttle means you don't have to drive to the bus stop parking lot. Just 'park and ride' from your campsite. The shuttle is a good deal. It makes the trip along narrow, curvy Bear Lake Road much more enjoyable. The large, level clearing on the edge of the campground must cover a half square mile. Its presence helps provide an unrestricted view of the neighboring peaks to the south. Sites in the C and D Loops generally have the best views. This camp would be preferable to Moraine Park or Aspenglen Campgrounds for rv's. The panorama from Moraine Park may be more distant and broad, but that in no way overshadows Glacier Basin's spectacular vista. You might agree that, on balance, this is the park's best campground.

LONGS PEAK
Rocky Mountain National Park

Location: North-central Colorado in eastern Rocky Mountain National Park.

Access: From Colorado State Highway 7 at milepost 9 (9 miles south of Estes Park, 4 miles north of Meeker Park), turn west onto a gravel (becomes paved) park access road; proceed 1 mile, then swing sharply right onto a paved campground access road for 0.2 mile to the campground.

Facilities: 26 campsites for tent camping only; sites are small to medium-sized, with fair separation; parking pads are sandy gravel, small straight-ins or pull-offs; level tent spaces for all sites, including framed-and-gravelled tent pads for some sites; fire rings; b-y-o firewood; water at a central hydrant; restrooms, plus supplemental vaults; narrow, paved driveway; complete supplies and services are available in Estes Park.

Activities & Attractions: Hiking on Storms Pass and Longs Peak Trails; picnic area at the Longs Peak Trailhead; Twin Sisters Trailhead is located just to the east, across Highway 7; Lily Lake Visitor Center (Park Service and Forest Service operation), 2 miles north on Highway 7.

Natural Features: Located on a small flat at the base of a slope on a mountainside; sites are sheltered/shaded by light to medium-dense conifers and a few aspens; 14,255' Longs Peak rises a couple of miles southwest; elevation 9000'.

Season, Fees & Phone: Open all year, subject to weather and road conditions, with limited services October to May; $9.00 for a site, $5.00 for the park entrance fee; 3 day limit June to September; Rocky Mountain National Park headquarters, Estes Park, (303) 586-2371.

Camp Notes: The edge of this mountainside ledge drops off sharply, offering nearly unrestricted views north and east across the Tahosa Valley to the peaks beyond. The atmosphere at Longs Peak Campground is typically serene, especially in the autumn when the leaves turn golden and the crisp Rocky Mountain air is freshened after the departure of summer vacationers. A choice camp for canvasbacks.

OLIVE RIDGE
Roosevelt National Forest

Location: North-central Colorado south of Estes Park.

Access: From Colorado State Highway 7 at milepost 13 +.6 (14 miles south of Estes Park, 6 miles northwest of the junction of Colorado State Highways 7 & 72 at Raymond), turn west onto a short stretch of paved road to a "T"; turn south (left), go 0.1 mile on a paved road, then turn west (right) into the campground.

Facilities: 56 campsites in 3 loops; site size is small+ to large, with fairly good to excellent separation; parking pads are gravel, reasonably level, mostly short to medium-length straight-ins, plus some medium-length pull-offs; most sites have framed-and-gravelled tent pads; fire rings and barbecue grills; limited firewood is available for gathering; water at faucets throughout; vault facilities; gravel driveways; gas and camper supplies in Allenspark, 1 mile south; complete supplies and services in Estes Park.

Activities & Attractions: A half-dozen foot trails lead from near here up into the mountain areas of Rocky Mountain National Park to the west; amphitheater; nice playground.

Natural Features: Located on a gently rolling slope on the eastern boundary of Rocky Mountain National Park; most sites are adequately shaded/sheltered by tall conifers and some aspens over a forest floor of tall grass and small plants; timbered mountains are visible in the distance; elevation 8300'.

Season, Fees & Phone: May to late October; $8.00; 14 day limit; Boulder Ranger District (303) 444-6600 (live) or (303) 443-5236 (recorded message).

Camp Notes: Since this is a popular trailhead, and also the forest campground that's closest to Rocky Mountain Park, it may be filled to capacity on peak summer weekends. It warrants consideration as an excellent alternative to the overworked park camps. (The campground's namesake seems to be lost in history. Was the ridge christened for the hue of the local vegetation; or for a long-forgotten, experimental orchard planted by a settler; or, perhaps, was it named for Popeye's goylefriend?)

PEACEFUL VALLEY
Roosevelt National Forest

Location: North-central Colorado west of Boulder.

Access: From Colorado State Highway 72 at milepost 50 (6 miles north of Ward, 18 miles north of Nederland, 4 miles south of Raymond, 30 miles south of Estes Park), turn west onto an access road signed for "Middle St. Vrain Recreation Area"; go west for 0.2 mile on a gravel road to the campground.

Facilities: 21 campsites; sites are medium to large, with average separation; parking pads are gravel, mostly average-length, straight-ins, although many are double-wide; some nice level tent spots with framed-and-gravelled tent pads are nestled in among the trees; fireplaces and/or barbecue grills at each site; firewood is available for gathering in the area; water at a hand pump; vault facilities; gravel driveways; camper supplies in Ward; adequate supplies and services are available in Nederland.

Activities & Attractions: Trailhead for the Middle St. Vrain Trail; four-season usability by hikers, equestrians, 4-wheel-drive enthusiasts, snowmobilers, and cross-country skiers; trout fishing on the stream.

Natural Features: Located on a forested flat in a small valley along the north bank of Middle St. Vrain Creek; willows and brush line the creek, but the campsites are in a more open forest setting; enough conifers and medium-tall aspens dot the campground to provide adequate shelter/shade in most sites; bordered by forested hills; Indian Peaks Wilderness lies a few miles to the west, along the Continental Divide; elevation 8500'.

Season, Fees & Phone: May to late October, with limited services before Memorial Day and after Labor Day; $7.00; 14 day limit; Boulder Ranger District (303) 444-6600 (live) or (303) 443-5236 (recorded message).

Camp Notes: This campground is indeed in a pleasant valley. However, since users of the trailhead and nearby Camp Dick Campground must pass through this camp, there may be considerable local traffic past your campsite.

CAMP DICK
Roosevelt National Forest

Location: North-central Colorado west of Boulder.

Access: From Colorado State Highway 72 at milepost 50 (6 miles north of Ward, 4 miles south of Raymond), turn west at a sign "Middle St. Vrain Recreation Area"; proceed 0.8 mile on a gravel access road (past Peaceful Valley Cg.) to Camp Dick.

Facilities: 34 campsites; sites are generously medium-sized, with fairly good separation; parking pads are gravel, mostly medium-length straight-ins, though some are spacious enough for larger rv's; adequate space for large tents in most sites; many units have large, framed-and-gravelled tent pads; fireplaces and/or barbecue grills; firewood is available for gathering in the area; water at a hand pump; vault facilities; gravel driveways; camper supplies in Ward; adequate supplies and services are available in Nederland.

Activities & Attractions: Jumping-off point for several foot, horse, snowmobile, cross-country skiing and 4-wheel drive trails; stream fishing for small trout.

Natural Features: Located on a large, open flat in a narrow valley bordered by low, timbered ridges along Middle St. Vrain Creek on the east slope of the Rocky Mountains; campsites are located in an open forest around a central grassy 'infield'; some sites are located in small 'pockets' of vegetation; Indian Peaks Wilderness lies to the west; elevation 8500'.

Season, Fees & Phone: May to October; $7.00; 14 day limit; Boulder Ranger District (303) 444-6600 (live) or (303) 443-5236 (recorded message).

Camp Notes: Many sites in this campground have a fairly substantial amount of privacy. Most sites are along the creekbank, with good shelter/shade, and generally a good breeze. Extra parking is provided for trail users.

Colorado 97

PAWNEE
Roosevelt National Forest

Location: North-central Colorado west of Boulder.

Access: From Colorado State Highway 72 at milepost 44 +.1 on the north edge of the settlement of Ward (36 miles south of Estes Park, 12 miles north of Nederland), turn west onto a paved local road at a "National Forest Recreation Area, 5 miles" sign; drive westerly for 5 miles on a paved access road; turn north (right) into the campground.

Facilities: 55 campsites in 2 loops; sites are medium to large, level, and generally well separated; most parking pads are gravel, medium-length, straight-ins; very good tent spots in most sites; some sites have framed tent pads; fire rings and barbecue grills; some firewood is available for gathering in the area; water at faucets; vault facilities; gravel driveways; camper supplies in Ward; adequate supplies and services are available in Nederland.

Activities & Attractions: Fishing in Brainard Lake, nearby Red Rock Lake, and other lakes in the area; a number of trailheads and picnic grounds are in the vicinity.

Natural Features: Located high in the Rocky Mountains just east of Brainard Lake; some of the tallest peaks of the Rockies are visible across the lake to the west; (the Peaks all have Indian names: Navajo, Pawnee, Piute, Apache); most campsites are well sheltered/shaded by medium-tall conifers with only a little underbrush; elevation 10,400'.

Season, Fees & Phone: July to October; $9.00; 5 day limit; Boulder Ranger District (303) 444-6600 (live) or (303) 443-5236 (recorded message).

Camp Notes: The drive along the winding access road from Highway 72 passes through some very lovely scenic country. There are commanding views of the valley off to the south. Although the lake isn't visible from the campground, it's "right over there".

Colorado 98

KELLY-DAHL
Roosevelt National Forest

Location: North-central Colorado west of Boulder.

Access: From Colorado State Highway 119 at milepost 21 +.9 (3.5 miles south of Nederland, 22 miles north of Idaho Springs), turn east at a "Forest Campground" sign; drive east for 0.1 mile on a gravel access road into the campground.

Facilities: 46 campsites in 2 loops; most sites are medium-sized, with nominal to good separation; parking pads are gravel, short+ to medium+ and reasonably level; adequate space for a large tent in most sites; fire rings and barbecue grills; some firewood is available for gathering in the area; water at central faucets; vault facilities; gravel driveways; adequate supplies and services are available in Nederland.

Activities & Attractions: Playground; several creeks and lakes in the area offer fishing; a number of local trails wind through the mountains.

Natural Features: Located on a level hilltop in the Rocky Mountains; an open grassy area forms the center of the campground, but most of the sites are in among medium-dense timber; Beaver Creek flows through the valley to the north and there are several small mountain lakes in the area; the campground straddles the Boulder-Gilpin county line; elevation 8600'.

Season, Fees & Phone: May to October; $7.00; 14 day limit; Boulder Ranger District (303) 444-6600 (live) or (303) 443-5236 (recorded message).

Camp Notes: There are some really super views in several directions from in and around the campground. The camp is locatd along the Peak to Peak Scenic Byway. Plan an early arrival (or a rez, if it's on the reservation system) on weekends.

Colorado 99

REVEREND'S RIDGE
Golden Gate Canyon State Park

Location: North-central Colorado west of Denver.

Access: From Colorado State Highway 119 at milepost 15 +.8 (10 miles south of Nederland, 8 miles north of Black Hawk), turn east onto Gilpin County Road 2 (gravel) and proceed 1 mile to the park boundary and a paved park road; at a 3-way intersection at a point 0.1 mile beyond the beginning of the pavement, turn north (left) onto the campground access road and follow it for 0.4 mile to the campground.

Facilities: 106 campsites, including many park 'n walk tent sites, in 10 loops; sites range from medium to very large, with fair to very good separation; parking pads are gravel, short straight-ins or pull-offs for tent sites, or very long pull-throughs for rv's; some additional leveling will probably be required; fair to very good tenting possibilities; some sites have large, framed tent pads; fire rings; gathering firewood on nearby national forest lands prior to arrival, or b-y-o, is recommended; water at central faucets; restrooms; showers; holding tank disposal station; paved main roadway, gravel loop driveways; limited supplies and services are available in Nederland and Black Hawk.

Activities & Attractions: Panorama Point has a covered observation deck with fantastic views; campground amphitheater for scheduled interpretive programs.

Natural Features: Located on timbered slopes in the Rocky Mountains at the northwest corner of the park; sites receive light to medium shade/shelter from tall conifers, with minimal low-level vegetation; elevation 9000'.

Season, Fees & Phone: Open all year, subject to weather and road conditions, with limited services October to May; 14 day limit; please see Appendix for reservation information and standard Colorado state park fees; park office (303) 592-1502.

Camp Notes: Panorama Point has one of the finest views of the Central Rockies available anywhere in the state. The panorama encompasses a 100-mile succession of peaks running perpendicular to your line of vision. Reverend's Ridge is the larger of the park's two principal campgrounds. It's an excellent facility that reportedly is seldom filled to capacity.

Colorado 100

ASPEN MEADOW
Golden Gate Canyon State Park

Location: North-central Colorado west of Denver.

Access: From Colorado State Highway 119 at milepost 15 +.8 (10 miles south of Nederland, 8 miles north of Black Hawk), turn east onto Gilpin County Road 2 (gravel) and proceed 1 mile to the park boundary and a paved park road; continue easterly, (the road shortly becomes gravel) past Panorama Point, then southeast, for 1.9 miles to a 3-way intersection; turn south (right) and continue for another 0.1 mile to the campground. (Continuing ahead at the 3-way intersection will take you to the Rifleman Phillips Group Camp).

Facilities: 35 campsites, mostly park 'n walk tent sites; (a group camp is available in the nearby Rifleman Phillips area); sites are small, with nominal to good separation; parking spaces are gravel, mostly short straight-ins; framed-and-gravelled tent pads in many sites; fire rings; b-y-o firewood; vault facilities; gravel driveways; limited supplies and services are available in Nederland and Black Hawk.

Activities & Attractions: Short trail down to the Dude's Fishin' Hole, plus other hiking and horse trails in the area.

Natural Features: Located in a medium-dense forest of aspens *-and conifers in the Rocky Mountains; a large meadow lies adjacent to the camp area; elevation 9000'.

Season, Fees & Phone: May to September; please see Appendix for reservation information and standard Colorado state park fees; 14 day limit; park office (303) 592-1502.

Camp Notes: Some of Aspen Meadow's campsites overlook a deep, forested canyon; others have quite respectable views out to the south and east. More than a half-million visitors enjoy Golden Gate Canyon each year, and some are tent campers who find a measure of accessible tranquility at Aspen Meadow.

Colorado 101

COLD SPRINGS
Arapahoe National Forest

Location: North-central Colorado west of Denver.

Access: From Colorado State Highway 119 at milepost 12 +.5 (200 yards south of the junction of State Highways 119 & 46), 11 miles north of Black Hawk), turn west into the campground.

Facilities: 47 campsites, including several walk-ins, in several loops; sites are generally large and well separated; parking pads are gravel, of various sizes and shapes, ranging from medium to long straight-ins to pull-throughs; many pads may require additional leveling; adequate, but sloped, space for large tents; fire rings or barbecue grills; some firewood is available for gathering; water at several faucets; vault facilities; gravel driveways; limited supplies and services are available in Blackhawk, 6 miles south on Highway 119.

Activities & Attractions: Several hiking and 4-wheel-drive trails are located in and around Cold Springs Recreation Area; the views south into the valley are fantastic; a group camping area called Pickle Gulch is located 2 miles south; Golden Gate Canyon State Park, a few miles to the east, has a visitor center and a number of scenic attractions.

Natural Features: Located on a rolling hill in the Rocky Mountains; campground vegetation consists primarily of tall conifers and some aspens; elevation 9200'.

Season, Fees & Phone: May to September; $8.00; 14 day limit; Clear Creek Ranger District, Idaho Springs, (303) 567-2901 (nationwide), or 460-0379 (from the Denver metro area).

Camp Notes: Though many of the campsites are quite close to the road, there is considerable distance between most sites, so a feeling of space and 'elbow room' prevails. Some campsites have some magnificent views of The Rockies across a valley.

Colorado 102

COLUMBINE
Arapahoe National Forest

Location: East-central Colorado west of Denver.

Access: From the junction of Colorado State Highways 119 & 279 in the town of Black Hawk, travel westerly on Highway 279 to and through the bustling burg of Central City for 2.3 miles to a fork (by the "Boodle Gold Mill"); take the left fork (Forest Road 176, gravel) for another 1.3 miles, then hang a right into the campground. (Note: As you leave Central City, you'll be on the right road if you pass the opera house, the festival hall and the sheriff's office, all on your left.)

Facilities: 47 campsites; sites are small+ to medium+, with nominal to good separation; parking pads are gravel/dirt, short to medium-length straight-ins, some are extra-wide; a little additional leveling may be needed in about half of the sites; adequate space for tents; fire rings and barbecue grills; some firewood is available for gathering in the vicinity; water at several faucets; vault facilities; gravel driveway; adequate supplies and services are available in Central City.

Activities & Attractions: See *Camp Notes* section.

Natural Features: Located on gently to moderately sloping terrain in a good mixture of aspens and medium-height conifers, with some undercover; forested mountains surround the area; elevation 8600'.

Season, Fees & Phone: May to September; $8.00; 14 day limit; Clear Creek Ranger District, Idaho Springs, (303) 567-2901 (nationwide), or 460-0379 (from the Denver metro area).

Camp Notes: The campground is surrounded by nice-looking forest, and there are very good distant views in several directions. With the resurrection, reconstruction and refurbishment of the old mining town of Central City as the result of the reestablishment of legal gambling, you'll probably have quite a bit of company if you camp here. In the gold days, Central City was called "The richest square mile on earth". Maybe that moniker will once again be appropriate.

Colorado 103

IDLEWILD
Arapahoe National Forest

Location: North-central Colorado south of Winter Park.

Access: From U.S. Highway 40 at the south edge of the small community of Winter Park, turn east into the campground.

Facilities: 24 campsites in 2 loops; most sites are of ample size, with nominal to fair separation; sites in the lower section are a bit more level than those in the upper loop; parking pads are gravel, short straight-ins; adequate space for tents in most sites; fire rings; some firewood is available for gathering in the vicinity; water at several faucets; vault facilities; gravel driveways; limited supplies and services are available in Winter Park and other nearby communities.

Activities & Attractions: Scenic Berthoud Pass area (11,000'+) is a few miles south of here; several hiking trails and 4wd roads in the area; Arapahoe National Recreation area, with several major lakes, is about a half hour's drive north.

Natural Features: Located along a small creek in the Rocky Mountains; some sites are on a short bluff along the highway, the remaining sites are below the road, on a creekside flat; moderately dense conifer forestation shelters the campsites; timbered mountains rise east and west of the camping area; elev. 9000'.

Season, Fees & Phone: May to October; $8.00; 14 day limit; operated and maintained by a local service club; Sulphur Ranger District, Granby, (303) 887-3331 (live) or (303) 887-3165 (recorded message).

Camp Notes: While this campground hasn't a great deal to offer in terms of active recreation in its own right, it is still a nice, and usually nicely maintained, place. If you're in the area on a summer weekend and can't find a good campsite in the busy national recreation area up north, Idlewild may provide you with a good public camping opportunity. Camping may also be available at Robber's Roost, a smaller forest campground, south of here.

Colorado 104

SYLVAN LAKE
Sylvan Lake State Park

Location: West-Central Colorado east of Glenwood Springs.

Access: From Interstate 70 Exit 147 for Eagle (31 miles east of Glenwood Springs, 10 miles west of Wolcott), proceed south on a local connecting road for 0.3 mile to a "T" intersection; turn west (right) onto U.S. Highway 6/First Street, go 0.1 mile, then turn south (left) onto Capital Street and proceed 0.4 mile; at the end of Capital Street (by the Eagle County administration building), pick up Brush Creek Road/Eagle County Road 307 and head southerly out of town for 10 paved miles to a fork; take the right fork and continue south on gravel for another 4.6 miles; turn west (right) and go 0.1 mile down to the campground.

Facilities: 24 campsites in a creekside loop, plus approximately 15 camp/picnic sites in a lakeside area; creekside sites are medium-sized, reasonably level, with nominal separation; parking surfaces are grass, long pull-offs; lakeside sites are small park 'n walk units with short, straight-in parking slots; ample space for tents on a grassy surface in all sites; fire rings, plus a few barbecue grills; firewood is available for gathering on national forest lands in the vicinity; water at several faucets; restrooms in the creekside loop, vaults in the lakeside area; gravel driveways; adequate supplies and services are available in Eagle.

Activities & Attractions: Limited boating (wakeless); small boat launch and dock; windsurfing possibilities; trout fishing; short hiking trails.

Natural Features: Located along the shore of Sylvan Lake and along the banks of Brush Creek in the heart of the Rocky Mountains; campsites are on large sections of mown grass, but are unsheltered; completely encircled by mountains clad with a good mix of conifers and aspens; elevation 8500'.

Season, Fees & Phone: Principal season is May to October; 14 day limit; please see Appendix for standard Colorado state park fees; phone c/o Rifle Gap State Recreation Area.

Camp Notes: Everyone likes lake or stream views served with their campfire dinner and there are plenty of them here. Probably the best reason of all to come to this park is just to mentally saturate yourself with this little gem's outstanding natural qualities. True, there's not much shade in the camp area; but trees would only obstruct your view of the superscenic surroundings, anyway. Taking a short walk up the trails will get you into all the trees you could want.

Colorado 105

RUEDI CREEK
White River National Forest

Location: Central Colorado southeast of Glenwood Springs.

Access: From midtown Basalt (just off Colorado State Highway 82, 24 miles southeast of Glenwood Springs, 18 miles northwest of Aspen), travel east on Fryingpan River Road (hard-surfaced) for 15 miles to a point 1 mile past the dam; turn south and proceed 0.2 mile to the *Little Maud* area, or 0.5 mile to *Mollie B*, or 0.9 mile to *Little Mattie*.

Facilities: *Little Maud*: 22 campsites; *Mollie B*: 26 campsites; *Little Mattie*: 20 campsites; *all areas*: sites are small to medium-sized, generally quite sloped, with nominal to fair separation; parking pads are gravel, mostly straight-ins that vary from short to long; adequate space for medium to large tents on a grassy surface; fire rings; some firewood is available for gathering on adjacent forest lands; water at several faucets; restrooms in Little Maud & Mollie B; vault facilities in Little Mattie; holding tank disposal station; paved driveways; gas and camper supplies in Meredith, 6 miles east; limited supplies and services are available in Basalt.

Activities & Attractions: Fishing; boating; boat launch.

Natural Features: Located on a semi-open slope on a large bay on Ruedi Reservoir, an impoundment on the Fryingpan River; campground vegetation consists of flowering bushes, aspens, conifers and grass; the Continental Divide lies a dozen miles east; elevation 7800'.

Season, Fees & Phone: June to September; $8.00 for Little Maud and Mollie B, $6.00 for Little Mattie; 14 day limit; Sopris Ranger District, Carbondale, (303) 963-2266.

Camp Notes: Little Maud and Mollie B are look-alikes, but Little Mattie is decidedly different, and might be your first choice if you prefer a spot that's a little more sheltered and not in the thick of things. (It's in a small draw or side canyon just off of the bay.) The majority of the sites in the three camps have at least a minimal lake view.

Colorado 106

CHAPMAN
White River National Forest

Location: Central Colorado southeast of Glenwood Springs.

Access: From midtown Basalt (just off Colorado State Highway 82, 23 miles southeast of Glenwood Springs, 18 miles northwest of Aspen), travel east on Fryingpan River Road (hard-surfaced) for 29 miles to a point 6 miles past the east end of Ruedi Reservoir; turn south onto gravel for 0.2 mile to the campground.

Facilities: 84 campsites in 8 loops; sites vary from small to large, with fair to good separation; parking pads are gravel, mostly medium to long straight-ins, plus a few pull-throughs; some additional leveling may be needed; small to large, grassy tent areas, though many are sloped; fire rings; firewood is available for gathering; water at several faucets; vault facilities; gravel driveways; gas and camper supplies in Meredith, 5 miles west; limited supplies and services are available in Basalt.

Activities & Attractions: Stream and lake fishing; limited boating on Chapman Reservoir, a small impoundment on the river; foot trails; 4wd trails.

Natural Features: Located on forested flats and slopes along the banks of the Fryingpan River; sites are lightly to moderately sheltered/shaded by tall conifers and aspens; several prominent peaks are visible from the campground area; elevation 8800'.

Season, Fees & Phone: June to September; $6.00; 14 day limit; Sopris Ranger District, Carbondale, (303) 963-2266.

Camp Notes: The Fryingpan River is classified as a Premier Trout Stream--and even if you're not a fisherman, you'd still classify it as a Premier Scenic Stream. The trip up from Basalt, through a red rock canyon cut by the Fryingpan, is worth the time even if you don't camp. A small forest camp which you'll pass on the way up to Chapman is Dearhamer, at the east tip of Ruedi Reservoir. Dearhamer has 13 sites, water and vaults.

Colorado 107

SILVER BAR, SILVER BELL, SILVER QUEEN
White River National Forest

Location: Central Colorado southwest of Aspen.

Access: From Colorado State Highway 82 at milepost 39 +.8 (1 mile west of Aspen, 16 miles southeast of Basalt), turn southwest onto Maroon Creek Road (paved) and proceed 4.8 miles to Silver Bar, or 5.1 miles to Silver Bell, or 6 miles to Silver Queen, all on the east (left) side of the road.

Facilities: *Silver Bar*: 4 park n' walk campsites; *Silver Bell*: 4 campsites; *Silver Queen*: 6 campsites; *all camps*: sites are small to medium-sized, closely spaced but with fair to good visual separation, and generally a bit sloped; most parking pads are gravel, short straight-ins or pull-offs; enough space for a small to medium-sized tent in most sites; fire rings; some firewood is available for gathering in the vicinity; water at hand pumps; vault facilities; paved driveways; adequate supplies and services are available in Aspen.

Activities & Attractions: Foot trails; the Maroon Bells and Maroon Lake, 3-4 miles farther on up Maroon Creek Road; possibly stream fishing; Snowmass Wilderness lies a few miles south of the campgrounds.

Natural Features: Located on a streamside shelf and slope just above Maroon Creek in Maroon Creek Canyon in the Central Rockies; the canyon is bordered by rugged mountains sewn with patches of aspens, dotted with tall conifers, and laced with waterfalls, cascades and tricklets; sites are lightly sheltered by short aspens and a few tall conifers; elevation 8300' at Silver Bar, 8400' at Silver Bell, 9100' at Silver Queen.

Season, Fees & Phone: May to September; $8.00; 3 day limit; Aspen Ranger District (303) 925-3445 (office) or (303) 920-1664 (recorded message).

Camp Notes: Silver Bar seems to have the most level sites of this triplet of "Silver" camps, but the sites in the other areas offer a tad more in the way of privacy. Great views in all directions.

Colorado 108

MAROON LAKE
White River National Forest

Location: Central Colorado southwest of Aspen.

Access: From Colorado State Highway 82 at milepost 39 + .8 (1 mile west of Aspen, 16 miles southeast of Basalt), turn southwest onto Maroon Creek Road (paved) and proceed 9 miles to the campground.

Facilities: 44 campsites, including several park n' walk sites, in 3 sections; sites are generally small, with minimal to fairly good separation; parking pads are gravel, primarily short to medium-length straight-ins, plus a number of very long pull-throughs; most pads will require additional leveling; tent areas are small to medium-sized, and generally somewhat sloped; barbecue grills; some firewood is available for gathering along the road to the campground; water at several faucets; vault facilities; paved driveways; adequate supplies and services are available in Aspen.

Activities & Attractions: The Maroon Bells; foot trails.

Natural Features: Located on a slope near the north shore of Maroon Lake in a canyon bordered by steep-sided, jagged mountains; majority of sites are lightly sheltered by short aspens and a few tall conifers; elevation 9600'.

Season, Fees & Phone: May to September; $10.00; 3 day limit; Aspen Ranger District (303) 925-3445 (office) or (303) 920-1664 (recorded message).

Camp Notes: Actually, some of the best campsites are the cozy park n' walks tucked away up on a hillside in a stand of tall aspens. So bring a small tent and enjoy the view! Some other nice sites are along the lake's outlet stream. The Maroon Bells, a celebrated group of peaks which resemble that color and shape, are in full view at the far end of the lake. Once you've seen this spot, you'll understand why it enjoys the reputation it has earned. The beauty of this place is unreal in September.

Colorado 109

DIFFICULT
White River National Forest

Location: Central Colorado east of Aspen.

Access: From Colorado State Highway 82 at milepost 45 + .2 (4 miles east of Aspen, 34 miles west of Twin Lakes), turn south onto a narrow paved access road and proceed 0.6 mile down to the campground.

Facilities: 47 campsites in 2 loops; sites are comfortably sized and level, with fair to very good separation; parking pads are gravel and vary from short straight-ins to long pull-throughs; fireplaces; some firewood is available for gathering in the area; water at several faucets; vault facilities; paved driveways; adequate supplies and services are available in Aspen.

Activities & Attractions: The local scenery; the community of Aspen; breathtaking (quite literally) drive over 12,100' Independence Pass.

Natural Features: Located on a large flat along the Roaring Fork River; vegetation consists of aspens mixed with some conifers; high timbered ridges flank the campground on the north and south; views of the mountains in the Independence Pass area to the east; elevation 8000'.

Season, Fees & Phone: June to September; $8.00; 5 day limit; Aspen Ranger District (303) 925-3445 (office) or (303) 920-1664 (recorded message).

Camp Notes: This is the largest and best-equipped of the public campgrounds along this route. Some of the sites, though small, are neatly tucked into aspen-lined pockets.

WELLER
White River National Forest

Location: Central Colorado east of Aspen.

Access: From Colorado State Highway 82 at milepost 49 +.5, turn north into the campground.

Facilities: 11 campsites; sites are small, somewhat sloped, with fair to good separation; parking pads are sandy gravel, short to medium-length straight-ins; small to medium-sized tent areas; fire rings; firewood is available for gathering in the area; no drinking water; vault facilities; sandy gravel driveway (may be rutty); adequate supplies and services are available in Aspen.

Activities & Attractions: Good views.

Natural Features: Located on a slope in the Independence Pass area of the Central Rockies; campground vegetation consists of mostly tall, dense aspens and dense ground-level vegetation; timbered mountains all around; elevation 9200'.

Season, Fees & Phone: June to September; no fee; (donations appreciated); 5 day limit; Aspen Ranger District (303) 925-3445 (office) or (303) 920-1664 (recorded message).

Camp Notes: Two other small forest camps are east of here, higher up in the pass: Lincoln Gulch Campground, at the end of a narrow gravel road a half-mile off the south side of the highway at milepost 49 +.4, has 7 small sites and no drinking water; Lost Man Campground, just off the south side of the highway at milepost 55 +.3, has 9 small, sloped sites with short gravel pads in a stand of conifers. Both of the smaller camps are open generally in July and August only. (During a brief visit to Weller one summer we noted that there were *two* campground hosts taking up two campsites here. Two hosts in an 11-site camp? Gimme a break! This pair of palookas resided in rv's sporting license plates from the same state. Wanna guess which state?. Ed.)

TWIN PEAKS
San Isabel National Forest

Location: West-central Colorado south of Leadville.

Access: From Colorado State Highway 82 at milepost 75 +.4 (10 miles west of the junction of Highway 82 and U.S. Highway 24, 34 miles east of Aspen), turn south into the campground.

Facilities: 37 campsites; sites are fairly good-sized, with generally good separation; parking pads are gravel, medium-length straight-ins; some very nice walk-in sites are down along the creek; fire rings and/or barbecue grills; some firewood is available for gathering; water at central faucets; vault facilities; holding tank disposal station at White Star Campground, 5 miles east; gravel driveways; camper supplies, seasonally, 2.5 miles east in Twin Lakes Village; adequate supplies and services are available in Leadville, 26 miles north.

Activities & Attractions: Several foot trails in the area; boating, boat launch and fishing on Twin Lakes Reservoir; the drive over Independence Pass, a dozen miles west of here, is one you won't soon forget.

Natural Features: Located on a moderately timbered bluff above Lake Creek at the foot of Twin Peaks; Lake Creek flows swiftly through a narrow canyon and past the campsites here; Twin Lakes Reservoir is 3 miles east; the tallest peaks in the Colorado Rockies rise to nearly 14,500' a few miles north; el. 9600'.

Season, Fees & Phone: June to September; $7.00; 14 day limit; Leadville Ranger District (719) 486-0752.

Camp Notes: The campsites at Twin Peaks seem to have a bit more elbow room than the other campgrounds in the area. The high, rocky, canyon walls and the towering peaks lend a special atmosphere to the setting. Subjectively, this is one of the nicest campgrounds along Highway 82. Independence Pass must have been named for the annual date that the highway opens--in some years, it's just about the Fourth of July by the time the road is free of snow.

PARRY PEAK
San Isabel National Forest

Location: West-central Colorado south of Leadville.

Access: From Colorado State Highway 82 at milepost 76 +.3 (9 miles west of the junction of Highway 82 and U.S. Highway 24, 35 miles east of Aspen), turn south into the campground.

Facilities: 26 campsites; sites are mostly average in size, level, with fairly good separation; parking pads are gravel, medium to long straight-ins; adequate level space for tents in most sites; some sites have framed-and-gravelled tent pads; fire rings; some firewood is available for gathering in the area; water at central faucets; vault facilities; holding tank disposal station at White Star Campground, 4 miles east; gravel driveways; camper supplies in season, 1.5 miles east in Twin Lakes Village; adequate supplies and services are available in Leadville 25 miles north.

Activities & Attractions: Several foot trails in the area; nearby Twin Lakes Reservoir provides boating and fishing opportunities; visitor center at the power plant on the reservoir.

Natural Features: Located at the foot of Parry Peak in the central Rocky Mountains; campground vegetation is primarily moderately dense, medium-height conifers, plus some aspens; Lake Creek flows swiftly over a rocky creekbed through the campground; Twin Lakes Reservoir is 2 miles east; elevation 9500'.

Season, Fees & Phone: June to September; $7.00; 14 day limit; Leadville Ranger District (719) 486-0752.

Camp Notes: A few of the campsites are located very close to the highway, so traffic noise could be a concern. But many of the sites are right along the creekbank, so the rushing stream drowns out the sounds of some of the rushers-by. Parry Peak Campground is surprisingly much more sheltered than the forest camps just a few miles east.

Colorado 113

WHITE STAR
San Isabel National Forest

Location: West-central Colorado south of Leadville.

Access: From Colorado State Highway 82 at milepost 79 +.8 (5.5 miles west of the junction of Highway 82 and U.S. Highway 24, 38 miles east of Aspen), turn south into the campground.

Facilities: 66 campsites, including several walk-ins, in 3 loops; sites are average in size, with minimal to nominal separation; parking pads are gravel, short to medium-length straight-ins; pads may require additional leveling; adequate space for medium to large tents, but the space may be a bit sloped; some sites have framed-and-gravelled tent pads; fire rings or barbecue grills; b-y-o firewood; water at hand pumps; vault facilities; holding tank disposal station; gravel driveways; camper supplies in season, 1 mile west, in Twin Lakes; adequate supplies and services are available in Leadville, 21 miles north.

Activities & Attractions: Fishing; boating; boat launch; day use area on the lake shore; Mt. Elbert Trailhead is located 1.5 miles north near Lakeview Campground; visitor center at the Mt. Elbert Power Plant, 1 mile east; scenic drive through Independence Pass, to the west.

Natural Features: Located on the north shore of Twin Lakes Reservoir; sites are on hilly terrain, in a variety of settings ranging from very open to nestled in among small aspens and pines; the tallest peak in Colorado, Mount Elbert, at 14,433', is 5 miles to the northwest; elevation 9400'.

Season, Fees & Phone: May to September; $7.00; 10 day limit; Leadville Ranger District (719) 486-0752.

Camp Notes: White Star would be an excellent choice for sun-worshipers. For when the sun shines, it shines mightily in this lightly forested camp. Some of the sites, particularly the walk-ins, have commanding views of the Independence Pass area.

Colorado 114

LAKEVIEW
San Isabel National Forest

Location: West-central Colorado south of Leadville.

Access: From Colorado State Highway 82 at milepost 81 +.3 (4 miles west of the junction of Highway 82 and U.S. Highway 24, 40 miles east of Aspen), turn north onto a paved access road; proceed up the winding road for 1 mile, then turn south (left) into the campground.

Facilities: 59 campsites in 7 loops; sites are medium-sized, with fair to good separation; parking pads are gravel, medium-length straight-ins; some sites have very nice tent spots located on beds of evergreen needles, other sites have framed-and-gravelled tent pads; fireplaces or barbecue grills; probably best to b-y-o firewood; water at faucets; vault facilities; holding tank disposal station at nearby White Star

Campground; gravel driveways; limited supplies in season, 3 miles west in Twin Lakes; adequate supplies and services are available in Leadville, 19 miles north.

Activities & Attractions: Mt. Elbert Trailhead; adjacent day use and parking area; fishing and boating on Twin Lakes; boat ramp at White Star Campground; visitor center on the lake at the Mt. Elbert Power Plant; the drive to the west along Highway 82 over Independence Pass offers unforgettably spectacular scenery, (the road is open for only a couple of months each year.)

Natural Features: Located on a pine, aspen and sage dotted hillside overlooking Twin Lakes Reservoir; sites have limited shelter/shade; Colorado's tallest mountain, Mount Elbert, towers to 14,433' just 5 miles to the west; elevation 9500'.

Season, Fees & Phone: May to September; $8.00; 10 day limit; Leadville Ranger District (719) 486-0752.

Camp Notes: The vista from almost all the sites across the valley and to towering peaks beyond is fantastic. The campsites are placed to provide each camper with ample elbow room.

Colorado 115

HORNSILVER
White River National Forest

Location: Central Colorado northwest of Leadville.

Access: From U.S. Highway 24 at milepost 155 (10 miles southeast of Minturn, 21 miles northwest of Leadville), turn east or west into the campground. (See below).

Facilities: 12 campsites in 2 sections on both sides of the highway--5 units on the west side of the highway, and 7 units on the east side; most sites are average-sized, with good separation; parking pads are gravel, level, medium to long straight-ins; large tent areas; fire rings; firewood is available for gathering in the vicinity; water at a hand pump; vault facilities; gravel driveways; limited supplies in Minturn; adequate supplies and services are available in Leadville.

Activities & Attractions: Classic Rocky Mountain scenery; remains of historic Camp Hale, a U.S. Army training ground for mountain troops, 6 miles southeast.

Natural Features: Located in a canyon along the Eagle River; the smaller camping area is situated on a flat close to the river; the larger section is on a level hilltop a short distance away; a mixture of tall pines and some aspens provide moderate shelter within the campground; high ridges east and west; elev. 8800'.

Season, Fees & Phone: May to October; $7.00; 10 day limit; Holy Cross Ranger District, Minturn, (303) 827-5715 (office) or (303) 827-5687 (recorded message).

Camp Notes: Camper's choice: the smaller loop along the river, but only a few yards from the highway; or the slightly larger section above and away from the road. This campground is available for use a little later in the year than others in the vicinity. Another good choice might be Blodgett, with 6 sites, which can be reached from milepost 156 +.1, then 0.4 mile southwest on a gravel road. Blodgett is a dandy little spot along the river with some good views. Oh, incidentally, if you're interested in Rocky Mountain real estate, there's a town for sale just north of here.

Colorado 116

CAMP HALE
White River National Forest

Location: Central Colorado northwest of Leadville.

Access: From U.S. Highway 24 at milepost 160 +.1 (15 miles southeast of Minturn, 16 miles northwest of Leadville), turn northeast, pass through a stone and mortar entrance way, and continue 0.15 mile to a "T" intersection; turn southeast (right) and proceed parallel the highway on a paved road for 1.2 miles to the campground.

Facilities: 21 campsites; most sites are large and level, with fair separation; parking pads are gravel, long straight-ins; large tent areas; fire rings; firewood is available for gathering in the vicinity; water at a hand pump; vault facilities; paved driveways; limited supplies in Minturn; adequate supplies and services are available in Leadville,

Activities & Attractions: Remains of historic Camp Hale; information signs; paved foot path meanders through and around the recreation area.

Natural Features: Located along a stream at the south edge of a large valley, in a stand of short to medium-height conifers; about half the sites are sheltered by trees, others are more open; tremendous views across the valley to the Gore Range, east of here; elevation 9200'.

Season, Fees & Phone: May to October; $7.00; 10 day limit; Holy Cross Ranger District, Minturn, (303) 827-5715 (office) or (303) 827-5687 (recorded message).

Camp Notes: This is a real find! Not only is this an excellent campground, but a visually appealing and historically significant site as well. Camp Hale served as the World War II training ground of the U.S. Army 10th Mountain Division, the first and only mountain infantry division. Only the concrete foundations of the 400 buildings which once stood here remain. You don't have to be a military history enthusiast to appreciate the significance of what took place here half a century ago.

Colorado 117

SILVER DOLLAR
Turquoise Lake/San Isabel National Forest

Location: Central Colorado west of Leadville.

Access: From U.S. Highway 24 in midtown Leadville, turn west onto West 6th Street and proceed 0.8 mile to a "T" intersection; turn north (right) onto Lake County Road 4 and travel 3.4 miles north then west; turn north (right) onto a paved local road and proceed 0.35 mile; turn west (left) onto the boat ramp/campground access road (paved) for 0.4 mile; continue on gravel for a final 0.3 mile to the campground.

Facilities: 45 campsites; overall, sites are small to medium-sized, with nominal to fair separation; parking pads are gravel, short to medium-length straight-ins, and some are extra-wide; many pads may require a little additional leveling; most sites have framed-and-gravelled tent pads; barbecue grills and fire rings; firewood is available for gathering in the area; water at central faucets; restrooms; gravel driveways; adequate supplies and services are available in Leadville.

Activities & Attractions: Fishing; boating; boat launch; boat trailer parking.

Natural Features: Located on rolling, forested terrain above the east shore of Turquoise Lake; medium-dense conifers, plus some aspens, provide adequate shelter/shade for most sites; boggy/marshy areas lie adjacent to the campsites; elev. 9900'.

Season, Fees & Phone: May to September; $9.00; 10 day limit; Leadville Ranger District (719) 486-0752.

Camp Notes: Of the several 'standard' campgrounds in the area (excluding Belle of Colorado tent camp), Silver Dollar is usually the least inhabited. But if you're a boater, this might be the place of choice because of the camp's closeness to the lake's main boat launch facilities. And if you're interested in observing (and experiencing) Rocky Mountain marsh life, Silver Dollar will provide the opportunity.

Colorado 118

MOLLY BROWN
Turquoise Lake/San Isabel National Forest

Location: Central Colorado west of Leadville.

Access: From U.S. Highway 24 in midtown Leadville, turn west onto West 6th Street and proceed 0.8 mile to a "T" intersection; turn north (right) onto Lake County Road 4 and travel 3.4 miles north then west; turn north (right) onto a paved local road and proceed 1.5 miles; turn west onto the campground access road (paved) and continue for 0.6 mile to the campground.

Facilities: 49 campsites; sites are of average size, with fair to good separation; parking pads are sandy gravel, mostly short to medium-length straight-ins which will require additional leveling; medium to large tent areas, mostly sloped; fire rings; firewood is available for gathering in the area; water at central faucets; restrooms; holding tank disposal station; paved driveways; adequate supplies and services are available in Leadville.

Activities & Attractions: Trout fishing (including Mackinaw trout); boating; boat launch, boat trailer parking, 1 mile south; nature trail.

Natural Features: Located on a conifer-covered slope along the east shore of Turquoise Lake; long, sandy beach adjacent to the campground; elevation 9900'.

Season, Fees & Phone: May to September; $9.00; 10 day limit; Leadville Ranger District (719) 486-0752.

Camp Notes: Less than a half-mile past the turnoff to Molly Brown is Belle of Colorado Campground. It's a tent-camping only spot with 19 park n' walk sites on sloping terrain several yards above the lake, just down from a paved parking lot. Most of the units have both barbecue grills and fire rings, and there's central water and restrooms. Many of Belle of Colorado's sites have good lake views through the trees. It would make a good stop for the many backpacking travelers and cyclists who roam the region around historic, interesting Leadville.

Colorado 119

BABY DOE & FATHER DYER
Turquoise Lake/San Isabel National Forest

Location: Central Colorado west of Leadville.

Access: From midtown Leadville at the intersection of Colorado State Highway 24 (Harrison Avenue) and West 6th Street, turn west and continue past the medical center and railroad tracks to a "T" intersection; turn right onto Lake County Road #4; continue for a total of 5.2 miles from Highway 24 to the entrance to Turquoise Lake Recreation Area; at a point 0.2 mile past the recreation area boundary, turn northerly (right) and follow a winding, paved road for 3 miles around the east side of the lake; turn southwest (left) onto a paved access road for a final 0.5 mile to the campground.

Facilities: *Baby Doe*: 50 campsites; *Father Dyer* (formerly Baby Doe Annex): 26 campsites; sites are medium-sized, with nominal to fair separation; parking pads are gravel, and some are pull-throughs spacious enough for large rv's; some sites have good tent spots; fire rings; b-y-o firewood is suggested; water at faucets; restrooms; adequate supplies and services are available in Leadville.

Activities & Attractions: Boating; boat launch at Matchless, near the recreation area entrance; fishing; Turquoise Lake foot trail follows along the north and east shore of the lake; museums and historic sites in and around Leadville.

Natural Features: Located on a rolling slope along the northeast shore of Turquoise Lake, an impoundment created by Sugar Loaf Dam on Lake Fork of the Arkansas River; campground vegetation consists of tall conifers and a small amount of underbrush; peaks rise above 14,000' along the Continental Divide to the west; elevation 9900'.

Season, Fees & Phone: May to September; $9.00 in Baby Doe, $8.00 in Father Dyer; 10 day limit; Leadville Ranger District (719) 486-0752.

Camp Notes: Baby Doe is the largest campground on the lake. "Baby Doe" doesn't refer to a critter of the forest; it was the nickname of the wife of one of Leadville's leading citizens back in the late 1800's.

Colorado 120

MAY QUEEN
Turquoise Lake/San Isabel National Forest

Location: Central Colorado west of Leadville.

Access: From midtown Leadville at the intersection of Colorado State Highway 24 (Harrison Avenue) and West 6th Street, turn west onto West 6th and continue past the medical center and railroad tracks to a "T" intersection; turn right onto Lake County Road #4; continue for a total of 5.2 miles from Highway 24 to the entrance to Turquoise Lake Recreation Area; continue across the dam and then along the south shore of the lake for another 5.3 miles on a paved road; turn east (right) onto a gravel access road for the last 0.5 mile to the campground.

Facilities: 26 campsites; sites are small to medium-sized, with zero to fair separation; parking pads are gravel, level, and some are longer pull throughs; most sites are level enough for tent-pitching; fire rings; b-y-o firewood is suggested; water at faucets; restrooms, plus supplemental vault facilities; gravel driveway; adequate services and supplies are available in Leadville.

Activities & Attractions: Boating; boat launch; adjacent day use area; fishing; Turquoise Lake foot trail follows the north shore of the lake from here.

Natural Features: Located on a grassy flat along the estuary of Lake Fork of the Arkansas River at the western tip of Turquoise Lake; most campsites are out on the open flat; a few sites are located in among the trees along a small hill on the north edge of the flat; the tallest peaks of the Rockies rise a few miles south of here; elevation 9900'.

Season, Fees & Phone: May to September; $8.00; 10 day limit; Leadville Ranger District (719) 486-0752.

Camp Notes: This campground, off by itself and away from the mainstream of activity at Turquoise Lake, has simple 'accommodations'. But the scenic views from here are super. It also serves as an excellent fishing camp.

Colorado 121

HEATON BAY
Arapahoe National Forest

Location: Central Colorado east of Frisco.

Access: From Interstate 70 Exit 203 for Frisco/Breckenridge, go south on Colorado State Highway 9 for 0.1 mile; at the first traffic light on the north edge of Frisco, turn east (left) onto Lusher Court/U.S. 6; proceed east/northeast (paralleling the Interstate) for 1.3 miles; turn east (right) onto a paved access road and continue for 0.2 mile to the campground.

Facilities: 83 campsites in 4 loops; sites are medium to large, with nominal to fairly good separation; parking pads are paved, tolerably level, mostly medium to medium+ straight-ins, plus a few long pull-throughs; most sites have good tent-pitching possibilities; fire rings, plus some barbecue grills; very little firewood is available for gathering, b-y-o is recommended; water at central faucets; vault facilities; paved driveways; public holding tank disposal station in Breckenridge (extra charge); complete supplies and services are available in the Frisco-Dillon-Silverthorne area.

Activities & Attractions: Boating; boat launches at Dillon and Pine Cove; fishing.

Natural Features: Located along the northwest shore of Dillon Reservoir in the Blue River Valley; the campground is in an open conifer forest with gentle slopes and small hills, on a point of land between Heaton Bay and Giberson Bay; some campsites are along a small lagoon; Dillon Reservoir was formed by damming the Blue River; peaks of the Rocky Mountains rise in all directions; elevation 9100'.

Season, Fees & Phone: Late May to late September; $9.00; 7 day limit; Dillon Ranger District (303) 468-5400 (office) or (303) 468-5435 (recorded recreation message).

Camp Notes: Views across the lake and of the surrounding mountains are terrific. There aren't many campgrounds in the West that have more convenient Interstate access. If you can't get a spot here in summer, try again in September. It's even more terrific then.

Colorado 122

PEAK ONE
Arapahoe National Forest

Location: Central Colorado south-east of Frisco.

Access: From Colorado State Highway 9 at milepost 95 +.3 (1 mile south of Frisco, 8 miles north of Breckenridge), turn northeasterly onto a paved access road signed for "Peninsula Recreation Area"; proceed 1.3 miles; turn west (left) into the campground. (Note: If you're traveling Interstate 70, take Exit 203, then travel southerly for 2 miles to the "Peninsula" turnoff.)

Facilities: 79 campsites in 3 loops; sites are medium-sized, with fair to fairly good separation; parking pads are paved or gravel, most are medium-length straight-ins, though some are large enough for good-sized vehicles; many sites have good to excellent tent areas; barbecue grills and/or fire rings; limited firewood is available for gathering in the area, b-y-o is recommended; water at central faucets; restrooms; paved driveways; complete supplies and services are available in the Frisco-Dillon-Silverthorne area.

Activities & Attractions: Boating; boat launch nearby at Pine Cove; fishing; several foot and 4wd trails in the area, including Miners Creek Trail past Rainbow Lake.

Natural Features: Located on gently rolling/hilly terrain on a peninsula on the south shore of Dillon Reservoir; sites are lightly to moderately shaded/sheltered by conifers; the peninsula is flanked by Frisco Bay (*really!*) on the west, and Blue River Arm to the east; rugged peaks of the Rockies rise in all directions; elevation 9100'.

Season, Fees & Phone: May to September; $9.00; 14 day limit; Dillon Ranger District (303) 468-5400 (office) or (303) 468-5435 (recorded recreation message).

Camp Notes: Peak One offers what possibly is the best camping on Dillon Reservoir. Its name is derived from the northernmost of a string of summits in the Tenmile Range that rise about two miles southwest of the campground. (Peak 1, Peak 6, Peak 10, etc.) Nearby Pine Cove also has camping (of sorts) for 55 vehicles in a large parking lot near the boat launch, a few tables and fire rings, central water and vaults. Just continue on the Peninsula road past the turnoff to Peak One for another 0.3 mile to the Pine Cove Camplot.

PROSPECTOR
Arapahoe National Forest

Location: Central Colorado between Frisco and Dillon.

Access: From Colorado State Highway 9 at milepost 93 (3 miles south of Frisco, 6 miles north of Breckenridge), turn northeasterly onto Swan Mountain Road/Road 1 (paved, signed for "Swan Mountain Recreation Area") and travel northeast for 3 miles; turn northwest onto a gravel access road and proceed 0.7 mile to the campground.

Facilities: 106 campsites in 5 loops; sites are medium-sized, with nominal to good separation; parking pads are gravel, mostly medium-length straight-ins; adequate space for tents; fire rings and/or barbecue grills; some firewood is available for gathering in the vicinity; water at central faucets; vault facilities; gravel driveways; limited+ supplies in Breckenridge; adequate+ supplies and services are available in Frisco.

Activities & Attractions: Fishing.

Natural Features: Located in a medium-dense conifer forest on a peninsula near the southeast shore of Dillon Reservoir; the reservoir, with 24 miles of shoreline, was formed by the damming of the Blue River; 11,000' to 12,000' peaks rise in all directions around the lake; elevation 9100'.

Season, Fees & Phone: May to September; $8.00; 14 day limit; Dillon Ranger District (303) 468-5400 (office) or (303) 468-5435 (recorded recreation message).

Camp Notes: Prospector is the last of the Dillon Reservoir campgrounds to open and first to close each summer. Its brief season and its somewhat remote location help it maintain its freshness from year to year.

KENOSHA PASS
Pike National Forest

Location: Central Colorado southwest of Denver.

Access: From U.S. Highway 285 at milepost 203 +.2 (20 miles northeast of Fairplay, 19 miles west of Bailey) turn north-west and proceed 100 yards to the campground.

Facilities: 25 campsites; sites are basically medium-sized, with fair to good separation; parking pads are gravel, short to medium straight-ins; some pads may require a little additional leveling; adequate space for medium-sized tents in most sites; fireplaces; firewood is available for gathering in the area; water at several faucets; vault facilities; gravel driveways; gas and groceries in Jefferson, 4 miles west, or Grant, 8 miles east; limited supplies and services are available in Bailey and Fairplay.

Activities & Attractions: Fine scenery; Colorado Trailhead.

Natural Features: Located on a rolling slope at the summit of Kenosha Pass; campsites are moderately sheltered/shaded; the campground is surrounded by aspen-covered mountains, conifer-clothed mountains and barren-topped mountains; to the east is Platte Canyon; just to the west is South Park, an enormous, high mountain valley; elevation 10,000'.

Season, Fees & Phone: May to November; $8.00; 14 day limit; South Park Ranger District, Fairplay, (719) 836-2031.

Camp Notes: There are phenomenal views from in and around the campground, and from nearby, highway vista points. The panoramas of South Park from an overlook about a half mile west of the campground are stunning.

LODGEPOLE
Pike National Forest

Location: Central Colorado southwest of Denver.

Access: From U.S. Highway 285 at milepost 199 in the hamlet of Jefferson (16 miles northeast of Fairplay, 4 miles southwest of Kenosha Pass, 24 miles southwest of Bailey), turn northwest onto Michigan Creek Road (paved, then gravel) and proceed 2 miles to a 3-way intersection; turn north (right) onto a gravel road and continue for 2.4 miles; turn west (left) into the campground.

Facilities: 35 campsites; sites are medium+ in size, with fair to good separation; parking pads are gravel, medium to medium+, mostly straight-ins, plus a few pull-throughs; a little additional leveling will be needed on some pads; medium to large tent areas on an earth/rock surface, some are slightly sloped; fire rings; firewood is available for gathering in the area; water at hand pumps; vault facilities; gravel driveways; gas and camper supplies are available in Jefferson.

Activities & Attractions: Fishing on Jefferson Creek; fishing, boating on Jefferson Lake, 1.6 miles (the last 1.2 miles are steep and narrow); Colorado Trail; Beaver Ponds, 0.7 mile north.

Natural Features: Located on a flat below a slope a few yards from Jefferson Creek in the Rocky Mountains; sites are sheltered/shaded by light to medium-dense, tall conifers, plus some aspens; elevation 9900'.

Season, Fees & Phone: May to September, possibly available at other times, subject to weather conditions; $8.00; 14 day limit; South Park Ranger District, Fairplay, (719) 836-2031.

Camp Notes: A small camp near Lodgepole that's certainly worth considering is Aspen Campground, 0.3 mile north. It has a dozen level, slightly more private sites in a stand of aspens and conifers several yards from the stream.

Colorado 126

JEFFERSON CREEK
Pike National Forest

Location: Central Colorado southwest of Denver.

Access: From U.S. Highway 285 at milepost 199 in the hamlet of Jefferson (16 miles northeast of Fairplay, 4 miles southwest of Kenosha Pass, 24 miles southwest of Bailey), turn northwest onto Michigan Creek Road (paved, then gravel) and proceed 2 miles to a 3-way intersection; turn north (right) onto a gravel road and travel 5.6 miles; turn west (left) for 0.1 mile to the campground.

Facilities: 17 campsites; sites are small to medium-sized, tolerably level, with fair separation; parking pads are gravel, mostly short to medium-length straight-ins plus a few medium+ pull-throughs; medium to large, earth/stone tent areas; fire rings; firewood is available for gathering in the general area; water at a hand pump; vault facilities; gravel driveway; gas and camper supplies are available in Jefferson.

Activities & Attractions: Fishing on Jefferson Creek; fishing, boating on Jefferson Lake, 1.6 miles north (the last 1.2 miles are paved, but narrow and steep); Colorado Trail; Beaver Ponds, 0.5 mile south.

Natural Features: Located on a short shelf at the bottom of a slope in a valley a few yards from Jefferson Creek in the Rocky Mountains; sites receive light to medium shelter/shade from medium-tall conifers, plus light underbrush; elevation 10,100'.

Season, Fees & Phone: May to September, possibly available at other times, subject to weather conditions; $8.00; 14 day limit; South Park Ranger District, Fairplay, (719) 836-2031.

Camp Notes: The campground's namesake is a cold, deep clear, inviting stream during most of the summer. There's good Rocky Mountain scenery up at Jefferson Lake, as well as some nice picnic spots just above the shore. (No camping at the lake, nor anywhere else in this area, other than in campgrounds.)

Colorado 127

MICHIGAN CREEK
Pike National Forest

Location: Central Colorado southwest of Denver.

Access: From U.S. Highway 285 at milepost 199 in midtown Jefferson (16 miles northeast of Fairplay, 24 miles southwest of Bailey), turn north onto Michigan Creek Road (paved, then gravel); travel 5.1 miles to the campground.

Facilities: 13 campsites; sites are medium-sized, reasonably level, with adequate separation; parking pads are gravel, mostly medium-length, straight-ins; fairly good tent-pitching possibilities; fireplaces; firewood is available for gathering in the area; water at a hand pump; vault facilities; gravel driveway; gas and groceries in Jefferson; limited supplies and services are available in Fairplay.

Activities & Attractions: Jeep trails in the area lead up toward the Great Divide; fishing on Michigan Creek; fishing and boating on nearby Jefferson Lake; several historically significant communities in this region.

Natural Features: Located in a moderately dense conifer forest along Michigan Creek, a typically crystal-clear mountain stream which flows through the campground; the campground is situated at the base of the mountains on the north edge of South Park, an enormous, high valley; the Continental Divide is a few miles to the west; elevation 10,000'.

Season, Fees & Phone: May to September, but may also be available at other times, without services or fee, subject to weather conditions; $8.00; 14 day limit; South Park Ranger District, Fairplay, (719) 836-2031.

Camp Notes: Michigan Creek itself is a mountain fresh rivulet that runs through a meadow surrounded by dense forest. (Some campers have described this as a "little jewel" of a place to camp.) Since it's off on its lonesome, Michigan Creek tends to be less-visited than the other camps in the area.

Colorado 128

BUFFALO
Pike National Forest

Location: Central Colorado southwest of Denver.

Access: From U.S. Highway 285 at milepost 229 at Pine Junction (6 miles northeast of Bailey, 7 miles southwest of Conifer), turn southeast onto Pine Valley Road/County Road 126 (paved) and proceed 10 miles to a point 0.1 mile northwest of the Buffalo Creek Work Center; turn southwest (right) onto Forest Road 243 (paved for 0.2 mile then gravel) and continue for 5.6 miles to a fork; turn south (left) for a final 0.1 mile to the campground. (Note: another approach worth mentioning is from County Road 126, at a point 4 miles south of the work center, then west 5 miles on Forest Road 550. It's a narrow, sandy gravel, trail that just *might* be in better condition than FR 243.)

Facilities: 41 campsites; sites are medium+ in size, with nominal to fair separation; parking pads are gravel/earth, short to long straight-ins which will require additional leveling; large, sloped, grass/earth tent areas; fireplaces or fire rings; some firewood is available for gathering; water at several faucets; vault facilities; dirt/gravel driveways; gas and groceries in Pine Junction.

Activities & Attractions: Stream fishing; fishing and limited boating on Wellington Lake, 4 miles southwest.

Natural Features: Located on a grassy, tree-dotted slope just above Buffalo Creek in the Rocky Mountains; sites receive light shelter from tall conifers; encircled by a rail fence (probably to ward off the local grazing bovines); elevation 7400'.

Season, Fees & Phone: June to September; $7.00; 14 day limit; South Platte Ranger District, Lakewood, (303) 236-7386 (office) or (303) 236-0900 (recorded message).

Camp Notes: You'll pass two other small campgrounds along FR 243 on the way to Buffalo: Baldy, with a half-dozen walk-in sites on a lightly timbered, grassy slope, accessed by crossing a bridge across the creek; and Tramway, with about five sites, tucked-away just off the south side of FR 243. Baldy is signed as handicapped-accessible. Both camps are former picnic grounds.

Colorado 129

KELSEY
Pike National Forest

Location: Central Colorado southwest of Denver.

Access: From U.S. Highway 285 at milepost 229 at Pine Junction (6 miles northeast of Bailey, 7 miles southwest of Conifer), turn southeast onto Pine Valley Road/Jefferson County Road 126 (paved) and travel 17 miles to a point 7 miles south of the Buffalo Creek Work Center; turn northwest (right) onto a paved access road for 0.1 mile to the campground. **Alternate Access:** From Colorado State Highway 67 in Deckers, proceed north on County Road 126 for 8 miles to the camp turnoff.

Facilities: 18 campsites; sites are medium to large, with generally good separation; parking pads are paved, short to medium+, primarily straight-ins, which probably will require additional leveling; adequate space for medium-sized tents, but typically sloped; fireplaces or fire rings; some firewood is available for gathering in the area; water at a hand pump; vault facilities; paved driveway; gas and camper supplies in Deckers.

Activities & Attractions: Trout fishing on the South Platte River, 5 miles south.

Natural Features: Located on a lightly forested, grassy slope dotted with boulders; surrounded by timbered mountains; some excellent, distant views; elevation 8000'.

Season, Fees & Phone: June to September; $6.00; 14 day limit; South Platte Ranger District, Lakewood, (303) 236-7386 (office) or (303) 236-0900 (recorded message).

Camp Notes: If a campground near the pavement with a solid, but unremarkable, name like this one isn't your first choice, you could always trip up to Top-of-the-World Campground. It can be reached from County Road 126 at a point 5 miles north of Kelsey Campground and 2.2 miles south of Buffalo Creek, then on a narrow, sandy gravel road for 1.8 miles. The road begins in a southeasterly direction off the highway, then swings sharply north as it climbs to the campground at 7500'. Top-of-the-World has a half-dozen sites but no drinking water.

Colorado 130

LONE ROCK
Pike National Forest

Location: Central Colorado southwest of Denver.

Access: From U.S. Highway 285 at milepost 229 at Pine Junction (6 miles northeast of Bailey, 7 miles southwest of Conifer), turn southeast onto Pine Valley Road/Jefferson County Road 126 (paved) and travel 25 miles to a point 15 miles south/southeast of the Buffalo Creek Work Center; turn south onto a paved access road for 0.1 mile down into the campground. (If you're approaching from this direction, it'll be a sharp right-hand turn off the highway.) **Alternate Access:** From Colorado State Highway 67 in the hamlet of Deckers, proceed west on County Road 126 for 0.7 mile to the campground turnoff.

Facilities: 13 campsites; sites are small, with very little separation; most parking pads are paved, short pull-offs or straight-ins; additional leveling probably will be required; ample, though sloped, space for large tents; fire rings; gathering firewood on forest lands enroute, or b-y-o, are suggested; water at several faucets; vault facilities; paved driveways; gas and camper supplies are available in Deckers.

Activities & Attractions: Trout fishing; rafting.

Natural Features: Located on a lightly forested, grassy slope in a small, red-walled canyon just above the South Platte River; surrounded by timbered mountains; elevation 6400'.

Season, Fees & Phone: June to September; $7.00; 4 day limit; South Platte Ranger District, Lakewood, (303) 236-7386 (office) or (303) 236-0900 (recorded message).

Camp Notes: The South Platte has earned considerable renown as an excellent trout fishery. Camping is also permitted at the Wigwam area, 2.2 miles west of Lone Rock on County Road 126. There are a half-dozen or so, mostly secluded, walk-in camp/picnic sites, with a large parking lot, water and vaults on a semi-sheltered flat along Wigwam Creek. If you usually try to avoid congested campgrounds, Wigwam, or nearby Kelsey (see info), might deserve a look.

Colorado
South Central
Please refer to the Colorado map in the Appendix

Colorado 131

PAINTED ROCKS
Pike National Forest

Location: Central Colorado west of Colorado Springs.

Access: From Colorado State Highway 67 at milepost 83 +.9 (7 miles north of Woodland Park), turn west onto Painted Rocks Road (gravel), and proceed 0.4 mile to the campground, on the left side of the road.

Facilities: 11 campsites; sites are generally on the small side, with nominal to fair separation; parking pads are dirt/gravel, medium-length straight-ins which will probably require a little additional leveling; adequate, but sloped, space for a large tent in most sites; fire rings; b-y-o firewood is recommended; water at several faucets; vault facilities; gravel/earth driveways; adequate supplies and services are available in Woodland Park.

Activities & Attractions: Painted Rocks.

Natural Features: Located on a grassy, moderately forested slope adjacent to an open field; several groups of short, reddish sandstone rock formations dot the surrounding terrain; a small stream flows near the campground; surrounded by grassy, conifer-covered hills; higher mountains are visible in the distance; elevation 7800'.

Season, Fees & Phone: May to September; $8.00; 14 day limit; Pikes Peak Ranger District (719) 636-1602.

Camp Notes: This appears to be one of those unspectacular, but unexplainably very popular, campgrounds. True, the small (some are perhaps 25 or 30 feet high) reddish rock formations hold a certain amount of fascination. But it is probably the setting--tall grass, tall conifers, low hills--combined with the eroded stone, that provides an interesting blend of the ordinarily pleasant and the slightly unusual.

Colorado 132

SOUTH MEADOWS & COLORADO
Pike National Forest

Location: Central Colorado west of Colorado Springs.

Access: From Colorado State Highway 67 at milepost 82 +.4 (5.5 miles north of the city of Woodland Park), turn west into South Meadows Campground; or at milepost 83 +.6 (6.5 miles north of Woodland Park), turn east into Colorado Campground.

Facilities: *South Meadows*: 54 campsites; *Colorado*: 47 campsites; *both camps*: sites are arranged in single complex loops in both campgrounds; sites are medium to large in South Meadows, small to medium-sized in Colorado; fair to good separation in both areas; parking pads are paved, medium to long straight-ins or pull-throughs; some additional leveling may be needed; large, slightly sloped tent areas; fireplaces or fire rings; b-y-o firewood; water at several faucets; vault facilities; paved driveways; adequate supplies and services are available in Woodland Park.

Activities & Attractions: Pleasant, forested setting; fishing.

Natural Features: Located on forested slopes in the Rocky Mountains; campground vegetation consists of medium-dense, tall conifers and grass; South Meadows is located on the edge of a meadow with a small stream; Manitou Lake is 0.7 mile north of Colorado; Pikes Peak is visible to the south from in and near the campgrounds; elevation 8500'.

Season, Fees & Phone: May to September, but either South Meadows or Colorado is also available with limited services at other times; $9.00; 14 day limit; Pikes Peak Ranger District, Colorado Springs, (719) 636-1602.

Camp Notes: South Meadows may have a slight edge over Colorado. A number of campsites in South Meadows have a very pleasant view of the stream and meadow just below the campground. But the distant views from Colorado and its proximity to tiny Manitou Lake are two things in its favor.

Colorado 133

MEADOW RIDGE & THUNDER RIDGE
Rampart Reservoir/Pike National Forest

Location: Central Colorado northwest of Colorado Springs.

Access: From U.S. Highway 24 in midtown Woodland Park at the intersection of U.S. 24, Fairview Street, and Midland Avenue (0.8 mile east of the junction of U.S. 24 & Colorado State Highway 67), proceed east on Midland Avenue for 0.2 mile to a "T" (at the school); turn north (left) onto Baldwin Avenue (which becomes Rampart Range Road) and continue north, then east, for 2.5 miles to a "Y" intersection; turn south (right) onto a paved road and proceed 1.5 miles to a 4-way intersection at the end of the pavement; turn right and follow the gravel road southeasterly for 4 miles; turn northeast (left) onto the lake access road (paved) for 0.8 mile, then left for a final 0.6 mile to Meadow Ridge; or continue on the lake road for 0.15 mile farther, then left 0.25 mile to Thunder Ridge.

Facilities: *Meadow Ridge*: 19 campsites; *Thunder Ridge*: 22 campsites; *both camps*: sites are small to medium-sized, with nominal to fairly good separation; parking pads are packed gravel, of various lengths and types; some additional leveling may be required; small to large tent areas, generally a little sloped; fire rings; firewood is available for gathering; water at faucets throughout; vault facilities; paved driveways; adequate supplies and services are available in Woodland Park.

Activities & Attractions: BPW Nature Trail; trail to the lake; trail to the Air Force Academy; fishing; boating; boat launch.

Natural Features: Located on adjacent ridgetops in the Rocky Mountains near the southwest side of Rampart Reservoir; campground vegetation consists of tall conifers, aspens, tall grass and wildflowers; elevation 9100'.

Season, Fees & Phone: May to September; $9.00; 14 day limit; Pikes Peak Ranger District (719) 636-1602.

Camp Notes: It's worth the trip just to see the incredible distant views from the last few miles of road to the lake!

Colorado 134

MUELLER
Mueller State Park

Location: Central Colorado west of Colorado Springs.

Access: From U.S. Highway 24 at milepost 278 +.1 in the town of Divide (7 miles west of the city of Woodland Park, 24 miles west of Colorado Springs, 13 miles east of the community of Lake George), travel south on Colorado State Highway 67 for 6 miles to milepost 66 +.2; turn west (right) onto the paved park access road and proceed 0.15 mile to the park entrance, then another mile to the campground.

Facilities: 90 campsites, including 78 with electrical hookups and 12 walk-in tent sites; (a group camp with 'pods' for 3 small groups is also available); sites are small+ to medium-sized, with nominal to fair separation; parking pads are paved, medium to long straight-ins or long pull-throughs; many pads will require additional leveling; enough space for small to medium-sized tents in many hookup units; large, gravelled tent pads for walk-in sites; fire rings; firewood is available for gathering; water at several faucets; restrooms with showers, plus auxiliary vault facilities; coin-op laundry; holding tank disposal station; paved driveways; gas and groceries+ in Divide; adequate supplies and services are available in Woodland Park.

Activities & Attractions: 90 miles of designated hiking, mountain bike and horse trails; bicycling on 5 miles of paved park roads; riding stables (concession); limited backcountry fishing for small trout; group meeting room in the camper service building; several day use areas.

Natural Features: Located on steep, forested terrain in the heart of the Rocky Mountains; local vegetation consists of some grassy slopes dotted with trees, bordered by a dense conifer forest intermixed with stands of tall aspens; most camp sites are moderately shaded/sheltered; elevation 9200'.

Season, Fees & Phone: Open all year, subject to weather and road conditions, with limited services October to April; 14 day limit; please see Appendix for reservation information and standard Colorado state park fees; park office (719) 687-2366.

Camp Notes: Nearly all of Mueller's 20 square miles is backcountry. But you don't have to be a hiker, a horseperson, or a hoofed critter to enjoy this place. From the long chain of view areas on the ridgetop above the campground the panoramas are little short of spectacular in just about any direction.

Colorado 135

ROUND MOUNTAIN
Pike National Forest

Location: Central Colorado west of Colorado Springs.

Access: From U.S. Highway 24 at milepost 259 +.4 (20 miles east of Hartsel, 26 miles west of Woodland Park, 46 miles west of Colorado Springs), turn north onto a gravel access road and proceed 0.25 mile to the campground.

Facilities: 16 campsites; sites are medium to large, with good separation; parking pads are gravel, basically level, medium+ to long straight-ins; excellent tent-pitching possibilities; fireplaces; limited firewood is available for gathering; gathering of firewood enroute, or b-y-o, is suggested; water at a hand pump; vault facilities; gravel driveway; gas and camper supplies in Hartsel; adequate supplies and services are available in Woodland Park.

Activities & Attractions: Small national forest visitor center and viewpoint at Wilkerson Pass.

Natural Features: Located on a hilltop 5 miles east of the summit of Wilkerson Pass in the Rocky Mountains; campground vegetation consists of light to moderately dense, tall conifers, small aspens, and tall grass; Round Mountain lies about a mile northwest of here; elevation 8600'.

Season, Fees & Phone: May to September, but may also be available at other times, with reduced services and no fee; $7.00; 14 day limit; Pikes Peak Ranger District, Colorado Springs, (719) 636-1602.

Camp Notes: From Wilkerson Pass there are some extraordinary views of the great valley west of here known as South Park. For that matter, the views to the east from the campground area and from some sites are pretty terrific as well. A few miles east of Round Mountain is another forest camp called Happy Meadows that probably appeals mostly to trout fishermen. From milepost 264 +.1 (a mile west of the hamlet of Lake George), go north on Park County Road 77 for 1.3 miles, then easterly on a gravel access road for a mile. Happy Meadows has a half dozen sites, a hand pump and vaults. The facilities aren't much, but the pleasant setting along the South Platte is appealing, and the fishing is generally good.

Colorado 136

ELEVEN MILE: NORTH SHORE
Eleven Mile State Recreation Area

Location: Central Colorado west of Colorado Springs.

Access: From U.S. Highway 24 at milepost 264 +.5 (0.8 mile northwest of the town of Lake George, 26 miles east of Hartsel), turn west (i.e., left if approaching from Lake George), onto Park County Road 90 (paved) and travel 4 miles; bear southwest (left) onto County Road 92 (also paved) and continue for 6 miles to the park entrance; the principal camp loops are within a half-mile of the entrance, left or right off the main road.

Alternate Access: From U.S. Highway 24 at milepost 249 +.9 (10 miles east of Hartsel, 15 miles west of Lake George), turn southeast onto Park County Road 23 (paved) and travel 3 miles to a 3-way junction; turn southeast (left) onto Park County Road 59 (paved) and travel 2.5 miles, then pick up County Road 92 and continue southeast above the north shore of the reservoir for a final 4 miles to the North Shore area. (Note: The Alternate Access would save about 15 miles for travelers on U.S. 24 eastbound from Hartsel.)

Facilities: *North Shore*, *Rocky Ridge*, *Ponderosa Ridge*, *Puma Hills*, *Rocky Flats*: approximately 100 campsites in the foregoing areas; sites are small+ to medium-sized, with minimal to fairly good separation; parking pads are sandy gravel, of all lengths, mostly straight-ins, plus a few pull-offs; a little additional leveling will be required in many sites; medium to large tent areas, some are sloped; fire rings or barbecue grills; b-y-o firewood is recommended; water at hand pumps; vault facilities; holding tank disposal station; sandy gravel driveways; camper supplies nearby; gas and groceries in Lake George.

Activities & Attractions: Fishing; trail around the lake; boating; boat launch and dock; playground; amphitheater.

Natural Features: Located on a grassy, boulder-strewn, conifer-dotted slope above the north shore of 3400-acre Eleven Mile Reservoir on the South Platte River; campsites are unsheltered or lightly sheltered by conifers or large rocks; the reservoir lies in a broad valley, surrounded by timber-topped mountains; breezy; elevation 8600'.

Season, Fees & Phone: Open all year, subject to weather and road conditions, with limited services October to April; 14 day limit; please see Appendix for standard Colorado state park fees; park office (719) 748-3401.

Camp Notes: Each of the principal camp areas is locally termed a "campground"; but their similarities make them individual sections of one huge campground. The most popular camp is the North Shore section because it's the closest to the water's edge. But the sites farther up the slope provide a broader view, and a number of them are tucked in among large rock formations. The scenery is terrific--open, tallgrass slopes extend hundreds of yards up from the lake shore until they meet the forest on the upper levels of the mountains. Sunsets here can be incredible.

Colorado 137

ELEVEN MILE: SOUTH SHORE
Eleven Mile State Recreation Area

Location: Central Colorado west of Colorado Springs.

Access: From U.S. Highway 24 at milepost 264 +.5 (0.8 mile northwest of the town of Lake George, 26 miles east of Hartsel), turn west (i.e., left, from Lake George), onto Park County Road 90 (paved) and travel 4 miles; bear southwest (left) onto County Road 92 (also paved) and continue for 6 miles to the park entrance; continue northwest (past the north shore camp and day use areas) on County Road 92 (still paved) for 6 miles beyond the northwest tip of the reservoir to a 3-way junction; turn southwest (left) onto Park County Road 59 (paved for the first mile, then gravel) and travel southwest then southeast for 2 to 9 miles to the south shore camp areas; the principal south shore campground is at *Witcher's Cove*, near the southeast tip of the lake. **Alternate Access:** See *Eleven Mile: North Shore*, above.

Facilities: *Witcher's Cove*: 31 campsites; 'open' camping is also available in several other small, south shore areas (except the designated fishing access sites); sites are small, with minimal separation; parking pads are gravel, mostly straight-ins; medium to large areas for tents; fire rings; b-y-o firewood; water from a hand pump near the boat launch; vault facilities; gravel driveways; camper supplies at a small store on the north shore; gas and groceries in Lake George.

Activities & Attractions: Fishing for cutthroat and rainbow trout; boating; boat launch.

Natural Features: Located along the south shore of Eleven Mile Reservoir; campsites are unshaded/unsheltered; a long line of high mountains rise from the south shore; elevation 8600'.

Season, Fees & Phone: April to October; 14 day limit; please see Appendix for standard Colorado state park fees; park office (719) 748-3401.

Camp Notes: There's nary a tree anywhere along the entire south shore of the lake. (The closest trees to Witcher's Cove are at the southeast tip of the lake near the dam.) There's some disagreement among assorted brochures and maps as to what the reservoir and the recreation area are called and how the names are spelled. "Eleven Mile", "Eleven-Mile", "Elevenmile", "Elevenmile Canyon" (and maybe some others) all have been used in the state and federal spelling bee. (A half-dozen miles south of here is "Thirtynine Mile Mountain", or is it.....? Ed.)

Colorado 138

BLUE MOUNTAIN
Pike National Forest

Location: Central Colorado west of Colorado Springs.

Access: From U.S. Highway 24 at milepost 265 +.3 in the small community of Lake George (27 miles east of Hartzell, 20 miles west of Woodland Park, 40 miles west of Colorado Springs), turn south onto Park County Road 96 (gravel) and proceed 0.85 mile to a fork in the road; take the left fork and continue 0.65 mile to the campground access road; turn west (right) for 0.2 mile to the campground.

Facilities: 21 campsites; sites are small to medium-sized, with fairly good separation; parking pads are gravel, mostly short straight-ins which probably will require additional leveling; medium to large, but sloped, tent areas; fireplaces; limited firewood is available for gathering; gathering of firewood on forest lands prior to arrival, or b-y-o, is recommended; water at a hand pump; vault facilities; gravel/dirt driveway; gas and groceries in Lake George; adequate supplies and services are available in Woodland Park.

Activities & Attractions: Fishing on the South Platte River.

Natural Features: Located on a moderately forested, rolling hillside in the Rocky Mountains; campground vegetation consists primarily of tall conifers and some grass; cone-shaped Blue Mountain is in view from the campground; elevation 8200'.

Season, Fees & Phone: May to September, but may be available with limited services at other times, subject to weather conditions; $8.00; 14 day limit; Pikes Peak Ranger District, Colorado Springs, (719) 636-1602.

Camp Notes: Blue Mountain Campground is the first of a string of campgrounds in the Elevenmile Canyon area. Since it's substantially larger than most of the other campgrounds, and is not right along the river, the chances of getting a campsite on a summer weekend are probably better here.

Colorado 139

RIVERSIDE
Pike National Forest

Location: Central Colorado west of Colorado Springs.

Access: From U.S. Highway 24 at milepost 265 +.3 in the small community of Lake George (20 miles west of Woodland Park, 27 miles east of Hartzell), turn south onto Park County Road 96 (gravel) and proceed along`the east shore of Lake George for 0.9 mile to a fork; continue on the right fork along the river for 1 mile; turn east (left) into the campground.

Facilities: 19 campsites, including about a dozen park n'walk units; sites are medium to large, with fairly good spacing but nominal visual separation; parking surfaces are gravel, basically level, medium to long, of assorted styles; large tent areas, some are sloped; framed tent/table areas for some park n' walks; fire rings; limited firewood is available for gathering in the area, so gather enroute or b-y-o to be sure; water at a hand pump; vault facilities; gravel driveway; gas and groceries in Lake George.

Activities & Attractions: Trout fishing; campfire programs.

Natural Features: Located on a flat and on a hillside near the east bank of the South Platte River in Elevenmile Canyon in the Rocky Mountains; some sites are essentially unsheltered, others are lightly sheltered by conifers; elevation 8000'.

Season, Fees & Phone: May to October; $8.00; 14 day limit; Pikes Peak Ranger District, Colorado Springs, (719) 636-1602.

Camp Notes: Though there are no riverside sites as such, the local views from Riverside's campsites are very pleasant indeed. (Some park n' walks on the hillside have river views.) The surface of the main gravel road is typical Colorado Corrugation, but you can always pray for a grader and a steamroller to precede you. This is the first of several camps near the river between the highway and Elevenmile Reservoir. (Incidentally, there's no reservoir access from the canyon road.) The others, including the largest, Spillway, are 6-10 miles southeast of here.

Colorado 140

BUFFALO SPRINGS
Pike National Forest

Location: Central Colorado northeast of Buena Vista.

Access: From U.S. Highway 285 at milepost 170 (13 miles south of Fairplay, 8 miles north of Antero Junction, 24 miles north of Buena Vista), turn west onto Buffalo Peaks Road (gravel) and proceed 0.9 mile to the campground access road; turn south, and continue for 0.2 mile to the campground.

Facilities: 17 campsites; sites are large, with good to excellent separation; parking pads are dirt/gravel, short to medium-length straight-ins; some pads may require a little additional leveling; large, tolerably level, tent areas; fireplaces; firewood is available for gathering in the area; water at a hand pump; vault facilities; pack-it-in/pack-it-out system of trash removal; gravel driveway; limited supplies and services are available in Fairplay.

Activities & Attractions: Access to several trails west of the campground: Rough and Tumbling Creek, 5 miles, Salt Creek, 5 miles, and Lynch Creek, 7.5 miles.

Natural Features: Located on a gentle slope at the base of a timbered hill in the central Rocky Mountains; campground vegetation consists of moderately dense, tall conifers and some short aspens; grassy, partially timber-covered hills in the immediate area; small, seasonal streams nearby; the campground is located near the west edge of South Park, an enormous, nearly treeless valley; campground elevation 9000'.

Season, Fees & Phone: May to October, but may be available for use as early as March and as late as November, depending upon weather conditions; no fee (subject to change); 14 day limit; South Park Ranger District, Fairplay, (719) 836-2031.

Camp Notes: There probably isn't a nicer, easier to reach campground within a half-hour's drive of this spot. And the fact that it's a freebie makes it extra-appealing.

Colorado 141

COTTONWOOD LAKE
San Isabel National Forest

Location: Central Colorado west of Buena Vista.

Access: From U.S. Highway 24 at its intersection with Main Street in midtown Buena Vista, travel westerly on West Main/Chaffee County Road 306 (paved) for 8.1 miles; turn south (left) onto Chaffee County Road 344 (paved for a short distance, then good gravel), and proceed 4 miles (past the picnic ground and along the north shore of the lake) to a fork; take the right fork into the campground.

Facilities: 28 campsites; sites are medium-sized, with fair to very good separation; parking pads are gravel, medium-length straight-ins, and most will require additional leveling; adequate space for tents, but most spaces are sloped; some firewood is available for gathering in the general vicinity; water at several faucets; vault facilities; gravel driveway; adequate supplies and services are available in Buena Vista.

Activities & Attractions: Trout fishing; limited boating (hand-propelled craft only); several hiking trails in the vicinity.

Natural Features: Located in a canyon/narrow valley just east of the Continental Divide in the Rocky Mountains; sites are on a slope above the northwest shore of small Cottonwood Lake, and are lightly sheltered/shaded by aspens, plus conifers in the surrounding area; elevation 9600'.

Season, Fees & Phone: May to October; $8.00; 7 day limit; Salida Ranger District (719) 539-3591.

Camp Notes: If you're planning to do some fishin', a cartopper or a 'belly boat' might be helpful. But lots of people--from kids to old timers--just fish from one of the many small spots along the north shore. There appears to be a 'dropoff' just offshore that's within an easy cast. ('Insider' tip: The locals don't use the classic Spanish pronunciation of *Buena Vista* (which means "Good View"). Instead, *Buena* is pronounced *by*ew-nuh, like the "byew" in "butane" or "bucolic". Go figure.)

Colorado 142

COLLEGIATE PEAKS
San Isabel National Forest

Location: Central Colorado west of Buena Vista.

Access: From U.S. Highway 24 at its intersection with Main Street in midtown Buena Vista, travel west on West Main/Chaffee County Road 306 (paved) for 12.3 miles; (you'll pass the turnoff to Cottonwood Lake about 8 miles out); turn south (left) onto a paved access road for a final 0.1 mile down into the campground.

Facilities: 56 campsites in 2 sections; sites are medium to medium+, with generally good separation; parking pads are gravel, mostly short to medium-length straight-ins; additional leveling will be needed in many sites; small to medium-sized tent areas, may be sloped; fire rings or fireplaces; firewood is available for gathering in the area; water at hand pumps; vault facilities; gravel driveways; adequate supplies and services are available in Buena Vista.

Activities & Attractions: Avalanche Trailhead, 2 miles east; scenic drive across Cottonwood Pass, 7 miles west.

Natural Features: Located along and above the north bank of Cottonwood Creek in a canyon on the east slope of the Continental Divide in the Rocky Mountains; sites receive light to medium shade/shelter from conifers and aspens; elevation 9800'.

Season, Fees & Phone: May to October; $8.00; 14 day limit; Salida Ranger District (719) 539-3591.

Camp Notes: Collegiate Peaks is named for the chain of 14,000' mountains which dramatically rise north and south of here. Extending about 15 miles along the west edge of the Upper Arkansas River Valley are (north to south) Mounts Oxford, Harvard, Columbia, Yale and Princeton.

Colorado 143

MT. PRINCETON, CHALK LAKE, CASCADE
San Isabel National Forest

Location: Central Colorado southwest of Buena Vista.

Access: From U.S. Highway 285 at milepost 142 +.5 in Nathrop (7 miles south of Buena Vista, 16 miles north of Poncha Springs), turn west onto Chaffee County Road 162 (paved) and travel 8.5 miles to Mt. Princeton; or continue for an additional 0.5 mile to Chalk Lake; or for another 0.8 mile on gravel beyond Chalk Lake to Cascade; all are on the south side of the road.

Facilities: *Mt. Princeton*: 17 campsites; *Chalk Lake*: 21 campsites, mostly walk-ins; *Cascade*: 23 campsites; *all camps*: sites are small to medium-sized, with nominal to quite good separation; parking pads are gravel, mainly medium-length straight-ins; some pads will require a little additional leveling; medium to large, mostly level tent spots; some sites have framed tent pads; fire rings, plus some barbecue grills; some firewood is available for gathering in the area; water at hand pumps; vault facilities; sandy gravel driveways; gas and groceries in Nathrop; limited supplies and services are available in Buena Vista.

Activities & Attractions: Fishing; very limited boating on tiny Chalk Lake.

Natural Features: Located in a canyon on a streamside flat (Mt. Princeton), or a streamside/lakeside flat (Chalk Lake), or a near-streamside flat (Cascade), along Chalk Creek; majority of sites are quite well sheltered/shaded by conifers and aspens; closely bordered by lofty, barren-topped peaks; elevation 8700'.

Season, Fees & Phone: May to September; $9.00; 7 day limit; Salida Ranger District (719) 539-3591.

Camp Notes: You probably wouldn't go wrong in selecting just about any of the spots in these camps. Subjectively, the nod goes to Mt. Princeton and Cascade. All three camps are plenty busy. If you plan to do some boating on diminutive Chalk Lake, bring a vessel that operates on 'D' batteries.

Colorado 144

HECLA JUNCTION
Arkansas Headwaters State & Federal Recreation Area

Location: Central Colorado north of Salida.

Access: From U.S. Highway 285 at milepost 135 +.4 (16 miles south of Buena Vista, 8 miles northwest of Poncha Springs, turn east onto Chaffee County Road 194 (gravel) and proceed 2.5 miles to the park.

Facilities: 12 campsites; sites are small, with nominal separation; parking pads are gravel, short straight-ins; small to medium-sized areas for tents; fire rings; no drinking water; vault facilities; gravel driveway; limited to adequate supplies and services are available in Poncha Springs, Buena Vista, or Salida, 10 miles southeast.

Activities & Attractions: River floating; launch area; reportedly excellent trout fishing downstream of this area.

Natural Features: Located in Brown's Canyon along the west bank of the Arkansas River; scattered small pines and junipers provide minimal to very light shade/shelter; elevation 7400'.

Season, Fees & Phone: Open all year, subject to road conditions; principal camping season is May to October; 14 day limit; please see Appendix for standard Colorado state park fees; park office, Salida, (719) 539-7289.

Camp Notes: Brown's Canyon is one of the prettiest sections along the river. Although the camp is used a lot by floaters and backpackers, it would make a simple but scenic, reasonably accessible stop for just about anyone.

Colorado 145

MONARCH PARK
San Isabel National Forest

Location: Central Colorado east of Gunnison.

Access: From U.S. Highway 50 at milepost 202 +.4 (3 miles northeast of Monarch Pass summit, 46 miles east of Gunnison, 20 miles west of Salida), turn south onto Chaffee County Road 231, and proceed 0.9 mile south (parallels the highway, which lies in a north-south line in this section) to the campground.

Facilities: 38 campsites in 2 loops; most sites are large and well spaced; parking pads are gravel straight-ins or pull-throughs, average or better in length; some sites are built on a gentle hillside, with steps leading up to the table and tent areas; fireplaces; a limited amount of firewood is available in the area; gathering of firewood prior to arrival, or b-y-o, is suggested; water at a hand pump; vault facilities; gravel driveways; gas and groceries are available in Sargents, 14 miles southwest and in Poncha Springs, 15 miles east.

Activities & Attractions: Wildlife project involving "silted beaver ponds" was instituted here to improve fish habitat; several trails in the area leading to small, high mountain lakes; footbridge across the stream.

Natural Features: Located in moderately dense timber on the edge of a small, mountain park (meadow) on the east slope of the Continental Divide near the summit of Monarch Pass; a small stream, part of the headwaters of the South Arkansas River, flows through the campground; bordered by high, timbered ridges and peaks; elevation 10,500'.

Season, Fees & Phone: June to September; $7.00; 14 day limit; Salida Ranger District (719) 539-3591.

Camp Notes: Because of its altitude, this campground is at its prime for only a few weeks out of the year. But it is really a dandy little spot as far as atmosphere and scenery are concerned.

Colorado 146

GARFIELD
San Isabel National Forest

Location: Central Colorado east of Gunnison.

Access: From U.S. Highway 50 at milepost 203 +.9 (5 miles east of Monarch Pass summit, 48 miles east of Gunnison, 18 miles west of Salida), turn south and drive across a bridge into the campground.

Facilities: 11 campsites; sites are small to medium-sized, level, with fairly good separation; parking pads are gravel, short to medium-length straight-ins, plus a few pull-throughs; maneuvering may be a little difficult for larger vehicles, but there is a turnaround at the east end of the campground; small tent areas; fireplaces; some firewood is available for gathering in the area; water at a hand pump; vault facilities; gravel driveway; gas and groceries in Poncha Springs, 13 miles east; virtually complete supplies and services are available in Salida.

Activities & Attractions: Fishing; several mountain trails in the area lead to small, high mountain lakes; a number of old, or still-operating, mines are in the area.

Natural Features: Located along the South Arkansas River on the east slope of the Continental Divide just east of the summit of Monarch Pass; campsites all have tall conifers, willows and leafy underbrush that provide a substantial amount of shelter/shade; the river flows through a narrow canyon here, flanked by high, rocky, timbered ridges; elevation 10,000'.

Season, Fees & Phone: June to September; $7.00; 14 day limit; Salida Ranger District (719) 539-3591.

Camp Notes: Even though this campground is right along a fairly busy highway, the riverfront setting makes it a pleasant place to stop for a night. It's also a good place to use as a base when exploring the region.

Colorado 147

ANGEL OF SHAVANO
San Isabel National Forest

Location: Central Colorado west of Salida.

Access: From U.S. Highway 50 at milepost 210 +.5 in Maysville (7 miles west of Poncha Springs, 11 miles east of Monarch Pass), turn north onto Chaffee County Road 240 (paved for the first 3 miles, then gravel) and travel 4 miles; turn south (left) onto County Road 240A (gravel) for 0.1 mile into the campground. (Note: If you blink, you'll miss Maysville.)

Facilities: 20 campsites; sites are small to medium-sized, reasonably level, with minimal to fair separation; parking pads are gravel, mostly short+ straight-ins, plus a few medium-length pull-offs; small to medium-sized areas for tents; fire rings; firewood is available for gathering in the area; water at a hand pump; vault facilities; gravel driveway; gas and groceries in Poncha Springs; virtually complete supplies and services are available in Salida, 11 miles east.

Activities & Attractions: Angel of Shavano Trailhead; picnic area; sports field; possible stream fishing for small trout.

Natural Features: Located in a canyon on a gently sloping flat in an aspen grove along and near the North Fork of the South Arkansas River; several sites are in the open, most are moderately shaded by tall aspens interspersed with a few conifers; bordered by densely forested hills and mountains; a very prominent peak, Mount Shavano, rises to 14,229' just north of the campground; campground elevation 9200'.

Season, Fees & Phone: May to October; $7.00; 14 day limit; Salida Ranger District (719) 539-3591.

Camp Notes: Mount Shavano's 'Angel' is formed by the pattern of clefts, gullies and ravines on the mountainside, which, especially when dusted with snow, resembles the image of a winged spirit. Continuing past Angel of Shavano on the main gravel road for another 6.5 miles will take you to North Fork Reservoir Campground. The road follows the river and is steep, winding and rough for much of that distance. It levels out once you get up on top at 11,000'. North Fork has a half-dozen sites, vaults, and is accessible only during midsummer. The scenery is very good and there are several hiking trails in the vicinity.

Colorado 148

O'HAVER LAKE
San Isabel National Forest

Location: Central Colorado south of Salida.

Access: From U.S. Highway 285 at milepost 121 +.5 (5 miles south of Poncha Springs, 2.4 miles north of the summit of Poncha Pass), turn southwest onto Chaffee County Road 200 (gravel) and proceed 2.3 miles to a fork/3-way intersection; bear right onto Chaffee County Road 202 and continue for another 1.3 miles (past a 4-way intersection) to the campground. (Note: There often is heavy traffic on this road; the last half-mile to the lake is a bit steep and narrow.)

Facilities: 29 campsites; sites are medium+ in size, with fair to fairly good separation; parking pads are gravel/earth, medium-length straight-ins plus a few long pull-throughs; additional leveling will be needed in some sites; large, though generally sloped, tent areas; fire rings; firewood is available for gathering in the general area; water at hand pumps; vault facilities; gravel driveways; gas and groceries are available in Poncha Springs; virtually complete supplies and services are available in Salida.

Activities & Attractions: Fishing; handicapped-access fishing platform; motorless boating; trail around the lake.

Natural Features: Located around the shore of O'Haver Lake on the east slope of the Rockies near the Continental Divide; sites are lightly sheltered by conifers and aspens; some sites are shoreside, others are a few yards from the water's edge; 13,000' to 14,000' peaks rise west and south of the lake; elevation 9200'.

Season, Fees & Phone: June to September; $9.00; 7 day limit; Salida Ranger District (719) 539-3591.

Camp Notes: On a reasonably clear, calm morning, the nearby peaks are brilliantly mirrored on the lake's surface. Add to the scene the smoke from a campfire, the soft giggles of kids and the splash of a rising trout, and a lot of campers will agree: "It just doesn't get any better than this!"

Colorado 149

BUFFALO PASS
Rio Grande National Forest

Location: South-central Colorado southeast of Gunnison.

Access: From Colorado State Highway 114 at milepost 35 +.3 (35 miles southeast of the junction of Highway 114 & U.S. Highway 50 near Gunnison, 4 miles east of the summit of North Cochetopa Pass, 27 miles northwest of Saguache), turn south onto a gravel road and proceed 0.7 mile to the campground.

Facilities: 30 campsites; sites are medium to medium+, with fair to very good separation; parking pads are gravel, short to long straight-ins, plus a couple of long pull-throughs; some additional leveling will be needed on many pads; plenty of space for tents, though they may be sloped; fireplaces; b-y-o firewood is suggested; no drinking water; gravel driveway; limited supplies and services are available in Saguache.

Activities & Attractions: Scenery and seclusion.

Natural Features: Located on a hillside in the Cochetopa Hills high on the east slope of the Continental Divide; sites are lightly shaded in an open forest of tall conifers and aspens on a grassy surface; encircled by conifer-cloaked hills and mountains garnished with aspen groves and grassy slopes; elevation 9100'.

Season, Fees & Phone: May to October; no fee (subject to change), contributions accepted; 14 day limit; Saguache Ranger District (719) 655-2553.

Camp Notes: Some campsites have quite respectable views toward the hills and mountains in the north across a valley. This could be a nice, cool, serene place to escape to on a midsummer weekend that's hot in the valleys far below and busy in all of the campgrounds along lakes and streams in the major rec areas. For a quick reference: The campground is a shade more than 200 miles from Denver, so it might be possible to leave the metro area late in the afternoon and still roll in here about nightfall.

Colorado 150

COALDALE & HAYDEN CREEK
San Isabel National Forest

Location: Central Colorado southeast of Salida.

Access: From U.S. Highway 50 at milepost 241 +.7 on the west edge of the hamlet of Coaldale (19 miles southeast of Salida), turn southwest onto Hayden Creek Road (paved for the first 1.5 miles, then gravel) and travel 3.8 miles to Coaldale Campground, on the east (left) side of the road; or continue past Coaldale for another 1.5 steep and narrow miles to Hayden Creek Campground. (Notes: You'll pass a large private campground just before you reach Coaldale Cg.; see *Camp Notes* for additional access info for Hayden Creek Cg.)

Facilities: *Coaldale*: 7 campsites; *Hayden Creek*: 11 sites; most sites are small park 'n walk or walk-in units, with generally good separation; parking surfaces are gravel, short straight-ins; small tent spots; fire rings; firewood is available for gathering in the area; no drinking water; vault facilities; narrow, gravel driveways, very limited turnaround space; virtually complete supplies and services are available in Salida.

Activities & Attractions: Possible fishing for small trout; Rainbow Trail passes through Hayden Creek Cg. as it skirts the foothills to Salida; 4wd trail across Hayden Pass.

Natural Features: Located in a densely forested canyon along Hayden Creek; most sites are streamside and are very well sheltered by cottonwoods and conifers; closely bordered by forested mountains; deer are plentiful in this area; elevation 7800' at Coaldale, 8000' at Hayden Creek.

Season, Fees & Phone: May to October; no fee (subject to change); 14 day limit; Salida Ranger District (719) 539-3591.

Camp Notes: It's easy enough to reach Coaldale Campground. No sweat. But it's a bit of a drill getting up to Hayden Creek without a solid vehicle, preferably a 4wd during inclement conditions. Neither of these small camps is used very often because they're perceived by most campers as being "too closed in". But that perception could be turned into a 'plus' during a holiday weekend. If you're a camper who enjoys hauling his gear and grub a few yards across a footbridge to a cozy little place by a nice, rushing stream, one of these sites might be just your spot.

Colorado 151

ALVARADO
San Isabel National Forest

Location: Central Colorado northwest of Walsenburg.

Access: From Colorado State Highway 69 at milepost 55 +.3 (3.5 miles south of Westcliffe, 62 miles northwest of Walsenburg), head due west on Road 140 (paved) for 4.7 miles to a "T" intersection; turn south (left) onto Road 141/Willow Lane (paved); go south on Road 141 for 0.2 mile, then the road becomes gravel and winds and climbs in a generally westerly direction up the mountainside for another 2.2 miles to the campground. (Note: Road 140 is called "Schoolfield Road" on some forest maps; the northbound section opposite the Highway 69 turnoff to Alvarado may be signed as "Rosita Road".)

Facilities: 45 campsites; sites are medium to large, with good to excellent separation; parking pads are gravel, short to medium+ straight-ins; additional leveling will be needed on many pads; medium to large tent areas; fire rings; firewood is available for gathering in the area; water at several faucets; vault facilities; gravel, rocky driveways; limited supplies and services are available in Westcliffe.

Activities & Attractions: Commanding views; trailheads for the Comanche and Venable Trails (hiking and horse routes) that cross the Sangre de Cristo Range.

Natural Features: Located on a mountainside on the east slope of the Sangre de Cristo Range overlooking an expansive valley far below to the east; sites receive light to medium shade/shelter from tall conifers and some aspens; small streams cascade down the mountainside in the area; elevation 9000'.

Season, Fees & Phone: May to October; $7.00; 14 day limit; San Carlos Ranger District, Canon City, (719) 275-4119.

Camp Notes: Alvarado's campsites are in several clusters and loops scattered across a good-sized piece of this mountainside 1200' above the valley floor. At night, the lights of Westcliffe and the friendly farm lights all over the valley can be seen twinkling far below. Another forest campground that's accessible from the same great valley east of the Sangre de Cristos is Lake Creek Campground. From Highway 69 at milepost 71 +.5 on the south edge of Hillside (11 miles north of Westcliffe), travel southwest on a local gravel road for 0.5 mile, then head almost due west for three more miles. Lake Creek has ten small streamside sites, vaults, no drinking water, in a forested setting where the valley plain meets this magnificent mountain range.

Colorado 152

NORTHERN PLAINS & JUNIPER BREAKS
Lake Pueblo State Recreation Area

Location: Southern Colorado west of Pueblo.

Access: From U.S. Highway 50 at milepost 307 +.4 (7 miles west of Interstate 25 Exit 101 in Pueblo, 29 miles east of Canon City), turn south onto McCollough Boulevard and travel 4.3 miles to a 3-way intersection; then pick up Nichols Road and follow it south and east for another mile to the park's northwest entrance station; just past the entrance, turn south (right) and proceed 1.1 miles to a 3-way intersection; turn west (right) and go 0.2 mile to *Northern Plains* Campground; or from the entrance station continue easterly on the main north shore road for 1.7 miles, then turn south into *Juniper Breaks* Campground. (Note: Access is also possible from Colorado State Highway 96; follow the basic directions for Arkansas Point Campground, below, then travel north along the dam, then west along the north shore to the campgrounds.)

Facilities: *Northern Plains*: 214 campsites, including 197 with electrical hookups, in 3 major loops; (a group camp is also available); sites are medium-sized, with nominal to fair separation; parking pads are paved, medium to long, extra-wide straight-ins, or long pull-throughs; additional leveling will be needed on many pads; large, grassy tent areas; ramadas (sun/partial wind shelters) in many sites; fire rings; b-y-o firewood; water at central faucets; restrooms with showers; coin-op laundry; holding tank disposal station; paved driveways; *Juniper Breaks*: 86 campsites; sites are small+, with minimal to nominal separation; parking pads are paved, medium-length straight-ins; medium to large areas for tents; fire rings; b-y-o firewood; water at central faucets; vault facilities; paved driveways; complete supplies and services are available along U.S. 50 near I-25 in Pueblo.

Activities & Attractions: Boating; boat launch; windsurfing; fishing for largemouth, smallmouth and spotted bass; several miles of hiking, bicycling and horse trails; paved fitness trail; large amphitheater and small playgrounds in Northern Plains Campground; model airplane field.

Natural Features: Located on a large, grassy bluff above the northwest shore of 4000-acre Pueblo Reservoir; the Rocky Mountains rise just to the west; vegetation consists of prairie grass and scattered trees; typically breezy; square miles of open fields border the north shore; elevation 4900'.

Season, Fees & Phone: Northern Plains, open May to October; Juniper Breaks, open all year, with limited services October to April; Northern Plains: 14 day limit; please see Appendix for reservation information and standard Colorado state park fees; park office (719) 561-9320.

Camp Notes: Lake Pueblo is particularly popular with avid boaters. When you combine all this water in one easily accessible spot close to population centers, (within a two-hour drive for half of the state's population) and within view of the Rockies, you can readily see why. The camp areas don't have a lot of natural shade, but you can duck under a ramada (or jump into the shower) if it gets too sunny and warm.

Colorado 153

ARKANSAS POINT
Lake Pueblo State Recreation Area

Location: Southern Colorado west of Pueblo.

Access: From Colorado State Highway 96 at milepost 49 (8 miles west of Interstate 25 in Pueblo, 19 miles east of Wetmore), turn northwest onto the park access road and travel 0.8 mile to the southeast entrance station (by the park visitor center); swing south (left) into the campground. (Note: Access is also possible from U.S. Highway 50; follow the directions to Northern Plains Campground, above, but continue east along the north shore, then south along the dam to Arkansas Point Campground.

Facilities: 94 campsites with electrical hookups; sites are medium-sized, with minimal to nominal separation; parking pads are paved, medium-length extra-wide straight-ins or long pull-throughs; additional leveling will be required in most sites; medium to large tent areas; fire rings; b-y-o firewood; water at central faucets; restrooms with showers; coin-op laundry; paved driveways; complete supplies and services are available along Highway 96 in Pueblo.

Activities & Attractions: Boating; boat launch; marina; fishing for warm water species; large visitor center with displays and audio-visual programs.

Natural Features: Located along, and on a hill above, the southeast shore of Lake Pueblo; campsites overlook the marina and a bay, and are minimally shaded by scattered hardwoods; a rocky bluff forms the south backdrop of the area; elev. 4900'.

Season, Fees & Phone: May to September; 14 day limit; please see Appendix for reservation information and standard Colorado state park fees; park office (719) 561-9320.

Camp Notes: There are some excellent displays in the park visitor center across from the campground. Most of them describe and depict the reservoir project, but many also relate to the area's fish and wildlife.

Colorado 154

GREENHORN MEADOWS
Greenhorn Meadows/Colorado City Park

Location: South-central Colorado south of Pueblo.

Access: From Colorado State Highway 165 at milepost 33 +.4 (3 miles west of Interstate 25 Exit 74 for Colorado City), turn south onto the park access road for 0.2 mile to the campground.

Facilities: 50 campsites, including 10 with electrical hookups, in 2 loops; sites are average to large, with nominal to good separation; parking pads are gravel, short to medium-length, mostly straight-ins; some pads may require minor additional leveling; mostly large, grassy tent spots, some nestled in among hardwoods next to the river; fireplaces or barbecue grills; b-y-o firewood is recommended; pack-it-in/pack-it-out system of trash removal; water at several faucets; restrooms; gravel driveways, including a ford across the river to sites on the south side; limited+ supplies and services are available in Colorado City.

Activities & Attractions: Sports fields; playground; nearby municipal golf course and swimming pool.

Natural Features: Located along the north and south banks of Greenhorn Creek, a few miles east of the Wet Mountains of the Rockies; campground vegetation consists of scattered conifers, hardwoods, and a little brush along the river; the stream flows through a somewhat narrow valley between gently rolling hills which merge with the higher foothills; campsites are situated in a grassy meadow or along the rocky cliffs at the edge of the meadow; elevation 6200'.

Season, Fees & Phone: May to October; $8.00 for a standard site, $10.00 for a hookup site; park office (719) 676-3452.

Camp Notes: Greenhorn Meadows Campground is in a very pleasant setting, conveniently close to the Interstate. It's also just 10 miles east of the mountains in San Isabel National Forest. There's lots of grassy space for tents and plenty of shade courtesy of big hardwoods. So if you're a canvasback camper, this spot might suit you better than the forest camps up the highway.

Colorado 155

SOUTHSIDE
Lake Isabel/San Isabel National Forest

Location: Southern Colorado southwest of Pueblo.

Access: From Colorado State Highway 165 at milepost 19 (17.7 miles west of Colorado City and Interstate 25 Exit 74, 19 miles south of the junction of State Highways 165 & 96), turn southwest onto a paved access road and proceed 0.4 mile; turn south (left) into the campground.

Facilities: 8 campsites; sites are very small and tightly spaced; parking pads are medium-length, parallel pull-throughs; not much space for tents; fire rings and barbecue grills; firewood is available for gathering; water at hand pumps; vault facilities; gravel driveway; limited+ supplies and services are available in Colorado City.

Activities & Attractions: Lake Isabel handicapped trail; fishing and motorless boating on nearby Lake Isabel; scenic mountain drive along Highway 165 with expansive views of the Great Plains to the east.

Natural Features: Located in a forested canyon along the St. Charles River in the Wet Mountains; vegetation consists of tall conifers and some aspens; elevation 8800'.

Season, Fees & Phone: May to September; $8.00; San Carlos Ranger District, Canon City, (719) 275-4119.

Camp Notes: Of the trio of camps in the Lake Isabel Recreation Area (also see St. Charles and Cisneros campgrounds), Southside is the closest to the lake. Since it's also the smallest, it may be to your advantage to scout the other spots for a campsite.

Colorado 156

SAINT CHARLES
Lake Isabel/San Isabel National Forest

Location: Southern Colorado southwest of Pueblo.

Access: From Colorado State Highway 165 at milepost 19 (17.7 miles west of Colorado City and Interstate 25 Exit 74, 19 miles south of the junction of State Highways 165 & 96), turn southwesterly onto a paved access road and proceed 1 mile; turn south (left) onto a gravel access road for another 0.3 mile, then swing north (right) into the campground.

Facilities: 15 campsites; sites are medium-sized, with good to excellent separation; parking pads are gravel, reasonably level, medium-length straight-ins; many sites have framed-and-gravelled tent pads; fire rings; firewood is available for gathering; water at hand pumps; vault facilities; gravel driveway; limited+ supplies and services are available in Colorado City.

Activities & Attractions: Fishing and motorless boating on nearby Lake Isabel; possible stream fishing for small trout.

Natural Features: Located in a forested canyon along the brush-lined St. Charles River in the Wet Mountains; sites are well sheltered by tall conifers and short aspens; elevation 8800'.

Season, Fees & Phone: May to September; $8.00; San Carlos Ranger District, Canon City, (719) 275-4119.

Camp Notes: St. Charles is in a relatively wide spot in an otherwise narrow canyon, so there's generally a bit more potential sunshine available here. Quite a few sites are streamside, or nearly so. Overall, this may be the best of the three local camps.

CISNEROS
Lake Isabel/San Isabel National Forest

Location: Southern Colorado southwest of Pueblo.

Access: From Colorado State Highway 165 at milepost 19 (17.7 miles west of Colorado City and Interstate 25 Exit 74, 19 miles south of the junction of State Highways 165 & 96), turn southwesterly onto a paved access road and proceed 1 mile; turn south (left) onto a gravel access road and go 0.6 mile (past the turnoff to St. Charles Campground) to a fork; take the left fork for a final 0.1 mile to the campground.

Facilities: 15 park n' walk or walk-in campsites; sites are small to medium-sized, with fairly good separation; gravel parking areas for small vehicles; most sites have adequate space for a small to medium-sized tent, but it may be sloped; fire rings and barbecue grills; firewood is available for gathering in the area; water at hand pumps; vault facilities; gravel driveway; limited+ supplies and services are available in Colorado City.

Activities & Attractions: Fishing and motorless boating on nearby Lake Isabel; Cisneros Trailhead.

Natural Features: Located on hilly, rocky terrain along a small stream in the Wet Mountains along the east slope of the Rockies; most sites are well sheltered by tall conifers and some aspens and underbrush; flanked by high, steep mountains; elevation 8800'.

Season, Fees & Phone: May to September; $7.00; San Carlos Ranger District, Canon City, (719) 275-4119.

Camp Notes: Cisneros is one of the larger camps (in terms of number of sites) designed for tent and small vehicle campers in Colorado. (If you're in an rv and have a yen to take a look-see, keep in mind that there's very limited turnaround room in here.)

PINYON FLATS
Great Sand Dunes National Monument

Location: South-central Colorado northeast of Alamosa.

Access: From U.S. Highway 160 at a point 16.5 miles east of Alamosa and 7 miles west of Blanca, turn north onto Colorado State Highway 150; proceed 18 miles to the park entrance; the campground is 1.8 miles farther.

Facilities: 88 campsites in 2 tiered loops; (a group camp is also available); most sites are small+ to medium-sized, with fair to fairly good separation; parking pads are hard-surfaced, fairly level, mostly short straight-ins, some are extra-wide; tent areas are reasonably level, and adequate for large tents; fire rings; b-y-o firewood; water at central faucets; restrooms; holding tank disposal station; showers and camper supplies, just south of the park; adequate+ supplies and services are available in Alamosa.

Activities & Attractions: Hiking across the sand dunes, just a few minutes walk west of the campsites; visitor center; trails from the park travel parallel to creekbeds through Mosca Pass and Medano Pass over the crest of the Sangre de Cristos.

Natural Features: Located between vast, 700-feet-high sand dunes to the west and the Sangro de Christo Mountains to the east; a fairly constant breeze sweeps across the dunes, through the campground, and up the west slopes of the mountains; deer frequently pass through the campground; campground vegetation includes piñon pines, yucca and brush; elevation 8200'.

Season, Fees & Phone: Open all year, with limited services November to April; $8.00 for a site, $5.00 for the park entrance fee; 14 day limit; park headquarters (719) 378-2312.

Camp Notes: Pinyon Flats Campground is situated in a truly unique setting--between the high-desert sand and the towering mountains. It may get a bit warm in the heat of summer, so consider spring or autumn for a visit. Quite honestly, this is a spot well worth going 20 miles out of the way for. Note the Americanized spelling of the campground's name, *Pinyon*, versus the traditional Spanish *Piñon*.

PIÑON & YUCCA
Lathrop State Park

Location: Southern Colorado west of Walsenburg.

Access: From U.S. Highway 160 at milepost 302 +.1 (3.2 miles west of Walsenburg, 11 miles east of the junction of U.S. 160 and Colorado State Highway 12 near La Veta), turn north into the park and go 0.2 mile to a 3-way intersection just past the visitor center; turn east (right) and proceed 0.2 mile to *Yucca* Campground; or continue past Yucca Campground and head northerly (across the top of Martin Lake dam on the east side of the lake) for 1.1 mile to *Piñon* Campground.

Facilities: *Piñon*: 78 campsites, many with electrical hookups, in 4 loops; sites are generously medium-sized, with nominal to fairly good separation; parking pads are gravel, fairly level, medium to long pull-throughs; virtually all sites have good tent areas, many have framed and leveled tent pads; fire rings; b-y-o firewood; water at several faucets; restrooms with showers; laundry facilities; holding tank disposal station; paved driveways; *Yucca*: 16 campsites; (a group camp is also available); sites are medium-sized, with good separation; parking pads are gravel, medium-length straight-ins; a few pads may require a little additional leveling; medium to large tent areas; fire rings; b-y-o firewood; water at several faucets; vault facilities; gravel driveways; adequate supplies and services are available in Walsenburg.

Activities & Attractions: Fishing for stocked trout, tiger muskie and catfish; boating; boat launches; windsurfing; sandy swimming beach; several miles of hiking and bicycling trails; small visitor center; small playground; 9-hole public golf course; amphitheater for scheduled summer weekend campfire programs; extensive day use facilities.

Natural Features: Located in a valley bordered by low, pine-topped hills on the east slope of the Rocky Mountains; campground vegetation consists of tall grass dotted with short pines and junipers; (b-y-o extra shade is suggested); small Martin Lake and Horseshoe Lake are within the park; Spanish Peaks rise to 12,683' and 13,623' south of the park; elevation 6400'.

Season, Fees & Phone: Open all year, with limited services in winter; 14-day limit; please see Appendix for reservation information and standard Colorado state park fees; park office (719) 738-2376.

Camp Notes: Park traffic thins out to a trickle by mid-September, even on weekends. That's somewhat surprising, considering the really nice camping facilities in Piñon Campground and the extraordinary vistas. Comparatively mild winter temperatures in this locale allow use of this park virtually year 'round. Spanish Peaks can be viewed from just about anywhere in the park. Called *Hua Jatolla*s ("Breasts of the World") by the Indians who believed that all life emanated from them, the stunning pair of mountains has also been known as *Dos Hermanos* ("Two Brothers") "Dream Mountains", and "Twin Peaks".

Colorado 160

PURGATOIRE
San Isabel National Forest

Location: Southern Colorado northwest of Trinidad.

Access: From Colorado State Highway 12 at milepost 30 +.8 (30 miles south of the junction of Colorado 12 with U.S. 160, 40 miles northwest of Trinidad), turn west onto North Fork Road; proceed west 0.1 mile to a "T" intersection; take the right leg of the "T"; continue up the road for 4.3 miles to the campground.

Facilities: 25 campsites; most sites are of ample size, fairly well spaced, and relatively level, considering the terrain; most parking pads are gravel/grass straight-ins; ample space for tents; fire rings; firewood is available for gathering; water at a hand pump; vault facilities; gravel driveways; gas and groceries in La Veta, 27 miles north; complete supplies and services are available in Trinidad.

Activities & Attractions: Stream fishing; 2 small local lakes on the east side of Highway 12--North Lake, near milepost 30, and Monument Lake, near milepost 33--provide fishing and limited boating opportunities.

Natural Features: Located on a somewhat open hillside surrounded by aspens and some conifers, on the east slope of the Sangre de Cristo Range, along the North Fork of the Purgatoire River; elevation 9700'.

Season, Fees & Phone: May to September; $7.00; 14 day limit; San Carlos Ranger District, Canon City, (719) 275-4119.

Camp Notes: Here's a case of it being not so much the campground, but the surroundings, that might attract someone to this area. There are some excellent views of the Sangre de Cristo Range from nearby. Some of the campsites are very nice indeed, and the campground has the appearance of being under-used. Another nearby national forest campground is Cuchara, along Cucharas Creek, on a gravel forest road just west of Colorado Highway 12 near milepost 20. Lots of traffic there, though.

CARPIOS RIDGE
Trinidad State Recreation Area

Location: Southern Colorado west of Trinidad.

Access: From Colorado State Highway 12 at milepost 66 +.5 (3 miles west of Interstate 25 Exit 14A in Trinidad, 66 miles south of the junction of State Highway 12 & U.S. Highway 160), turn south to the park entrance station, then proceed 0.5 mile to the campground. (Note for I-25 travelers: From the freeway exit, Highway 12 zigzags at least a half-dozen times on its way out of town, so be watchful of the "Colorado 12 Thataway" arrows planted near intersections.)

Facilities: 62 campsites, including 49 with electrical hookups; sites are small to medium-sized, fairly level, with minimal to nominal separation; parking pads are gravel, short+ to medium-length straight-ins (although there are 20 yards of clear overhang area behind some pads); most sites have large, framed tent pads; fireplaces; b-y-o firewood; water at several faucets; restrooms with showers; coin-op laundry; holding tank disposal station; paved driveways; virtually complete supplies and services are available in Trinidad.

Activities & Attractions: Boating; boat launch; windsurfing; fishing for rainbow trout, bass, walleye, channel cat and panfish; 1.5-mile Levsa Canyon Nature Trail (a nice guide pamphlet is available), and the 0.75-mile Carpios Ridge Trail both start and end near the camp area; (an extension of the Levsa Canyon Trail continues several miles west to the old mining town of Cokedale); amphitheater; limited hunting in season; Corps of Engineers visitor center one-half mile east; day use areas.

Natural Features: Located on a gently rolling, flat-topped ridge overlooking the north shore of 900-acre Trinidad Lake; many of the campsites are in the open, some have limited shelter/shade provided by pines and junipers; prominent, flat-topped, 9700' Fisher's Peak rises across the valley to the east; elevation 6300'.

Season, Fees & Phone: Open all year, with limited services November to April; 14 day limit; please see Appendix for reservation information and standard Colorado state park fees; park office (719) 846-6951.

Camp Notes: This might prove to be an excellent, convenient stop if you're entering or leaving Colorado via Interstate 25. There aren't many public campgrounds north of here, in Colorado, or south, in New Mexico, with easy access from I-25.

Colorado
East

Please refer to the
Colorado map in the Appendix

SOUTH BAY
Horsetooth Reservoir/Larimer County Park

Location: North-central Colorado west of Fort Collins.

Access: From Interstate 25 Exit 265, travel west on Colorado State Highway 68 for 4.5 miles; turn north (right) onto U.S. 287 (College Avenue); proceed 1 mile; turn west (left) onto Horsetooth Road and head west for 1.9 miles; turn south (left) onto Taft Hill Road and continue south for 0.6 mile; turn west (right) onto Road 38E and continue west and south on a paved, winding road for 3 final miles to the campground. (Got that?)

Facilities: 150 campsites in 3 loops; sites are small to medium-sized, with nominal separation; parking pads are paved, mostly level, short to medium+, mostly straight-ins; small to medium-sized tent spots; fireplaces; b-y-o firewood is recommended; water at several faucets; vault facilities; paved driveways; camper supplies at a store nearby; complete supplies and services are available in Fort Collins.

Activities & Attractions: Boating; boat launch and marina; fishing; swimming; hiking nearby and in Lory State Park.

Natural Features: Located on the southwest shore of Horsetooth Reservoir at the base of the Laramie Mountains of the Central Rockies; campground vegetation consists of sparse grass, and a few small trees and bushes; some sites are on a bluff overlooking the lake, some are right at the water's edge; the lake is surrounded by rocky, tree-dotted bluffs; Horsetooth Mountain rises to 7255' just a few miles to the west; elevation 5400'.

Season, Fees & Phone: Open all year, with limited services in winter; $6.00; 14 day limit; Larimer County Parks Department, Fort Collins, (303) 679-4570.

Camp Notes: South Bay is the most easily accessible campground in the park. Others are scattered along the shore of the reservoir and are less developed. Views from atop the nearby mountains are spectacular.

Colorado 163

COTTONWOOD SHORES
Boyd Lake State Recreation Area

Location: Northern Colorado east of Loveland.

Access: From U.S. Highway 34/East Eisenhower Boulevard at milepost 92 +.8 (3.5 miles west of Interstate 25 Exit 257B, 1 mile east of the junction of Highway 34 & U.S. Highway 287 in midtown Loveland), turn north onto North Madison Avenue and travel north for 1.4 miles; turn east (right) onto Larimer County Road 24E and go 1.2 miles east and north to the park entrance station; continue past the entrance for another 0.1 mile to a major 4-way intersection, (you'll be pointed east here); turn south (right) and go 0.3 mile to the campground.

Facilities: 148 campsites in 6 loops; sites are medium-sized, with nominal separation; parking pads are paved, essentially level, medium+ pull-throughs; ample space for large tents; fire rings; b-y-o firewood; water at several faucets; restrooms with showers; holding tank disposal station; paved driveways; complete supplies and services are available in Loveland.

Activities & Attractions: Large, sandy swimming beach; playgrounds; volleyball courts; boating; boat launch; windsurfing and sailing; fishing for bass, catfish, crappie, perch and walleye.

Natural Features: Located along the west shore of Boyd Lake, on the plains east of the Front Range of the Rocky Mountains; campground vegetation consists of a line of cottonwoods along the lake shore (hence the name), plus scattered conifers on a surface of mown grass; majority of the campsites are minimally to very lightly shaded; typically breezy; elevation 5000'.

Season, Fees & Phone: Open all year, with limited services October to April; 14 day limit; please see Appendix for reservation information and standard Colorado state park fees; park office (303) 669-1739.

Camp Notes: Boyd Lake provides fairly comfortable camping opportunities conveniently close to Colorado's population center. (Loveland is within 50 miles of Denver.) As a bonus, it's also within striking distance of some super, high mountain country.

Colorado 164

BARBOUR PONDS
Barbour Ponds State Recreation Area

Location: Northern Colorado east of Longmont.

Access: From Interstate 25 Exit 240 for Longmont/Colorado State Highway 119 (17 miles south of Fort Collins, 30 miles north of Denver), travel west on State Highway 119 for 1 mile to milepost 62 +.5; turn north (right) onto Road 7 (gravel) and proceed 0.5 mile, then the road swings east (right) and becomes Road 24 1/2; continue east for another 0.75 mile, then turn north (left) into the park entrance; from just inside the entrance, swing west/northwest (left) onto the park driveway for another 0.4 mile to an intersection; turn left or right to the campsites.

Facilities: 60 campsites in 2 loops; (a small group camp is also available); sites are small, generally level, with minimal separation; parking pads are sand/dirt, medium-length straight-ins; medium to large areas for tents; small ramadas (sun/partial wind shelters) for many sites; fire rings; b-y-o firewood; water at a hand pump; vault facilities; holding tank disposal station; sand/dirt driveways; gas and groceries on Highway 119; complete supplies and services are available in Longmont.

Activities & Attractions: Fishing for bass, channel cat, crappie, also trout (seasonally); limited boating (hand, sail, or electric power); Muskrat Run nature trail; small playground.

Natural Features: Located around the shores of 4 ponds, and the banks of St. Vrain Creek, Idaho Creek and Last Chance Ditch, on the plains east of the Front Range of the Rockies; vegetation consists of scattered large hardwoods, grass and some marshland; elevation 4900'.

Season, Fees & Phone: Open all year; 14 day limit; please see Appendix for reservation information and standard Colorado state park fees; phone c/o Boyd Lake State Park.

Camp Notes: Barbour Ponds originally were sand and gravel pits excavated for highway construction. Seepage and underground springs gradually filled the big holes. You can see and hear the freeway from just about every campsite; you can smell it, taste it, and *feeelll* it, too. It's the small cost of convenient camping. All campsites have pond views, such as they are. In counterbalance, the distant mountain vistas and their accompanying sunsets are really good.

Colorado 165

CHERRY CREEK
Cherry Creek State Recreation Area

Location: Northern Colorado southeast of Denver.

Access: From Interstate 225 Exit 4 for Parker Road/Colorado State Highway 83 (4 miles northeast of the junction of Interstates 225 & 25 in southeast Denver), travel southeast on Parker Road for 1 mile to East Lehigh Avenue; turn southwest (right) onto a paved park access road and proceed 1.7 miles southwest and west to the East Gate entrance station, then to a major 4-way intersection just beyond the entrance; turn north (right) and travel 0.9 mile to the campground.

Facilities: 91 campsites in 5 loops; (a group camp is also available); sites are small+ to medium-sized, level, with nominal to fair separation; parking pads are paved, medium-length straight-ins or pull-offs; ample space for large tents; fire rings; b-y-o firewood; water at many faucets; restrooms with showers; coin-op laundry; holding tank disposal station; paved driveways; complete supplies and services are available along Parker Road.

Activities & Attractions: Very large, sandy swimming beach; fishing for trout, walleye, bass, tiger muskie, crappie and catfish; boating; boat launch; 8 miles of paved hiking/jogging/bicycling trails throughout the park; 10 miles of horse trails; riding stables (operated by concessionaire); extensive day use facilities nearby.

Natural Features: Located near the east shore of Cherry Creek Reservoir, a U.S. Army Corps of Engineers flood-control project; campsites are unshaded to nicely shaded by large hardwoods on a surface of mown grass (b-y-o shade 'just in case'); most of the park consists of large tracts of open fields with stands of hardwoods and a few conifers; elevation 5400'.

Season, Fees & Phone: Open all year; 14 day limit; please see Appendix for reservation information and standard Colorado state park fees; park office (303) 779-6144.

Camp Notes: The campground is in the shadow of a cluster of high-rise apartments and motels, but the Front Range of the Rockies can be seen rising from behind the dam from most campsites, too. It's one of the nicest (and handiest) 'big city' camps in the Rockies.

Colorado 166

CHATFIELD
Chatfield State Recreation Area

Location: Northern Colorado south of Denver.

Access: From U.S. Highway 85/Santa Fe Drive at milepost 196 (4.3 miles south of the junction of U.S. 85 & Colorado State Highway 470 near Littleton, 12 miles north of Interstate 25 Exit 183 at Castle Rock), turn west onto Titan Road and travel 2 miles to Douglas County Road 3/Roxborough Park Road; turn north onto Road 3 and proceed 2 miles north/northwest to the park entrance station, then a final 0.5 mile to the campground.

Facilities: 153 campsites, including 51 with electrical hookups, in 3 loops; (a very large group camp area is also available); sites are medium-sized, level or nearly level, with nil to zip separation; parking pads are paved pull-throughs; medium to large tent areas; fire rings; b-y-o firewood; water at several faucets; restrooms with showers; holding tank disposal station; paved driveways; small playground; complete supplies and services are available in Littleton.

Activities & Attractions: Boating; boat launch; marina; fishing for bass, perch, crappie, catfish and trout on the lake and on the South Platte River upstream of the lake; several miles of hiking, bicycling and horse trails; short trails in a nature area; model airplane field; swimming beach in the park's West Shore area; extensive day use areas.

Natural Features: Located on gently sloping terrain covered by mown grass, along the south shore of Chatfield Lake, a reservoir on the South Platte River; camp loops are situated a few hundred yards above the lake shore; some large hardwoods and small evergreens dot the campground, but the majority of sites are essentially unsheltered; the Front Range of The Rockies is in view to the west; elevation 5500'.

Season, Fees & Phone: April to October; 14 day limit; please see Appendix for reservation information and standard Colorado state park fees; park office (303) 791-7275.

Camp Notes: With miles of trails, 1400 acres of water, a large, sandy swim beach and even a model airplane field, there's certainly enough to do here. Heron Overlook, southwest of the campground, is a popular spot for both human and avian fishermen. (The dead trees left standing in the water just offshore as "fish attractors" also serve as roosts for the big birds.)

Colorado 167

CROW VALLEY
Pawnee National Grassland

Location: Northeast Colorado east of Fort Collins.

Access: From Colorado State Highway 14 at milepost 176 +.1 (0.2 mile west of Briggsdale, 61 miles west of Sterling, 23 miles east of Ault), turn north onto Weld County Road 77 (paved); proceed north 0.3 mile to the recreation area access road; turn west onto the gravel road and continue 0.3 mile (past the day use area) to the campground.

Facilities: 5 campsites; sites are generously medium-sized, level, with fair to excellent spacing between sites, but with minimal visual separation; parking pads are gravel, medium+ straight-ins; excellent, large, grassy areas for tents; fire rings and barbecue grills; b-y-o firewood; water at central faucets; vault facilities; pack-it-in/pack-it-out system of trash removal; gravel driveway; nearest source of supplies and services (limited+) is Ault.

Activities & Attractions: Sports field (with backstop); amphitheater; day use area with large shelter complete with a hooded (chimneyed) barbecue grill.

Natural Features: Located in a small hollow on the Great Plains of Eastern Colorado; campground vegetation consists of short to tall grass, and large hardwoods which provide fair to very good shelter/shade in all sites; large, open grassy 'infield' within the loop; surrounded by many, many miles of nearly treeless, very gently rolling prairie; elevation 4900'.

Season, Fees & Phone: April to October; $7.00; 7 day limit; Pawnee National Grassland Headquarters, Greeley, (303) 353-5004 (Fort Collins Metro phone).

Camp Notes: So who says Colorado's only good camping is in the mountains? This is a really neat little place. OK, so there isn't a lake or a river to dip your toes into. But there's a sea of grass that's perfect for prairie puttering.

Colorado 168

JACKSON LAKE: WEST SHORE
Jackson Lake State Recreation Area

Location: Northeast Colorado northwest of Fort Morgan.

Access: From Interstate 76 Exit 66 for Goodrich/Wiggins (14 miles west of Fort Morgan, 70 miles northeast of Denver), travel north on Colorado State Highway 39 for 7.5 miles to the hamlet of Goodrich; continue north (straight ahead) on Colorado State Highway 144 to a point 0.4 mile north of Goodrich; at a "T" intersection a few yards north of milepost 11 on Highway 144, turn west (left) onto a paved access road and proceed west, then north, for 2.3 miles to the park boundary; from there, continue north for 0.8 mile to 1.5 miles to the camp areas (*Lakeside*, *Cove*, and *Pelican*). **Alternate Access:** From the junction of U.S. Highway 34 & Colorado State Highway 144 (32 miles southeast of Greeley), head northeast on State Highway 144 for 8 miles to Goodrich and continue as above.

Facilities: *Lakeside*, *Cove*, and *Pelican* areas: 78 campsites in 3 major areas, plus boat-in, walk-in and 'open' camping areas; sites are small, with minimal to nominal separation; parking pads are sandy gravel, reasonably level, mostly short to medium-length straight-ins; most pads are reasonably level; adequate space for small to medium-sized tents in most units; fire rings; b-y-o firewood; water at several faucets; restrooms with showers, also vault facilities; holding tank disposal station; gravel driveways; gas and groceries are available in Goodrich.

Activities & Attractions: Fishing for walleye, bass, catfish perch and crappie; fishing jetty; boating; boat launch; windsurfing; marina/boat rental; designated swimming area; cross-country skiing and other winter pastimes; day use areas.

Natural Features: Located along the west shore of 2700-acre Jackson Lake in a large, shallow basin north of the South Platte River; some sites have shelter/shade provided by large hardwoods, other sites have minimal shade; many sites are within a few feet of the lake; large beaches; surrounded by gently rolling prairie; elevation 4400'.

Season, Fees & Phone: Open all year, with limited services in winter; 14 day limit; please see Appendix for reservation information and standard Colorado state park fees; park office (303) 645-2551.

Camp Notes: Jackson Lake, like many of the big ponds on the Plains, has an abundance of sand along its shore, which substantially bolsters the "beach" mood here. Although the facilities are, as one visitor commented, "unremarkable", the lake and prairie views are quite good from most sites.

Colorado 169

JACKSON LAKE: SOUTH SHORE
Jackson Lake State Recreation Area

Location: Northeast Colorado northwest of Fort Morgan.

Access: From Interstate 76 Exit 66 for Goodrich/Wiggins (14 miles west of Fort Morgan, 70 miles northeast of Denver), travel north on Colorado State Highway 39 for 7.5 miles to the hamlet of Goodrich; continue north (straight ahead) on Colorado State Highway 144 to a point 0.4 mile north of Goodrich; at a "T" intersection a few yards north of milepost 11 on Highway 144, turn west (left) onto a paved access road and proceed west, then north, for 2.3 miles to the park boundary; turn east onto a gravel access road into the South Shore area. (For Alternate Access see Jackson Lake, West Shore, above.)

Facilities: 20 campsites in 2 loops; sites are small, with minimal to nominal separation; parking pads are sandy gravel, mostly short to medium-length straight-ins; most pads are reasonably level; adequate space for small to medium-sized tents in most sites; small ramadas (sun/partial wind shelters) for table areas in some sites; fire rings; b-y-o firewood; water at several faucets; restrooms with showers; gravel driveways; gas and groceries are available in Goodrich.

Activities & Attractions: Designated swimming beach; fishing.

Natural Features: Located along and near the south shore of Jackson Lake; campsites are in a stand of hardwoods on a small knoll several yards south of the shoreline; elevation 4400'.

Season, Fees & Phone: Open all year, with limited services November to April; 14 day limit; please see Appendix for standard Colorado state park fees; park office (303) 645-2551.

Camp Notes: It's an easy task to swing into the South Shore camp just after entering the park to take a quick look before going on up the pike to the West Shore areas. The West Shore is not only many times larger than the South Shore but, subjectively, it's just "better" as well.

Colorado 170

FOSTER GROVE & NORTH COVE
Bonny State Recreation Area

Location: Eastern Colorado near the Colorado-Kansas border.

Access: From U.S. Highway 385 at milepost 210 +.8 (23 miles north of Interstate 70 Exit 437 or Exit 438 at Burlington, 8 miles south of the junction of U.S. 385 & U.S. 36 near Idalia), turn east onto Road 3 (a sandy gravel park access road) and go 1.7 miles to the park entrance station; just past the entrance, turn south (right) to *Foster Grove* Campground; or continue northeasterly on the main park road past the Foster Grove turnoff for an additional 4 miles to the *North Cove* area.

Facilities: *Foster Grove*: 49 campsites; sites are small, essentially level, with minimal to nominal separation; parking pads are gravel, medium to medium+ straight-ins or pull-throughs; plenty of space for tents; fire rings; b-y-o firewood; water at several faucets; restrooms, plus auxiliary vaults; holding tank disposal station; gravel driveway; *North Cove*: 20 primitive campsites, group camp area and vault facilities; limited to adequate supplies and services are available in Burlington.

Activities & Attractions: Boating; boat launch at North Cove; short trail to the lake shore; small playground; x-c skiing and other quiet winter activities; self-guided nature trail at North Cove; waterfowl and limited upland game hunting in season.

Natural Features: Located in bottomland near the north-west shore of Bonny Reservoir (Foster Grove); most campsites are lightly to moderately shaded by mature hardwoods on large, open grassy areas; closely bordered by dense woodland and well-irrigated farmland; located on a long, slender cove on the northeast corner of the reservoir (North Cove); the reservoir is surrounded by high plains; elevation 3700'.

Season, Fees & Phone: Open all year, with limited services October to May; Foster Grove: 14 day limit; please see Appendix for standard Colorado state park fees; park office (303) 354-7306.

Camp Notes: The north shore areas described above are less popular than those closer to the lake shore and the highway (see the south shore areas below); hence, they'll be less *populated* as well. However, at

Foster Grove you'll probably have plenty of company from assorted wild walking and winged critters who've taken up residence in the adjoining woods and fields. The very fertile bottomland at Foster Grove stands in exceptional contrast to the open slopes and plains surrounding it.

Colorado 171

WAGON WHEEL & EAST BEACH
Bonny State Recreation Area

Location: Eastern Colorado near the Colorado-Kansas border.

Access: From U.S. Highway 385 at milepost 209 +.7 (22 miles north of Interstate 70 Exit 437 or Exit 438 at Burlington), turn east onto Road 2 (a sandy gravel park access road) and travel 3.9 miles to the park entrance station; after passing through the entrance, continue ahead to Wagon Wheel Campground, or turn right and go 1.9 miles to the East Beach Campground.

Facilities: *Wagon Wheel*: 61 campsites in 6 loops; sites are medium-sized, with minimal to fair separation; parking pads are paved or gravel, short to medium-length straight-ins, which will require additional leveling; medium to large tent spots; a few sites have small ramadas (sun/wind shelters); fire rings; b-y-o firewood; water at several faucets; restrooms with showers; holding tank disposal station; paved/gravel driveways; *East Beach*: 38 campsites; sites are small, somewhat sloped, with minimal separation; parking surfaces are gravel, mostly short straight-ins; generally large areas for tents; small ramadas (sun/partial wind shelters) for some sites; fire rings; b-y-o firewood; water at hand pumps; vault facilities; gravel driveways; camper supplies at the marina; adequate supplies and services in Burlington.

Activities & Attractions: Boating; boat launch; fishing for most standard warm water species, including bass, catfish, walleye, northern pike and the ever-elusive Great Plains wiper; designated swimming areas; small playground; cross-country skiing, ice fishing, and other winter pursuits.

Natural Features: Located in a large basin on the south shore of Bonny Reservoir, a flood-control impoundment on the South Fork of the Republican River; vegetation consists of light to medium-dense hardwoods and a few short pines on a grassy surface; campsites in Wagon Wheel are unshaded to moderately shaded and a few have lake views; many East Beach sites lack natural shade/shelter and are situated near the base of the dam, close to the lake shore; bordered by high plains; elevation 3700'.

Season, Fees & Phone: Open all year, with limited services October to April; 14 day limit; please see Appendix for reservation information and standard Colorado state park fees; park office (303) 354-7306.

Camp Notes: Bonny may prove to be a boon to Interstate 70 travelers who discover that the next public parks in slate-level Eastern Colorado and Western Kansas are many, many miles from here. If you're planning on staying for a while, Wagon Wheel Campground would be the spot to check out first of all the campgrounds in the recreation area.

Colorado 172

LAKE HASTY
John Martin Reservoir/Corps of Engineers Park

Location: Southeast Colorado northeast of La Junta.

Access: From U.S. Highway 50 at milepost 414 +.9 (in midtown Hasty, 21 miles west of Lamar, 35 miles east of La Junta), turn south onto a gravel access road (signed for John Martin Reservoir); proceed 2.4 miles south to a fork; take the left (east) fork and continue for 0.8 mile to the campground.

Facilities: 51 campsites in 2 loops, plus dispersed camping; sites are mostly average-sized, with fair to good separation; parking pads are gravel, level, medium to long, mostly straight-ins; virtually all sites have large, level, grassy tent spots; fireplaces, plus some barbecue grills; b-y-o firewood; water at several faucets; restrooms, plus auxiliary vault facilities; holding tank disposal station; gravel driveways; camper supplies in Hasty; adequate supplies and services are available in La Junta.

Activities & Attractions: Visitor center at the dam; amphitheater; motorless boating; fishing; swimming beach nearby; day use area with lawns, playground and horseshoe courts.

Natural Features: Located on the Arkansas River below John Martin Reservoir; campground vegetation consists of grass and an assortment of mature hardwoods; sites are situated in a grassy pocket with rolling hills on 3 sides and the reservoir to the south; farmland stretches for miles in every direction; elev. 4100'.

Season, Fees & Phone: Open all year, with limited services and no fee October to April; $6.00; 14 day limit; John Martin Reservoir CoE Project Office (719) 336-3476 or (719) 679-9631.

Camp Notes: This is it for southeast Colorado. It's the best public campground for many, many miles in any direction.

Montana

Public Campgrounds

The Montana map is located in the Appendix on page 199.

Montana

West

Montana 1

YAAK RIVER
Kootenai National Forest

Location: Northwest Montana northwest of Libby.

Access: From U.S. Highway 2 at a point 7 miles southeast of the Montana-Idaho border and 7 miles northwest of Troy, turn southwest from either side of the Yaak River bridge (one loop is on each side of the river) into the campground.

Facilities: 43 campsites in 2 loops, including 29 sites in the loop east of the river and 14 sites in the west loop; sites are average or better in size, and fairly well spaced; parking pads are paved, level, medium to long straight-ins or long pull-throughs; good-sized tent areas; fireplaces; firewood is available for gathering in the area; water at several faucets; vault facilities; paved driveways; limited+ supplies and services are available in Troy.

Activities & Attractions: Fishing; Yaak Falls is west on Highway 2 then north on Highway 508 (8 miles total distance); Boulder City ghost town a few miles northwest (accessible from Highway 2 in Idaho); a number of 4wd trails provide access to mountain lakes and streams in the surrounding area.

Natural Features: Located on a forested flat slightly above the confluence of the Yaak and Kootenai Rivers; campground vegetation consists of tall conifers with light to dense underbrush and a pine needle carpet; the Purcell Range of the Rocky Mountains lies to the east and the Cabinet Mountains rise to the south; elevation 1900'.

Season, Fees & Phone: May to September; $7.00; 14 day limit; Three Rivers Ranger District, Troy, (406) 295-4693.

Camp Notes: Many of these nice campsites are perched right on the edge of a short bluff overlooking the river. There are some great views of the streams and the timbered ridges across the wide Kootenai River. The point of lowest elevation in Montana, a mere 1820 feet above sea level, is just a few miles from here along the Kootenai.

Montana 2

BAD MEDICINE
Kootenai National Forest

Location: Northwest corner of Montana southwest of Libby.

Access: From Montana Highway 56 at milepost 16+.5 (35 miles southwest of Libby, just north of the Sanders/Lincoln County Line), turn west onto a gravel forest road; drive 0.7 mile to a fork; take the right fork 1 more mile to the campground; (the left fork leads to Ross Creek and the Giant Cedars Scenic Area).

Facilities: 16 campsites; sites are mostly average-sized with fair to good separation; parking pads are paved, short to medium-length straight-ins; many pads may require some additional leveling; most sites have at least small spots level enough for tents; fireplaces; firewood is available for gathering; water at several faucets; vault facilities; narrow, paved driveways; limited supplies and services are available in Troy, 22 miles north.

Activities & Attractions: Boating; boat launch and docks; fishing; Ross Creek Giant Cedars Scenic Area, 4 miles west, has a 0.9 mile self-guided nature trail and 250-foot-tall cedars; Cabinet Mountain Wilderness is to the east.

Natural Features: Located on a forested hillside on the west shore of Bull Lake on the Bull River; campground vegetation consists of tall, fairly dense conifers over a forest floor of pine needles; peaks of the Cabinet Range are visible across the lake from many sites; elevation 2200'.

Season, Fees & Phone: May to September; $6.00; 14 day limit; Three Rivers Ranger District, Troy, (406) 295-4693.

Camp Notes: Bad Medicine Campground is located in one of the greenest valleys in Montana. The drive through the superscenic Bull River Valley between two crests of the Cabinet Mountains is in itself worth the trip. Another nearby campground, Spar Lake, is on a gravel road several miles west of Highway 56 mile 25. Spar Lake has a half-dozen sites, drinking water and vaults. It's on a very small lake about a thousand feet higher in elevation than Bad Medicine and is said to have very good fishing.

Montana 3

BULL RIVER
Kootenai National Forest

Location: Northwest Montana south of Libby.

Access: From Montana State Highway 200 at milepost 11 +.1 (0.7 mile southeast of the junction of Montana State Highways 200 and 56, 4.5 miles northwest of Noxon), turn northeast onto a gravel access road and proceed 0.1 mile to the campground.

Facilities: 18 campsites in 2 terraced loops; sites are small to medium-sized, with generally good separation; parking pads are gravel, short to medium-length straight-ins; some pads may require additional leveling; sites in the lower loop, just above the water's edge, are a little more open and level and better for tent-pitching than the upper loop's sites; fireplaces; firewood is available for gathering in the area; water at several faucets; restrooms, plus auxiliary vault facilities; gravel driveways; camper supplies at a nearby resort; nearest source of adequate supplies and services is Sandpoint, Idaho, 46 miles northwest.

Activities & Attractions: Boating; boat launch and floating docks; fishing; swimming; hiking trails nearby.

Natural Features: Located on a forested hillside at the confluence of the Bull River and Clark Fork of the Columbia River near Cabinet Gorge Reservoir; campground vegetation is fairly dense, with tall conifers, hardwoods, primroses, and ferns; forested peaks of the Bitterroot Range rise to the west; the Cabinet Mountains rise to the east; elevation 2200'.

Season, Fees & Phone: May to October; $7.00; 14 day limit; Cabinet Ranger District, Trout Creek, (406) 827-3533.

Camp Notes: The atmosphere at Bull River is somewhat reminiscent of a coastal rain forest. The campground is surrounded by some of the greenest hillsides and forested peaks in this part of the state.

Montana 4

NORTH SHORE
Kootenai National Forest

Location: Northwest Montana south of Libby.

Access: From Montana State Highway 200 at milepost 26 +.7 (27 miles southeast of the Montana-Idaho border, 2 miles northwest of the community of Trout Creek), turn west/southwest and proceed 0.5 mile on a gravel access road to the campground.

Facilities: 12 campsites; sites are medium-sized, with fair to good separation; parking pads are grass/gravel, mostly level, medium-length straight-ins; some good tent-pitching opportunities; fireplaces; some firewood is available for gathering in the area; water at several faucets; vault facilities; oiled gravel driveway; limited supplies are available in Trout Creek.

Activities & Attractions: Boating; boat launch and floating docks; fishing; self-guided nature trail describes local vegetation; large day use area with sheltered picnic tables; Trout Creek hosts an annual Huckleberry Festival.

Natural Features: Located on a rolling, forested hillside above Noxon Reservoir, created by Noxon Rapids Dam across Clark Fork of the Columbia River; most sites are in a forested setting with tall conifers and light underbrush; the Cabinet Mountains tower to the east while the Bitterroot Mountains rise just to the west; elevation 2200'.

Season, Fees & Phone: May to September; $6.00; 14 day limit; Cabinet Ranger District, Trout Creek, (406) 827-3533.

Camp Notes: A really picturesque lake is just over the rise from these campsites. Forested mountains are visible in every direction. North Shore Campground is nestled right in the midst of some of the most inviting country in Montana.

THOMPSON FALLS
Thompson Falls State Recreation Area

Location: Northwest Montana northwest of Missoula.

Access: From Montana State Highway 200 at milepost 49 +.6 (1 mile west of the community of Thompson Falls, a few yards east of the Clark Fork bridge, 5 miles southeast of Belknap), turn north onto a paved local access road and proceed 1 mile; turn west (left) into the park and proceed 0.3 mile to the campground.

Facilities: 19 campsites; sites are medium-sized, generally level, with nominal to fairly good separation; parking pads are gravel, medium-length straight-ins or long pull-throughs; medium to large tent areas; fire rings; some firewood is available for gathering in the general area, b-y-o to be sure; water at several faucets; vault facilities; paved driveway; limited+ supplies and services are available in Thompson Falls.

Activities & Attractions: Boating; boat launch; fishing for trout, bass and ling; museum in Thompson Falls; day use areas.

Natural Features: Located on the east bank of the wide and deep Clark Fork of the Columbia River, between the Bitterroot Range and the Cabinet Mountains; campsites are on a flat near river level; sites receive very light to light-medium shade/shelter from tall pines; high, steep-sided, timbered Flatiron Ridge rises from the opposite bank of the river; Noxon Rapids Reservoir is a few miles downstream of the park; elevation 2400'.

Season, Fees & Phone: May to September; please see Appendix for standard Montana state park fees; phone c/o Montana Dept. of Fish Wildlife & Parks Office, Kalispell, (406) 752-5501; summer park phone (406) 827-3732.

Camp Notes: With all of the mountains around here, you would expect the elevation to be a lofty one. Actually, Thompson Falls' elevation is one of the lowest of all public campgrounds in Montana. It tops those on the Great Plains of far Eastern Montana by only a couple-hundred feet. Warm days and mild nights spring through fall are the general rule. Thompson Falls on Clark Fork was named for David Thompson, geographer and explorer for the Northwest Company, a British fur-trading firm. He built a trading post near here in 1809. Thompson was the greatest geographer of his day in British North America.

LOGAN
Logan State Recreation Area

Location: Northwest Montana west of Kalispell.

Access: From U.S. Highway 2 at milepost 77 +.1 (45 miles west of Kalispell, 45 miles southeast of Libby), turn south into the campground.

Facilities: 47 campsites in 2 loops; sites are generally small, tolerably level, with minimal to nominal separation; parking pads are gravel, mostly short to medium-length straight-ins; adequate room for medium to large tents in most sites; fire rings; b-y-o firewood is recommended; water at central faucets; restrooms, plus auxiliary vault facilities; holding tank disposal station; gravel driveways; gas and camper supplies at Happy's Inn, 5 miles west; adequate supplies in Libby; complete supplies and services are available in Kalispell.

Activities & Attractions: Boating; boat launch and docks; fishing for rainbow trout, kokanee salmon, largemouth bass and perch; designated swimming area.

Natural Features: Located on the north shore of Middle Thompson Lake, between the Cabinet Mountains and the Salish Mountains; tall Douglas fir and ponderosa pines provide moderate shade/shelter for most campsites; several sites are near the lake shore; heavily timbered mountains are visible across the lake to the south; elevation 3500'.

Season, Fees & Phone: May to mid-September; please see Appendix for standard Montana state park fees; phone c/o Montana Dept. of Fish Wildlife & Parks Office, Kalispell, (406) 752-5501; summer park phone (406) 293-7190.

Camp Notes: All three Thompson Lakes are right along this highway. Surrounded by verdant slopes, they're very pleasantly picturesque.

McGREGOR LAKE
Kootenai National Forest

Location: Northwest Montana west of Kalispell.

Access: From U.S. Highway 2 at milepost 85+.5 (37 miles west of Kalispell, 53 miles east of Libby, 13 miles east of Happy's Inn); turn south onto a gravel access road; proceed 0.2 mile to campground entrance.

Facilities: 12 park 'n walk campsites; sites are located in an infield meadow with pull-off parking within a few feet; parking is in a gravel lot, and is not really designed for level, in-vehicle sack-outs; some large, grassy tent areas; barbecue grills and/or fireplaces; b-y-o firewood is recommended; water at faucets; vault facilities; pack-it-in/pack-it-out system of trash removal; gravel driveways; camper supplies at a nearby resort; complete supplies and services are available in Kalispell.

Activities & Attractions: Boating; boat ramp; fishing (including ice fishing in winter); several forest roads in the area provide rough, gravel access to the mountain areas nearby.

Natural Features: Located on the west shore of McGregor Lake between two crests of the Rocky Mountains; campground vegetation consists of tall grass and young trees; the McGregor Lake basin has room for little more than just the lake, the campground on its breezy open slope, and the roadway; the lake and campsites are near the base of 6300' peaks; the Salish Mountains are visible across the lake to the east; elevation 3900'.

Season, Fees & Phone: Open all year, subject to weather conditions, with limited services in winter; $6.00; 14 day limit; Fisher River Ranger District, Libby, (406) 293-7773.

Camp Notes: A typically breezy, sunny and open hillside is the setting for this campground. Views across the lake to the east and the forested slopes beyond are outstanding. Superscenic U.S. 2. between Kalispell and Libby passes through nearly a hundred miles of what is still largely wild country.

McGILLIVRAY
Kootenai National Forest

Location: Northwest Montana northeast of Libby.

Access: From Montana State Highway 37 (southbound from Eureka) near milepost 17 at Libby Dam (17 miles northeast of Libby, 50 miles southwest of the junction of Highway 37 & U.S. Highway 93 in Eureka), turn west and proceed across the top of the dam to the west side of the lake; turn north (right) onto Forest Road 228 (paved) and travel 7 miles to milepost 10 +.3; turn east (right) onto a paved access road for 0.1 mile to a "T"; turn northerly (left) and proceed 0.3 mile to the campground. **Alternate Access:** From Highway 37 (north-eastbound from Libby) at milepost 13 +.6 (13 miles east of Libby) turn north onto Forest Road 228 and travel 10 miles (along the west side of Lake Koocanusa and past Libby Dam) to milepost 10 +.3; turn east into the recreation area and continue as above.

Facilities: 50 campsites in 2 loops; sites are small+ to medium-sized, with good to excellent separation; parking pads are hard-packed, oiled gravel, mostly medium to long straight-ins; a bit of additional leveling may be needed in about half of the sites; tent space varies from small to large; fireplaces; firewood is available for gathering; water at several faucets; restrooms; paved driveways; adequate supplies and services are available in Libby.

Activities & Attractions: Boating; boat launch; designated swimming beach nearby; several short trails in the area; small amphitheater; 2 picnic areas with shelters; group day use areas (available by reservation only); horseshoe courts; fishing; Corps of Engineers visitor center on the west side of the dam.

Natural Features: Located on a bench/bluff a short distance above the west shore of Lake Koocanusa, a major reservoir on the Kootenai River created by a Corps of Engineers dam; the lake is 90 miles long, with a maximum depth of 370'; campsites are well sheltered by tall conifers and dense undergrowth; the lake is closely flanked by densely timbered mountains; elevation 2500'.

Season, Fees & Phone: May to November; $7.00; 14 day limit; Fisher River Ranger District, Libby, (406) 293-7773.

Camp Notes: Fjord-like Lake Koocanusa straddles the U.S.-Canada international boundary, and roughly half of the lake's surface lies on either side of the border. The name of the lake suggests that it might be of Indian origin, right? Nope. A group of locals appointed to a commission to name the man-made lake came up with a man-made contrivance for the new reservoir. They took the *Koo*tenai River, *Can*ada, and tacked-on *USA* to form *Koocanusa*. Neat, huh?

Montana 9

PECK GULCH
Kootenai National Forest

Location: Northwest Montana southwest of Eureka.

Access: From Montana State Highway 37 at milepost 45 +.7 (20 miles southwest of the junction of Highway 37 & U.S. Highway 93 in Eureka, 30 miles north of Libby Dam), turn west onto a paved, steep, narrow access road (Forest Road 7942) and proceed down 0.5 mile, then turn left into the campground.

Facilities: Approximately 25 campsites; (overflow and group camp areas are also available); sites are small to small+, level, with zip sep; parking pads are gravel, short+ straight-ins or long pull-throughs or pull-offs; plenty of space for big tents; fire rings; gathering of firewood on national forest side roads prior to arrival is recommended; water at several faucets; vault facilities; waste water receptacles; paved or gravel driveways; nearest reliable source of supplies and services (adequate) is Eureka.

Activities & Attractions: Boating; boat launch; fishing for plentiful small kokanee salmon, also rainbow (kamloops) trout.

Natural Features: Located on a flat along the east shore of Lake Koocanusa; vegetation in the campground consists mostly of mown grass; b-y-o shade; a steep, densely timbered hill forms the eastern backdrop for the campground; the high, timbered Selirk Mountains rise from the lake's west shore, the Purcell Mountains are to the east; elevation 2500'.

Season, Fees & Phone: May to November; $7.00; 14 day limit; Rexford Ranger District, Eureka, (406) 296-2536.

Camp Notes: Boating campers might be interested in exploring a large bay on an inlet on the opposite shore from Peck Gulch. It's one of the few sizeable shoreline indents along the middle third of the lake. Another nearby recreation site that is under development is Rocky Gorge, located off the west side of Highway 37 at milepost 40 +.5. Reportedly there are plans for adding camping facilities or for allowing self-contained camping in the large existing parking lot. (A call to the local ranger district may provide you with current info.)

Montana 10

REXFORD BENCH
Kootenai National Forest

Location: Northwest Montana west of Eureka.

Access: From Montana State Highway 37 at milepost 61 +.4 (5.5 miles west of the junction of Highway 37 & U.S. Highway 93 in Eureka, 45 miles north of Libby Dam), turn north onto a paved road and go 0.1 mile to a fork; swing onto the right fork and go 0.25 mile to another fork; bear right into the campground.

Facilities: 52 campsites in 2 loops; sites are medium-sized, with fair to good separation; parking pads are hard-surfaced, medium to long, double-wide straight-ins, plus a few pull-throughs; a little additional leveling may be needed in some sites; medium to large areas for tents; fire rings; some firewood is available for gathering nearby, b-y-o to be sure; water at several faucets; restrooms; holding tank disposal station; paved driveways; adequate supplies and services are available in Eureka.

Activities & Attractions: Nature trail; foot trail down to the boat ramp; small program area; boating; boat launch, designated swimming beach and day use area nearby.

Natural Features: Located on a bench (bluff) above the north-east shore of Lake Koocanusa; most sites are lightly to moderately sheltered by conifers above a surface of tall grass; the lake is bordered by densely forested mountains; elevation 2600'.

Season, Fees & Phone: May to November; $8.00; 14 day limit; Rexford Ranger District, Eureka, (406) 296-2536.

Camp Notes: Nice, hilltop environment here. This is certainly one of the better-equipped camps in this part of the state. You can fairly easily walk down the quarter-mile trail from the campground to a dandy little picnic area near the boat launch. For a nearby freebie, you might check out the four-site primitive spot called Camp 32. It's located two miles southeast of Highway 37 from milepost 55 +.5. Camp 32 has tables, fire facilities, vaults, but no drinking water.

NORTH DICKEY LAKE
Kootenai National Forest

Location: Northwest Montana Southwest of Eureka.

Access: From U.S. Highway 93 at milepost 163 +.4 (15 miles southeast of Eureka, 36 miles northwest of Whitefish), turn west onto the Trego Road (paved) and proceed 0.3 mile; turn easterly (left) onto a paved access road for 0.2 mile to the campground.

Facilities: 25 campsites; sites are small+ to medium-sized, with nominal to fairly good separation; parking pads are paved, medium to medium+, mostly double-wide straight-ins; a little additional leveling may be necessary; small to medium-sized areas for tents, but they may be slightly sloped; fire rings; b-y-o firewood; water at faucets; vault facilities; paved driveways; adequate supplies and services are available in Eureka.

Activities & Attractions: Fishing; boating; boat launch and dock; designated swimming beach; small campfire circle.

Natural Features: Located on hilly terrain above the north-west shore of Dickey Lake; campground vegetation consists mostly of moderately dense tall conifers; the lake is bordered by densely forested mountains; elevation 3100'.

Season, Fees & Phone: May to November; $7.00; 14 day limit; Rexford Ranger District, Eureka, (406) 296-2536.

Camp Notes: Some of the most beautiful country in Montana can be enjoyed while driving this segment of '93'. There's another campground on Dickey Lake that's a bit more remote and roughcut than North Dickey. South Dickey Campground, reached via a two-mile, narrow gravel road from near mp 160, has eight campsites, a hand pump and vaults near the south-west shore.

WHITEFISH LAKE
Whitefish Lake State Recreation Area

Location: Northwest Montana north of Kalispell.

Access: From U.S. Highway 93 at milepost 129 +.1 (by the golf course, 2 miles west of Whitefish, 49 miles southeast of Eureka), turn north onto a paved local access road (an angle right if coming from Whitefish, a sharp left if approaching from Eureka); follow the access road northerly past the golf course and across the railroad tracks for 1 mile; just across the railroad tracks, hang a left into the park.

Facilities: 44 campsites; sites are small to medium-sized, with minimal to good separation; parking pads are gravel, straight-ins or pull-offs, and vary in length from short to long; some pads may require a little additional leveling; a level, grassy area is available for tents; fire rings; b-y-o firewood; water at several faucets; restrooms, plus auxiliary vaults; paved driveways; adequate+ supplies and services in Whitefish.

Activities & Attractions: Sandy beach; boating; boat launch; fishing for the famous Superior whitefish.

Natural Features: Located along a small bay on the west shore of Whitefish Lake; picnic sites are on a lightly shaded, grassy lakeshore flat; campsites are on a slope and on a grassy flat, lightly to moderately shaded/sheltered by hardwoods and conifers; the lake is surrounded by densely forested mountains; the Whitefish Range, with peaks rising to almost 7000', is visible across the lake to the east; elevation 3000'.

Season, Fees & Phone: May to September; please see Appendix for standard Montana state park fees; phone c/o Montana Department of Fish Wildlife & Parks Office, Kalispell, (406) 752-5501; summer park phone (406) 862-3991.

Camp Notes: There's only one little hitch to camping here: the railroad. An occasional choo-choo rummmmmbles and honnnks past on the tracks a few yards above the park. Irrespective of that, this is still a great little spot on a beautiful little lake. It's close enough to town to provide convenience, but not so close that it seems urban.

BIG CREEK
Flathead National Forest

Location: Northwest Montana on the west edge of Glacier Park.

Access: From the junction of Going-to-the-Sun Road and Camas Road at Apgar Village, travel northwest on Camas Road (paved) for 12 miles to a major "T" junction; turn southwest (left) onto Forest Road 210/Montana Secondary 486 (gravel, with a paved section) and proceed 2.5 miles; turn easterly (left) for a few yards to a "T", then turn southerly (right) and go a final 0.4 mile to the campground. (Note: If you desire to bypass Glacier NP and travel directly to the campground from the Kalispell-Columbia Falls area, take Montana Secondary 486 for 19.5 miles, much of it paved, to the campground.)

Facilities: 22 campsites in 2 loops; (7 small group sites in a separate group loop are also available); sites are medium to large, level, with fair separation; parking pads are gravel, short+ to medium+ straight-ins; adequate space for tents; fire rings; some firewood is available for gathering in the area; water at a hand pump; vault facilities; gravel driveways; nearest gas and groceries are in West Glacier; adequate supplies and services are available in Columbia Falls.

Activities & Attractions: Fishing; floating.

Natural Features: Located on a flat in a forested canyon above the west bank of the North Fork of the Flathead River, just downstream of the river's confluence with Big Creek; campsites are moderately to densely sheltered by tall conifers; bordered by 6600' Huckleberry Mountain to the east, forested mountains to the west; elevation 3400'.

Season, Fees & Phone: $6.00; May to October; 14 day limit; Glacier View Ranger District, Columbia Falls, (406) 892-4372.

Camp Notes: To be openly candid about it: This isn't the most attractive place in Northwest Montana. Most of the unattractiveness emanates from the several square miles of mountainside scars still left after the disastrous Huckleberry Burn of 1967. Still, Big Creek presents a useable alternative to the camps in the park which are often more congested. About half of Big Creek's sites have river views, and some of them are nearly streamside.

Montana 14

FISH CREEK
Glacier National Park

Location: Northwest Montana in western Glacier National Park.

Access: From the junction of Going-to-the-Sun Road and Camas Road at Apgar Village, travel northwest on Camas Road for 2 miles; turn east (right) onto North Fork Road (paved) and continue for 1.2 miles to a "T"; turn southerly (right) into the campground.

Facilities: 179 campsites in 4 loops; sites are small+ to medium-sized, with fairly good separation; most parking pads are packed gravel, medium to long pull-throughs; most pads will require minor to major additional leveling; tent spots vary from level and large, to small and sloped; fireplaces; b-y-o firewood is recommended; water at several faucets; restrooms; paved driveways; gas and groceries in West Glacier.

Activities & Attractions: Hiking; boating; boat launch at Apgar; amphitheater for ranger-naturalist programs; visitor center in Apgar; North Fork Road leads north toward some backcountry gravel travel and hiking trails.

Natural Features: Located on hilly terrain above the south-west shore of Lake McDonald, where Fish Creek enters the lake; sites are moderately to densely sheltered by tall conifers above a dense undercover of bushes and young evergreens; bordered by densely forested mountains; elevation 3200'.

Season, Fees & Phone: June to September; $10.00 for a site, $5.00 for the park entrance fee; 7 day limit; Glacier National Park Headquarters, West Glacier, (406) 888-5441.

Camp Notes: Of all of the major Glacier campgrounds (with the possible exception of Many Glacier Campground), Fish Creek subjectively has the nicest forest environment. Overall, the privacy factor is probably best, as well. Fish Creek is a bit off the beaten path, so the atmosphere is somewhat more relaxed and quieter than some of the other park campgrounds. This is an excellent base camp from which to explore the less-visited, but rewardingly magnificent northwest corner of Glacier Park.

Montana 15

BOWMAN LAKE
Glacier National Park

Location: Northwest Montana in northwest Glacier Park.

Access: From the junction of Going-to-the-Sun Road and Camas Road at Apgar Village, travel northwest on Camas Road (paved) for 12 miles to a "T" junction; turn north (right) onto Forest Road 210/Montana Secondary 486 (gravel) and head north/northwest for another 14 miles to the settlement of Polebridge;

from Polebridge, follow the signed route northeasterly (past the Park Service Ranger Station) for a final 6 miles to the campground. (Note: Much of the route is narrow, winding, and often washboardy.)

Facilities: 48 primitive campsites in 2 loops; sites are small to small+, with fair separation; parking surfaces are gravel/earth, short to medium-length straight-ins or pull-offs; small to medioum-sized areas for tents; fireplaces; firewood is available for gathering in the area; water at central faucets; vault facilities; gravel driveways; gas and groceries are available in West Glacier.

Activities & Attractions: Boating; boat launch; fishing; hiking trail from here leads along the north shore of the lake into the high country; day use area.

Natural Features: Located near the southwest tip of Bowman Lake; campsites receive light to moderate shade/shelter from tall conifers; the 6-mile-long lake is bordered by high, forested ridges; elevation 4000'.

Season, Fees & Phone: May to September; $8.00 for a site, $5.00 for the park entrance fee; 7 day limit; Glacier Park Headquarters, West Glacier, (406) 888-5441.

Camp Notes: Backpackers and boaters find this to be a convenient base camp or jumping off point for trips to the upper end of the lake. It takes a lot of extra effort to reach Bowman Lake (and Kintla Lake, described below). But it's worth it to see this wild country at least once.

Montana 16

KINTLA LAKE
Glacier National Park

Location: Northwest Montana in northwest Glacier Park.

Access: From the junction of Going-to-the-Sun Road and Camas Road at Apgar Village, travel northwest on Camas Road (paved) for 12 miles to a "T" junction; turn north (right) onto Forest Road 210/Montana Secondary 486 (gravel) and head north/northwest for another 14 miles to the settlement of Polebridge; from Polebridge, follow the signed route northeasterly (past the Park Service Ranger Station and the turnoff to Bowman lake Campground) then northwesterly for a final 15 miles to the campground. (Note: Much of the road is narrow, winding and typically washboardy.)

Facilities: 12 primitive campsites; sites are small, somewhat sloped, with nominal separation; parking surfaces are gravel/ earth, short straight-ins or pull-offs; medium-sized tent areas; fireplaces; firewood is available for gathering in the area; water at a central faucet; vault facilities; gravel driveway; nearest gas and groceries are in West Glacier.

Activities & Attractions: Boating; small boat ramp; fishing; foot trail from here leads along the north shores of Kintla and Upper Kintla Lakes into the high country.

Natural Features: Located on sloping terrain just above the southwest shore of Kintla Lake; sites receive light-medium shade from conifers; the lake is closely flanked by high, forested ridges; elevation 4000'.

Season, Fees & Phone: May to September; $8.00 for a site, $5.00 for the park entrance fee; 7 day limit; Glacier Park Headquarters, West Glacier, (406) 888-5441.

Camp Notes: *Kintla* is an Indian word meaning "sack" or "bag". It refers to the Indians' belief (perhaps from actual experience as much as from pure legend) that anyone unlucky enough to take a tumble into the lake was quickly engulfed by its icy depths, as if a sack had been drawn tightly closed over them. Superstitions associated with the lake notwithstanding, the scenery and sense of remoteness here are superb.

Montana 17

APGAR
Glacier National Park

Location: Northwest Montana in western Glacier National Park.

Access: From Going-to-the-Sun Road at a point 1 mile northeast of Apgar Village, 8 miles southwest of Lake McDonald Lodge, and 28 miles west of Logan Pass, turn north-west onto the *east* end of the Apgar loop road and proceed 0.5 mile, then swing south (left) into the campground. (Note: You can also get to the campground by entering the Apgar loop road at the *west* end of the loop and picking your way eastward through the traffic in the village; the principal access is simpler and less congested for both east or west bound travelers.)

Facilities: 194 campsites in 4 loops; (hike-bike sites and a group loop are also available); sites are medium to medium+ in size, with nominal to fair separation; parking pads are hard-surfaced, medium-length pull-offs or long pull-throughs; a little additional leveling may be needed on some pads; large tent spots; fireplaces; b-y-o firewood is recommended; water at several faucets; restrooms; holding tank disposal station; paved driveways; ranger station; camper supplies in Apgar Village; gas and groceries in West Glacier; nearest complete supplies and services are in Kalispell, 35 miles southwest.

Activities & Attractions: Visitor center; boating; boat launch; fishing; amphitheater for ranger-naturalist programs; scenic drive along Going-to-the-Sun Road over Logan Pass.

Natural Features: Located on gently rolling terrain near the south-east shore of Lake McDonald; sites are all situated among tall conifers, some underbrush and grass; encircled by forested mountains and prominent peaks; elevation 3200'.

Season, Fees & Phone: Open all year, subject to weather conditions, with limited services October to May; $10.00 for a site, $5.00 for the park entrance fee; 7 day limit; Glacier National Park Headquarters, West Glacier, (406) 888-5441.

Camp Notes: The Lake McDonald country is some of the most beautiful around. The many interesting things to see and do in and around Apgar make this spot a good place to stay for a day or two. The Going-to-the-Sun Road drive over Logan Pass is one superscenic experience. (Because of the vehicle size restrictions in Logan Pass, Apgar might serve as a good place to park a trailer or a long motorhome and head out solo.)

SPRAGUE CREEK
Glacier National Park

Location: Northwest Montana in western Glacier National Park.

Access: From Going-to-the-Sun Road at a point 8 miles northeast of Apgar Village, 0.8 mile southwest of Lake McDonald Lodge, 22 miles southwest of Logan Pass, turn north-west into the campground.

Facilities: 25 campsites in 2 loops; no towed vehicles permitted; sites are rather small and closely spaced; parking pads are paved, fairly level, short straight-ins; most sites have spaces roomy enough for small to medium-sized tents; fire rings; b-y-o firewood is suggested; water at several faucets; restrooms; paved driveways; camper supplies at Lake McDonald Lodge; gas and groceries in West Glacier.

Activities & Attractions: Hiking; boating; fishing (fair) for trout on the lake; day use area; Going-to-the-Sun Road across 6600' Logan Pass is one of the most spectacular scenic drives in the country.

Natural Features: Located on the north-east shore of Lake McDonald where Sprague Creek flows into the lake, in the Rocky Mountains; sites are situated on or around gently rolling knolls; campground vegetation consists of medium-dense, tall conifers and hardwoods; elevation 3200'.

Season, Fees & Phone: June to September; $10.00 for a site, $5.00 for the park entrance fee; 7 day limit; Glacier National Park Headquarters, West Glacier, (406) 888-5441.

Camp Notes: Campers with tents and small vehicles get a nice break here. There are a number of campsites situated along the lake shore (and away from the roadway). Most of the sites have at least a glimpse of 9.5-mile-long, 472-feet-deep, beautiful Lake McDonald.

AVALANCHE CREEK
Glacier National Park

Location: Northwest Montana in western Glacier National Park.

Access: From Going-to-the-Sun Road at a point 5.5 miles northeast of Lake McDonald Lodge, 15 miles northeast of Apgar Village, 15 miles southwest of Logan Pass, turn southeast into the campground.

Facilities: 87 campsites in 2 loops; (a small hike-bike camp area and a group site are also available); sites are medium-sized, basically level, with fair to good separation; parking pads are packed gravel, long pull-throughs; medium to large tent areas; fireplaces; campfire wood is available for gathering in the surrounding area; water at faucets throughout; restrooms; holding tank disposal station; paved driveways; ranger station; camper supplies at Lake McDonald; gas and groceries in West Glacier.

Activities & Attractions: Self-guided "Trail of the Cedars"; hiking trail leads up to Avalanche Lake and Monument Falls; amphitheater for ranger-naturalist programs; picnic area with river access, across the roadway; superscenic drive to the east over Logan Pass.

Natural Features: Located near the confluence of Avalanche Creek with McDonald Creek; campsites are well-sheltered by medium to dense, very tall conifers and small hardwoods; surrounded by very dense forest; peaks rise sharply to almost 9000' just behind the campground; elevation 3300'.

Season, Fees & Phone: June to September; $10.00 for a site, $5.00 for the park entrance fee; 7 day limit; Glacier National Park Headquarters, West Glacier, (406) 888-5441.

Camp Notes: One of the most spectacular scenic drives in the country commences (or ends, obviously, depending on your direction of travel), just northeast of this campground. From there on east, Going-to-the-Sun Road follows a steep, winding, and narrow route with magnificent vistas through Logan Pass.

Montana 20

RISING SUN
Glacier National Park

Location: Northwest Montana in eastern Glacier National Park.

Access: From Going-to-the-Sun Road at a point 6 miles west of the St. Mary Entrance Station and 14 miles east of Logan Pass, turn north into the campground.

Facilities: 83 campsites in 2 loops; most sites are small and closely spaced; parking pads are gravel, short to medium-length straight-ins; some pads might need a little additional leveling; most sites can handle a medium-sized tent; fireplaces; b-y-o firewood is recommended; water at several faucets; restrooms; holding tank disposal station; paved driveways; camper supplies and showers at the adjacent general store; gas and groceries+ in St. Mary, 7 miles east.

Activities & Attractions: Major visitor center, 6 miles east; ranger-guided activities and evening programs; launch tours on St. Mary Lake (extra charge); spectacular scenery along Going-to-the-Sun Road.

Natural Features: Located on gently sloping terrain in a wide valley/basin just across the roadway from 9 mile-long St. Mary Lake; granite peaks tower thousands of feet above the valley floor; summer weather is marked by mild sunny days and cool nights, with an occasional afternoon cloudburst; elevation 4600'.

Season, Fees & Phone: June to September; $10.00 for a site, $5.00 for the park entrance fee; 7 day limit; Glacier National Park Headquarters, West Glacier, (406) 888-5441.

Camp Notes: Rising Sun is considered by many to be the premier camp spot along Going-to-the-Sun Road. A never-to-be-forgotten experience is the sight of the morning sun's glow on the glacier-carved cliffs.

Montana 21

ST. MARY
Glacier National Park

Location: Northwest Montana in eastern Glacier National Park.

Access: From Going-to-the-Sun Road at a point 0.4 mile west of the St. Mary Entrance Station and 20 miles east of Logan Pass, turn north into the campground.

Facilities: 152 campsites in 3 loops; sites are small to small+, with minimal to fair separation; most parking pads are gravel pull-throughs spacious enough to accommodate large rv's; many pads may require some additional leveling; lots of large, grassy tent spots; fireplaces; b-y-o firewood is recommended; water at several faucets; restrooms; holding tank disposal station; paved driveways; gas and groceries+ in St. Mary, 1 mile east.

Activities & Attractions: Major park visitor center nearby; ranger-guided hikes and activities; St. Mary Lake launch tours (extra charge); good base from which to explore the park.

Natural Features: Located in the Rocky Mountains on the bank of the St. Mary River, and near the northeast tip of 9-mile-long St. Mary Lake; campground vegetation ranges from grass and sage slopes toward the northwest to a few trees and bushes closer to the river; sheer granite peaks of the Rocky Mountains tower above the basin; elevation 4500'.

Season, Fees & Phone: Open all year, with limited services October to June; $10.00 for a site; $5.00 for the park entrance fee; 7 day limit; Glacier National Park HQ (406) 888-5441.

Camp Notes: Glacier National Park offers some of the most magnificent mountain scenery of the Northern Rockies--or anywhere, for that matter. Some of the best views of the St. Mary basin are available from campsites higher up on this campground's gentle slope.

MANY GLACIER
Glacier National Park

Location: Northwest Montana in northeast Glacier Park.

Access: From U.S. Highway 89 at milepost 39 +.9 at the south edge of the hamlet of Babb (8 miles north of St. Mary, 10 miles south of the U.S.-Canada border), head west on Many Glacier-Swiftcurrent Road for 7.5 miles to the Many Glacier Entrance Station; continue ahead for another 5 miles to a point 0.8 mile past the turnoff to the Many Glacier Hotel; turn south (left) into the campground.

Facilities: 109 campsites in a single complex loop; (a small group camp is also available); sites are medium-sized, level, with fair to good separation; parking pads are packed gravel, medium to long pull-throughs or pull-offs; ample space for tents; fireplaces or fire rings; a very limited amount of firewood is available for gathering, b-y-o is recommended; water at several faucets; restrooms; holding tank disposal station; paved driveways; ranger station; camper supplies near the hotel; gas and groceries in Babb.

Activities & Attractions: Hiking trails; limited boating; boat launch.

Natural Features: Located in a narrow valley on a flat along the north bank of Swiftcurrent River; campsites are moderately sheltered/shaded by medium-tall conifers and some hardwoods; Swiftcurrent Lake is a few hundred yards east; very imposing mountains loom above the valley north and south of the campground; elevation 4900'.

Season, Fees & Phone: June to September; $10.00 for a site, $5.00 for the park entrance fee; 7 day limit; Glacier National Park Headquarters, West Glacier, (406) 888-5441.

Camp Notes: Incredible views of the fortress-like peak that towers over the south edge of the campground. This is *most* impressive! Without a doubt, Many Glacier is one of the park's finest places to camp.

TWO MEDICINE
Glacier National Park

Location: Northwest Montana in southeast Glacier Park.

Access: From Montana State Highway 49 at a point 4 miles north of East Glacier and 8 miles south of the junction of Highway 49 & U.S. 89 west of Browning, turn west onto Two Medicine Road; travel 7.5 miles to the campground.

Facilities: 99 campsites in 3 loops; sites are small+ to medium-sized, with good separation; parking pads are packed gravel, medium+ to long pull-throughs; many pads will require additional leveling; ample spaces for tents, but many are sloped; fireplaces; b-y-o firewood is suggested; water at central faucets; restrooms in each loop; holding tank disposal station; paved driveways; camper supplies at the camp store; limited supplies and services are available in East Glacier.

Activities & Attractions: Hiking trails; limited boating (10 hp max.); boat launch; day use area; ranger-guided activities; scenic launch tours on Two Medicine Lake (extra charge).

Natural Features: Located along Two Medicine River just east of the shore of Two Medicine Lake in the Rocky Mountains; a trio of lakes--Lower Two Medicine, Two Medicine, and Upper Two Medicine--are nestled at the base of 9513' Rising Wolf Mountain; some sites are on a riverside flat, most are on slopes above the stream; campground vegetation varies from open grassy sections to medium-dense stands of conifers; most sites are moderately sheltered/shaded; elevation 5200'.

Season, Fees & Phone: Mid-June to early September; $10.00 for a site; $5.00 for the park entrance fee; 7 day limit; Glacier National Park Headquarters, West Glacier, (406) 888-5441.

Camp Notes: There are majestic peaks *all over the place* here! Unlike Logan Pass and the Going-to-the-Sun Road, Two Medicine is one of those places in the park that doesn't get a lot of hoopla and holler. But it's in a truly unforgettable setting. A small, primitive camp in this corner of the park that's also off the well-worn track is Cut Bank Campground. It's a dozen air miles north of Two Medicine, accessible from U.S. 89 milepost 17 +.3 (17 miles northwest of Browning), then west for 5 miles on a gravel road. Cut Bank has 18 small campsites, drinking water and vaults, along the North Fork of Cut Bank Creek in a narrow valley bordered by classic Northern Rockies peaks.

DEVIL CREEK
Flathead National Forest

Location: Northwest Montana south of Glacier National Park.

Access: From U.S. Highway 2 at milepost 190 (20 miles west of East Glacier, 36 miles east of West Glacier), turn south into the campground.

Facilities: 14 campsites for hard-sided vehicles only; sites are fairly good sized, with average to good separation; parking pads are paved, short or medium-length straight-ins; some pads are double-wide; virtually all pads will require additional leveling; no tents permitted; fire rings; firewood is available for gathering in the vicinity; water at central faucets; vault facilities; paved driveways; limited supplies and services are available in East Glacier.

Activities & Attractions: Fishing on Bear Creek; Devil Creek Trail for foot and equestrian travel.

Natural Features: Located in Bear Creek Canyon on a moderate slope at the confluence of Devil Creek and Bear Creek on the west slope of the Continental Divide; campground vegetation consists of medium-tall conifers mixed with some small aspens and light undercover; elevation 4600'.

Season, Fees & Phone: June to September; $6.00; 14 day limit; Hungry Horse Ranger District (406) 287-5243.

Camp Notes: Glacier National Park's southern boundary is just across the highway from here. Bear Creek Canyon (also called John Stevens Canyon) is quite narrow, but there are some relatively open views off to the north and west. This is grizzly country, thus the "no camping in tents, tent trailers or sleeping on the ground" directive. The scenic drive along U.S. 2 through Marias Pass, east of here, is super-duper.

SUMMIT
Lewis and Clark National Forest

Location: Northwest Montana south of Glacier National Park.

Access: From U.S. Highway 2 at milepost 197 + .9 (11 miles west of East Glacier, 45 miles east of West Glacier), turn south into the campground.

Facilities: 22 campsites in 2 loops; sites are medium-sized, with fair to good separation; parking pads are paved, short+ to medium+ straight-ins; some pads are double-wide; many pads may require a little additional leveling; several good tent spots; fire rings or fireplaces; firewood is available for gathering in the area; water at several faucets; vault facilities; paved driveways; limited supplies and services are available in East Glacier.

Activities & Attractions: Theodore Roosevelt Memorial monument just west of the campground entrance; Glacier Park's Autumn Creek Trailhead is north of the highway near the settlement of Summit; cross-country skiing.

Natural Features: Located on a gentle slope on the Continental Divide at Marias Pass Summit; heavy timber plus some hardwood undercover provides ample shelter for all sites; a small creek flows past a number of the campsites; the rugged peaks of the Rocky Mountains in Glacier National Park are prominent to the north; elevation 5200'.

Season, Fees & Phone: June to September; $6.00; 14 day limit; Rocky Mountain Ranger Dist., Choteau, (406) 466-5341.

Camp Notes: The granite Roosevelt Monument that stands along the south side of the highway just west of the campground was constructed in 1931 to honor the conservationist President's leadership in matters of forest and stream. Originally, the 60-foot obelisk was raised between the east and west bound lanes of the Roosevelt International Highway, but it was relocated a few yards southward to its present site some years later.

LAMBETH
Lambeth State Recreation Area

Location: Northwest Montana northwest of Polson.

Access: From U.S. Highway 93 at milepost 82 +.8 (abeam of midtown Dayton, 20 miles north of Polson, 30 miles south of Kalispell), turn west onto Montana Secondary Highway 352/Lake Mary Ronan Road; travel northwest for 6 paved miles to the end of the pavement; at a fork in the road, take the right fork and continue on a gravel road for 1 more mile, then swing left into the park and the campground just beyond the entrance.

Facilities: 31 campsites; sites are small+ to medium-sized, with fair to good separation; parking pads are gravel, fairly level, most are short to medium-length straight-ins, plus a number of long pull-throughs; some nice tent spots; fire rings; some firewood is available for gathering in the vicinity; water at several faucets; vault facilities; gravel driveway; groceries in Elmo, 5 miles southwest of Dayton; adequate supplies and services are available in Polson.

Activities & Attractions: Boating; boat launch; fishing for trout, kokanee salmon and bass; swimming area; (good swimming, especially for ducks--don't they like to hang out in reeds along the shore?).

Natural Features: Located in the Salish Mountains on the east shore of Lake Mary Ronan; sites are situated on a forested bluff slightly above the lake; vegetation consists of moderately dense, tall conifers, some hardwoods, and considerable undercover; timbered hills and mountains encircle the 3-square-mile lake; elevation 3700'.

Season, Fees & Phone: May to September; please see Appendix for standard Montana state park fees; phone c/o Montana Department of Fish Wildlife & Parks Office, Kalispell, (406) 752-5501; summer park phone (406) 849-5082.

Camp Notes: One great advantage of this campground is the quiet, secluded atmosphere that comes from being seven miles from the main highway. The forested slopes around the lake are lush and green, and some sites in the campground have views of the lake. Fishing can be very good here, and the lake's 'fishing fleet' can number several dozen boats.

Montana 27

WEST SHORE
Flathead Lake State Park

Location: Northwest Montana south of Kalispell.

Access: From U.S. Highway 93 at milepost 92 +.8 (19 miles south of Kalispell, 35 miles north of Polson), turn east onto a paved, somewhat steep, narrow, access road leading 0.2 mile down to the park entrance; one camp loop is just to the right of the entrance; or continue ahead for another 0.2 mile to 0.5 mile to the remaining camp loops. (Watch for "no trailers" signs in certain areas.)

Facilities: 30 campsites in 3 principal areas, plus a few hilltop walk-in sites; sites are small to medium-sized, with nominal to fair separation; parking pads are gravel, mostly short to medium-length straight-ins; many pads will require additional leveling; some fairly good tent spots; fire rings; some firewood is available for gathering in the vicinity, b-y-o is recommended; water at several faucets; vault facilities; paved or gravel driveways; gas and groceries+ are available in Lakeside, 5 miles north.

Activities & Attractions: Boating; sailing; small boat launch; excellent fishing for lake trout and perch; pebble-gravel beach near the day use area; interpretive exhibits at the overlook.

Natural Features: Located on and above the west shore of Flathead Lake; campsites are in a light-medium to medium-dense mixture of conifers, hardwoods, and underbrush; small (privately owned) Goose Island; the Salish Mountains rise to the west, the Mission Mountains to the east; elevation 2900'.

Season, Fees & Phone: Open all year, with limited services October to May; $8.00; park office, Kalispell, (406) 752-5501; summer phone for this unit (406) 884-3901.

Camp Notes: This area is located on the shore of one of the West's most beautiful lakes. Flathead Lake was named for the Indians who occupied this valley. Its 188 square miles make it the largest freshwater lake west of the Mississippi River. Most of the lakeshore property is either privately owned or is held by the Flathead tribe. If you're a camper looking for a trailer site, consider swinging into the first camp loop on the right just inside the park. Driveways throughout most of this compact park unit are narrow and steep, and some have tight turns. Most of the campsites are back in the woods away from the shore, but have lake views through the trees.

Montana 28

ELMO
Flathead Lake State Park

Location: Northwest Montana north of Polson.

Access: From U.S. Highway 93 at milepost 78 +.1 (1 mile north of the community of Elmo, 4 miles south of Dayton, 18 miles north of Polson), turn south into the campground.

Facilities: 50 campsites; sites are medium-sized, with nominal separation; parking pads are gravel, mostly long pull-offs or pull-throughs; some pads may require a little additional leveling; (most of the parking pads are cut parallel to the steepish slope, so leveling isn't a big problem); some sites are designated for tents only, with plenty of grassy space for tents; fire rings; b-y-o firewood; water at central faucets; restrooms with coin-op showers; holding tank disposal station; paved/gravel driveway; groceries in Elmo; adequate supplies and services are available in Polson.

Activities & Attractions: Boating; sailing; small boat launch and dock; fishing; pebble beach.

Natural Features: Located on an open, southward-facing, grassy slope just above Big Arm, a large bay on the west shore of Flathead Lake; most campsites are situated along the open slope, a few tent campsites are lakeside; a few trees along the shoreline provide shelter for some sites; forested peaks are visible across the lake; Wild Horse Island is a few miles offshore; elev. 2900'.

Season, Fees & Phone: Open all year; principal season is April to October; please see Appendix for standard Montana state park fees; park office, Kalispell, (406) 752-5501; summer phone for this unit (406) 849-5744.

Camp Notes: Elmo is a great place, especially for anyone who really likes a lot of sun and a fairly reliable breeze. Reportedly, many campers briefly stop here, say "I want trees", and then go on to the park's other units at Big Arm or West Shore. But the views are actually a little better from this open slope than at the more forested park units.

Montana 29

BIG ARM
Flathead Lake State Park

Location: Northwest Montana north of Polson.

Access: From U.S. Highway 93 at milepost 74 +.5 (3 miles southeast of Elmo, 14 miles north of Polson), turn east onto a paved access road and proceed 0.3 mile to the campground. (Note: For southbound travelers, the park turnoff is a hard, 180° left turn, possibly across heavy oncoming traffic.)

Facilities: 62 campsites; sites are very small to small+, with nominal to fair separation; parking surfaces are gravel, mostly short to medium-length straight-ins or pull-offs; many pads may require a little additional leveling; mostly small to medium-sized tent spots; assorted fire appliances; b-y-o firewood; water at several faucets; central restrooms, plus auxiliary vaults; narrow, paved or gravel/dirt driveways; groceries in Elmo; adequate supplies and services are available in Polson.

Activities & Attractions: Boating; sailing; boat launch and dock; fishing; gravelly/rocky beach.

Natural Features: Located on the southwest shore of Big Arm, a major bay on the west shore of Flathead Lake; campsites are among hardwoods and tall conifers that provide fairly good shade/shelter; a few other sites are on a grassy, juniper-dotted slope a few yards from the lake; most campsites are right along the lake shore; Wild Horse Island State Park lies 4 miles northeast offshore of this park unit; the forested peaks of the Mission Range are visible across the lake; elevation 2900'.

Season, Fees & Phone: May to September; please see Appendix for standard Montana state park fees; park office, Kalispell, (406) 752-5501; summer phone for this unit (406) 849-5255.

Camp Notes: Many of the campsites at Big Arm, although very small, are at the water's edge. (Bring a greased shoehorn if you have a large tent or vehicle.) As seen from the edgewater camps, impressive Wild Horse Island seems closer than its four-mile distance. A trip on U.S. 93 can be one of Montana's most scenic and most pressure-packed experiences. The vehicles of many locals have been seen sporting bumper stickers reading:

> I Drive Highway 93
> Pray For Me

Montana 30

WAYFARERS
Flathead Lake State Park

Location: Western Montana southeast of Kalispell.

Access: From Montana State Highway 35 at milepost 30 + .9 in Bigfork (0.2 mile north of the junction of State Highway 35 & Montana Secondary Highway 209, 2.7 miles south of the junction of State Highways 35 & 83, 17 miles southeast of Kalispell), turn west onto a paved access road and proceed west then south (past private homes and a private resort) for 0.4 mile to the park entrance; the campground is toward the south end of the park.

Facilities: 30 campsites, including a half-dozen designated tent camping sites; sites are small to average in size, with fair to good separation; parking pads are gravel, short to medium-length straight-ins, or long pull-throughs; additional leveling will probably be required in most sites; areas for tents are medium to large in the standard sites, spacious in the tents-only sites, though most are a little sloped; barbecue grills or fireplaces; b-y-o firewood is recommended; water at several faucets; restrooms; holding tank disposal station; paved driveway (steep and narrow in some sections); adequate supplies and services are available in Bigfork.

Activities & Attractions: Boating; boat launch; pier; fishing for lake trout and perch; large, level, grassy recreation field; large day use area.

Natural Features: Located on the northeast shore of Flathead Lake; the lake is in the wide Flathead Valley between the Mission Range to the east and the Salish Mountains to the west; most campsites are on a forested hill with tall conifers, a few hardwoods and moderate underbrush; tent sites are on a rolling, grassy flat rimmed by trees; Swan River inlet is just north of the park; elevation 2900'.

Season, Fees & Phone: Open all year, with limited services October to April; please see Appendix for standard Montana state park fees; park office, Kalispell, (406) 752-5501; summer phone for this unit (406) 837-4196.

Camp Notes: Wayfarers is in a lush, green, lakeside environment. The forest provides some neat little glades and cubby holes for campers who like a little extra measure of seclusion. The campground is conveniently close to the shops and other attractions in Bigfork. (Bigfork has often been described in promotional literature as "quaint", but it's a nice place to visit anyway.)

Montana 31

FINLEY POINT
Flathead Lake State Park

Location: Northwest Montana northeast of Polson.

Access: From Montana State Highway 35 at milepost 6 + .1 (6 miles northeast of Polson, 25 miles south of Bigfork), turn west onto Finley Point Road (paved, across Highway 35 from the Finley Point Volunteer Fire Department station); travel 1 mile west and north; turn west (left) onto South Finley Point Road (paved) and continue for 3 more miles westerly; turn left into the park entrance and proceed 0.3 mile down to the campground.

Facilities: 16 campsites, some with electrical hookups, for camper-boaters using the slips; sites are very small, level, with zero separation; parking slots are paved, medium-length straight-ins; enough space for a small tent behind each slot; fire rings; b-y-o firewood; water at central faucets; water closets; paved driveway; camper supplies on Highway 35; adequate services and supplies are available in Polson.

Activities & Attractions: Boating; boat launch; 16 slips for boats up to 25' are rented with each campsite; fishing for lake trout and perch; designated swimming area.

Natural Features: Located on the southeast corner of Flathead Lake near the 'Narrows' just north of Polson Bay; the park is in an open forest of tall conifers; high, forested mountains encircle the lake; elevation 2900'.

Season, Fees & Phone: May to September; $13.00 for a standard site, $15.00 for a hookup site, (includes slip rental); 7-day limit; reservations accepted; please see Appendix for additional reservation information; park office, Kalispell, (406) 752-5501; summer phone for this unit (406) 887-2715.

Camp Notes: Finley Point has a highly unusual arrangement for a state park campground. The camp slots here are comparable in size to the so-called "enroute" campsites in California state parks, which are designed for quick one-nighters by self-contained rv's before moving on to their next port of call. In this case, though, there's 'package deal' for boater-campers and a longer stay limit than in the California camps. Perhaps elbow room is a moot problem for the typical user. Chances are that most of your time would be spent afloat on Flathead Lake, coming ashore just to catch some shut-eye, or grab a hot meal, or re-stock the cooler.

SWAN LAKE
Flathead National Forest

Location: Northwest Montana southeast of Kalispell.

Access: From Montana State Highway 83 at milepost 71 +.9 (0.5 mile north of the community of Swan Lake, 16 miles southeast of Bigfork), turn east onto a paved access road for 0.1 mile into the campground.

Facilities: 44 campsites, including some double-occupancy sites, in 3 loops; sites are medium-sized, basically level, and fairly well separated; parking pads are paved, short to medium-length straight-ins; many nice, large, grassy tent spots; fireplaces; b-y-o firewood is recommended; water at several faucets; restrooms, plus vault facilities; paved driveways; gas and groceries in Swan Lake; adequate supplies and services are available in Bigfork.

Activities & Attractions: The campground is just a few hundred yards across the highway from an extensive day use area with landscaped lawns, paved trails, boat ramp, and beach with designated swimming area; a covered "view deck" provides a sheltered place from which to watch an occasional summer storm sweep across the valley and lake; boating; fishing, said to be especially good for kokanee salmon and northern pike at this end of the lake, also for bull trout.

Natural Features: Located on a forested flat near the southeast corner of Swan Lake; the Mission Mountains are visible across the lake to the west, and peaks of the Swan Range of the Rockies rise to the east; campground vegetation consists of a light to moderately dense mixture of tall conifers and hardwoods on a grassy forest floor; elevation 3100'.

Season, Fees & Phone: May to October; $8.00; 14 day limit; Swan Lake Ranger District (406) 837-5081.

Camp Notes: The Swan and Clearwater Valleys form a 90-mile-long verdant trough harboring a number of small, scenic lakes. Swan Lake certainly competes for the "most beautiful" title. It's very popular with water sports enthusiasts, but an equally noteworthy feature is the national forest "park" just across the highway. The dandy day use facility is one of the more inviting public picnic and play areas in this part of the state. As you peruse this campground's description and read down through the other seven write-ups which follow, you'll note that each area is, without exception, along or very near to a lake and/or major stream. "Is this good camping, or what!"

HOLLAND LAKE
Flathead National Forest

Location: Northwest Montana northeast of Missoula.

Access: From Montana State Highway 83 at milepost 35 +.5 (6 miles south of the community of Condon, 20 miles north of Seeley Lake), turn east onto Holland Lake Road; proceed east and northeast (first on pavement, then on gravel) for 2.8 miles to the Larch Loop, or another 0.9 mile to the Bay Loop.

Facilities: 41 campsites, including many available for multiple occupancy, in 2 loops; (in effect, as many as 60 or 70 camping units could use the loops); (overflow camping and a group camp are also available); most sites are small to medium-sized, with nominal separation; parking pads are gravel, mostly short to medium-length straight-ins, plus a few pull-throughs; tent sites are basically smallish; (sites and pads in the Larch Loop tend to be larger than those in the Bay Loop); fire rings; firewood is available for gathering in the area; water at several faucets; vault facilities; holding tank disposal station; narrow, one way, gravel driveways; gas and groceries+ in the Condon-Swan Valley area.

Activities & Attractions: Boating; boat launch; fishing; day use area; large designated swimming area; convenient hiker access to the Bob Marshall Wilderness.

Natural Features: Located in the western foothills of the Swan Range of the Rockies on the northwest shore of Holland Lake; Larch Loop sites are on a knoll/bluff overlooking the lake; Bay Loop sites are on a small shelf right above the lake shore; campground vegetation consists of towering conifers, some hardwoods, and a moderate amount of underbrush; elevation 4200'.

Season, Fees & Phone: May to October; $8.00; 14 day limit; Swan Lake Ranger District (406) 837-5081.

Camp Notes: Holland Lake's scenery, including the lake itself, the surrounding forested hills, a picturesque waterfall, and the spectacular peaks of the Continental Divide makes the short side trip off the

cop.1

main highway worth the effort, even if just for a look. Unlike all other lakeside campgrounds in the Swan-Clearwater corridor, the views here are eastward instead of westerly. And what exceptional views they are! If you don't absolutely insist on a lakeshore site, grab one of the nice spots in the Larch Loop on the way in.

Montana 34

LAKE ALVA
Lolo National Forest

Location: Western Montana northeast of Missoula.

Access: From Montana State Highway 83 at milepost 26 +.1 (11 miles north of the community of Seeley Lake, 18 miles south of Condon), turn west onto a steep paved access road and proceed 0.3 mile to a "T"; turn right into the campground.

Facilities: 41 campsites in 2 loops; (a group camp is also available, by reservation); sites are medium to large, with good to excellent separation; parking pads are hard-surfaced, medium to medium+ straight-ins; many pads will require some additional leveling; about half the sites have spots level and roomy enough for large tents, remaining sites can handle small tents; fireplaces; some firewood is available for gathering in the vicinity; water at hand pumps; vault facilities; paved driveways; limited+ supplies and services are available in Seeley Lake.

Activities & Attractions: Boating; boat ramp; fishing; day use area; pebble beach with designated swim area; a number of forest roads lead from here into the nearby mountains.

Natural Features: Located on a forested hillside above the northeast shore of Lake Alva, one of a chain of lakes along the Clearwater River; the lake lies between two crests of the Rockies, the Mission Mountains to the west and the peaks of the Continental Divide in the Bob Marshall Wilderness to the east; tall conifers and underbrush shelter most campsites; elevation 4200'.

Season, Fees & Phone: May to October; $8.00; 14 day limit; Seeley Lake Ranger District (406) 677-2233.

Camp Notes: Quite a few of Lake Alva's campsites are configured as long slots notched out of the surrounding dense forest, so they offer a good measure of privacy and seclusion. For more elbow room, you could always meander down to the nice picnic area along the lake shore.

Montana 35

BIG LARCH
Lolo National Forest

Location: Western Montana northeast of Missoula.

Access: From Montana State Highway 83 at milepost 15 +.7 (a mile north of midtown Seeley Lake, 28 miles south of Condon), turn west onto a paved access road; proceed 0.4 mile west and south to a fork, then take the left fork into the campground.

Facilities: 50 campsites in 3 loops; sites are medium to large, level, with good separation; parking pads are hard-surfaced, primarily medium-length straight-ins; some nice, fairly large tent areas are situated in among the trees; fire rings or fireplaces; firewood is available for gathering in the area; water at several faucets; vault facilities; paved driveways; limited+ supplies and services are available in Seeley Lake.

Activities & Attractions: Boating; boat launch; fishing; day use area; designated swimming beach; self-guided nature trail; interpretive programs on summer weekends.

Natural Features: Located near the east shore of Seeley Lake in the Rocky Mountains; campground vegetation consists of tall conifers and a considerable quantity of underbrush on a thick forest carpet of evergreen needles and leaves; the valley is bordered by the Swan Range to the east and the Mission Range to the west; elevation 4000'.

Season, Fees & Phone: May to October; $8.00; 14 day limit; Seeley Lake Ranger District (406) 677-2233.

Camp Notes: Big Larch is convenient to the highway, the setting is inviting, the sites are good-sized, and the surrounding scenery is some of the most beautiful in Montana. The drive along gently winding Highway 83 through the Swan and Clearwater Valleys intermittently affords glimpses of unforgettable scenery--of many splendid lakes fringed by green slopes--against a backdrop of the Mission Range, one of the most scenic series of peaks in Montana.

RIVER POINT
Lolo National Forest

Location: Western Montana northeast of Missoula.

Access: From Montana State Highway 83 at milepost 14 (south of midtown Seeley Lake, 14 miles north of the junction of State Highways 83 & 200), turn west onto Boy Scout Camp Road (paved, signed for "West Side Seeley Lake Recreation Sites"); proceed west-northwest for 2.1 miles, then turn north (right) into the campground.

Facilities: 27 campsites; sites are small+ or better in size, generally level, and most are well separated; parking pads are hard-surfaced, medium-length straight-ins; small to medium+ tent spots; fireplaces; plenty of firewood is available for gathering in the surrounding area; water at several faucets; vault facilities; gravel driveways; limited+ supplies and services are available in Seeley Lake.

Activities & Attractions: Fishing; boating; boat ramp at nearby Seeley Lake Campground; foot trail to the beach; Clearwater River Canoe Trail; day use area; Seeley Lake Game Preserve, adjacent.

Natural Features: Located in a valley near the southwest shore of Seeley Lake, surrounded by the forested slopes of the Rocky Mountains; the Clearwater River exits Seeley Lake at this point; campground vegetation consists of towering timber dripping with moss, and brush which separate the sites nicely; elev. 4000'.

Season, Fees & Phone: June to September; $8.00; 14 day limit; Seeley Lake Ranger District (406) 677-2233.

Camp Notes: As it departs Seeley Lake, the Clearwater is a wide, deep stream worthy of its name. If you have a shallow-draft vessel, you may be able to explore the waters for quite a distance downstream. You may also be able to tie up your craft a few yards from one of several campsites near the riverbank.

SEELEY LAKE
Lolo National Forest

Location: Western Montana northeast of Missoula.

Access: From Montana State Highway 83 at milepost 14 (on the south side of the town of Seeley Lake, 14 miles north of the junction of State Highways 83 & 200), turn west onto Boy Scout Camp Road (paved, signed for "West Side Seeley Lake Recreation Sites"); proceed west-northwest for 3.3 miles (past River Point Cg.); turn northeast (right) into the campground.

Facilities: 29 campsites in 2 loops; sites are medium to large, level, with good separation; parking pads are hard-surfaced, and most pads are of the straight-in variety spacious enough to accommodate larger rv's; many nice large, level, grassy spots for tents; fire rings; firewood is available for gathering in the area; water is available at several faucets; restrooms; paved driveways; limited+ supplies are available in Seeley Lake.

Activities & Attractions: Boating; boat ramp; fishing; a short foot trail leads from the campground down to a sandy beach with a designated swim zone; day use area.

Natural Features: Located near the middle-west shore of Seeley Lake in a Rocky Mountain valley; vegetation consists of moderately dense tall conifers, moderate underbrush and grass; elevation 4000'.

Season, Fees & Phone: June to September; $8.00; 14 day limit; Seeley Lake Ranger District (406) 677-2233.

Camp Notes: To a good number of campers familiar with the Seeley Lake resort area, this campground has an edge over its neighbor, River Point. It does have a couple of advantages, including a number of sites with lake views through the trees. It's very popular on summer weekends, so you'll probably want to plan to arrive early. Whichever camp you choose, there's a good chance your neighborhood will be visited by one or several of the many deer which reside in the surrounding dense forest.

PLACID LAKE
Placid Lake State Recreation Area

Location: Western Montana east of Missoula.

Access: From Montana State Highway 83 at milepost 10 +.1 (10 miles north of the junction of State Highways 200 & 83, 5 miles south of the community of Seeley Lake), turn west onto North Placid Lake Road (gravel); travel west for 3.1 miles (the access road takes a left/right jog at 2.8 miles from the highway), then turn south (left) into the campground. (Note: The highway turnoff point is a bit difficult to see on the approach until you're almost on top of it.)

Facilities: 42 campsites; sites are small+, with nominal to fairly good separation; parking pads are gravel, medium-length straight-ins, plus some long pull-throughs; some pads will require additional leveling; many good tent spots; fire rings; b-y-o firewood is recommended; water at central faucets; restrooms, plus auxiliary vault facilities; gravel driveways; limited supplies and services are available in Seeley Lake.

Activities & Attractions: Boating; boat launch and dock; designated swimming area; fishing.

Natural Features: Located on a forested flat along the north shore of Placid Lake in the Clearwater River Valley; vegetation consists of tall conifers, some hardwoods, moderate underbrush and grass; the lake is nestled at the foot of high, heavily timbered mountains; elevation 4100'.

Season, Fees & Phone: May to November; 14 day limit; please see Appendix for standard Montana state park fees; phone c/o Montana Dept. of Fish Wildlife & Parks Office, Missoula, (406) 542-5500.

Camp Notes: The 90-mile Clearwater River-Swan River corridor along Highway 83 is one of the most popular recreation areas in Montana. Because Placid Lake is a bit removed from the mainstream of traffic, a site here is slightly more likely to be available than in some of the other camping areas in the valleys. The setting at Placid Lake is certainly just as beautiful as any of the others, though!

Montana 39

SALMON LAKE
Salmon Lake State Recreation Area

Location: Western Montana northeast of Missoula.

Access: From Montana State Highway 83 at milepost 7 (7 miles north of the junction of State Highways 200 & 83, 8 miles south of the community of Seeley Lake), turn west onto a gravel park access road to a fork; bear left into the campground.

Facilities: 21 campsites; sites are small+, with nominal to fair separation; parking pads are gravel, acceptably level, medium-length straight-ins, plus some long pull-throughs; medium to large tent areas; fire rings; b-y-o firewood is recommended; water at several faucets; restrooms; gravel driveways; limited supplies and services are available in Seeley Lake.

Activities & Attractions: Boating; boat launch and dock; fishing; designated swimming area; trail along the lakeshore.

Natural Features: Located along the east shore of Salmon Lake; the campground is a few yards inland, on a gently rolling flat, with a moderately dense cover of conifers, underbrush and grass; the lake lies in the Clearwater River Valley, flanked by densely forested mountains to the east and west; elevation 3800'.

Season, Fees & Phone: May to November; 14 day limit; please see Appendix for standard Montana state park fees; phone c/o Montana Dept. of Fish Wildlife & Parks Office, Missoula, (406) 542-5500.

Camp Notes: Four-mile long, quarter-mile wide Salmon Lake comes complete with several, small, tree-covered islands (some of which are inhabited) that award added interest to an already scenic location. For a pleasant diversion from camp chores, you might take a stroll out to the nice picnic sites at the end of a small point of land in the park's main day use area nearby.

Montana 40

RUSSELL M. GATES
Russell M. Gates State Recreation Area

Location: Western Montana east of Missoula.

Access: From Montana State Highway 200 at milepost 35 +.5 (0.1 mile west of the Missoula-Powell county line, 37 miles west of Lincoln, 3.5 miles east of the junction of State Highways 200 & 83 at Clearwater Junction) turn south into the campground.

Facilities: 12 campsites; sites are small, level, with fair separation; parking pads are gravel, mostly medium-length straight-ins; small to medium-sized tent spots; fire rings; some firewood is available for gathering in the area; no drinking water; vault facilities; gravel driveway; limited+ supplies and services are available in Lincoln.

Activities & Attractions: Fishing; rafting/floating.

Natural Features: Located on a flat along the north bank of the Blackfoot River; sites are moderately shaded/sheltered by tall conifers; bordered by forested hills and mountains; elev. 3800'.

Season, Fees & Phone: May to October; 14 day limit; please see Appendix for standard Montana state park fees; phone c/o Montana Department of Fish Wildlife & Parks Office, Missoula, (406) 542-5500.

Camp Notes: Beautiful river views. The Blackfoot is one of the most pleasantly scenic streams in the Northern Rocky Mountains. This dandy little wayside camp is adjacent to the Blackfoot River recreation corridor, which includes a number of fishing and boating access points. (The Blackfoot was the setting for the classic book and subsequent film, *A River Runs Through It*, which was centered around trout fishing and family life in early twentieth century Montana.)

Montana 41

CASCADE
Lolo National Forest

Location: Northwest Montana northwest of Missoula.

Access: From Montana State Highway 135 at milepost 16 +.2 (6 miles southwest of the junction of State Highways 135 and 200, 16 miles east of the junction of Interstate 90 Exit 33 and State Highway 135 at St. Regis), turn south (i.e., right if arriving from the Interstate) into the campground. (Note: The campground driveway is one-way; if you're headed south-west on Highway 135, it will be necessary to drive past the campground, then swing sharply left across the highway into the entrance.)

Facilities: 11 campsites; sites are small+, with good to excellent separation; parking pads are paved, short to medium-length straight-ins, some are extra wide; a little additional leveling may be necessary; most sites have small tent spaces, a few have large tent spots; fire rings; firewood is available for gathering in the area; water at a central hand pump; vault facilities; narrow, one-way, paved driveway; limited supplies and services are available in St. Regis, 16 miles south and Plains, 16 miles northwest.

Activities & Attractions: Hiking; Cascade Falls Nature Trail (about a mile); fishing; a small sandy beach across the highway provides access to the river.

Natural Features: Located in a timbered canyon (or narrow valley) along Clark Fork of the Columbia River; campground vegetation consists of moderately dense, tall conifers, hardwoods, and dense undergrowth; Cascade Creek flows down past the campground to the river; a forested hillside rises behind the campground and a rocky, tree-dotted canyon wall lies across the river; bordered by hills and mountains; elevation 2600'.

Season, Fees & Phone: May to September; $7.00; 14 day limit; Plains Ranger District (406) 826-3821.

Camp Notes: The all-too-brief trip on Highway 135 along Clark Fork is one of the prettiest short drives in Western Montana. When the river level is right, you'll see rafters having a lot of fun on this stretch of the wide stream. The preferred sites at Cascade Campground obviously are those away from the highway, but nighttime traffic on Highway 135 is fairly light, and the dense vegetation provides an effective sound barrier.

Montana 42

CABIN CITY
Lolo National Forest

Location: Far Western Montana northwest of Missoula.

Access: From Interstate 90 Exit 22 (3 miles east of DeBorgia, 12 miles west of St. Regis), from the north side of the freeway turn northeast onto Old Highway 10 (toward Camels Hump) and proceed 1.7 miles; turn north (left) onto Twelve Mile Road (gravel); continue for 0.2 mile, then turn west (left) onto the campground access road for 0.5 mile into the campground.

Facilities: 12 campsites; sites are fairly spacious, with good to very good separation; parking pads are gravel, mostly level, medium to medium+ straight-ins; lots of room for big tents; fireplaces or fire rings; plenty of firewood is available for gathering; water at several faucets; vault facilities; gravel driveway; limited supplies and services are available in St. Regis.

Activities & Attractions: Stream fishing; Camels Hump and Buzzards Gulch lie to the east and are accessible by rough trails.

Natural Features: Located in a fairly densely forested area on the west slope of the Bitterroot Range; campground vegetation consists of very tall conifers and some second growth timber; Twelve Mile Creek is a couple-hundred yards from the campground; elevation 3200'.

Season, Fees & Phone: May to October; $6.00; 14 day limit; Superior Ranger District (406) 822-4233.

Camp Notes: Forest tranquility and convenient seclusion are found here at a little-used campground not far from the Interstate. The fairly spacious, though simple, sites at Cabin City should help insure enough convenient solitude for virtually any camper.

Montana 43

SLOWAY
Lolo National Forest

Location: Northwest Montana west of Missoula.

Access: From Interstate 90 (eastbound) take Exit 37 (4 miles east of St. Regis, 10 miles west of Superior), drive east on the south frontage road (Old Highway 10) for 2.6 miles; turn south (right) into the campground. **Alternate Access:** From I-90 (westbound) take Exit 43 then proceed 3.2 miles west on the south frontage road to the campground.

Facilities: 21 campsites; most sites are fairly good sized and well separated; parking pads are gravel, medium to long straight-ins or pull-throughs; some pads may require additional leveling; large, open, grassy areas for tents; fireplaces, plus some barbecue grills; limited firewood may be available for gathering in the surrounding area; water at several faucets; vault facilities; gravel driveways; limited supplies and services are available in St. Regis.

Activities & Attractions: Fishing on Clark Fork; Lookout Pass Recreation Area, 40 miles to the west, offers fabulous vistas of the mountains.

Natural Features: Located in the Bitterroot Range in an open forest on the north bank of Clark Fork of the Columbia River; some sites are in open grassy areas and others are in brushy, forested areas; terrain is slightly irregular, with some sites in little hollows and others on little knolls; elevation 2700'.

Season, Fees & Phone: May to September; $7.00; 14 day limit; Superior Ranger District (406) 822-4233.

Camp Notes: There are some really top-notch campsites here, including several that overlook Clark Fork. Timbered ridges are visible in all directions. In contrast to Quartz Flat Campground (below), very little freeway noise reaches the campground.

Montana 44

QUARTZ FLAT
Lolo National Forest

Location: Northwest Montana west of Missoula.

Access: From Interstate 90 (either eastbound or westbound) near milepost 60 (10 miles east of Superior, 35 miles west of Missoula), take the exit for "Rest Area/Quartz Flat Campground"; drive past the rest area parking lot; one loop is on each side of I-90; the loops are linked by a single-lane underpass.

Facilities: 52 campsites in 2 distinct loops, with 24 sites on the north side of I-90 and 28 sites on the south side; sites are medium-sized with fair to good separation; parking pads are paved and level; some pads are spacious enough for very large rv's; most tent spots are level and will accommodate large tents; fireplaces and barbecue grills; some firewood is available for gathering in the area; water at central faucets; restrooms, plus auxiliary vault facilities; holding tank disposal stations; paved driveways; gas and groceries in Lozeau, 5 miles west; limited+ supplies and services are available in Superior.

Activities & Attractions: Fishing on Clark Fork; hiking trail leads to the river; superscenic drive toward Lookout Pass, 60 miles west at the Montana-Idaho border.

Natural Features: Located in the Clark Fork Valley in the densely forested Bitterroot Range of the Rocky Mountains; vegetation consists of very tall conifers, very little underbrush and an evergreen needle carpet; the Clark Fork flows westward past the north loop of the campground and ultimately to the Columbia River; elevation 2800'.

Season, Fees & Phone: May to September; $8.00; 14 day limit; Superior Ranger District (406) 822-4233.

Camp Notes: Even though the campground boundary skirts the Interstate right-of-way, the atmosphere at Quartz Flat is remarkably "woodsy". For being so conveniently close to a major trans-continental route, it merits consideration.

Montana 45

BEAVERTAIL HILL
Beavertail Hill State Recreation Area

Location: Western Montana southeast of Missoula.

Access: From Interstate 90 Exit 130 for Beavertail Road (25 miles east of Missoula, 54 miles west of Deer Lodge), proceed south on a gravel road for 0.3 mile; turn east onto a park access road and drive 0.1 mile to the campground.

Facilities: 17 campsites; all sites are fairly spacious, level, with fair to good separation; parking pads are gravel, mostly long pull-throughs or pull-offs; excellent tent-pitching opportunities; fire rings; b-y-o firewood is recommended; water at central faucets; restrooms; gravel driveway; camper supplies at nearby lodges; complete supplies and services are available in Missoula.

Activities & Attractions: Good fishing on Clark Fork and nearby side streams, particularly Rock Creek, one of Montana's famed 'blue ribbon' trout streams (accessed from I-90 Exit 126, 4 miles west of here); limited hiking along the river bank.

Natural Features: Located in a valley on the north-west bank of Clark Fork of the Columbia River; light to medium shelter/shade is provided by tall hardwoods and some conifers; several sites are right along the river; a rail fence around the perimeter of the recreation area adds a finishing touch (and keeps out stray livestock); flanked by timbered hills and ridges along both sides of the river valley; elevation 3600'.

Season, Fees & Phone: May to September; 14 day limit; please see Appendix for standard Montana state park fees; phone c/o Montana Department of Fish Wildlife & Parks Office, Missoula, (406) 542-5500.

Camp Notes: This spot is nearly ideal for Interstate travelers. It's far enough off the highway that road noise isn't much of a concern. The campground often fills on midsummer Friday and Saturday evenings, but sites are usually available at other times.

Montana 46

LEE CREEK
Lolo National Forest

Location: Far Western Montana southwest of Missoula.

Access: From U.S Highway 12 at milepost 6 (6 miles east of Lolo Pass, 26.5 miles west of Lolo, Montana), turn south into the campground.

Facilities: 22 campsites in 2 loops; sites in the lower section are large and well spaced; sites in the upper loop are smaller, sloped, a little closer together, but still well spaced; parking pads are gravel, medium to long straight-ins; most units are suitable for rv's, and about three-fourths are good for tents; fireplaces or fire rings; firewood is available for gathering; water at faucets throughout; vault facilities; gravel driveways; limited+ supplies and services are available in Lolo.

Activities & Attractions: Self-guiding nature trail along Lee Creek; fishing for small trout on Lolo Creek; small national forest visitor information center at Lolo Pass.

Natural Features: Located at the confluence of Lee Creek, a side stream, with Lolo Creek, the main stream in this watershed; the campground is situated in a moderately dense conifer forest; units 1-5 are streamside spots just as you enter the campground; the remainder of the sites are on a knoll directly to the east of the lower units; low timbered ridges lie north and south of the campground; elk and black bear are in the area; count on cool nights even in midsummer; elevation 4600'.

Season, Fees & Phone: May to early September; $6.00; 14 day limit; Missoula Ranger District (406) 329-3750.

Camp Notes: U.S. 12 was constructed less than a half-century ago. Prior to that time the only way to penetrate the wilderness in the Lolo Creek, Montana and Clearwater River, Idaho watersheds was on foot or horseback. Except for the sinuous strip of pavement that closely follows the main streams, not much has changed since Lewis and Clark forged their way through here on the way to and from the Coast two centuries ago.

LEWIS AND CLARK
Lolo National Forest

Location: Far Western Montana southwest of Missoula.

Access: From U.S. Highway 12 at milepost 17 (15.5 miles west of the community of Lolo, Montana, 17 miles east of Lolo Pass), turn south off the highway onto a gravel road, and continue across a wooden bridge to the campground.

Facilities: 18 campsites; sites are medium to large and well spaced; parking pads are gravel straight-ins, and most are reasonably level but a bit snug for large trailers; fireplaces; firewood is available for gathering; water at faucets throughout; vault facilities; gravel driveway; nearest reliable source of limited supplies is Lolo; complete supplies and services are available in Missoula, 27 miles northeast.

Activities & Attractions: Fishing on Lolo Creek; small national forest visitor center at Lolo Pass.

Natural Features: Located on a hillside in a narrow valley bordered by low, timbered mountains; dense, tall timber and low-level brush shelters the campground; Lolo Creek flows between the camp area and the highway; a small side stream runs along the west side of the campground; elevation 3800'.

Season, Fees & Phone: May to mid-September; $6.00; 14 day limit; Missoula Ranger District (406) 329-3750.

Camp Notes: A number of historic information signs along U.S. 12 in this area note the passage of Lewis and Clark and the Corps of Discovery through this valley in 1804-05. One of the expedition's campsites was apparently on or very near this spot. This is the easternmost public campground along the 220-mile segment of Highway 12 between Lewiston, Idaho, and Missoula, Montana. Supplies and services are hard to come by. It might be a good idea to fill up with gas and groceries in one of the big towns before you embark on your adventure through one of the most wild and beautiful regions in the Rockies.

CHARLES WATERS
Bitterroot National Forest

Location: Western Montana south of Missoula.

Access: From U.S. Highway 93 at milepost 70 +.4 (4.5 miles south of Florence, 3.5 miles north of Stevensville), turn west onto Bass Creek Road (paved, but narrow); continue west for 2 miles to the recreation area entrance, then an additional 0.1 mile to the campground.

Facilities: 17 campsites; most sites are large, level, fairly well separated, and would be excellent for either tents or rv's; most parking pads are gravel straight-ins; plenty of tent space; fireplaces or fire rings; some firewood is available for gathering in the area; water at faucets throughout; vault facilities; most driveways are paved; limited supplies in Florence; adequate supplies in Stevensville; complete supplies and services are available in Missoula, 24 miles north.

Activities & Attractions: Nature trail and fitness trail; Bass Creek Trailhead (access to the Selway-Bitterroot Wilderness) just west of the campground.

Natural Features: Located on a lightly forested flat, nestled up against the eastern foothills of the Bitterroot Range; large open grassy areas, with a profusion of wildflowers during most of the summer; black bears have been sighted near the campground, so safeguard your vittles; elevation 3600'.

Season, Fees & Phone: May to October; $6.00; 14 day limit; Stevensville Ranger District (406) 777-5461.

Camp Notes: The recreation area in which the campground is situated is named after a prominent University of Montana forestry professor and researcher who used this locale as an outdoor laboratory. Nice place.

LAKE COMO
Bitterroot National Forest

Location: Western Montana south of Missoula.

Access: From U.S Highway 93 at milepost 35 + .5 (11 miles south of Hamilton, 35 miles north of Lost Trail Pass), turn west onto a gravel road (often quite rough); drive 3.4 miles to a fork in the road; take the right fork and continue for another 1.2 miles; the campground is at the west end of the recreation area.

Facilities: 12 campsites in a single large loop; sites are spacious, with good separation; parking pads are gravel, short to medium-length straight-ins; large tent spots; pads and tent areas a reasonably level even though the campground is on a hill; fire rings; some firewood is available for gathering in the area; water at a hand pump; vault facilities; gravel driveways; gas and groceries+ in Darby, 4.7 miles south of the Lake Como turnoff; adequate supplies and services are available in Hamilton.

Activities & Attractions: Designated swimming area with a gravel beach nearby; day use area with tables and barbecue grills; fishing; boating; foot trail around the lake.

Natural Features: Located on a knoll on the northeast shore of Lake Como, below the foothills of the rugged Bitterroot Range; a moderately dense conifer forest, with some low vegetation, covers the campground; a marsh with lily pads is in the center of the loop; a great variety of animals and birds, particularly migratory waterfowl reside near, or visit the lake; elevation 4200'.

Season, Fees & Phone: May to October; $6.00; 14 day limit; Darby Ranger District (406) 821-3913.

Camp Notes: Several Lake Como camp spots have good lake views. There are some breathtaking vistas which are reminiscent of the Teton Range in Wyoming. The lake was named for Como, the home town in northern Italy of Father Ravalli, the pioneering Jesuit missionary to Montana's Flathead Indians.

Montana 50

ROMBO
Bitterroot National Forest

Location: Western Montana south of Missoula.

Access: From the junction of U.S. Highway 93 and Montana Secondary Highway 473 near Conner (17 miles south of Hamilton, 31 miles north of Lost Trail Pass), turn west onto Secondary 473 (paved, may be signed for "Painted Rocks Lake); head southwest for 15.5 miles; bear left at the major "Y" intersection, and continue on West Fork Road for 3 additional miles; turn northwest (right) onto the gravel campground access road for a final 0.1 mile to the campground.

Facilities: 19 campsites in 2 loops; all sites are good-sized, level, and fairly private; parking pads are gravel, medium-length straight-ins; fire rings; firewood is available for gathering; water at faucets; vault facilities; gravel driveways; camper supplies in Conner, 18 miles east near U.S. 93; nearest source of adequate supplies is Hamilton.

Activities & Attractions: Easy riverbank access; good fly fishing; boating and fishing on Painted Rocks Lake.

Natural Features: Located on a moderately timbered flat on the West Fork of the Bitterroot River; the river valley is bordered by heavily timbered mountains; many sites have good views of the river and mountains; Painted Rocks Lake is 7 miles west on a gravel road; elevation 4500'.

Season, Fees & Phone: June to September; $6.00; 14 day limit; West Fork Ranger District, Darby, (406) 821-3269.

Camp Notes: The West Fork of the Bitterroot River is a beautiful mountain stream which runs crystal clear during most of the year. Rombo is a very nice campground which sees relatively little use. This might be a good spot for campers who would like to settle in for a few days away from the Montana mainstream. Another local, forest campground, Boulder Creek, located several miles east of Rombo on a gravel side road just north of Secondary 473, has a half-dozen sites, no water and no fee. If you're willing to enter some additional mileage on your vehicle's 'odo', Painted Rocks SRA can be reached by just staying on West Fork Road for another ten miles (7 are gravel) past Rombo. Painted Rocks is on the shore of a good-sized lake of the same name. It has 18 sites, drinking water, vaults and appropriate fees.

Montana 51

INDIAN TREES
Bitterroot National Forest

Location: Southwest Montana south of Missoula.

Access: From U.S. Highway 93 at milepost 7 + .1 (40 miles south of Hamilton, 7 miles north of Lost Trail Pass), turn west onto a gravel road (Forest Road 729) directly across the highway from a Montana Highway Department maintenance yard; the road immediately jogs to the south; proceed south 0.5 mile, then bear west (right) and continue for 0.2 mile (past private property) to the campground.

Facilities: 17 campsites; most sites are small to medium in size, with fair separation; parking pads are paved or gravel, short straight-ins, plus a couple of pull-throughs; about half the sites are suitable for tents; fire rings; firewood is available for gathering; water at a hand pump; vault facilities; paved driveway; camper supplies in Sula, 6 miles north; nearest sources of adequate supplies are Hamilton, or Salmon, Idaho, 53 miles south.

Activities & Attractions: A historical sign marks the site of one of Lewis and Clark's camps, just south of here; magnificent views in Lost Trail Pass.

Natural Features: Located on a forested hillside in the Bitterroot Range; sites are fairly well sheltered by some tall ponderosa pines, but mostly smaller mountain hardwoods; large, open, grassy areas lies in and around the campground; a small creek completes the setting; elevation 5100'.

Season, Fees & Phone: June to September; $6.00; 14 day limit; Sula Ranger District (406) 821-3201.

Camp Notes: Scarred ponderosa pines found here suggested the name for the camp. The Flathead Indians used the cambium layer of the bark as a sweet and chewy treat. The practice was discontinued as sugar was introduced to the Indians by the White Man.

Montana 52

MAY CREEK
Beaverhead National Forest

Location: Southwest Montana west of Wisdom.

Access: From Montana State Highway 43 at milepost 9 + .4 (9 miles east of Lost Trail Pass, 16.5 miles west of Wisdom), turn south onto a gravel access road for 0.1 mile to the campground.

Facilities: 21 campsites; sites are generally large, level and well separated; most parking pads are long, gravel straight-ins; large, well cleared tent spots; fire rings and barbecue grills; firewood is available for gathering; water at faucets; vault facilities; gravel driveways; limited supplies and services are available in Wisdom.

Activities & Attractions: Big Hole National Battlefield and Visitor Center, 8 miles east, marks the site of a major encounter between 800 fleeing Nez Percé Indians and a makeshift local U.S. Army force of 200 soldiers; fishing for small trout on nearby streams; foot trails.

Natural Features: Located in a valley at the confluence of Joseph, May and Stevenson Creeks; tall conifers with very little underbrush shelter the camp area; the campground is bordered by a lush mountain meadow on the west, timber on the east; many sites look out across the meadow; densely forested hills and mountains lie in the surrounding area; elevation 6400'.

Season, Fees & Phone: June to mid-September; $6.00; 14 day limit; Wisdom Ranger District (406) 689-3243.

Camp Notes: The scenery in this region changes dramatically in just a few miles: very fertile and forested near May Creek Campground and to the west; much drier and more rugged a dozen miles east near Big Hole. The historical significance of the route that passes the campground is twofold: Lewis and Clark traveled past this spot on their way West; Chief Joseph and the Nez Percé also came through here on their flight from Oregon in the summer of 1877.

Montana 53

BANNACK
Bannack State Park

Location: Southwest Montana west of Dillon.

Access: From Interstate 15 Exit 59 for Jackson/Wisdom (3 miles south of Dillon), head westerly on Montana Secondary Highway 278 for 18 miles to the Bannack turnoff (well marked) at milepost 17 + .7; turn south onto a local gravel road and travel south for 3 miles; (at 2.9 miles the road passes through a ranch yard); as the road divides just south of the ranch, follow the left fork easterly for 1.3 miles, then turn south (right) and proceed 0.1 mile down into the campground.

Facilities: 25 campsites in two sections; one section is near the old town of Bannack, the other is 0.1 mile west of the first; sites are average in size, generally level, with nominal separation; parking areas are gravel or dirt, of assorted types and lengths; large, grass/earth tent spots; fire rings; b-y-o firewood; water at hand pumps; vault facilities; (restrooms at the visitor center); gravel/dirt driveways; horse corrals; adequate+ supplies and services are available in Dillon.

Activities & Attractions: Historic ghost town of Bannack; small visitor center; Bannack Days, celebrated annually during the third weekend in July.

Natural Features: Located in a small valley on the north bank of Grasshopper Creek; dense, brushy, hardwood vegetation lines the creek; campsites are on a creekside flat and are lightly shaded by large hardwoods; the surrounding terrain consists primarily of sage plains and very high, dry hills and mountains in all directions; elevation 5900'.

Season, Fees & Phone: Open all year, with limited services in winter; 14 day limit; please see Appendix for standard Montana state park fees; park office (406) 834-3413.

Camp Notes: Bannack was born after a placer strike in 1862, and the new town quickly became Montana's first major gold camp. In 1864 Bannack became Montana's first territorial capital. Less than a year later, many of the town's residents--as well as the territorial capital--had moved to richer diggins at Alder Gulch in Virginia City. Bannack is now a ghost town, preserved in a state of arrested decay. About two-dozen major historic buildings, and a dozen or more lesser structures remain. You can gain quite an appreciation of life in the gold days from visiting this park. *The* best time to visit is during Bannack Days. It's a home grown get-together of Montanans and others who might be called "Bannack Backers". The three-day gathering includes frontier cooking, quilting, blacksmithing, gold panning, cross-town telegraphy, black powder shoots and other demos related to the frontier lifestyle.

Montana 54

FLINT CREEK
Deerlodge National Forest

Location: Western Montana northwest of Butte.

Access: From Montana State Highway 1 (old U.S. 10A) at milepost 30 +.3 (8 miles south of Philipsburg, 21 miles west of Anaconda), turn west then south onto a gravel road paralleling the highway; proceed 0.1 mile to the campground.

Facilities: 10 campsites plus overflow parking; sites are small to medium-sized, level, very well spaced with fair to good visual separation; parking pads are gravel, smallish straight-ins or long pull-throughs; some nice grassy tent spots; water at a faucet at the south end of the campground; vault facilities; pack-it-in/pack-it-out trash removal system; firewood is available for gathering in the vicinity; gravel driveway; limited supplies and services are available in Philipsburg.

Activities & Attractions: Ghost towns and a number of old mining sites in the surrounding area; superscenic drive along Highway 1, part of the Anaconda-Pintlar Scenic Route; boating and fishing on Georgetown Lake, a few miles southwest.

Natural Features: Located in Flint Creek Canyon between the Flint Creek Range to the east and peaks above 8000' in the Sapphire Mountains to the west; campground vegetation along the outer edge, away from the grassy creekbank, consists of fairly dense conifers, hardwoods, and underbrush; sites are strung out for 0.3 mile along Flint Creek, a classic mountain stream which flows by the campsites; elevation 5700'.

Season, Fees & Phone: June to September; no fee (subject to change); 14 day limit; Philipsburg Ranger District (406) 859-3211.

Camp Notes: Most Flint Creek sites are creekside. This is a delightfully pleasant spot. The crystal clear creek bubbles over granite rocks between a pair of intensely green, forested walls.

Montana 55

PHILIPSBURG BAY
Deerlodge National Forest

Location: Western Montana northwest of Butte.

Access: From Montana State Highway 1 (old U. S. 10A) at milepost 27 +.3 (11 miles south of Philipsburg, 18 miles northwest of Anaconda), turn southwest onto "Georgetown Lake Road"; continue on the paved access road to a sign for "Philipsburg Bay Campground"; turn left and continue on a steep, paved driveway down to the campground (a total of 1.5 miles from Highway 1).

Facilities: 69 campsites in 3 loops; sites are average or better in size, with generally good separation; parking pads are paved, medium to long, and some pads may require additional leveling; nice spots for tents on a forest floor of pine needles; fireplaces; some firewood is available for gathering in the area; water at hand pumps; vault facilities; paved driveways; camper supplies on the north shore of the lake at a small store and resort; limited supplies in Philipsburg; adequate supplies and services are available in Anaconda.

Activities & Attractions: Boating; boat launch; fishing; ghost towns and wilderness access points are accessible by forest roads.

Natural Features: Located along the shore of Philipsburg Bay on Georgetown Lake, in the Rocky Mountains a few miles west of the Continental Divide; sites are on a slope in an open forest of tall, thin pines and very little underbrush; the Anaconda Range, the Flint Creek Range, and the Sapphire Mountains encircle the large lake; elevation 6400'.

Season, Fees & Phone: May to September; $8.00; 14 day limit; Philipsburg Ranger District (406) 859-3211.

Camp Notes: Georgetown Lake is a natural mountain beauty surrounded by grassy slopes and forested mountains. The rugged granite peaks of the Anaconda-Pintlar Wilderness area are visible across the lake in the distance.

Montana 56

PINEY
Deerlodge National Forest

Location: Western Montana northwest of Butte.

Access: From Montana State Highway 1 at milepost 27 +.3 (18 miles northwest of Anaconda, 11 miles south of Philipsburg), turn southwest onto the Georgetown Lake Road; continue on the paved access road to a sign for "Piney Campground"; turn left and continue on a steep paved driveway down to the campground (a total of 2.8 miles from the highway).

Facilities: 36 campsites; sites are medium to medium+ in size, with fairly good separation; parking pads are paved, medium to long, most pads are fairly level; some nice spots for tents on a grassy forest floor; a few sites on a hillside have steps leading from the parking pads to the tables; fireplaces; some firewood is available for gathering in the area; water at hand pumps; vault facilities; paved driveways; camper supplies nearby; adequate supplies and services are available in Anaconda.

Activities & Attractions: Boating; boat launch; fishing; forest roads provide access to ghost towns and wilderness trailheads.

Natural Features: Located on Piney Bay of Georgetown Lake, a large, natural lake surrounded by the forested peaks of the Anaconda Range, the Flint Creek Range, and the Sapphire Mountains; campground vegetation consists of very tall, thin pines and some underbrush; elevation 6400'.

Season, Fees & Phone: May to September; $8.00; 14 day limit; Philipsburg Ranger District (406) 859-3211.

Camp Notes: Most campsites at Piney have a view of beautiful Georgetown Lake through the trees. A number of sites are close enough to the shore to allow campers to tie up their boats within a few yards of their tents.

Montana 57

LODGEPOLE
Deerlodge National Forest

Location: Western Montana northwest of Butte.

Access: From Montana State Highway 1 at milepost 26 +.9 (11 miles southeast of Philipsburg, 18 miles west of Anaconda, 0.4 mile south of the Georgetown Lake Road turnoff), turn northeast into the campground.

Facilities: 31 campsites; sites are average or better in size, with good separation; parking pads are gravel and some are spacious enough to accommodate large vehicles; some pads may require additional leveling; some designated tent sites are situated farther away from the highway; fireplaces; firewood is available for gathering in the area; water at faucets; vault facilities; paved driveways; camper supplies on the north shore of the lake; adequate supplies and services are available in Anaconda.

Activities & Attractions: Scenic drive along the east shore of Georgetown Lake on the Anaconda-Pintler Scenic Route; boating; Red Bridge boat ramp directly across Highway 1 from the campground; fishing.

Natural Features: Located on a hill above the east shore of Georgetown Lake in the Rocky Mountains a few miles west of the Continental Divide; campground vegetation, denser here than in other local campgrounds, consists of tall pines and a considerable amount of undergrowth; the area is surrounded by the forested peaks of the Anaconda Range, the Flint Creek Range, and the Sapphire Mountains; elevation 6400'.

Season, Fees & Phone: May to September; $7.00; 14 day limit; Philipsburg Ranger District (406) 859-3211.

Camp Notes: Lodgepole Campground is on a hillside across the highway from Georgetown Lake. The stop is certainly convenient and there's often room for one more camper here, even when nearby Philipsburg Bay and Piney campgrounds are packed.

Montana 58

LOST CREEK
Lost Creek State Park

Location: Western Montana northwest of Butte.

Access: From Montana State Highway 1 at milepost 5 +.6 (6 miles west of Interstate 90 Exit 208, 3 miles east of Anaconda) turn northeast onto Montana State Highway 48 and proceed 0.2 mile; turn north (left) onto Montana Secondary Highway 273 and head due north for 1.9 miles; turn west (left) onto a paved local road and travel 4 miles west/northwest to the end of the pavement; pick up a gravel road and travel northwest for another 1.8 miles to the park entrance, then 1.4 miles to the campground.

Facilities: 20 camp/picnic sites; sites are medium-sized, with fair separation; parking pads are gravel, short to medium-length straight-ins; many pads will require additional leveling; some sites are suitable for smaller tents; fire rings; b-y-o firewood is recommended; water at a hand pump; vault facilities; pack-it-in\pack-it-out trash removal system; gravel driveways; adequate+ supplies and services are available in Anaconda, 3 miles west of the junction of Highways 1 & 48.

Activities & Attractions: Scenic views; paved trail leads 125 yards up to Lost Creek Falls Viewpoint; interpretive placards.

Natural Features: Located in a deep canyon in the eastern foothills of the Flint Creek Range of the Rocky Mountains; Lost Creek Falls is a few yards from the campground; vegetation consists mostly of tall conifers, sections of hardwoods and varying amounts of undercover; elevation 6000'.

Season, Fees & Phone: May to October; 14 day limit; please see Appendix for standard Montana state park fees; phone c/o Montana Department of Fish Wildlife & Parks Office, Missoula, (406) 542-5500.

Camp Notes: Quite a few of the park's attractive campsites are located right along rushing, tumbling Lost Creek. Many visitors come to see the small falls that leaps from rock to rock on its way down the hill. The falls drops 20 to 50 vertical feet, depending upon how many levels you include in your estimate. However, the sheer cliffs and granite palisades that tower over the campground may be the best reasons to come and stay a while.

Montana
West Central
Please refer to the Montana map in the Appendix

Montana 59

LAKE FRANCIS
City of Valier Recreation Area

Location: North-central Montana northwest of Great Falls.

Access: From Montana State Highway 44 at milepost 13 +.8 on the west edge of the city of Valier (14 miles west of Interstate 15 Exit 348, 14 miles east of U.S. 89), turn west onto Teton Avenue; drive west (past the airport) for 0.4 mile, then the road curves south for 0.6 mile; turn west (right) into the campground.

Facilities: Approximately 20 camp/picnic sites; sites are medium-sized, level, with nominal separation; parking pads are gravel/earth, small to large pull-offs or straight-ins; good tent-pitching opportunities; fireplaces; b-y-o firewood; water at a central faucet; restrooms; holding tank disposal station; gravel driveways; gas and groceries+ are available in Valier.

Activities & Attractions: Boating; boat launch; fishing for warm-water species; sports/play areas.

Natural Features: Located on the east shore of Lake Francis on the west edge of the Great Plains; a line of bushes and medium-sized hardwoods serve as a wind break and very light shade for some sites; (b-y-o shade); the Northern Rockies rise about 35 miles west; typically breezy; elevation 3600'.

Season, Fees & Phone: Open all year, subject to weather conditions, with limited services October to May; $6.00; weekly rates available; Valier City Hall (406) 279-3721.

Camp Notes: Lake Francis and its campground are situated in the middle of a vast prairie that stretches for miles and miles and miles in every direction. From your campsite, looking westward across the lake and the plains beyond, you can view the peaks of the Rockies rising above the horizon.

Montana 60

ASPEN GROVE
Helena National Forest

Location: Western Montana northwest of Helena.

Access: From Montana State Highway 200 at milepost 78 +.7 (7 miles east of Lincoln, 4 miles west of the junction of Montana State Highway 200 and County Highway 279), turn south onto a gravel access road; proceed 0.5 mile to the campground.

Facilities: 19 campsites in 2 loops; sites are medium-sized, with fair to good separation; parking pads are gravel, basically level short to medium-length straight-ins, and some are double-wide; many really good tent-pitching spots; fireplaces; firewood is available for gathering in the surrounding area; water at several faucets; vault facilities; gravel driveways; limited supplies and services are available in Lincoln.

Activities & Attractions: Fishing; hiking; picnic area 0.3 mile east; access to several mountain lakes is gained by driving north on nearby Copper Creek Road.

Natural Features: Located along the Blackfoot River on the edge of a sage flat in the Rocky Mountains; steep canyon walls rise to the south, across the river, and a more open valley lies to the north; sites are situated among aspens, scattered conifers and tall grass; elevation 4800'.

Season, Fees & Phone: June to September; $6.00; 14 day limit; Lincoln Ranger District (406) 362-4265.

Camp Notes: There are some super vast vistas all up and down this valley. The city of Lincoln also has a small public campground. It's located in a grove of tall conifers at milepost 72 near the east end of town, on the south side of the highway.

Montana 61

CROMWELL DIXON
Helena National Forest

Location: West-central Montana west of Helena.

Access: From U.S. Highway 12 at milepost 27 +.5 at the summit of MacDonald Pass (17 miles west of Helena, 16 miles east of Avon, 28 miles east of Interstate 90 at Garrison Junction), turn south onto a paved access road, (signed for "MacDonald Pass Recreation Area"), then almost immediately swing west (right) and proceed 0.5 mile to a fork; continue straight ahead (the left fork) onto gravel for 0.1 mile into the campground.

Facilities: 14 campsites; sites are medium to large, wit61fair to very good separation; parking pads are sandy gravel, short to medium+ straight-ins, some are double-wide; minor additional leveling may be required on some pads; some really nice, sheltered tent spots; fire rings; a small amount of firewood is available for gathering in the surrounding area, b-y-o to be sure; water at a hand pump; vault facilities; gravel driveway; complete supplies and services are available in Helena.

Activities & Attractions: Scenic overlook just east of the campground offers very impressive views of McDonald Pass and Helena Valley to the east; the drive along Highway 12 across MacDonald Pass offers first-rate scenery; (the pass is named for Alexander "Red" MacDonald, the manager of a tollgate on this road back in the late 1800's); some hiking and 4-wheel-drive trails lead into the mountains from near the campground.

Natural Features: Located in a stand of conifers on the Continental Divide; in addition to moderately dense tall conifers, campground vegetation consists of a considerable amount of underbrush and a thick carpet of evergreen needles; encircled by a large, subalpine park (meadow); elevation 6300'.

Season, Fees & Phone: June to September; $6.00; 14 day limit; Helena Ranger District (406) 449-5490.

Camp Notes: In September 1911, pioneer aviator Cromwell Dixon earned a $10,000 prize when he became the first pilot to fly an airplane over the Continental Divide. Dixon flew his plain plane across the Great Divide through MacDonald Pass and over the campground area which now bears his name.

Montana 62

HOLTER LAKE
Public Lands/BLM Recreation Site

Location: West-central Montana north of Helena.

Access: From Interstate 15 Exit 226 for Wolf Creek (34 miles north of Helena, 55 miles south of Great Falls), from the east side of the freeway, drive southeast to a "T" intersection, then turn east (left) onto a frontage road; continue east for 3 miles (just over the Missouri River Bridge); turn south (right) onto Beartooth Road (gravel, somewhat steep and winding); drive south for 2.4 miles; turn westerly (right) into the campground.

Facilities: 27 campsites; sites are small to medium-sized, with minimal to nominal separation; parking pads are gravel, mostly double-wide straight-ins; many good tent spots are situated on a grassy, gentle slope; fire rings and barbecue grills; water at several faucets; vault facilities; pack-it-in/pack-it-out system of trash removal; paved driveway; gas and limited groceries in Wolf Creek; complete supplies and services are available in Helena.

Activities & Attractions: Boating; boat ramp; fishing; prairie dog town, 2.2 miles south along the access road.

Natural Features: Located in the Rocky Mountains on the east shore of Holter Lake, a reservoir on the Missouri River created by Holter Dam; Gates of the Mountains Wilderness lies to the east; peaks which comprise the Continental Divide are visible to the west; all sites are situated on a breezy slope with good lake views; elevation 3500'.

Season, Fees & Phone: Open all year with limited services in winter; $7.00; 14 day limit; Bureau of Land Management Office, Butte, (406) 494-5059.

Camp Notes: The prevailing sunny and breezy conditions at this campground accentuate the beautiful blue lake with its backdrop of forested Rocky Mountain foothills and peaks. No wonder this very spot was chosen as a campsite by the Lewis & Clark Expedition on July 18, 1805. Holter Lake is a four-season recreation area. Even in mid-January you'll occasionally see fly fishermen working the Missouri below the frozen lake where ice fishermen are doing their own thing.

Montana 63

LOG GULCH
Public Lands/BLM Recreation Site

Location: West-central Montana north of Helena.

Access: From Interstate 15 Exit 226 for Wolf Creek (34 miles north of Helena, 55 miles south of Great Falls) from the east side of the freeway, drive southeast to a "T" intersection; turn east (left) onto a frontage road and proceed easterly for 3.3 miles (just over the Missouri River Bridge); turn south (right) onto Beartooth Road, (gravel) and travel south for 4.4 miles to the park boundary; continue ahead for another 2.3 miles to the campground. (Note: Beartooth Road has several steep and twisty sections.)

Facilities: 44 campsites in 2 sections; sites vary from small and fairly well separated to spacious with no separation; parking pads are gravel, short to long pull-throughs or straight-ins; many pads may require additional leveling; large spots for tents, though some may be rocky or sloped; assorted fire appliances; b-y-o firewood is recommended; water at a central faucet; vault facilities; gravel driveways; gas and limited groceries in Wolf Creek; complete supplies and services are available in Helena.

Activities & Attractions: Boating; boat launch and docks; fishing for rainbow, brown, brook trout, also walleye, perch, kokanee salmon; prairie dog town, 2 miles north.

Natural Features: Located along the east shore of Holter Lake, a reservoir on the Missouri River; vegetation varies from open areas of sparse grass to short conifers and sheltering hardwoods; closely bordered by partially forested hills and mountains; elevation 3500'.

Season, Fees & Phone: Open all year with limited services in winter; $7.00; 14 day limit; Bureau of Land Management Office, Butte, (406) 494-5059.

Camp Notes: Campsites at Log Gulch are situated immediately across the roadway from the east shore of Holter Lake. There are exceptional views across the lake from most of the campground. A candid word: Beartooth Road is a dusty, one-vehicle-per-minute thoroughfare in midsummer, even in mid-week; so don't expect yourself or your passengers to enthusiastically exclaim, "Ah, Wilderness!"

Montana 64

MISSOURI RIVER ROAD
Missouri River Road State Recreation Area

Location: West-central Montana between Helena and Great Falls.

Access: From Interstate 15 (northbound) Exit 219 for Spring Creek/Recreation Road (27 miles north of Helena), go to the east side of the Interstate, then travel north on the Recreation Road to the recreation sites; **Alternate Access:** From I-15 (southbound) take Exit 247 for Hardy Creek and travel south on the Recreation Road to the recreation sites. **Alternate-Alternate Access:** From I-15 Exit 226 for Wolf Creek, proceed to the east side of the Int4rstate to a "T" intersection; turn north or south onto the Recreation Road to the recreation sites. (Note: Recreation Road mileposts are numbered south to north, beginning with Mile 0 at freeway Exit 219 and ending just north of Mile 31 at freeway Exit 247; also, 3 minor freeway exits between Exit 226 and Exit 247 will also take you to the Road.)

Facilities: 7 small, roadside camp/picnic areas, with 3 to 6 campsites in each area; most areas can handle a few medium to large vehicles and tents; no drinking water; vault facilities; gas and limited groceries in Wolf Creek.

Activities & Attractions: Scenic drive; boating; boat launches; fishing (most common trout are cutthroats).

Natural Features: Located along the banks of Little Prickly Pear Creek and the Missouri River in their respective canyons; the stream banks are intermittently lined with hardwoods; virtually all sites are within a few yards of the streams; canyon walls are partially timbered with conifers; elevation 3400'.

Season, Fees & Phone: Open all year, subject to weather conditions; no fee (subject to change); 3 day limit; phone c/o Montana Department of Fish Wildlife & Parks Office, Great Falls, (406) 454-3441.

Camp Notes: Missouri River Recreation Road winds through 32 highly scenic miles of canyons and valleys. (The entire passage is generally called "Wolf Creek Canyon"). The road is the well-maintained leftover of what was the old main highway through the canyon prior to construction of the Interstate. Where are the best spots to camp along the Road? Probably in the northern half. It's the most geologically dramatic area.

Montana 65

BLACK SANDY
Black Sandy State Recreation Area

Location: West-central Montana north of Helena.

Access: From Interstate 15 Exit 200 for Lincoln Road/Montana Secondary Highway 453 (8 miles north of Helena, 26 miles south of Wolf Creek) head east on Secondary 453 for 5.1 miles to a "T" junction; turn north (left) onto Hauser Lake Dam Road (gravel) and proceed 3 miles to the campground.

Facilities: Approximately 25 camp/picnic sites; sites are small, tolerably level, with zip separation; parking surfaces are gravel, short straight-ins/pull-offs; enough room for small to medium-sized tents in some sites; fire rings; some firewood may be available for gathering in the vicinity, b-y-o is recommended; water at a central faucet; vault facilities; holding tank disposal station; gravel driveways; complete supplies and services are available in Helena.

Activities & Attractions: Boating; boat launch and courtesy dock; fishing.

Natural Features: Located on the west shore of Hauser Lake, a reservoir on the Missouri River; sites are unshaded or lightly shaded/sheltered by large hardwoods along the lake shore; bordered by hills and low mountains partially covered with conifers; elevation 3500'.

Season, Fees & Phone: April to October; 14 day limit; please see Appendix for standard Montana state park fees; phone c/o Montana Department of Fish Wildlife & Parks Office, Helena, (406) 444-4720.

Camp Notes: Because of their lakeside location, the sites here are very much in demand during most of the summer. (Lakeside, indeed. In a year with abundant runoff, your trailer tongue may be lapping lake water.) Tenters can successfully camp in some of the sites here, but the area really is better-suited to self-contained users. Expect a lot of close-quartered company.

SILOS
Canyon Ferry State Park

Location: West-central Montana southeast of Helena.

Access: From U.S. Highways 12/287 at milepost 70 (8 miles north of Townsend, 26 miles southeast of Helena), turn east onto a gravel road and proceed 1.1 miles to the park.

Facilities: Approximately 15 camp/picnic sites scattered along the lake shore in several sections; (a group camp is available by reservation); campsites are generally large and level; some good tent spots, but probably more suitable for vehicle camping; fireplaces or fire rings; b-y-o firewood; water at central faucets and hand pumps; vault facilities; gravel/dirt driveways; limited supplies and services in Townsend.

Activities & Attractions: Fishing for rainbow and brown trout, also perch; boating; boat launches.

Natural Features: Located in a large valley on a grassy plain on the west shore of Canyon Ferry Lake; a few tall hardwoods scattered along the shore provide limited shelter from the elements; high, timbered mountains rise east and west of the valley; windy; antelope abound in this area; elevation 3800'.

Season, Fees & Phone: Open all year, with limited services in winter; 14 day limit; please see Appendix for standard Montana state park fees; park office (406) 444-4475.

Camp Notes: Silos provides the easiest access to Canyon Ferry Lake on the west shore. The area was named for two old brick silos which still stand near the main highway. Also in this vicinity is the state park's White Earth unit. It's 5.5 miles east of the highway via a gravel road from milepost 64 +.7. White Earth has a dozen camp/picnic sites near the lake shore, a hand pump, vaults and boat ramp.

INDIAN ROAD
Canyon Ferry State Park

Location: West-central Montana southeast of Helena.

Access: From U.S. Highways 12/287 at milepost 76 +.5 (1 mile north of the junction of U.S. 12 & 287 in Townsend, 31 miles southeast of Helena, 0.2 mile south of the Missouri River Bridge), turn east onto Centerville Road (gravel) and proceed 0.1 mile to the park.

Facilities: 12 camp/picnic sites; sites are average or better in size, level, with nominal separation; parking pads are gravel, mostly straight-ins or pull-offs spacious enough to accommodate medium to large vehicles; tent spots are large and grassy; barbecue grills; b-y-o firewood; water at several faucets; vault facilities; gravel driveways; limited supplies and services are available in Townsend.

Activities & Attractions: Boating; boat launch for river access; fishing; Canyon Ferry Lake, a few hundred yards downstream of this area, offers boating, fishing and other water recreation.

Natural Features: Located near the south-east bank of the Missouri River just south of Canyon Ferry Lake; park vegetation consists of large areas of mown grass bordered by scattered, large hardwoods; the Big Belt Mountains rise to almost 10,000' to the east; peaks of the Continental Divide rise to above 9000' just to the west; elevation 3800'.

Season, Fees & Phone: Open all year, with limited services in winter; 14 day limit; please see Appendix for standard Montana state park fees; park office (406) 444-4475.

Camp Notes: The Journals of Lewis and Clark mention an "Indian road" along the river in this area which was used by Captain Clark to scout the countryside. Indian Road would be an excellent campground to use in spring or fall, or anytime the weather is cool. The winged critters which dwell in the backwater slough pond near the river shouldn't be overly aggressive in cooler weather. (Interestingly enough, the Journals also mention that "The mosquitos are very troublesome" along this section of the river.) It's fairly low in altitude so there should be relatively light amounts of snow (except for a few days after a storm). A fresh dusting of snow on the high peaks which completely surround this valley glistens iridescently in soft autumn sunlight.

RIVERSIDE
Canyon Ferry State Park

Location: West-central Montana southeast of Helena.

Access: From the junction of U.S. Highways 12/287 and Montana Secondary Highway 284 (11 miles southeast of Helena, 22 miles north of Townsend), turn east onto Secondary 284 and follow this paved road easterly across the Canyon Ferry Dam to the north shore; at a point 1 mile east of the dam (just east of the turnoff to the visitor center) turn north (left) onto a paved access road and proceed 1.1 miles down to the campground.

Facilities: 18 campsites, plus overflow room for another several dozen vehicles; sites are small, tolerably level, and closely spaced; parking pads are gravel, medium-length straight-ins or pull-offs; a bit of additional leveling will be needed; medium to large areas for tents; ramadas (sun shelters) for a couple of sites; fire rings; water at a central faucet; vault facilities; gravel driveways; gas, camper supplies and laundry at the marina on the northeast shore of the lake.

Activities & Attractions: Fishing; handicapped-access fishing platform; boating; boat launch and courtesy dock.

Natural Features: Located in a canyon on the east bank of the Missouri River below Canyon Ferry Dam; a few large hardwoods and bushes are in the area, but most campsites are unshaded; bordered by evergreen-dotted hills; elevation 3600'.

Season, Fees & Phone: Open all year, with limited services in winter; 14 day limit; please see Appendix for standard Montana state park fees; park office (406) 444-4475.

Camp Notes: One of the favorite places at Canyon Ferry Lake isn't on the lake at all. Riverside is packed full of campers, picnickers and fishers (both persons and pelicans) throughout much of the summer. Boat fishermen anchor on the river below the dam and line-up in orderly rows with their bows pointed upstream as if they were positioned in a liquid parking lot.

Montana 69

COURT SHERIFF
Canyon Ferry State Park

Location: West-central Montana southeast of Helena.

Access: From the junction of U.S. Highways 12/287 and Montana Secondary Highway 284 (11 miles southeast of Helena, 22 miles north of Townsend), turn east onto Secondary 284 and follow this paved road easterly across Canyon Ferry Dam and around to the northeast shore of the lake to the recreation area, a total of 11 miles from the main highway.

Facilities: Approximately 40 campsites; sites are small+ to medium-sized, acceptably level, with nominal separation; parking pads are gravel/dirt, mostly short to medium-length straight-ins, plus some long pull-throughs; medium to large tent spots; fire rings; b-y-o firewood is recommended; water at central faucets and a hand pump; vault facilities; (nearby Bureau of Reclamation Visitor Center has restrooms); gravel driveways; small store, gas, laundromat and showers 0.6 mile south on Route 284; complete supplies and services are available in Helena.

Activities & Attractions: Small, gravel, designated swimming beach; boating; fishing for rainbow and brown trout; Canyon Ferry Dam Visitor Center, (Bureau of Reclamation) 0.6 mile north, has outdoor displays about the construction of the dam.

Natural Features: Located on Cave Bay on the northeast corner of Canyon Ferry Lake; campground vegetation consists of grass, short pines and junipers, plus a few hardwoods; hills and mountains with some patchy timber are in the surrounding area; fairly dry environment; elevation 3800'.

Season, Fees & Phone: Open all year, subject to weather conditions, with limited services October to May; 14 day limit; please see Appendix for standard Montana state park fees; park office (406) 444-4475.

Camp Notes: The local views are good--across the small bay and over to the west shore. This is the northernmost camping area on the lake proper. Court Sheriff now also encompasses the former small site known as "Ponderosa" (which you may still see referenced on some maps and literature).

Montana 70

CHINAMAN'S
Canyon Ferry State Park

Location: West-central Montana southeast of Helena.

Access: From the junction of U.S. Highways 12/287 and Montana Secondary Highway 284, (11 miles southeast of Helena, 22 miles north of Townsend), turn east onto Secondary 284; travel east, then around the north end of Canyon Ferry Lake, across the dam, then southerly along the east side of the lake for 11.2 miles; turn west (right) and go 0.1 mile to the campground.

Facilities: 50 campsites in several sections; sites are small to medium-sized, with nominal to fair separation; parking pads are gravel, short to medium+ straight-ins or pull-offs; many pads will require additional leveling; small to medium-sized tent spots, some are level; fire rings; b-y-o firewood is recommended; water at a hand pump; vault facilities; gravel driveway; gas and groceries+, 0.2 mile south on Route 284; complete supplies and services are available in Helena.

Activities & Attractions: Boating; boat launch, dock; fishing.

Natural Features: Located in a narrow, moderately sloping coulee/draw bordering Chinaman Cove on the east shore of Canyon Ferry Lake; some hardwoods and small pines provide limited shelter/shade; timbered hills and mountains lie in the surrounding area; elevation 3800'.

Season, Fees & Phone: Open all year, subject to weather conditions, with limited services October to May; 14 day limit; please see Appendix for standard Montana state park fees; park office (406) 444-4475.

Camp Notes: Chinaman's facilities are minimal, but the rustic, sheltered atmosphere appeals to many campers. Another basic campground near here is Jo Bonner, two miles south of Chinaman's. Jo Bonner's 15 sites are in a considerably more open setting than Chinaman's, but the facilities are similar.

Montana 71

HELLGATE
Canyon Ferry State Park

Location: West-central Montana southeast of Helena.

Access: From the junction of U.S. Highways 12/287 & Montana Secondary Highway 284 (11 miles southeast of Helena, 22 miles north of Townsend), turn east onto Secondary 284; travel east, then around the north end of Canyon Ferry Lake and across the dam, then southerly along the east side of the lake for 17 miles to the Hellgate access road at mile 17 +.1; turn southwest (right) and proceed 0.7 mile to the campground. **Alternate Access:** From U.S. 12 at milepost 2 +.4 (2.4 miles east of the junction of U.S. 12 & 287 in Townsend), head northerly on Montana Secondary 284 parallel to and above the east shore of Canyon Ferry Lake for 16.5 miles to the Hellgate access road and continue as above.

Facilities: 47 campsites; sites are small+, with minimal to fair separation; parking pads are gravel, level, short to medium-length, wide straight-ins; many sites have good, grassy tent spots, but some are sloped; about 10 units have small ramadas over tables; barbecue grills or fireplaces; b-y-o firewood; water at central faucets and hand pumps; vault facilities; (restrooms in the day use area); gravel driveways; gas and groceries+, 5 miles north on Route 284; complete supplies and services are available in Helena.

Activities & Attractions: Excellent boating and fishing (rainbow and brown trout, perch); boat launch and dock; designated swimming area; day use area.

Natural Features: Located on a long peninsula at the lower end of Hellgate Gulch on the east shore of Canyon Ferry Lake; the easternmost section has a long stand of hardwoods, other areas are much more exposed; quite a few waterfront campsites; gravel beach; the lake is flanked by high mountain ranges east and west; elevation 3800'.

Season, Fees & Phone: Open all year, subject to weather conditions, with limited services October to May; 14 day limit; please see Appendix for standard Montana state park fees; park office (406) 444-4475.

Camp Notes: There's little question that this is the best camping facility on Canyon Ferry Lake. Campsites at the tip of a point on the lake are very exposed to the elements, but do they have a view! Many sites along the south shore of a long, slender bay are at water's edge and are better sheltered. The name "Hellgate" dates back to the gold mining days of the 1800's. Some of the most profitable placer diggings in Montana were in the mountains just southeast of this recreation area. Back in the 1860's and 70's, Montana Bar (a *gravel* bar) in Confederate Gulch (now part of Lewis and Clark National Forest) had the far-reaching reputation as "the richest acre of ground in the world".

Montana 72

SKIDWAY
Helena National Forest

Location: West-central Montana southeast of Helena.

Access: From U.S. Highway 12 at milepost 22 (10 miles west of the junction of U.S. 12 & U.S. 89 south of White Sulphur Springs, 23 miles east of Townsend), turn south onto a gravel access road drive up on a narrow, winding road for 1.5 miles to the campground. (Note: the entrance to the access road comes up suddenly, especially from the east, so watch closely.)

Facilities: 11 campsites in 2 loops; sites are fairly large, with generally excellent separation; parking pads are gravel straight-ins, quite well leveled, considering the terrain; some pads are spacious enough to accommodate large rv's; some nice sheltered spaces for tents; fireplaces and/or fire rings; firewood is available for gathering; water at a hand pump; vault facilities; gravel driveways (may be a bit tight for a larger vehicle); limited supplies and services are available in Townsend.

Activities & Attractions: Great views from the campground across a canyon toward forested ridges and mountains; foot and 4wd trails lead into the mountains from near the campground and from several places along Highway 12; fishing on Deep Creek, a few miles to the west.

Natural Features: Located in the Big Belt Mountains at a summit near the source of Deep Creek which flows westerly toward the Missouri River; campground vegetation consists of tall conifers, aspens, and moderately dense underbrush, on a forest carpet of grass and wildflowers; elevation 5900'.

Season, Fees & Phone: May to September; no fee; 14 day limit; Townsend Ranger District (406) 26-3425.

Camp Notes: The setting for this campground is secluded--in among the trees--yet because of the views, a mountaintop atmosphere prevails. The site spacing provides each camper with somewhat better than average privacy and quiet.

Montana 73

MISSOURI HEADWATERS
Missouri Headwaters State Park

Location: Southwest Montana west of Bozeman.

Access: From Interstate 90 Exit 278 for Three Forks/Trident (28 miles west of Bozeman, 57 miles east of Butte), at the north side of the freeway, travel northeast/east on Montana State Highway 2 (toward Trident) for 2 miles; turn north onto Montana Secondary Highway 286 and proceed 1.5 miles to the park boundary; the campground is just ahead, on the west (left) side of the park road.

Facilities: 15 campsites; most sites are small+, level, and are fairly closely spaced; parking pads are gravel, adequate for medium-length vehicles; lots of grassy areas for tents; fire rings; b-y-o firewood is recommended; water at faucets; vault facilities; holding tank disposal station; gravel driveways; nearest supplies are in Three Forks (limited), and Logan (camper supplies), 3 miles west or east, respectively; complete supplies and services are available in Bozeman.

Activities & Attractions: Natural and historical exhibits throughout the park; hilltop observation point and interpretative plaza; settler's log cabin on display in the campground; fishing; boat launch; canoeing, rafting; several day use areas.

Natural Features: Located at the confluence of the Jefferson, Madison and Gallatin Rivers, which join to form the great Missouri River; tall hardwoods are along the river banks, but otherwise the terrain is quite open and basically semi-arid; bordered by rocky bluffs and hills, with views of distant peaks; elevation 4100'.

Season, Fees & Phone: Open all year, with limited services October to April; 14 day limit; please see Appendix for standard Montana state park fees; phone c/o Montana Dept. of Fish Wildlife & Parks Office, Bozeman, (406) 994-4042.

Camp Notes: Their quest for the fabled Northwest Passage had brought Meriwether Lewis and William Clark and their Corps of Discovery to this meeting place of the waters. In late July 1805, they camped here for several days. After some deliberation, they named the Three Forks of the Missouri--the Jefferson, Madison, and Gallatin Rivers--on July 28, 1805. (You've heard of Jefferson and Madison. But Gallatin? He was President Jefferson's Secretary of the *Treasury*. Nice move, Meriwether. Ed.). Three Forks must have held a certain mystique for these first explorers, as it does for many campers today. The following July, on the return trip to the East, Captain Clark and his party camped here again. (On their way back home, Lewis and Clark divided their command and set off on different routes through Montana in order to optimize the use of their congressional credit card.) This park marks the beginning of the Missouri River, the main artery for the largest watershed system in the United States.

LEWIS AND CLARK CAVERNS
Lewis and Clark Caverns State Park

Location: Southwest Montana east of Butte.

Access: From Interstate 90 (eastbound) at Exit 256 for Cardwell/Boulder (31 miles east of Butte, 22 miles west of Three Forks), go to the south side of the freeway, then swing east (left) onto Montana State Highway 2; travel easterly for 7 miles to milepost 7 +.4; turn north (left) into the park; proceed north on the paved main park road for 0.3 mile, then turn west (left) into the campground. **Alternate Access:** From Interstate 90 (westbound) at Exit 274 for Three Forks/Ennis/Helena, at the south side of the freeway, head west on State Highway 2/U.S. Highway 287 for 11 miles; at that point, U.S. 287 splits off to the south, but continue west on State Highway 2 for another 5 miles to the park turnoff and continue as above.

Facilities: 45 campsites; sites are average-sized, fairly well spaced but with minimal visual separation; parking pads are gravel, fairly level, medium to long; some large, level tent sites; barbecue grills; b-y-o firewood; water at several faucets; restrooms, plus vault facilities; gravel driveways; limited supplies in Whitehall, 10 miles west, and Three Forks, 18 miles east.

Activities & Attractions: Guided tours of spectacular limestone caverns (2 miles, 2 hours); visitor centers; short nature trail; amphitheater for campfire programs in summer.

Natural Features: Located on a moderate slope in the Jefferson River Canyon in the Tobacco Root Mountains; campground vegetation consists of mostly sage and grass, plus scattered hardwoods; elevation 4200'.

Season, Fees & Phone: Open all year, with limited services in winter; 14 day limit; please see Appendix for standard Montana state park fees; park office (406) 287-3541.

Camp Notes: The caverns, of course, are a popular attraction. But the terrific views out in the light of day make this a worthwhile stop for campers. Many anglers have a high regard for trout fishing on the Jefferson, and that might be an enjoyable way to wait for the next scheduled tour time or to pass the hours 'til it's dark enough to enjoy a campfire. If you do decide to take one of the tours, bring something warm to wear, good grippy shoes, and a camera with a potent flash. It's OK to take pix just about anywhere except in the batroom. (The *fledermausen* that hang upside down from the ceiling above your group-gathering place are a bit skittish in bright light--and you don't want to provoke a startling incident.)

RED MOUNTAIN
Bear Trap Recreation Area/BLM

Location: Southwest Montana west of Bozeman.

Access: From Montana State Highway 84 at milepost 8 +.5 (8 miles east of Norris, 28 miles west of Bozeman), turn northerly onto a gravel access road and go 0.1 mile to the campground.

Facilities: 8 campsites; (a small group camp is also available); sites are medium-sized, level, well spaced, but with no visual separation; parking pads are gravel, mostly long pull-throughs; large tent areas; fire rings; b-y-o firewood; water at a hand pump; vault facilities; gravel driveway; gas and camper supplies in Norris; complete supplies and services in Bozeman.

Activities & Attractions: Some of the better trout fishing in Montana; rafting is popular.

Natural Features: Located on a riverside flat in Madison River Canyon; sites are unsheltered; bordered by semi-forested hills; Red Mountain rises to 5700' about a mile north of the campground; elevation 4500'.

Season, Fees & Phone: Open all year, subject to weather conditions, with limited services in winter; $6.00; Bureau of Land Management Office, Dillon, (406) 683-2337.

Camp Notes: The Madison River is considered to be "Blue Ribbon" trout habitat. According to wildlife biologists' reports, an average of about 4500 legal trout inhabit each mile of the river. There's good river access from the south bank of the Madison for more than four miles along this route. Plenty of fly fishing action. Equip yourself accordingly.

RUBY CREEK
West Madison Recreation Area/BLM

Location: Southwest Montana southwest of Bozeman.

Access: From U.S. Highway 287 at milepost 30 +.8 (7 miles south of Cameron, 31 miles north of the Montana-Idaho border), turn west at a point just south of the Indian Creek Bridge; drive west for 0.8 mile (and across the McAtee Bridge); turn south onto a hard-surfaced road and continue south for 2.6 miles; turn east (left) into the campground.

Facilities: 28 campsites in 2 loops; sites are large, level, with minimal to nominal separation6 parking pads are gravel, medium to medium+ straight-ins; tent spots are large, but a bit rocky; fireplaces and fire rings; you'd have to range out pretty far to gather much firewood, so b-y-o is recommended; water at hand pumps; vault facilities; gravel driveways; limited supplies and services are available in Ennis, 18 miles north.

Activities & Attractions: River floating; boat ramp at the McAtee Bridge; fishing on the Madison is generally very good to outstanding; nearby backcountry roads for exploring the mountains; Wall Creek Game Range; Yellowstone National Park is an hour's drive to the south.

Natural Features: Located on a vast, rocky, grassy, sage flat along the west bank of the Madison River; a few short hardwoods grow along Ruby Creek, which flows between the 2 loops and into the Madison River; the Madison Range rises to the east and the peaks of the Gravelly Range rise to the west; elev. 5600'.

Season, Fees & Phone: Open all year, subject to weather conditions, with limited services in winter; $6.00; Bureau of Land Management Office, Dillon, (406) 683-2337.

Camp Notes: A great campground for those who appreciate the "wide open spaces". The campsites are good-sized, but the only separation between most of them is distance, and neat rows of boulders which have been planted along the driveways and parking pads. There are unrestricted views of sharp mountain peaks to the east and west, and of the great Madison River Valley to the north and south.

LOCH LEVEN
South Madison Recreation Area/BLM

Location: Southwest Montana southwest of Bozeman.

Access: From U.S. Highway 287 at milepost 22 +.7 (17 miles south of Cameron, 22 miles north of the Montana-Idaho border), turn west onto a paved access road; proceed west for 0.2 mile, then bear north (right) onto a gravel road and continue for 0.9 mile to the campground.

Facilities: 11 campsites; sites are large, with nominal separation; parking pads are gravel, mostly level, medium+ straight-ins; tent spots are large and level, but may be a bit rocky; barbecue grills and/or fire rings; b-y-o firewood is recommended; water at a hand pump; vault facilities; gravel driveway; limited supplies and services are available in Ennis, 26 miles north.

Activities & Attractions: Fishing (reportedly excellent); river floating; small gravel boat launch is located 0.5 mile south, at Palisades Picnic Area; nearby backcountry roads for those who wish to explore the surrounding mountains; Hebgen Lake Visitor Center, 17 miles south, describes the results of the 1959 Madison Canyon Earthquake.

Natural Features: Located on the grassy east bank of the Madison River in the Madison River Valley between the Madison Range and the Gravelly Range; the surrounding hillsides are sage-covered, but the campsites themselves have only bunchgrass for a camp carpet; a few bushes grow near the water's edge; a high, steep, rocky bluff rises from the river's west bank; typically breezy; elevation 5700'.

Season, Fees & Phone: Open all year, subject to weather conditions, with limited services in winter; $6.00; Bureau of Land Management Office, Dillon, (406) 683-2337.

Camp Notes: Loch Leven Campground is in a fairly well protected location--on the valley floor, with a steep, rocky bluff to the west and a sage hillside to the east. The sites still have spectacular views of the river, up and down the valley, and of the mountains bordering the valley.

MADISON RIVER
Beaverhead National Forest

Location: Southwest Montana northwest of West Yellowstone.

Access: From U.S. Highway 287 at either milepost 14 +.6 or 14 +.8 (25 miles south of Cameron, 15 miles north of the Montana-Idaho border), proceed west across the river bridge for 0.25 miles to a fork; the left fork leads 0.7 mile along the river to Madison River Campground; (the right fork leads 100 yards to West Fork Campground).

Facilities: 10 campsites; sites are small to medium-sized, with nominal to fairly good separation; parking pads are gravel, medium to long straight-ins; some pads may need additional leveling; a few large, grassy, but somewhat sloped tent spots; fireplaces; limited firewood is available for gathering in the surrounding area; water at several faucets; vault facilities; pack-it-in/pack-it-out system of trash removal; gravel driveway; adequate supplies and services are available in West Yellowstone.

Activities & Attractions: Excellent fishing on the Madison; Hebgen Lake Earthquake Visitor Center, 10 miles east.

Natural Features: Located along the west bank of the Madison River in the Madison Valley between the Madison and Gravelly Ranges of the Rocky Mountains; campground vegetation varies from mostly grass on the east side, to tall conifers on the west; some sites are notched into the bordering hillside; elev. 5900'.

Season, Fees & Phone: May to September; $6.00; 14 day limit; Madison Ranger District, Ennis, (406) 682-4253.

Camp Notes: Madison River Campground serves well as a fishing camp. (The highway and the private residences just across the river aren't very conspicuous). West Fork Campground (see above for access) has several smaller, sometimes soggy, sites snuggled in among dense vegetation along the West Fork of the Madison River.

WADE LAKE
Beaverhead National Forest

Location: Southwest Montana northwest of West Yellowstone.

Access: From U.S. Highway 287 at milepost 9 +.7 (10 miles north of the Montana-Idaho border, 28 miles south of Cameron), turn west onto Wade Lake Road (gravel); travel 3.4 miles to a fork; take the right fork and proceed 1.7 miles; take a right fork again and continue 0.7 mile on a somewhat steep and twisty road to the campground.

Facilities: 12 campsites; sites are small to medium-sized, with fair to good separation; parking pads are gravel, short to medium-length straight-ins; most pads will require additional leveling; tent sites are at least medium-sized, but may be a bit sloped; fireplaces and fire rings; some firewood is available for gathering in the vicinity; water at several faucets and a hand pump; vault facilities; gravel driveways, a bit steep and narrow in places; adequate supplies and services are available in West Yellowstone, 35 miles east.

Activities & Attractions: Boating; small boat launch; fishing; foot trail leads off toward Cliff Lake Natural Area.

Natural Features: Located on a hillside above Wade Lake, one of several small, mountain lakes in the Madison River drainage; sites are scattered over a fairly steep hillside, with tall conifers, grass and underbrush; most sites have views of the lake through the trees; elevation 6300'.

Season, Fees & Phone: May to September; $8.00; 14 day limit; Madison Ranger District, Ennis, (406) 682-4253.

Camp Notes: Before taking the side trip off the highway in wet weather, you may want to inquire about the condition of the access road. The surprise setting--densely forested hills as opposed to the sage-covered slopes along the Madison River itself--is well worth the 6-mile drive. The scenery is terrific from the campground and from atop nearby ridges. Another nearby lakeside campground, Cliff Point, is located at Cliff Lake. To reach it, take the left fork instead of the second right fork (see Access, above). Cliff Point has 6 sites, drinking water and vaults.

HILLTOP
Beaverhead National Forest

Location: Southwest Montana northwest of West Yellowstone.

Access: From U.S. Highway 287 at milepost 9 +.7 (10 miles north of the Montana-Idaho state line, 28 miles south of Cameron), turn west onto Wade Lake Road (gravel); proceed 3.4 miles to a fork; take the right fork; continue 1.7 miles; at a second fork, take the left fork and continue for 0.1 mile; turn right and proceed up a steep road for 0.9 mile to the campground.

Facilities: 18 campsites; sites are unusually spacious, with fair to good separation; parking pads are gravel, long straight-ins; minor additional leveling may be necessary; some good, large tent sites, but they may be a bit sloped; fireplaces and fire rings; firewood is available for gathering in the vicinity; water at central faucets; vault facilities; gravel driveway; adequate supplies and services are available in West Yellowstone, about 35 miles east.

Activities & Attractions: Super-duper scenery from this vantage point; Cliff Lake and Wade Lake, both within a mile, have boating, fishing and wading; a number of 4wd trails lead off into the wilderness.

Natural Features: Located on Cliff Lake Bench on the east slope of the Gravelly Range of the Rocky Mountains; sites are on a hilltop overlooking the surrounding mountains, valleys and lakes; moderate vegetation in the campground consists of tall conifers, tall grass and light underbrush; a rail fence along much of the campground perimeter helps safeguard visitors who approach the fairly sharp and deep dropoff; elevation 6500'.

Season, Fees & Phone: May to September; $7.00; 14 day limit; Madison Ranger District, Ennis, (406) 682-4253.

Camp Notes: Terrific views in almost every direction: Cliff Lake to the south, a deep forested valley and canyon to the west, and the Madison Range through the trees to the east. If you don't have to have lakefront property, definitely check it out.

GREEK CREEK
Gallatin National Forest

Location: Southwest Montana south of Bozeman.

Access: From U.S. Highway 191 near milepost 58 (31 miles south of Bozeman, 58 miles north of West Yellowstone) turn east or west into the campground.

Facilities: 13 campsites in 2 loops; sites are small+, with nil to nominal separation; parking pads are paved, short to medium-length straight-ins; small tent areas; fire rings or fireplaces; some firewood is available for gathering in the area; water at a hand pump; vault facilities; paved driveways; gas and groceries in Big Sky, 11 miles south; complete supplies and services are available in Bozeman.

Activities & Attractions: Trout fishing (often very good); rafting/floating, usually in June and early July.

Natural Features: Located on a narrow flat along the Gallatin River in Gallatin Canyon; sites are moderately shaded/sheltered by conifers; closely crowded by steep, forested canyon walls; elevation 5600'.

Season, Fees & Phone: May to October; $8.00; 14 day limit; Bozeman Ranger District (406) 587-6920.

Camp Notes: Although it hasn't achieved the World Class status of the Madison River, the Gallatin nonetheless produces many respectable catches. If you're interested in trying your luck, your best bet probably would be to ask around the sports specialty shops in Bozeman or West Yellowstone to find out what's currently "hot" on the river. A couple bucks' investment in local tackle might net a few more fish. (Save your sales receipt. Ed.)

SWAN CREEK
Gallatin National Forest

Location: Southwest Montana south of Bozeman.

Access: From U.S. Highway 191 at milepost 57 +.3 (32 miles south of Bozeman, 57 miles north of West Yellowstone) turn east onto Swan Creek Road (paved), and proceed 0.4 mile or 0.8 mile to the 2 sections of the campground.

Facilities: 13 campsites in 2 sections; most sites are small to medium-sized, with nominal to fair separation; parking pads are reasonably level, mostly short to medium-length straight-ins; small tent areas; fire rings or fireplaces; firewood is available for gathering in the area; water at a hand pump; vault facilities; narrow, paved driveways; gas and groceries in Big Sky, 10 miles south; complete supplies and services are available in Bozeman.

Activities & Attractions: Very good to excellent trout fishing on the Gallatin River and possibly on Swan Creek; numerous gravel roads and hiking trails in the area.

Natural Features: Located on the south bank of Swan Creek, in a side canyon off the main Gallatin River Canyon; a substantial amount of small hardwoods and brush, but not much heavy timber, is within the campground; high, densely forested peaks and ridges loom over the canyon; the Gallatin Range is to the east, Spanish Peaks Wilderness is to the west; elevation 5700'.

Season, Fees & Phone: May to October; $8.00; 14 day limit; Bozeman Ranger District (406) 587-6920.

Camp Notes: Sites in Swan Creek's upper end are slightly larger than those in the lower section. Overall, this is probably the most desirable of the three campgrounds (Swan Creek, Greek Creek and Moose Flat) in this vicinity. If you have a large rv, you might consider Moose Flat Campground, 1 mile south, at milepost 56 +.2, on the west side of the highway. The campsites are on an unshaded sage flat along the river.

Montana 83

RED CLIFF
Gallatin National Forest

Location: Southwest Montana south of Bozeman.

Access: From U.S. Highway 191 at milepost 41 +.4 (6 miles south of Big Sky, 41 miles north of West Yellowstone), turn east and go across the Gallatin River Bridge into the campground.

Facilities: 70 campsites in 2 loops; sites are medium-sized or better, with fair separation; gravel parking pads are gravel, mostly medium-length straight-ins; sites toward the south end tend to be a bit more level than those on the north; some very nice tent spots among the trees or along the river; fire rings and/or barbecue grills; limited firewood is available for gathering, b-y-o is recommended; water at central faucets; vault facilities; gravel driveways; gas and groceries in Big Sky; adequate supplies and services are available in West Yellowstone.

Activities & Attractions: Excellent angling on the Gallatin River; picnic sites along the west bank of the river; Elk Horn Trailhead, with equestrian facilities, at the south end of the campground; surrounding mountains are accessible by 4wd trails; Yellowstone National Park is 40 miles south.

Natural Features: Located in Gallatin Canyon between the Madison Range and the Gallatin Range; some of sites are in an unshaded grassy area but most are in open forest of tall pines, light underbrush and a floor of grass or pine needles; the Gallatin River rushes by within a stone's throw of many sites; forested slopes border the river both east and west; elevation 6400'.

Season, Fees & Phone: June to September; $8.00; 14 day limit; Bozeman Ranger District (406) 587-6920.

Camp Notes: Sites are across the rushing river from the highway, so even though traffic is visible, the noise should be minimal. There's little question that this is the best roadside campground in Gallatin Canyon.

Montana 84

BEAVER CREEK
Gallatin National Forest

Location: Southwest Montana northwest of West Yellowstone.

Access: From U.S. Highway 287 at milepost 6 +.8 (24 miles northwest of West Yellowstone, 7 miles east of the junction of U.S. 287 and Montana State Highway 87), turn south onto a paved access road and proceed 0.7 mile to the campground.

Facilities: 65 campsites in 4 loops; most sites are fairly spacious and well separated; parking pads are gravel, mostly medium to long straight-ins; some pads are quite level, others will require additional leveling; good tenting in about half of the sites; fireplaces; firewood is available for gathering; water at faucets throughout; vault facilities; paved driveways; adequate supplies and services are available in West Yellowstone.

Activities & Attractions: Earthquake Visitor Center (Forest Service), 4 miles west; good fishing and boating on nearby lakes.

Natural Features: Located in an aspen grove on a grassy hill in the center of the Upper Madison River Valley; the valley is flanked by high, timber-covered ridges and peaks; Hebgen Lake and Quake Lake are directly to the east and west, respectively; Beaver Creek enters the river at this spot; elevation 6400'.

Season, Fees & Phone: June to mid-September; $8.00; 15 day limit; Hebgen Lake Ranger District (406) 646-7369.

Camp Notes: If the Yellowstone Park campgrounds are too crowded for you, Beaver Creek would be a good alternative. It's surprising that campgrounds in locations such as this so often go unnoticed by travelers to Yellowstone Country.

Montana 85

CABIN CREEK
Gallatin National Forest

Location: Southwest Montana northwest of West Yellowstone.

Access: From U.S. Highway 287 at milepost 8 +.5 (22 miles northwest of West Yellowstone, 9 miles east of the junction of U.S. 287 & Montana State Highway 87), turn north into the campground.

Facilities: 15 campsites; most sites are medium-sized, with minimal to average separation; parking pads are gravel, level, mostly medium length straight-ins; most sites have adequate level space for tents; fireplaces; firewood is available for gathering nearby; water at faucets; vault facilities in the campground, restrooms are available in the adjacent day use area; paved driveway; camper supplies at several small stores to the east; adequate supplies and services are available in West Yellowstone.

Activities & Attractions: Earthquake Visitor Center (Forest Service) 5 miles west; earthquake information exhibits and Cabin Creek Trail just east of the campground; excellent fishing and boating on nearby lakes.

Natural Features: Located in the Upper Madison River Valley, bordered by tall, timbered ridges and peaks; tall conifers plus some low-level vegetation shelter the campground; the Madison River is about 100 yards south; Hebgen Lake and Quake Lake are just east and west of the campground, respectively; wildlife includes deer, elk, black and grizzly bear; elevation 6300'.

Season, Fees & Phone: June to mid-September; $8.00; 15 day limit; Hebgen Lake Ranger District (406) 646-7369.

Camp Notes: This campground is in a nice creekside setting. If you prefer a campsite without highway activity, a good alternative might be Beaver Creek, two miles west. Either way, please keep your goods under guard, and let the local bruins buy their own dinner.

Montana 86

RAINBOW POINT
Gallatin National Forest

Location: Southwest Montana north of West Yellowstone.

Access: From U.S. Highway 191 at milepost 4 +.9 (5 miles north of West Yellowstone, 43 miles south of Big Sky), turn west onto a gravel forest road (should be signed for "Rainbow Point Campground); travel west-northwest for 3.2 miles, then turn north (right) and continue north and west for 1.8 miles; turn left into the campground.

Facilities: 85 campsites in 4 loops; sites are spacious, with fair to good separation; parking pads are gravel, level, medium-length double-wide, or long straight-ins; tents are not permitted because of potential bear visitations; fireplaces; ample firewood is available for gathering; water at several faucets; vault facilities; gravel driveways; adequate supplies and services are available in West Yellowstone.

Activities & Attractions: Boating; boat launch, 0.1 mile east; fishing; day use area; Yellowstone National Park's West Entrance is 10 miles south.

Natural Features: Located on a forested flat near the south shore of Hebgen Lake; vegetation in the campground consists of tall conifers and tall grass with varying amounts of second growth and underbrush; tall mountain peaks can be seen across the lake from the lakeshore; elevation 6600'.

Season, Fees & Phone: June to September; $9.00; 15 day limit; Hebgen Lake Ranger District, (406) 646-7369.

Camp Notes: In recent years, the campground has not been used to capacity, perhaps because of the strongly worded bear cautions issued by the public agencies. (A jackcamper was killed by a grizzly near here.) If you're self-contained and appreciate good boating opportunities, this is a good campground with plenty of elbow room.

BAKER'S HOLE
Gallatin National Forest

Location: Southwest Montana north of West Yellowstone.

Access: From U.S. Highway 191 at milepost 2 +.8 (2.8 miles north of West Yellowstone, 5 miles south of the junction of U.S. 191 & U.S. 287), turn east into the campground.

Facilities: 72 campsites; sites are generously medium sized, with fair separation; medium to long, level, paved parking pads; some designated trailer units; "closed to tents, tent trailers, pop-up vans or sleeping on the ground due to high bear frequency"; fireplaces; firewood is available for gathering; water at several faucets; vault facilities; paved driveways; adequate supplies and services are available in West Yellowstone.

Activities & Attractions: Very good fly fishing on the Madison; fishing and boating on nearby Hebgen Lake; 3 miles from the West Entrance to Yellowstone Park.

Natural Features: Located on the south bank of the last remaining wild segment of the Madison River; the campground is situated in an open pine forest; some campsites have a river view; tremendous views of the northeast corner of Yellowstone Park to the east; black and grizzly bears are in the area; elevation 6600'.

Season, Fees & Phone: June to September; $9.00; 15 day limit; Hebgen Lake Ranger District (406) 646-7369.

Camp Notes: This campground is named after the broad, flat valley in which it is located. Please note the above restrictions on the types of camping accommodations permitted here. Yellowstone's native residents have been known to prowl through the campground at night, looking for stray victuals that may have been left out on camp tables.

MANY PINES
Lewis and Clark National Forest

Location: Central Montana north of White Sulphur Springs.

Access: From U.S. Highway 89 at milepost 33 +.8 (37 miles north of White Sulphur Springs, 4 miles south of the hamlet of Niehart), turn west into the campground.

Facilities: 23 campsites in a large loop plus an extension; sites are medium-sized, with fair to good separation; parking pads are gravel, wide, fairly short straight-ins; most pads will probably require some additional leveling; about half of the sites would be ok for tent-pitching; some sites have tables situated on the hillside above their parking pads, with steps for access; barbecue grills and fire rings; firewood is available for gathering; water at a hand pump; vault facilities; pack-it-in/pack-it-out trash removal system; gravel driveway; camper supplies are available in Niehart, or Monarch 17 miles north; limited+ supplies and services are available in White Sulphur Springs.

Activities & Attractions: Many gravel roads and 4wd trails in the area; rockhounding.

Natural Features: Located on a forested hillside in the Little Belt Mountains, 5 miles north of the summit of Kings Hill Pass; Belt Creek flows between the campground and the highway; timbered ridges form the east-west boundary of the creek 'corridor'; elevation 6900'.

Season, Fees & Phone: May to October; $6.00; 14 day limit; Kings Hill Ranger District, White Sulphur Springs, (406) 547-3361.

Camp Notes: Although Many Pines certainly does live up to its name, the closed-in atmosphere of heavily forested campgrounds in some other regions is absent here. One possible consideration, though:

the campground is somewhat close to the highway, although nighttime traffic is nominal. You might want to check out Kings Hill Campground, 5 miles south. It's larger and bit farther from the road.

Montana 89

KINGS HILL
Lewis and Clark National Forest

Location: Central Montana north of White Sulphur Springs.

Access: From U.S. Highway 89 at milepost 28 +.5 (at Kings Hill Summit, 32 miles north of White Sulphur Springs), turn west into the campground.

Facilities: 21 campsites in a single large loop; (small group sites are also available); most sites are large, well separated and reasonably level; parking pads are gravel, mostly wide, medium-length straight-ins; a few pads are long pull-throughs; many good tent spots; fire rings and barbecue grills; firewood is available for gathering; water at central faucets; vault facilities; pack-it-in/pack-it-out trash removal system; gravel driveway; camper supplies in Niehart, 10 miles north; limited + supplies are available in White Sulphur Springs.

Activities & Attractions: Numerous gravel roads and 4wd trails in the region; Porphyry Peak Observation Point.

Natural Features: Located in a moderately dense conifer forest at the summit of Kings Hill Pass in the heart of the Little Belt Mountains; the campground extends for approximately 0.3 mile parallel to the highway; elevation 7400'.

Season, Fees & Phone: Mid-May to mid-September; $6.00; 14 day limit; Kings Hill Ranger District, White Sulphur Springs, (406) 547-3361.

Camp Notes: There are some terrific mountain vistas in the Kings Hill area. The climate in this part of the country is drier and a little less forested than in many of the other mountainous regions in Montana; consequently, the local ambience is one of openness and space. Bring an extra blanket.

Montana 90

JUMPING CREEK
Lewis and Clark National Forest

Location: Central Montana north of White Sulphur Springs.

Access: From U.S. Highway 89 at milepost 19 +.3 (22 miles north of White Sulphur Springs, 9 miles south of Kings Hill Summit), turn east/southeast onto the campground access road, and proceed 0.2 mile to the campground.

Facilities: 15 campsites; sites are large, level, and well-separated; parking pads are gravel, extra-wide, short to medium-length straight-ins; large tent areas; barbecue grills and fire rings; firewood is available for gathering; water at a hand pump; vault facilities; pack-it-in/pack-it-out trash removal; gravel driveway; limited + supplies are available in White Sulphur Springs.

Activities & Attractions: Fishing for small trout.

Natural Features: Located on the south bank of Jumping Creek; several sites are creekside; tall conifers, with very little low-level vegetation, shelter/shade the campsites; adjacent to meadows and grazing land; timbered mountains lie in the surrounding area; elevation 5700'.

Season, Fees & Phone: Mid-May to mid-September; $6.00; 14 day limit; Kings Hill Ranger District, White Sulphur Springs, (406) 547-3361.

Camp Notes: True to its name, Jumping Creek itself tumbles and gurgles and skips and bounces over its rocky bottom past the campground. Or did it perhaps get its name from the width of the stream--just wide enough to jump across in some spots? For the trout, try digging up a few local earthworms and drifting them in the riffles with a barbless hook and a split-shot sinker.

Montana 91

GRASSHOPPER
Lewis and Clark National Forest

Location: Central Montana east of White Sulphur Springs.

Access: From U.S. Highway 12 at milepost 49 (7 miles east of White Sulphur Springs, 50 miles west of Harlowton), turn south onto Fourmile Road (gravel); proceed 4.1 miles to a "T" intersection; turn right and continue for 0.2 mile to the campground.

Facilities: 12 campsites; most sites are quite spacious and well separated; parking pads are gravel, wide, short to medium-length straight-ins; some additional leveling may be required; adequate space for a large tent in most sites; barbecue grills and fire rings; firewood is available for gathering; water at a hand pump; vault facilities; pack-it-in/pack-it-out trash removal; gravel driveway; limited+ supplies are available in White Sulphur Springs.

Activities & Attractions: Several foot trails and 4wd roads in the vicinity; the historic mining community of Castle Town is 15 miles southeast of the "T" intersection; small corral for horses.

Natural Features: Located in a small "pocket" next to a meadow in the northern foothills of the high, densely forested Castle Mountains; a small creek (complete with footbridge) tumbles down through the center of the campground; a major elk herd makes its home in this region; elevation 5800'.

Season, Fees & Phone: May to October; no fee (subject to change); 14 day limit; Kings Hill Ranger District, White Sulphur Springs, (406) 547-3361.

Camp Notes: This is certainly one of the nicest forest campgrounds along U.S. 12. Inasmuch as it is located at the end of its own short access road, there usually isn't a lot of traffic in or near the campground except, perhaps, during elk hunting season. Definitely worth considering.

Montana 92

SPRING CREEK
Lewis and Clark National Forest

Location: Central Montana east of White Sulphur Springs.

Access: From U.S. Highway 12 at milepost 68 +.4 (26 miles east of White Sulphur Springs, 31 miles west of Harlowton), turn north onto Spring Creek Road; drive 2 miles on a paved surface, then another 2 miles on gravel, to the campground entrance, on the east side of the road.

Facilities: 10 campsites in 2 loops; sites are large and well separated; parking pads are gravel, short, wide straight-ins; adequate space for a large tent in most sites; fire rings; firewood is available for gathering in the vicinity; water at a hand pump; vault facilities; gravel driveways; camper supplies in Checkerboard, near milepost 63; limited+ to adequate supplies are available in White Sulphur Springs and Harlowton.

Activities & Attractions: Pleasant views; fishing for small trout; several good forest roads for easy exploration of the area.

Natural Features: Located on the bank of Spring Creek; most sites are streamside; hardwoods and some pines in the campground; situated in a narrow valley with low, timber-topped ridges along either side; elevation 5300'.

Season, Fees & Phone: May to October; $6.00; 14 day limit; Musselshell Ranger District, Harlowton, (406) 632-4391.

Camp Notes: This camp is located in a pleasant creekside setting surrounded by the more "open" forest lands typical of this part of Montana. It's just far enough off the main highway so it's conveniently accessible, but not overused.

Montana
East Central
Please refer to the Montana map in the Appendix

Montana 93

ACKLEY LAKE
Ackley Lake State Recreation Area

Location: Central Montana southwest of Lewistown.

Access: From U.S. Highway 87/Montana State Highway 200 at milepost 58 +.8 (20 miles west of Lewistown, 4 miles southeast of Moccasin), turn south onto Montana Secondary Highway 239 and travel 0.6 mile into and through the town of Hobson to a "T" intersection at the south end of town (by the high school); swing west (right) continuing on Secondary 239 for another 0.9 mile to a 3-way junction; turn south (left) onto Montana Secondary Highway 400 and go 3.3 miles (the road makes a couple of sharp curves); turn west (right, at an irrigation ditch) onto a gravel road and proceed 1 mile; turn south (left, at a large farm in a stand of hardwoods on the southwest corner of the intersection) and drive a final 0.9 mile on a gravel access road to the camping areas.

Facilities: Approximately 25 camp/picnic sites; (a small group site is also available); sites are small+ to medium-sized, most are tolerably level, with nominal separation; parking surfaces are gravel or grass, medium to long straight-ins or pull-offs; enough space for large tents; small ramadas (sun or sun/wind shelters) for about two-thirds of the sites; fire rings and/or barbecue grills; b-y-o firewood; water at a hand pump; vault facilities; pack-it-in/pack-it-out system of trash removal; gravel driveways; limited gas and groceries in Hobson; adequate+ supplies and services are available in Lewistown.

Activities & Attractions: Fishing for small rainbow trout (average 12"); boating; boat launch.

Natural Features: Located around the north and east shores of Ackley Lake; the lake lies in Judith Basin, an immense valley drained by the Judith River, which flows near the park; park vegetation consists mostly of tall grass and scattered hardwoods; most sites lack natural shade/shelter; mountain ranges rise in most directions around the Basin; elevation 3800'.

Season, Fees & Phone: Open all year, subject to weather and road conditions; principal season is May to October; 14 day limit; please see Appendix for standard Montana state park fees; phone c/o Montana Department of Fish Wildlife & Parks Office, Great Falls, (406) 454-3441.

Camp Notes: You'll probably want to b-y-o a little extra shade just in case the ramadas aren't large enough for your operation, or if you have to settle for an unsheltered site. Judith Basin is known for being one of Charlie Russell's favorite stomping grounds. Ol' Charlie, the "Cowboy Artist", is considered by all Montanans (and anyone else with artistic sensitivities) to be the greatest of the Western artists. Many of his drawings and paintings are scenes from in and around Judith Basin.

Montana 94

DEADMAN'S BASIN
Deadman's Basin State Recreation Area

Location: Central Montana northwest of Billings.

Access: From U.S. Highway 12 at milepost 120 +.4 (19 miles east of Harlowton, 11 miles west of Ryegate), turn north onto a gravel access road and proceed 0.6 mile to the park.

Facilities: 25 camp/picnic sites; sites are medium to large, with nominal to good separation; parking spaces are gravel/grass, spacious enough for large vehicles, though many may require some additional leveling; large, grassy tent spots; a few sites have small ramadas (sun shelters); a few barbecue grills or fire rings; definitely b-y-o firewood; no drinking water; vault facilities; gravel driveways; gas and groceries in Ryegate; limited+ supplies and services are available in Harlowton.

Activities & Attractions: Boating; small boat launch; windsurfing; typically good fishing.

Natural Features: Located on the south shore of a small, prairie lake in the Musselshell River Valley; sites are spread out for 2 miles along the shore; some sites are on a bluff overlooking the lake and some are lakeside; a few of the sites have some smaller shade trees but the others are very much in the open; the tallgrass hills around the rim of the basin are dotted with short pines; the Big Snowy Mountains are prominently visible to the north; typically breezy; elevation 4100'.

Season, Fees & Phone: Open all year, subject to weather and road conditions; no fee (subject to change); 14 day limit; phone c/o Montana Department of Fish Wildlife & Parks Office, Billings, (406) 252-4654.

Camp Notes: Deadman's Basin is particularly pleasant in late spring, when the prairie grass is green and the Big Snowy's are still wearing their winter caps. By midsummer, the basin becomes a gilt-rimmed bowl as the tall grass turns to gold in almost single-digit humidity levels. Windsurfers are just beginning to discover this place. If you're inclined toward campsites with drinking water and restrooms, you may find the small campground at Chief Joseph Park in Harlowton to be a useful U.S. 12 stop. The city park is located off the south side of the highway, almost directly across from the Wheatland County Court House. Chief Joseph has plenty of grass for tents, and a few sites with electrical hookups, for a modest fee.

SODA BUTTE
Gallatin National Forest

Location: South-central Montana just east of Yellowstone Park.

Access: From U.S. Highway 212 at milepost 5 (1 mile east of Cooke City, 5 miles east of the Yellowstone Park boundary, 60 miles west of Red Lodge), turn south into the campground. (Note: If you're approaching from Red Lodge and points east, this requires a hairpin left turn across traffic; from the west, it'll be the first right turn past the Cooke City marble orchard; although Soda Butte Campground and neighboring Colter Campground are located in Montana, they are accessible only through Wyoming via U.S. 212 or from Yellowstone Park.)

Facilities: 21 campsites; sites are medium-sized, with fair to fairly good separation; parking pads are gravel, medium-length straight-ins; additional leveling will be required in most sites; large grassy areas for tenting; fire rings; ample firewood is available for gathering; water at several faucets; vault facilities; gravel driveway; gas and camper supplies+ in Cooke City.

Activities & Attractions: Nearby trailheads for trips into the high lakes area of the Absaroka-Beartooth Wilderness; Cooke City has a number of seasonal festivals; Yellowstone Park.

Natural Features: Located on hilly terrain in a narrow valley along Soda Butte Creek in the Absaroka Range, just west of Colter Pass; most sites have some shelter/shade provided by tall conifers; the sites are spread out for almost half a mile along a pleasant creekside meadow; early in the season the grounds tend to be soggy, and the driveway may be rutty; elevation 7600'.

Season, Fees & Phone: June to September; $7.00; 14 day limit; Beartooth Ranger District, Red Lodge, (406) 446-2103.

Camp Notes: Soda Butte Creek is named for a large mineral formation in Yellowstone Park about 20 miles southwest of here. In 1870, the first prospectors arrived in this country via Soda Butte Creek. During the ensuing years, many gold seekers combed the nearby mountains, and in 1883 Cooke City was founded. At that time, the boomtown had 135 log cabins, two general stores and thirteen saloons.

COLTER
Gallatin National Forest

Location: South-central Montana just east of Yellowstone Park.

Access: From U.S. Highway 212 at milepost 6 (2 miles east of Cooke City, 6 miles east of the Yellowstone Park boundary, 59 miles west of Red Lodge) turn north into the campground.

Facilities: 23 campsites in 2 concentric loops; sites are quite spacious, with fairly good separation; parking pads are gravel straight-ins, long enough to accommodate most rv's; additional leveling may be required in some sites; some good tent spots; fireplaces; plenty of firewood is available for gathering in the area; water at several faucets; vault facilities; gravel driveways; gas and camper supplies+ in Cooke City.

Activities & Attractions: Foot trails into the wilderness areas; 4-wheel-drive trails lead toward Goose Lake and Lulu Pass; stream fishing.

Natural Features: Located on a hill in the Absaroka Range, just west of Colter Pass, on the edge of the Absaroka-Beartooth Wilderness; campground vegetation consists of tall conifers adjacent to a tallgrass meadow; the flames of the cataclysmic Yellowstone fires of '88 were conquered at the very edge of the campground; elevation 7600'.

Season, Fees & Phone: June to September; $7.00; 14 day limit; Beartooth Ranger District, Red Lodge, (406) 446-2103.

Camp Notes: This campground has a rather unusual arrangement. There is an interior grassy park (meadow) around which there is a loop of campsites, and around which there is *another* loop of campsites. All sites have plenty of elbow room, and there are some excellent mountain views from here. The campground is named for John Colter, a member of the Lewis and Clark Expedition. Colter, an irrepressible adventurer, was the first White man to explore the Yellowstone Country. His colorful tales about the area's steamy geological phenomena and strong sulfurous smells sparked newspaper articles that labeled the region "Colter's Hell".

BASIN & CASCADE
Custer National Forest

Location: South-central Montana south of Red Lodge.

Access: From U.S. Highway 212 at milepost 68 +.2 (on the south edge of Red Lodge, 24 miles north of the Montana-Wyoming border), turn west/southwest onto West Fork Road/Forest Road 71 (paved) and travel 2.8 miles to a fork; take the left fork (continuing on pavement) remaining on West Fork Road for another 4.3 miles; turn northerly (right) into Basin Campground; or continue past Basin Campground for another 3 miles on gravel, then turn south (left) into Cascade Campground.

Facilities: 30 campsites in each campground; sites are generally medium-sized, with nominal to fair separation; parking pads are hard-surfaced, short+ to medium-length straight-ins, many are double wide; a bit of additional leveling may be needed on some pads; fire rings; firewood is available for gathering nearby; water at hand pumps; vault facilities; paved driveways; adequate supplies and services are available in Red Lodge.

Activities & Attractions: Fishing for small planted trout on Wild Bill Lake, which you'll pass on the way to the campgrounds; Basin Trailhead near Basin Campground.

Natural Features: Located near the West Fork of Rock Creek in Granite Basin on the lower north slope of the Beartooth Range; campground vegetation consists mainly of conifers that provide light-medium to medium shelter/shade for most campsites; closely flanked by high, steep, rocky, slopes; elevation 6400' in Basin, 7000' in Cascade.

Season, Fees & Phone: May to October; $8.00; 10 day limit; Beartooth Ranger District, Red Lodge, (406) 446-2103.

Camp Notes: According to local folklore, many years ago a splinter faction of Crow Indians said "*adios*" (or whatever) to the main tribe and moved into these foothills. They painted their council teepee with red clay, from whence sprang the name of this locale. Some anthropologists theorize that, long before the Crow took up residence around present-day Red Lodge, prehistoric people found their way into this area. Evidence suggests that ambitious aboriginals may have wandered through here a couple of million years earlier than has been commonly believed.

PARKSIDE
Custer National Forest

Location: South-central Montana south of Red Lodge.

Access: From U.S. Highway 212 at milepost 57 +.3 (12 miles south of Red Lodge, 13 miles north of the Montana-Wyoming border, 56 miles northeast of Cooke City), turn west/southwest onto the paved Rock Creek Recreation Area Road/Forest Road 421; proceed 0.4 mile, then turn right into the campground.

Facilities: 16 campsites in 2 loops; sites are medium-sized, with good to very good separation; parking pads are paved, reasonably level, short to medium-length straight-ins, many are double-wide; medium to large tent areas; fire rings; firewood is available for gathering in the surrounding forest; water at a hand pump; vault facilities; paved driveways; adequate supplies and services are available in Red Lodge.

Activities & Attractions: Sightseeing along the Beartooth Highway; spectacular Rock Creek Viewpoint 8 miles south; road to Hellroaring Plateau; hiking trails to nearby lakes.

Natural Features: Located on slightly sloping flats along the banks of Rock Creek, nestled up against the rugged Beartooth Mountains; sites are well-sheltered by conifers; about half of the sites are streamside; deer, bear and bighorn sheep reside in the general area; elevation 6900'.

Season, Fees & Phone: May to October; $8.00; 10 day limit; Beartooth Ranger District, Red Lodge, (406) 446-2103.

Camp Notes: Some of the most breathtaking scenery available anywhere is within a short drive or hike from here. The rough, rocky, but driveable road to Hellroaring Plateau leads seven miles up the mountainside from the campground. The Plateau offers stunning views of the Beartooth-Absaroka region which few visitors experience. (Rough and rugged mechanical mountain goats with 4wd who pick their way around the rocks and over the washouts up to the Plateau are occasionally greeted at the top by Bugs--air-cooled, not airborne, Bugs.)

GREENOUGH LAKE
Custer National Forest

Location: South-central Montana south of Red Lodge.

Access: From U.S. Highway 212 at milepost 57 +.3 (12 miles south of Red Lodge, 13 miles north of the Montana-Wyoming border), turn west/southwest onto the paved Rock Creek Recreation Area Road/Forest Road 421; proceed 1 mile south and west (past the turnoff to Parkside Campground, above); turn south (left) for another 0.3 paved mile to the campground.

Facilities: 18 campsites; sites are medium-sized, essentially level, with nominal to good separation; parking pads are paved, medium to medium+ straight-ins; nearly all sites are suitable for tent camping; fire rings; firewood is available for gathering nearby; water at a hand pump; vault facilities; paved driveway; adequate supplies and services are available in Red Lodge.

Activities & Attractions: Short foot trail from the campground to tiny Greenough Lake (0.25 mile); several other major backcountry hiking trails, including Parkside National Recreation Trail, and primitive roads in the area; spectacular drive along the Beartooth Highway.

Natural Features: Located on a gently sloping flat near the confluence of Wyoming and Rock Creeks, in a canyon bordered by the towering peaks of the Beartooth Range; a mixture of pines and low hardwoods provides medium shade/shelter for campsites; elevation 6900'.

Season, Fees & Phone: May to October; $8.00; 10 day limit; Beartooth Ranger District, Red Lodge, (406) 446-2103.

Camp Notes: Of the trio of principal forest camps in Rock Creek Recreation Area, Greenough Lake has a slight edge in ambience over the other two. Perhaps that explains why it seems to be especially popular with tent campers, who are closer to their surroundings than their rv counterparts.

LIMBER PINE
Custer National Forest

Location: South-central Montana south of Red Lodge.

Access: From U.S. Highway 212 at milepost 57 +.3 (12 miles south of Red Lodge, 13 miles north of the Montana-Wyoming border), turn west/southwest onto the paved Rock Creek Recreation Area Road/Forest Road 421; proceed 1.2 miles south and west (past the turnoffs to Parkside and Greenough Campgrounds, above); cross the short Rock Creek bridge, then roll south (left) into the campground.

Facilities: 13 campsites; sites are generally medium-sized, with fair to very good separation; parking pads are paved, short to medium-length straight-ins; a little additional leveling may be needed on some pads; fire rings; firewood is available for gathering nearby; water at a hand pump; vault facilities; paved driveway; adequate supplies and services in Red Lodge.

Activities & Attractions: Primarily sightseeing; rough, but passable, road to the astounding views from atop Hellroaring Plateau; several foot trails in the vicinity.

Natural Features: Located along the west bank of Rock Creek; campsites are sheltered by moderately tall conifers; the terrain is slightly more rolling and open than that of other campgrounds in the area; situated in a narrow valley/canyon virtually surrounded by the lofty peaks of the Beartooth Range; elevation 6900'.

Season, Fees & Phone: May to October; $8.00; 10 day limit; Beartooth Ranger District, Red Lodge, (406) 446-2103.

Camp Notes: Pleasant creekside atmosphere, plus excellent views, at Limber Pine. If, perchance, Limber Pine and the other two main camps in the Rock Creek cluster (Parkside and Greenough Lake) are filled, there are three bare-bones alternatives in this locale you could consider for a night's stay on public property. The closest is M-K Campground, two miles south of Limber Pine on a gravel road. The remaining duo consists of Sheridan and Ratine Campgrounds, located several miles north of here along a gravel side loop off the east side of U.S. 212. The turnoffs to Sheridan and Ratine are near mileposts 61 and 64.

COONEY
Cooney State Recreation Area

Location: South-central Montana southwest of Billings.

Access: From U.S. Highway 212 at milepost 90 +.7 in the burg of Boyd (22 miles southwest of Interstate 90 Exit 434 in Laurel, 22 miles north of Red Lodge), head west/southwest on Cooney Dam Road (paved for the first 3 miles, then gravel) for 7.1 miles to a 3-way intersection; turn south (left) onto a local gravel road and proceed 0.6 mile to a triangle intersection; turn west (right) onto another local gravel road and travel west/southwest on the south shore road from 0.6 mile to 4 miles to the Marshall Cove, Cottonwood, Fisherman's Point, and Red Lodge Creek camp areas.

(Note: there are at least 3 other ways of getting to Cooney, principally from State Highway 78, but all involve many more miles of gravel travel and none are any quicker than the access listed above--unless you're coming from Absarokee, Roscoe, Fishtail or the other major metropolitan areas near '78'.)

Facilities: *Marshall Cove, Cottonwood, Fisherman's Point, Red Lodge Creek*: approximately 60 campsites in 4 areas; (a few sites are also available in the reservoir's North Shore area); sites are small to medium-sized, most are tolerably level, with minimal to fair separation; parking surfaces are gravel or grass, short to medium+ pull-offs or straight-ins; adequate space for medium to large tents; ramadas (sun shelters) for a few sites; fire rings; b-y-o firewood; water at central hand pumps; vault facilities; gravel driveways; camper supplies at a local store; gas and groceries+ in Joliet, 5 miles north of Boyd.

Activities & Attractions: Fishing for rainbow trout and walleye; boating; boat launches; designated swimming area.

Natural Features: Located in a basin or small valley along the shore of Cooney Reservoir, an impoundment on Red Lodge Creek; sites in the Marshall Cove area are moderately shaded/sheltered, other areas are minimally to lightly shaded; bordered by grassy hills dotted with brush and some evergreens and hardwoods; the Beartooth Mountains rise to 13,000' a few miles south; elevation 4300'.

Season, Fees & Phone: Open all year, subject to weather, with limited services September to April; 14 day limit; please see Appendix for standard Montana state park fees; phone c/o Montana Department of Fish Wildlife & Parks Office, Billings, (406) 252-4654; summer park phone (406) 445-2326.

Camp Notes: Cooney SRA (usually called "Cooney Dam" by the locals) provides the only public camping facilities in the entire middle Yellowstone Valley. Subjectively, the 'best' subdivision is the Red Lodge Creek area--plenty of elbow room there. Local agriculture relies heavily on the reservoir for irrigation water, so by late summer the lake is usually drawn down to a puddle of its springtime self. Spectacular views of the majestic Beartooth Mountains from many points around the lake.

CAMP CREEK
Public Lands/BLM Recreation Site

Location: Central Montana southwest of Malta.

Access: From U.S. Highway 191 at milepost 109 (47 miles south of Malta, 21 miles north of the Missouri River bridge), turn west/northwest onto a wide, level gravel road, and proceed 6.5 miles to the Zortman intersection; continue straight ahead past the intersection for 0.6 mile to the campground access road; turn north/northeast (right), proceed 0.6 mile on a narrow road to the campground. **Alternate Access:** From U.S. 191 at milepost 118, turn west onto a gravel road, drive 9 miles to the Zortman intersection; turn right and continue as above.

Facilities: 13 campsites; sites are large and well-separated; parking pads are gravel, long pull-throughs or straight-ins; some additional leveling may be required; a few good tent spots; barbecue grills; firewood is available for gathering in the area; water at a hand pump; vault facilities; gas and camper supplies in Zortman; adequate supplies and services are available in Malta.

Activities & Attractions: Many old mining diggings in this region; the fifth largest gold mine in the U.S. is near here; limited fishing on Beaver Creek; hiking.

Natural Features: Located in a little 'pocket' near Beaver Creek on the east edge of the Little Rockies, a small, isolated mountain range situated between the Missouri Breaks and the prairie of the Montana 'Highline'; sites are sheltered by mountain hardwoods and conifers; elevation 4100'.

Season, Fees & Phone: April to November; no fee (subject to change); 14 day limit; Bureau of Land Management Office, Malta, (406) 654-1240.

Camp Notes: The Little Rockies area is a relatively 'undiscovered' part of Montana. Another small BLM campground, Montana Gulch, 9 miles from here near Landusky, lacks water, but is still a pleasant place to camp. The city of Malta also offers camping in its midtown city park at the junction of U.S. 2 & U.S. 191. Trafton Park has plenty of room for rv's or tents, water and restrooms, along the bank of the Milk River.

Montana

East

Please refer to the Montana map in the Appendix

Montana 103

FORT PECK WEST
Fort Peck Lake/Corps of Engineers Park

Location: Northeast Montana southeast of Glasgow.

Access: From Montana State Highway 24 at milepost 57 +.3 (0.6 mile northwest of the junction of State Highways 24 & 117 near the community of Fort Peck, 16 miles southeast of Glasgow), turn southwest at the information station and follow a paved road for 0.7 mile to the campground.

Facilities: 12 campsites, including 6 with electrical hookups; sites are small+ to medium-sized, with nominal separation; hookup sites have reasonably level, long, paved, pull-through pads, remainder of the sites have straight-ins; good tent-pitching spots; several sites have sheltered tables; fireplaces or barbecue grills; b-y-o firewood; water at central faucets; restrooms with showers; holding tank disposal station; paved driveways; gas and groceries at several small stores in the vicinity; adequate supplies and services are available in Glasgow.

Activities & Attractions: Excellent boating; boat launch; fishing for walleye, northern pike and similar species; tours of the Fort Peck Power Plant and Museum; nice playground in the nearby day use area.

Natural Features: Located on an exposed, grassy hill overlooking Fort Peck Lake; planted hardwoods offer some shade in the campground; semi-barren terrain in the vicinity, evergreen-dotted hills are nearby in the Pines area; abundance of wildlife; windy; elevation 2300'.

Season, Fees & Phone: Mid-May to mid-September; $6.00 for a standard site, $8.00 for a hookup site; 14 day limit; Fort Peck CoE Project Office (406) 526-3411.

Camp Notes: Although it is less sheltered than Downstream Campground, 2 miles east, the views here are more spectacular. Semi-primitive camping is also available at a small CoE camp in the Pines area, a dozen gravel miles west of here. The area also has a boat ramp. It's very pleasant at the Pines, but don't even *think* about heading in (or out) after rain or snow greases the gooey gravel surface. (What a trip!)

Montana 104

DOWNSTREAM
Fort Peck Lake/Corps of Engineers Park

Location: Northeast Montana southeast of Glasgow.

Access: From Montana State Highway 24 at milepost 55 +.1 (1.5 miles east of the junction of State Routes 24 and 117 near the community of Fort Peck, 55 miles north of the intersection of State Routes 24 and 200), turn north at the Fort Peck power substation; proceed north/northwest 0.8 mile down a steep, paved road, past the power plant, to the campground.

Facilities: 57 campsites, including 51 with electrical hookups; sites are large, level, with nominal separation; parking pads are paved, very long straight-ins; excellent tent-pitching spots; barbecue grills, plus some fireplaces; b-y-o firewood; water at several faucets; restrooms with showers; holding tank disposal station in Fort Peck; paved driveways; gas and groceries at several small stores in the vicinity; adequate supplies and services are available in Glasgow, 18 miles northwest.

Activities & Attractions: Excellent boating and fishing on Fort Peck Lake, or on the Missouri River below Fort Peck Dam; museum and visitor center; nature trail; amphitheater; large playground in the adjacent day use area.

Natural Features: Located on a large, grassy flat in a grove of hardwoods on the west bank of the Missouri River, just below Fort Peck Dam; elevation 2000'.

Season, Fees & Phone: Mid-May to mid-September, but available for camping with limited services and no fee at other times; 14 day limit; $6.00 for a standard site, $8.00 for a hookup site; Fort Peck CoE Project Office (406) 526-3411.

Camp Notes: Many campers consider Downstream to be the best of the public campgrounds in northeast Montana because of it's excellent facilities, and because of its nicely sheltered and shaded location.

Montana 105

AFTERBAY
Bighorn Canyon National Recreation Area

Location: South-central Montana southwest of Hardin.

Access: From Interstate 90 Exit 495 for Hardin, head west on Montana Secondary Route 313 for 43 miles to Fort Smith; at Fort Smith, continue straight ahead, past the water tower and the visitor center, for 1 mile to a point just at the west end of the housing project; bear right onto the gravel access road which leads down to the campground.

Facilities: 24 campsites on two tiers; sites are small and closely spaced; parking pads are gravel, small to medium-sized, level, mostly straight-ins; room for a tent in most sites, but the surface is rocky; fireplaces; b-y-o firewood; water at several faucets; restrooms; gravel driveways; camper supplies in Fort Smith; adequate supplies and services are available in Hardin.

Activities & Attractions: Visitor center; paved boat ramps nearby for floating the river; the boat launch which serves the main part of Bighorn Canyon Reservoir is 10 miles south; large playground nearby; campfire programs on summer weekends.

Natural Features: Located below Bighorn Canyon Dam on the shore of a secondary impoundment on the Bighorn River; a single line of mature hardwoods in the campground provides some shelter/shade; multi-colored bluffs and hills are in view from all sites; dry, windy climate; elevation 3300'.

Season, Fees & Phone: Open all year; no fee; 14 day limit; park headquarters, Fort Smith, (406) 666-2412.

Camp Notes: OK, Afterbay *is* 44 miles from the Interstate, and its facilities aren't world class. But its redeeming qualities are remoteness, year 'round availability, and proximity to some of the best boating and fishing in the region. And it's a freebie!

Montana 106

RED SHALE
Custer National Forest

Location: Southeast Montana west of Broadus.

Access: From U.S. Highway 212 at milepost 68 +.8 (6.3 miles east of Ashland, 59 miles west of Broadus), turn north into the campground.

Facilities: 14 campsites in 2 loops; most sites are large and well separated; parking pads are gravel, short, double-wide straight-ins that will probably require some additional leveling; large, level tent spots with a grass and pine needle base; fireplaces; some firewood is available for gathering in the vicinity; water at central faucets; vault facilities; gravel driveways; ranger station in Ashland; gas and groceries in Ashland; limited+ to adequate supplies and services are available in Broadus.

Activities & Attractions: Hiking; limited fishing nearby.

Natural Features: Located on two, small, grassy hilltops moderately covered with pines, but with very little underbrush; red earth, pine-covered hills lie throughout the area; Otter Creek, the major stream in this locale, is just west of here; elevation 2900'.

Season, Fees & Phone: May to October; $6.00; 14 day limit; Ashland Ranger District (406) 784-2344.

Camp Notes: This isn't what most people envision when they think of Eastern Montana. The territory around here is red and green, in contrast to the gold and brown of most of the eastern part of the state. There are some pleasant views of hills and low mountains from most sites. A nice, out-of-the-way place.

TONGUE RIVER RESERVOIR
Tongue River Reservoir State Recreation Area

Location: Southeast Montana southeast of Hardin.

Access: From Interstate 90 Exit 16 signed for "Decker Mont" (16 miles southeast of the Montana-Wyoming border, 7 miles north of Sheridan, Wyoming), drive east on Wyoming State Highway 339 for 1 mile to a "T" junction; turn north (left) onto Wyoming State Highway 338 and go north/northeast for 11 miles to the Wyoming-Montana border; pick up Montana Secondary Highway 314 and continue traveling northeast for another 10 miles (past the Decker Mine) to milepost 10 +.1; turn east onto a park access road (begins as paved, becomes gravel after a few yards) and proceed 0.4 mile to the park boundary; continue east then north for 0.2 miles to 2 miles to the camp areas.

Facilities: Approximately 60 primitive campsites; sites are randomly placed and spaced, with dirt/gravel/grass parking spaces large enough for most vehicles; large tent areas; fire rings; b-y-o firewood; no drinking water; pack-it-in/pack-it-out system of trash removal; gravel/dirt driveways; complete supplies and services are available in Sheridan.

Activities & Attractions: Boating; boat launch; fishing for bass, walleye, northern pike and crappie.

Natural Features: Located on a half-dozen points of land and bays along the west shore of 10-mile-long Tongue River Reservoir; vegetation on the hilly terrain consists of expanses of range grass with stands of hardwoods and flecks of junipers; campsites range from unshaded to lightly shaded; bordered by red and beige hills, bluffs and small mountains; elevation 3600'.

Season, Fees & Phone: Open all year, with limited services in winter; 14 day limit; please see Appendix for standard Montana state park fees; phone c/o Montana Department of Fish Wildlife & Parks Office, Miles City, (406) 232-4365.

Camp Notes: Simple, honest Western scenery here. A couple of good-sized islands on the reservoir provide an additional element of interest. Southeast Montana is coal country and the facilities in the recreation area have been funded by the local coal company. Environmentally preferred, low-sulphur coal is mined here and shipped via 'unit trains' comprised of hundreds of identical railroad cars to fuel-hungry Midwest power plants.

MAKOSHIKA
Makoshika State Park

Location: Eastern Montana south of Glendive.

Access: From Interstate 90 Exit 215 for Glendive (27 miles west of the Montana-North Dakota border, 37 miles northeast of Terry), travel south and west on Business Route I-94/Merrill Avenue through the center of town for 1.5 miles; at the far west end of Glendive, look for a very large Indian arrow pointing south (left); turn south, go through an underpass, and continue on a well-signed route south on Barry Street to Taylor, then west (right) on Taylor to Snyder, then south (left) on Snyder to the park boundary; continue ahead for 1.3 miles to the campground.

Facilities: 16 campsites adjacent to a small, paved parking lot; adequate space for large vehicles and tents; fire rings; b-y-o firewood; water at a central faucet; vault facilities; complete supplies and services are available in Glendive.

Activities & Attractions: Scenic views of badlands; nature trail; hiking trail; amphitheater for interpretive programs.

Natural Features: Located in an area of rocky, colorful badlands; vegetation consists of sparse grass and scattered pines and junipers; elevation 2200'.

Season, Fees & Phone: Open all year, with limited services in winter; 14 day limit; please see Appendix for standard Montana state park fees; park office (406) 365-8596.

Camp Notes: Makoshika (Mah-*koh*-shih-kah) is a Sioux word which has been variously translated as "badlands", "bad earth" or "hell cooled over". (In midsummer, you can drop the "cooled over" part.) The park is best-known for its radical geology, but in recent years it also has been the scene of some serious dinosaur digging. Interesting place, actually.

MEDICINE ROCKS
Medicine Rocks State Park

Location: Southeast Montana south of Baker.

Access: From Montana State Highway 7 at milepost 11 +.4 (24.5 miles south of Baker, 11 miles north of Ekalaka), turn west into the park entrance and follow a dirt road (not recommended for large trailers) which leads 0.8 mile to the camping area.

Facilities: Approximately 20 camp/picnic sites; sites are small to medium-sized, marginally level enough for rv's, and fairly good for tents; fire rings; b-y-o firewood; water at a hand pump; vault facilities; pack-it-in/pack-it-out system of trash removal; dirt driveways; gas and limited groceries are available in Ekalaka.

Activities & Attractions: Exploring the park on foot.

Natural Features: Located on an isolated ridge studded with strangely eroded sandstone formations; vegetation consists of short to medium-tall pines on a surface of tall grass; rolling prairie surrounds the park; forested hills and low mountains rise in the distance to the south; elevation 3400'.

Season, Fees & Phone: Available all year; no fee (subject to change); 14 day limit; phone c/o Montana Department of Fish Wildlife & Parks Office, Miles City, (406) 232-4365.

Camp Notes: The Indians believed "Big Medicine" emanated from this rocky island that rises above a sea of prairie grass. Much of the park's interest lies in its contrast with the surrounding terrain. A good place to sit and ponder the prairie.

MACNAB POND
Custer National Forest

Location: Southeast corner of Montana south of Baker.

Access: From the town of Ekalaka, (35 miles south of Baker) drive south on Montana Secondary Route 323 (paved) for 7.3 miles; turn east at the "MacNab Campground" and "Mill Iron" signs onto a gravel road (Mill Iron Road); proceed east for 0.3 mile, then turn north onto the campground access road, and continue for 0.7 mile to the campground.

Facilities: 10 campsites; sites are medium to large and adequately spaced; parking spots are gravel/dirt, large and level enough for rv's; satisfactory tent areas; fireplaces, plus some barbecue grills; a limited amount of firewood is available for gathering, b-y-o is suggested; water at a hand pump; vault facilities; pack-it-in/pack-it-out system of trash removal; gravel/dirt driveways; gas and limited groceries in Ekalaka; limited+ supplies and services are available in Baker.

Activities & Attractions: Remoteness; good deer hunting.

Natural Features: Located in an isolated section of the national forest; sparse to medium-dense pines, tall grass, and a little brush shelter the campground; low mountains and hills covered with medium-height pines border the area; elevation 3800'.

Season, Fees & Phone: Open all year; no fee (subject to change); 14 day limit; Sioux Ranger District, Camp Crook SD, (605) 797-4432.

Camp Notes: Considering this is Eastern Montana, the campground offers some really pleasant local and distant views. The town of Ekalaka (named for an Indian girl), had its start as a saloon in the 1860's--a watering hole for thirsty buffalo hunters and trappers. If you're looking for a place to get away from civilization that offers surprisingly easy access, maybe this is it.

Wyoming

Public Campgrounds

The Wyoming map is located in the Appendix on page 201.

Wyoming

Yellowstone Country

Please refer to the Wyoming map in the Appendix

Wyoming 1

MAMMOTH
Yellowstone National Park

Location: Northwest Wyoming in northern Yellowstone Park.

Access: From North Entrance Road at a point 5 miles south of the North Entrance to Yellowstone National Park at Gardiner, Montana and 1 mile north-east of Mammoth Village, turn northwest (i.e., right, if entering the park) into the campground.

Facilities: 87 campsites in several tiered loops; sites are small+, fairly level, with nominal to fair separation; parking pads are gravel, long pull-throughs; small tent areas; fireplaces; firewood is usually for sale, b-y-o is recommended; water at faucets; restrooms; paved driveways; gas, snacks and showers in Mammoth Village; gas and groceries+ are available in Gardiner, Montana.

Activities & Attractions: Nature walk along Hot Springs Terraces; museum at Mammoth Village has wildlife and historical displays; campfire programs during the summer; cross-country skiing and wildlife-watching opportunities in winter.

Natural Features: Located on a forested hillside (on the inside of a curve in the park road) above Gardner Valley; rocky mountains lie to the east, forested mountains south and west; vegetation consists of light to light-medium hardwoods, evergreens, tall grass and sage; at nearby Mammoth Hot Springs, steaming water cascades over a series of delicately colored rimstone pools creating a series of terraces; wildlife, especially deer and elk, frequent the camp area; elevation 6200'.

Season, Fees & Phone: Open all year, with limited services in winter; $8.00 for a site; $10.00 for the park entrance permit, (valid for 7 days in Yellowstone and Grand Teton National Parks); 7 day camping limit; Yellowstone Park Headquarters, Mammoth, (307) 344-7381.

Camp Notes: Mammoth Campground is right along the roadway in a heavy traffic area, but then it's also close to a number of interesting natural attractions as well. The Gardner Valley is a favorite winter retreat for wildlife and winter sports enthusiasts alike. A moderate microclimate, resulting in part from the warm waters of thermal activities, the topography, and the relatively low elevation, helps maintain favorable temperatures in winter. The campground is a few yards south of the 45th Parallel--halfway between the North Pole and the Equator.

Wyoming 2

INDIAN CREEK
Yellowstone National Park

Location: Northwest Wyoming in northwest Yellowstone Park.

Access: From Grand Loop Road at a point 12 miles north of Norris Junction and 9 miles south of Mammoth, turn west onto a paved access road and proceed 0.5 mile to the campground.

Facilities: 73 campsites in 2 loops; sites are small, with nominal separation; parking pads are gravel, mostly short, tolerably level straight-ins; a few designated rv sites have long pull-throughs; many sites have framed-and-gravelled tent pads; fire rings or fireplaces; b-y-o firewood; water at central faucets; vault facilities; hard-surfaced driveway; gas and groceries+ are available in Gardiner, Montana, 15 miles north.

Activities & Attractions: Campfire circle; fishing; access to the Howard Eaton Trail.

Natural Features: Located on a low hill a couple-hundred yards above the Gardner River, near the river's confluences with Indian Creek and Obsidian Creek; campsites receive very light to light-medium shade/shelter from medium-height conifers above a ground cover of sparse grass and small plants; elevation 7300'.

Season, Fees & Phone: June to early September; $7.00 for a site; $10.00 for the park entrance permit; 7 day limit; Yellowstone Park Headquarters, Mammoth, (307) 344-7381.

Camp Notes: The streams in this area look fishably inviting. Note the different spellings of the *Gardner* River and *Gardiner*, Montana, above. One of them isn't a typo. Both are named for the identical individual. It's not uncommon in the West for the same name to have slightly disparate 'official' spellings. To wit: *Casper*, Wyoming, taken from Fort *Caspar*; and *Kearney*, Nebraska, derived from Fort *Kearny*. In both cases, the forts were named for military heroes of the 1800's.

Wyoming 3

NORRIS
Yellowstone National Park

Location: Northwest Wyoming in northwest Yellowstone Park.

Access: From Grand Loop Road at a point 0.8 mile north of Norris Junction and 20 miles south of Mammoth (just north of the Gibbon River Bridge), turn east onto a paved access road and go 0.3 mile to the campground.

Facilities: 116 campsites, including a dozen walk-in sites, in 3 loops; sites are small to a generous medium, with nominal to fair separation; parking pads are paved, mostly short or short+ straight-ins, plus a few pull-throughs for medium-sized vehicles; many sites, especially in Loop C on the hillside, will require additional leveling; Loop A has a number of terrific tent sites; fire rings; b-y-o firewood; water at several faucets; restrooms; holding tank disposal station; paved driveways; gas and groceries+ are available in Canyon Village, 13 miles east.

Activities & Attractions: Museum just southwest of Norris Junction has information about the origin and peculiarities of the various thermal activities in the area; Museum of the National Park Ranger at the campground; campfire programs on summer evenings; fishing.

Natural Features: Located just north of Norris Geyser Basin; some sites are situated along a grassy streambank, most sites are on an adjacent hillside amid light-medium timber; the campground is near the confluence of the Gibbon River and Solfatara Creek; elevation 7500'.

Season, Fees & Phone: June to early September; $8.00 for a site; $10.00 for the park entrance permit; 7 day limit; Yellowstone Park Headquarters, Mammoth, (307) 344-7381.

Camp Notes: Norris Campground has some superb tent sites along a lush, green streambank. There are some good views of the very pleasant surrounding countryside, too. The meadow below the campground is a favorite munching spot of local elk.

Wyoming 4

MADISON
Yellowstone National Park

Location: Northwest Wyoming in western Yellowstone Park.

Access: From West Entrance Road, 0.1 mile west of Madison Junction and 14 miles east of the West Entrance to Yellowstone Park at West Yellowstone, turn south into the campground.

Facilities: 292 campsites in 8 loops; sites are small to medium in size, with nominal to fair separation; parking pads are paved, generally level, medium+ pull-throughs or short straight-ins; most sites have very good tent spots; fireplaces; firewood is usually for sale, b-y-o is recommended; water at central faucets; restrooms; holding tank disposal station; paved driveways; adequate supplies and services are available in West Yellowstone.

Activities & Attractions: Explorers Museum at Madison Junction; fly fishing on the Madison; several hiking trails nearby.

Natural Features: Located in a stand of light timber near the north bank of the Madison River; vegetation in the campground is light to light-medium conifers atop a forest floor of sparse grass and conifer needles; sites are on 3 levels, with most sites on a small bench above the river; in this segment the Madison flows through a meadow between Purple Mountain to the north and National Park Mountain to the south; elevation 6800'.

Season, Fees & Phone: May to October; $8.00 for a site; $10.00 for the park entrance permit; 7 day limit; Yellowstone Park Headquarters, Mammoth, (307) 344-7381.

Camp Notes: One of the West's premier streams, the Madison River, is born from the merger of the Firehole and Gibbon Rivers at this point. The loops of Madison Campground stretch for nearly half a mile along the river. The campground presents a good balance between shelter and openness, tent and rv camping.

TOWER FALLS
Yellowstone National Park

Location: Northwest Wyoming in northeast Yellowstone Park.

Access: From Grand Loop Road at a point 2.3 miles south of Tower Junction and 16 miles north of Canyon Junction, turn west onto a paved access road for 200 yards up to the campground.

Facilities: 32 campsites; sites are small, closely spaced, with very little visual separation; parking pads are surfaced, mostly short straight-ins plus a few medium-length pull-offs; pads will require additional leveling; some tent pads, but most tent spots are bare earth, sloped and on the small side; 'bear boxes'; fireplaces; b-y-o firewood; water at faucets; vault facilities; hard-surfaced driveways; gas and snacks in the Tower Junction-Tower Falls area; gas and groceries+ are available in Gardiner, Montana, 25 miles northwest.

Activities & Attractions: Tower Falls Observation Deck; amphitheater for ranger-naturalist programs; access to the Howard Eaton Trail; a wooden footbridge crosses the creek.

Natural Features: Located just above the point where Tower Creek drops 132 feet into the Yellowstone River via Tower Falls; sites are built into a hillside; some sites are lightly sheltered/shaded by conifers, other sites are unshaded; some views of a canyon from atop a hill near the sites; the Washburn Range lies to the west; elevation 6700'.

Season, Fees & Phone: May to September; $7.00 for a site; $10.00 for the park entrance fee; 7 day limit; Yellowstone Park Headquarters, Mammoth, (307) 344-7381.

Camp Notes: Because of its central location near significant tourist attractions and a major foot trail, and its small size, Tower Falls Campground is very often filled to capacity. One of the park's major foot passages, the Howard Eaton Trail, passes the campground. The trail is the foot-travelers' counterpart to the figure-8 Grand Loop Road, and it closely parallels the road along much of its course around the park.

CANYON
Yellowstone National Park

Location: Northwest Wyoming in central Yellowstone Park.

Access: From Grand Loop Road at Canyon Junction (16 miles north of Fishing Bridge, 12 miles east of Norris), go 0.2 mile east, then turn north (left) into the campground.

Facilities: 280 campsites in 12 loops; a number of loops are designated as tents-only areas; sites are small to medium-sized, with fair to good separation; parking pads are paved, short to medium-length straight-ins or pull-offs, or long pull-throughs; many pads may require some additional leveling; sites in the loops farthest from the entrance tend to be more level; fireplaces; firewood is usually for sale, b-y-o is highly recommended; water at several faucets; restrooms; coin-op showers and laundry nearby; paved driveways; gas and groceries+ in Canyon Village.

Activities & Attractions: Visitor center at Canyon Village; amphitheater for evening campfire programs; scenic drive on the canyon's west rim to several viewpoints of Upper and Lower Yellowstone Falls; the canyon's east rim drive provides access to other viewpoints; several hiking trails in the area.

Natural Features: Located on a series of gently-rolling, forested hills near the Grand Canyon of the Yellowstone River; campground vegetation is mainly medium-dense tall conifers with light underbrush; elevation 7900'.

Season, Fees & Phone: May to early September; $8.00 for a site; $10.00 for the park entrance permit; 7 day limit; Yellowstone Park Headquarters, Mammoth, (307) 344-7381.

Camp Notes: Canyon Campground is situated in a nicely forested setting. It's close to one of the major wonders of the park, and also to a good source of supplies. Many travelers establish a base of operations here, then take off on day trips to other Yellowstone attractions.

BRIDGE BAY
Yellowstone National Park

Location: Northwest Wyoming in central Yellowstone Park.

Access: From Grand Loop Road at a point 2 miles southwest of Lake Junction and 17 miles northeast of West Thumb Junction, turn north-west onto a paved access road; proceed 0.2 mile, then turn easterly (right) and go 0.1 mile to the campground entrance.

Facilities: 438 campsites in 9 loops; lower sites are small+, with paved, short+ straight-ins or medium+ pull-off/pull-through parking pads; upper sites have paved, short straight-ins or medium-length pull-off pads; additional leveling may be required on many pads, particularly in the upper levels; many pretty good tent sites in the upper loops; designated section for hike/bike campers; fire rings or fireplaces; firewood is usually for sale, b-y-o firewood is highly recommended; restrooms; water at central faucets; holding tank disposal station; gas and camper supplies are available at the marina.

Activities & Attractions: Amphitheater for evening programs; boating; boat launch; marina; fishing.

Natural Features: Located just east of Bridge Bay on the northwest shore of Yellowstone Lake, high in the Rocky Mountains; sites in the lower section (Loops A-D, #1-230) are on a huge, open, grassy, rolling slope flecked with a few conifers; upper sites (Loops E-I) are on hilly terrain and are lightly to moderately sheltered by conifers; the snug harbor shelters boats from the lake's frequent summer storms; elevation 7700'.

Season, Fees & Phone: May to October; $9.00 for a site; $10.00 for the park entrance permit; 7 day limit; reservations accepted, please see Appendix for reservation information; Yellowstone Park Headquarters, Mammoth, (307) 344-7381.

Camp Notes: It's almost a mile from the campground entrance to the most distant campsites in the upper section. The Bridge Bay area provides some good views of Yellowstone's super lake. With a typical summer water temperature in the low 40's and a maximum depth of 309 feet (in the center of West Thumb), it's one of the largest, coldest and deepest lakes in the West.

Wyoming 8

GRANT VILLAGE
Yellowstone National Park

Location: Northwest Wyoming in southern Yellowstone Park.

Access: From South Entrance Road at a point 2 miles south of West Thumb Junction and 20 miles north of the South Entrance to Yellowstone National Park, turn east and proceed 1 mile; turn north (left) for 0.4 mile to the campground.

Facilities: 399 campsites in 10 loops; (group sites are also available); sites are small to medium-sized, with fair to fairly good separation; parking pads are paved, mostly long pull-throughs, plus some short straight-ins; loops closest to the entrance have sites which tend to be closer together and reasonably level; loops farther north generally have slightly more spacious sites, with better separation, but which may require additional leveling; many nice tent spots; designated sites for hike/bike campers; fireplaces; firewood is usually for sale, or b-y-o; water at central faucets; restrooms; holding tank disposal station; gas, camper supplies and coin-op showers are nearby.

Activities & Attractions: Visitor center; boating; boat launch; fishing; geothermal activity in nearby West Thumb Geyser Basin; hiking trails lead to several smaller lakes in the area.

Natural Features: Located on a bluff above the southwest shore of West Thumb of Yellowstone Lake; campground vegetation consists of light-medium to medium dense tall conifers, considerable young growth, and underbrush which varies from very light to moderately dense; elevation 7700'.

Season, Fees & Phone: May to October; $8.00 for a site; $10.00 for the park entrance permit; 7 day limit; Yellowstone Park Headquarters, Mammoth, (307) 344-7381.

Camp Notes: Grant Village is a good place to use as an hq for exploring this corner of the park. Yellowstone Lake's wild, remote, unbelievably superscenic 'arms' can probably best be reached from here if you're lucky or prudent enough to have a boat with you.

Wyoming 9

LEWIS LAKE
Yellowstone National Park

Location: Northwest Wyoming in southern Yellowstone Park.

Access: From South Entrance Road at a point 10 miles south of West Thumb Junction and 12 miles north of the South Entrance to Yellowstone National Park, turn west onto a paved access road for 100 yards, then turn south (left) into the campground.

Facilities: 85 campsites in 4 loops; sites are medium-sized, with fair to good separation; parking pads are gravel, mostly medium-length straight-ins; additional leveling may be required at some sites; some large tent spots, but they may be a bit sloped; fireplaces; b-y-o firewood; water at several faucets; vault facilities; paved driveways; gas and camper supplies in Grant Village.

Activities & Attractions: Boating; boat launch; fishing; 5-mile foot trail to Shoshone Lake, accessible from a small parking area at the northeast corner of Lewis Lake.

Natural Features: Located on a forested hillside overlooking the south tip of Lewis Lake, which is fed by larger, more remote, Shoshone Lake via a short segment of the Lewis River; waters from the lakes plunge 37 feet at Lewis Falls, which is visible from the highway just south of the campground; campsites are lightly to moderately shaded/sheltered by conifers; surrounded by densely forested hills and mountains; elevation 7800'.

Season, Fees & Phone: June to September; $7.00 for a site; $10.00 for the park entrance fee; 7 day limit; Yellowstone Park Headquarters, Mammoth, (307) 344-7381.

Camp Notes: This campground appears to attract campers with tents and smaller vehicles, as well as those who wish to be a bit away from the hustle and bustle of the larger, more congested centers of activity. The atmosphere at Lewis Lake is likable, and views across the lake are terrific.

Wyoming 10

SLOUGH CREEK
Yellowstone National Park

Location: Northwest Wyoming in northeast Yellowstone Park.

Access: From Northeast Entrance Road at a point 22 miles southwest of the Northeast Entrance to Yellowstone National Park and 6 miles northeast of Tower Junction, turn north onto a gravel access road; proceed 2.2 miles to the campground.

Facilities: 29 campsites, including many park 'n walk or walk-in tent units; standard sites are small to medium-sized, with nominal to fair separation; parking pads are gravel, short straight-ins, plus a few medium-length pull-offs; tent sites have pull-off parking spaces; some very nice tent sites stretch for several hundred yards along the streambank; fire rings; b-y-o firewood; water at a hand pump; vault facilities; gas and snacks in the Tower Junction-Tower Falls area; gas and camper supplies+ are available in Cooke City, Montana, 26 miles northeast.

Activities & Attractions: Fishing; hiking; trailhead to McBride Lake is along the Slough Creek access road; elk and buffalo are often seen grazing in the nearby meadow.

Natural Features: Located at the head of a small valley along the grassy bank of Slough Creek, at its confluence with Buffalo Creek; sites vary from unshaded to moderately shaded; Slough Creek meanders through a narrow valley, a mountain meadow, a sage flat and then south into the Lamar River; bordered by timbered peaks and ridges; elevation 6300'.

Season, Fees & Phone: June to September; $7.00 for a site; $10.00 for the park entrance permit; 7 day limit; Yellowstone Park Headquarters, Mammoth, (307) 344-7381.

Camp Notes: Wide, deep Slough Creek lends an air of serenity to the campground. There are many really dandy streamside tent sites here. Far enough from the main stream of park traffic, the setting is more remote than most park campgrounds.

Wyoming 11

PEBBLE CREEK
Yellowstone National Park

Location: Northwest Wyoming in northeast Yellowstone Park.

Access: From Northeast Entrance Road at a point 9 miles west of the Northeast Entrance to Yellowstone National Park and 20 miles northeast of Tower Junction, turn north onto a paved access road and proceed 0.2 mile to the campground.

Facilities: 36 campsites; sites are mostly small to average-sized, with nominal to fair separation; parking pads are gravel, mostly short to medium-length straight-ins, plus several medium+ pull-offs; there are some super tent sites, including some park 'n walk units at the north end; bear boxes; fireplaces; b-y-o firewood; water at a hand pump; vault facilities; paved driveways; gas and camper supplies+ in Cooke City, Montana, 13 miles northeast.

Activities & Attractions: Fishing; a footbridge spans the creek; Pebble Creek Trail leads up to and around the north side of Barronette Peak; meadows and slopes here and in nearby Lamar Valley are favorite grazing areas for elk and buffalo.

Natural Features: Located in a valley on a flat and on a gentle slope along and near the bank of Pebble Creek; some sites are unsheltered, most are lightly shaded/sheltered by tall conifers on a grassy surface; 10,000' peaks border the valley; elev. 6900'.

Season, Fees & Phone: June to September; $7.00 for a site; $10.00 for the park entrance permit; 7 day limit; Yellowstone Park Headquarters, Mammoth, (307) 344-7381.

Camp Notes: Pebble Creek Campground is a particularly good place to stop if lots of open space and beautiful, far-reaching vistas are high on your list. The facilities are simple but the pastoral setting is truly impressive.

Wyoming 12

FOX CREEK
Shoshone National Forest

Location: Northwest Wyoming northeast of Yellowstone Park.

Access: From U.S. Highway 212 at a point 7 miles east of Cooke City, Montana, 6 miles west of the junction of U.S. 212 & Wyoming State Highway 296, 58 miles west of Red Lodge, Montana, turn north onto a gravel access road and go 0.1 mile to the campground.

Facilities: 27 campsites in 2 loops; sites are medium to medium+ in size, generally level, with good to very good separation; parking pads are gravel, short to medium-length straight-ins; medium to large tent areas; fire rings; firewood is available for gathering in the area; water at central faucets; vault facilities; gravel driveways; gas and camper supplies+ are available in Cooke City.

Activities & Attractions: The drive along Highway 212 is unforgettable; from this point west it climbs and twists a bit through Colter Pass in the Absaroka Range, and then continues westward into Yellowstone National Park; stream fishing for trout; hiking trail along Pilot Creek.

Natural Features: Located in a narrow valley where Fox Creek enters Clarks Fork of the Yellowstone River; campsites are on a heavily forested flat along and near the streambank; Pilot Peak and Index Peak of the Absaroka Range rise considerably above 11,000' about 2 miles west of the campground; elevation 7100'.

Season, Fees & Phone: June to September; $7.00; 14 day limit; Clarks Fork Ranger District, Powell, (307) 754-2407.

Camp Notes: Fox Creek maintains a remarkably isolated atmosphere, considering it's just off a U.S. highway. But then again, this isn't a garden-variety highway, either. Perhaps the most prominent pair of peaks in this part of the Rockies, Pilot and Index, loom imposingly over the campground. Chief Joseph's band of 800 Nez Percé Indians, fleeing from their homeland in Oregon and pursued by federal troops, passed this way in late summer of 1877. Some weeks later in northern Montana they would meet the Army in a final encounter at the Battle of the Bears Paw.

Wyoming 13

CRAZY CREEK
Shoshone National Forest

Location: Northwest Wyoming northeast of Yellowstone Park.

Access: From U.S. Highway 212 at a point 10 miles east of Cooke City, Montana, 2.5 miles west of the junction of U.S. 212 & Wyoming State Highway 296, 55 miles west of Red Lodge, Montana, turn south into the campground.

Facilities: 16 campsites; sites are average-sized, with nominal to fair separation; parking pads are gravel, mostly short+ to medium-length straight-ins, plus a couple of medium+ pull-throughs; a touch of additional leveling might be needed on a few pads; some nice tent sites; fire rings; firewood is available for gathering in the vicinity; water at central faucets; vault facilities; gravel driveway; gas and camper supplies+ in Cooke City.

Activities & Attractions: Superscenic drive along Highway 212 climbs over the Beartooth Plateau to the east and winds past the Absaroka Range on its way to Yellowstone National Park to the west; hiking trails lead to Crazy Creek Falls, to Crazy Lakes, and north into the Beartooth Wilderness; stream fishing.

Natural Features: Located on a blufftop above Clarks Fork of the Yellowstone River; campground vegetation consists of light-medium conifers and a few hardwoods over light undercover, bordered by much more dense forest in the surrounding area; Crazy Creek Falls is nearby, where the highway crosses the creek; lofty peaks of the Beartooth and Absaroka Ranges tower in all directions around the campground; elevation 6900'.

Season, Fees & Phone: June to September; $7.00; 14 day limit; Clarks Fork Ranger District, Powell, (307) 754-2407.

Camp Notes: There is a fantastic vista of Clarks Fork Valley and surrounding mountains from up on a knoll, just a few yards south of the campsites. Because so much of Wyoming consists of semi-arid plains, people in the western travel industry have an off-the-record adage: "Wyoming's best asset is Montana". Well, the drive across the Beartooth Highway and along Clarks Fork is certainly one of the most scenic trips not only in Wyoming but in all the West. Montanans have a tough time thinking up "Wyoming jokes" about this piece of country.

Wyoming 14

BEARTOOTH LAKE
Shoshone National Forest

Location: Northwest Wyoming northeast of Yellowstone Park.

Access: From U.S. Highway 212 (Beartooth Highway) at a point 9.5 miles east of the junction of U.S. 212 & Wyoming State Highway 296, 24 miles east of Cooke City, Montana and 41 miles southwest of Red Lodge, Montana, turn north-east onto a gravel access road; drive east for 0.5 mile to the campground. (Note: This is a hairpin right turn at the bottom of a steepish hill if you're coming from Red Lodge; the Beartooth Lake turnoff is 3.2 miles west of the turnoff to Island Lake Campground.)

Facilities: 21 campsites in 3 loops; sites are generally good-sized, mostly level, with nominal to fair separation; parking pads are gravel, short+ to medium-length straight-ins, plus a few long pull-throughs; some nice, large tent spots; fire rings; firewood is usually available for gathering in the vicinity; water at hand pumps; vault facilities; gravel driveways; gas and camper supplies are available in midsummer 2 miles east; gas and camper supplies+ are available in Cooke City.

Activities & Attractions: The Scenery!; limited boating; small boat launch; trout fishing; a foot trail leads around the lake; hiking trail across the top of the Beartooth Plateau.

Natural Features: Located on a forested hilltop above the south shore of Beartooth Lake in the Beartooth Mountains; campground vegetation consists of light to medium-dense tall conifers, light underbrush and a forest floor of sparse grass and pine needles; a few sites border a large mountain meadow; Beartooth Creek tumbles past several sites and down into Beartooth Lake; impressive red, pink and white Beartooth Butte rises dramatically to 10,500' directly across the lake; elevation 9000'.

Season, Fees & Phone: June to mid-September; $7.00; 14 day limit; Clarks Fork Ranger District, Powell, (307) 754-2407.

Camp Notes: The subalpine scenery at and near Beartooth Lake is superlative. About a quarter of a billion years of the earth's geological history lies open along the pastel flanks of Beartooth Butte for all to view. This is undoubtedly one of the most impressive small lakes in the Northern Rockies.

Wyoming 15

ISLAND LAKE
Shoshone National Forest

Location: Northwest Wyoming northeast of Yellowstone Park.

Access: From U.S. Highway 212 (Beartooth Highway) at a point 12.5 miles east of the junction of U.S. 212 & Wyoming State Highway 296, 27 miles east of Cooke City, Montana and 38 miles southwest of Red Lodge, Montana, turn north onto a gravel access road; proceed 0.2 mile, then swing left into the campground. (If you're approaching from Red Lodge, it might also be helpful to know that the Island Lake turnoff is 7.5 miles west of the West Summit of Beartooth Pass; if you arrive after dark, be especially careful to turn *left* into the campground, *not right* toward the boat ramp--unless you need a 40° rinse-off.)

Facilities: 20 campsites in 3 loops; sites are small to medium-sized, with fair to fairly good separation; parking pads are gravel, short to short+ straight-ins; most pads will require additional leveling; generally enough room for medium to large tents; fire rings; gathering of firewood on forest lands prior to arrival, or b-y-o, is recommended; water at several faucets; vault facilities; gravel driveways; gas and camper supplies are available in midsummer 1.5 miles west; gas and camper supplies+ are available in Cooke City.

Activities & Attractions: Limited boating; small boat launch; fishing for small trout; foot trail leads around the lake to Night Lake just over a rise to the north; several other hiking trails in the area; Yellowstone Park is within an hour's drive to the west.

Natural Features: Located on a hill above Island Lake high in the Beartooth Mountains; sites are perched on boulder-strewn hillsides overlooking Island Lake; campground vegetation consists of light-medium to medium conifers, light underbrush and tiny alpine plants; large meadows dotted with stands of conifers border the campground; typically breezy; the Beartooth Wilderness is to the north; elevation 9600'.

Season, Fees & Phone: June to mid-September; $7.00; 14 day limit; Clarks Fork Ranger District, Powell, (307) 754-2407.

Camp Notes: Island Lake is not quite at the top of the world, but very near it. Because of the high altitude, these campsites are often snowed-in until early July. Views of the alpine scenery and nearby snow-capped mountains are truly magnificent. Many, many travelers consider the drive along the Beartooth Highway to be the finest trip in the West. The passage over 11,000' Beartooth Pass is one of the most incredibly scenic journeys in the country. Don't miss it.

Wyoming 16

HUNTER PEAK
Shoshone National Forest

Location: Northwest Wyoming northeast of Yellowstone Park.

Access: From Wyoming State Highway 296/Forest Road 296 (Chief Joseph Scenic Highway) at milepost 4 +.8 (5 miles southeast of the junction of Highway 296 & U.S. Highway 212 east of Cooke City MT, 42 miles northwest of the junction of State Highways 296 & 120 north of Cody), turn west onto a paved access road and go 0.1 mile down into the campground.

Facilities: 9 campsites; sites are small to medium-sized, level, with nominal to fair separation; parking pads are gravel, short to medium-length straight-ins; enough room for most tents; fire rings; firewood is available for gathering in the area; 'bear boxes'; water at a hand pump; vault facilities; gravel driveway; gas and camper supplies+ in Cooke City, 20 miles northwest.

Activities & Attractions: Trout fishing (special regs, including use of artificial flies or lures only); Clarks Fork Trailhead.

Natural Features: Located in a small hollow on a flat along Clarks Fork of the Yellowstone River; sites receive light-medium to medium shelter from tall conifers and some bushes; closely bordered by tree-dotted hills and mountains; Hunter Peak rises above 9000' a mile southwest of the campground; elev. 6500'.

Season, Fees & Phone: June to September; $7.00; 14 day limit; Clarks Fork Ranger District, Powell, (307) 754-2407.

Camp Notes: Under normal summer circumstances, you probably wouldn't choose to travel the Chief Joseph road instead of taking the incredible trip across Beartooth Pass as your preferred route to or from Yellowstone. But if it's too early or too late in the season for the Beartooth road to be snow-free, or your itinerary includes Cody WY but not Red Lodge MT, this passage would make an excellent option. Four miles north of Hunter Peak, at milepost 1 +.2 is another forest camp, Lake Creek, with 6 sites, a hand pump and vaults along the stream of the same name.

Wyoming 17

DEAD INDIAN
Shoshone National Forest

Location: Northwest Wyoming northwest of Cody.

Access: From Wyoming State Highway 296/Forest Road 296 (Chief Joseph Scenic Highway) at milepost 25 +.1 (21.5 miles northwest of the junction of State Highways 296 & 120 north of Cody, 25.5 miles southeast of the junction of Highway 296 & U.S. Highway 212 east of Cooke City MT, turn north-west into the camp loops (one loop on either side of the stream).

Facilities: 10 campsites in 2 loops; sites are small, level, with nominal to fair separation; parking pads are gravel/earth, short straight-ins; small tent areas; fire rings; b-y-o firewood, or gather on forest lands prior to arrival, is suggested; water at a faucet; vault facilities; pack-it-in/pack-it-out trash removal; tight, gravel driveways; nearest supplies and services are available in Cody (complete) and Cooke City (gas and camper supplies+).

Activities & Attractions: Possible fishing for small trout; Dead Indian Trailhead; superscenic views from Dead Indian Pass (Dead Indian Hill Summit), 7.6 miles southeast.

Natural Features: Located on streamside flats flanking Dead Indian Creek in a valley in the Absaroka Range of the Rocky Mountains; sites receive are lightly shaded/sheltered by large hardwoods; closely bordered by steep sage slopes and slab-sided hills and mountains; elevation 6100'.

Season, Fees & Phone: June to September; no fee (subject to change); 14 day limit; Clarks Fork Ranger Dist. (307) 754-2407.

Camp Notes: Although it's much easier to arrive and leave this area via Cooke City because of the switchbacks between here and Dead Indian Pass, you'd miss much of the scenery if you didn't make your way over the Summit on your way in or out. An excellent trip. For a worthwhile side trip, take the road through Sunlight Basin for a half-dozen miles up to the ranger station. The Sunlight Road can be accessed from Highway 296 about two miles northwest of Dead Indian Campground.

Wyoming 18

PAHASKA
Shoshone National Forest

Location: Northwest Wyoming east of Yellowstone Park.

Access: From U.S. Highways 14/16/20 at milepost 1 + .9 (2 miles east of Yellowstone National Park, 50 miles west of Cody), turn south into the campground.

Facilities: 23 campsites in 2 loops; sites are small to medium-sized, essentially level, with nominal to fairly good separation parking pads are gravel, mostly short straight-ins, plus a few medium-length straight-ins and pull-offs; good-sized tent areas; fire rings; limited firewood in the area, so gathering of firewood prior to arrival, or b-y-o, is suggested; water at hand pumps; vault facilities; gravel driveways; gas and camper supplies at Pahaska Teepee, 0.1 mile east.

Activities & Attractions: Trout fishing; Pahaska-Sunlight Trailhead, a half mile east, leads into the Absaroka Wilderness.

Natural Features: Located in a canyon on a flat along the north bank of the North Fork of the Shoshone River; sites are sheltered by light-medium timber, plus some brush and tall grass; bordered by the high peaks of the Absaroka Range; elevation 6800'.

Season, Fees & Phone: June to September; $7.00; 14 day limit; Wapiti Ranger District, Cody, (307) 527-6241 (recording).

Camp Notes: Pahaska Teepee, a few yards east of the campground, was Buffalo Bill Cody's original hunting lodge. Since this is the forest campground that's closest to Yellowstone Park, it may fill a little earlier than the many others along the 30-mile stretch of highway east of here. In any regard, your choices of camping accommodations along the North Fork of the Shoshone River between Yellowstone and Cody are limited to the established campgrounds; jackcamping is not allowed.

Wyoming 19

THREE MILE
Shoshone National Forest

Location: Northwest Wyoming east of Yellowstone Park.

Access: From U.S. Highways 14/16/20 at milepost 3 (3 miles east of Yellowstone National Park, 49 miles west of Cody), turn south down into the campground.

Facilities: 33 campsites, including several park ' walk units, in 2 loops; sites are medium-sized, with fair to good separation; parking pads are gravel, short to medium+ straight-ins or medium-length pull-offs; a little additional leveling may be needed on some pads; adequate space for tents; fire rings; gathering of firewood prior to arrival, or b-y-o, is suggested; water at hand pumps; vault facilities; gravel driveways; gas and camper supplies at Pahaska Teepee, 1 mile west.

Activities & Attractions: Fishing.

Natural Features: Located in a canyon on a timbered slope above the north bank of the North Fork of the Shoshone River; sites are sheltered/shaded by medium-dense conifers, light underbrush and tall grass; bordered by the tall peaks of the Absaroka Range of the Rocky Mountains; elevation 6800'.

Season, Fees & Phone: June to September; $7.00; 14 day limit; Wapiti Ranger District, Cody, (307) 527-6241 (recording).

Camp Notes: Some very nice campsites here, especially the park 'n walk spots near the river's edge. Yellowstone National Park may very well be the more renowned attraction in the area, but the scenery in the Shoshone River Canyon, and Wapiti Valley farther east, are worth the visit. Another six campsites with standard facilities (pump, vaults, straight-in pads) are a mile east, at Sleeping Giant Campground. Sleeping Giant has a slightly more 'open' environment. Nice river views from there, too.

Wyoming 20

EAGLE CREEK
Shoshone National Forest

Location: Northwest Wyoming east of Yellowstone Park.

Access: From U.S. Highways 14/16/20 near milepost 7 (7 miles east of Yellowstone Park, 45 miles west of Cody), turn south onto a gravel access road for 0.1 mile to a "Y"; go right or left to the camp loops.

Facilities: 20 campsites in 2 loops; sites are fairly roomy, level, and generally well separated; parking pads are gravel, mostly short to medium-length straight-ins; plenty of tent space; fire rings or fireplaces; limited firewood is available for gathering in the vicinity, so b-y-o is suggested; water at hand pumps; vault facilities; gravel driveway; gas and camper supplies at Pahaska Teepee, 5 miles west.

Activities & Attractions: Fishing; hiking; Natural Bridge Trail leads south from just east of here; parking area for Eagle Creek foot trail that leads across the river via a footbridge from the campground into the Washakie Wilderness; Eagle Creek Trailhead with stock-handling facilities and parking, 1 mile east.

Natural Features: Located on a forested flat in a canyon along the North Fork of the Shoshone River; virtually all sites have views of the river; some are on the river's edge; vegetation consists of medium-dense tall conifers, plus a line of small hardwoods along the riverbank; elevation 6600'.

Season, Fees & Phone: June to September; $7.00; 14 day limit; Wapiti Ranger District, Cody, (307) 527-6241 (recording).

Camp Notes: There are some very respectable mountain views toward the south, particularly from the east loop. But you may prefer the overall atmosphere of the west loop a little better.

Wyoming 21

NEWTON CREEK
Shoshone National Forest

Location: Northwest Wyoming east of Yellowstone Park.

Access: From U.S. Highways 14/16/20 at milepost 14 +.3 (14 miles east of Yellowstone Park, 38 miles west of Cody), turn south onto a gravel access road for a few yards to a "T"; turn left and go down 0.1 mile into the campground.

Facilities: 31 campsites in 2 loops; sites are mostly medium-sized, a few are large, with nominal to fairly good separation; parking pads are gravel, short to medium-length straight-ins; a little additional leveling may be needed; fire rings; water at hand pumps; vault facilities; gravel driveways; gas and camper supplies at Pahaska Teepee, 13 miles west; complete supplies and services are available in Cody.

Activities & Attractions: Fishing; Blackwater Fire Memorial National Recreation Trail goes from near the campground up to Clayton Mountain at 11,715'.

Natural Features: Located in a narrow canyon on a slightly sloping, rolling shelf a few feet above the North Fork of the Shoshone River; some nice tent sites are in areas clear of underbrush but still shaded by tall conifers; closely bordered by high, partially timbered cliffs; elevation 6300'.

Season, Fees & Phone: June to September; $7.00; 14 day limit; Wapiti Ranger District, Cody, (307) 527-6241 (recording).

Camp Notes: Though none are streamside, many sites have good river views. A massive, fortress-like rock formation (called "Henry Ford Rock" according to maps) rises above the campground to the north. A rail fence extends the length of the campground and adds a nice touch to a good facility.

Wyoming 22

REX HALE & CLEARWATER
Shoshone National Forest

Location: Northwest Wyoming east of Yellowstone Park.

Access: From U.S. Highways 14/16/20 near milepost 15 +.5 (15 miles east of Yellowstone Park, 37 miles west of Cody), turn south into either of two entrances to Rex Hale; or at milepost 19 +.9, turn south into Clearwater.

Facilities: *Rex Hale*: 3 small, level campsites with short, gravel pads, medium-sized tent areas and fire rings; *Clearwater*: 6 park 'n walk camp/picnic sites, fire rings, gravel parking area; *both camps:* water at hand pumps, vault facilities, gravel driveways; complete supplies and services are available in Cody.

Activities & Attractions: Fishing; Firefighter Memorial, a large monument crafted of local stone, along the highway just west of Rex Hale Campground.

Natural Features: Located on streamside flats in a canyon along the north bank of the North Fork of the Shoshone River; sites are lightly shaded by hardwoods and a few conifers; elevation 6200' at Rex Hale, 6000' at Clearwater.

Season, Fees & Phone: May to September; $7.00; 14 day limit; Wapiti Ranger District, Cody, (307) 527-6241 (recording).

Camp Notes: Both of these camps may be small, with minimal facilities; but on the other hand, you won't have a lot of neighbors either, (except for picnickers at Clearwater). Good distant views from Clearwater.

Wyoming 23

ELK FORK
Shoshone National Forest

Location: Northwest Wyoming east of Yellowstone Park.

Access: From U.S. Highways 14/16/20 at milepost 22 +.1 (22 miles east of Yellowstone Park, 30 miles west of Cody), turn south onto a paved access road for 0.1 mile to the campground.

Facilities: 13 campsites; sites are small to medium-sized, level, with nominal to fair separation; parking pads are hard-surfaced, medium-length straight-ins, plus a couple of pull-offs; enough room for a big tent in most sites; fire rings; some firewood is available for gathering; water at a hand pump; vault facilities; paved driveway; complete supplies and services in Cody.

Activities & Attractions: Fishing; trailhead parking for hiking and horse trails leading south into the Washakie Wilderness.

Natural Features: Located in a side canyon on a flat along Elk Fork Creek, a tributary of the North Fork of the Shoshone River; sites receive very light to light-medium shade/shelter by large hardwoods, brush and a few junipers; closely bounded by the lower slopes of the Absaroka Range; elevation 6200'.

Season, Fees & Phone: May to October; $7.00; 14 day limit; Wapiti Ranger District, Cody, (307) 527-6241 (recording).

Camp Notes: Elk Fork is a sizeable stream and its bank makes a good spot for a campsite. This camp is often used by horsers as as a jumping-off spot for pack trips into the high country of the Absaroka Range. (Incidentally, the Indian name *Absaroka* is pronounced Ab-*soar*-kuh, not Ab-suh-*roe*-kuh, as it might first appear. If you didn't pronounce it quite correctly when you first saw the name, don't fret. Many of the regional TV and radio news dudes and dj's don't get it right, either.)

Wyoming 24

WAPITI
Shoshone National Forest

Location: Northwest Wyoming east of Yellowstone Park.

Access: From U.S. Highways 14/16/20 at milepost 22 +.2 (22 miles east of Yellowstone Park, 30 miles west of Cody), turn north into the campground.

Facilities: 40 campsites in 2 loops; sites are medium to large, level, with fair to excellent separation; parking pads are hard-surfaced, medium to long straight-ins; some nice tent sites; fire rings; some firewood is usually available for gathering; water at several faucets; vault facilities; paved driveways; complete supplies and services are available in Cody.

Activities & Attractions: Fishing; visitor information center at historic Wapiti Ranger Station, a quarter mile east, has historical markers and information about grizzly bears and their habitat.

Natural Features: Located on a wooded flat on the bank of the North Fork of the Shoshone River; sites receive light to light-medium shade/shelter from hardwoods and underbrush; a number of the sites are along the river's edge; bordering peaks of the Absaroka Range rise to 12,000'; elevation 6000'.

Season, Fees & Phone: May to October; $7.00; 14 day limit; Wapiti Ranger District, Cody, (307) 527-6241 (recording).

Camp Notes: *Wapiti* is of eastern American Indian origin, an Algonquin word meaning "pale white". It was a term used by the Indians to distinguish the light colored elk from the darker colored deer. The Wapiti Ranger Station next to the campground is considered to be the first home of the Forest Service. Established in 1891, the entire Northwest Wyoming region was known then as the "Yellowstone Park Timberland Reserve".

Wyoming 25

BIG GAME
Shoshone National Forest

Location: Northwest Wyoming east of Yellowstone Park.

Access: From U.S. Highways 14/16/20 at milepost 23 +.1 (23 miles east of Yellowstone Park, 29 miles west of Cody), turn north into the campground.

Facilities: 17 campsites; sites are medium to large, level, with fair to very good separation; parking pads are packed gravel, short to medium-length straight-ins and long-long pull-throughs; some nice tent spots on a grassy riverbank beneath the trees; fire rings; some firewood is usually available for gathering in the area; water at hand pumps; vault facilities; hard-surfaced driveways; complete supplies and services are available in Cody.

Activities & Attractions: Fishing for trout and whitefish; superscenic drive along the Shoshone River past a number of interesting rock formations (many will challenge your imagination); information turnout, 2 miles east, for the "Holy City" rock formations.

Natural Features: Located in the North Fork Shoshone River Canyon (Wapiti Valley); campground vegetation consists of mostly hardwoods and bushes; sites are stretched out in an elongated oval along the riverbank; peaks of the Absaroka Range rise to 12,000' nearby; elevation 6000'.

Season, Fees & Phone: May to October; $7.00; 14 day limit; Wapiti Ranger District, Cody, (307) 527-6241 (recording).

Camp Notes: Big Game is the easternmost campground that provides measurable shade along this highway. From here on east, Wapiti Valley is dramatically more arid. Grizzly and black bears occasionally have been sighted in the area, so camping in a hard-sided apparatus is encouraged. (Makes you wonder: Does the name of the campground refer to the local fauna, or to the large rv's that come to roost here? Ed.)

Wyoming 26

NORTH FORK
Buffalo Bill State Park

Location: Northwest Wyoming west of Cody.

Access: From U.S. Highways 14/16/20 at milepost 37 +.3 (14 miles west of Cody, 38 miles east of Yellowstone National Park), turn south onto a gravel access road and go 100 yards, then turn west (right) and proceed 0.5 mile to the campground. **Additional Access** for the boat launch area camp: From U.S. 14/16/20 near milepost 43 (6 miles east of North Fork Campground), turn south into the campground.

Facilities: Approximately 50 campsites, including 6 park 'n walk tent sites; (two dozen additional sites with pull-through or straight-in parking pads, drinking water and vaults are available in the boat launch area); sites are medium-sized, tolerably level, with nominal separation; parking pads are gravel, long pull-throughs; some designated tent spots with framed pads and small wind shelters; fire rings; b-y-o firewood; water at several faucets; vault facilities; holding tank disposal station; gravel driveways; complete supplies and services are available in Cody.

Activities & Attractions: Boating; boat launch and dock near the east park boundary; fishing.

Natural Features: Located on a very large, grassy flat along the North Fork of the Shoshone River near the west end of Buffalo Bill Reservoir; North Fork area vegetation consists of acres of grass dotted with small hardwoods (b-y-o shade); the sheer walls of Sheep Mountain tower thousands of feet above the North Fork area; other peaks of the Absaroka Range rise to 12,000' south and west of the lake; (boat launch sites are on an unsheltered, windswept sage slope above the reservoir); elevation 5200'.

Season, Fees & Phone: Open all year, with limited services in winter; 14 day limit; please see Appendix for standard Wyoming state park fees; park office (307) 587-9227.

Camp Notes: Buffalo Bill Reservoir is located in an immense valley, so there are fantastic vistas in just about every compass direction. Lofty mountains with sheer cliffs tower over North Fork, which is about a half-mile from the west end of the lake. The 6000-acre reservoir covers much of lower Wapiti Valley and was formed behind Buffalo Bill Dam, which spans the slender Shoshone River Canyon.

Wyoming 27

SNAKE RIVER
Bridger-Teton National Forest

Location: Northwest Wyoming south of Yellowstone Park.

Access: From U.S. Highways 89/287/191 (John D. Rockefeller Jr. Parkway), at a point 4 miles south of Yellowstone National Park and 3 miles north of Grand Teton National Park, (immediately south of the Snake River Bridge), turn west onto a paved access road and proceed 0.2 mile to the campground.

Facilities: 24 campsites; sites are medium to medium+ in size, level, with nominal separation; parking pads are gravel, medium to long straight-ins or pull-throughs; some large, grassy tent spots; fireplaces; b-y-o firewood; water at several faucets; restrooms; gas, camper supplies and showers at a nearby lodge.

Activities & Attractions: Fishing; river floating; foot trail leads east into the Teton Wilderness; ranger-guided activities are scheduled during the summer.

Natural Features: Located near the headwaters of the legendary 1000-mile-long Snake River; virtually all sites are situated on the grassy south bank of the Snake; a number of sites are at river's edge; tall conifers provide some shelter/shade; peaks of the Teton Range rise to the south and west; elevation 6800'.

Season, Fees & Phone: June to early-September; $8.00; 14 day limit; phone c/o Grand Teton National Park Headquarters.

Camp Notes: This camp has an atmosphere quite different from that of the campgrounds in the nearby national parks. If you're looking for a camp spot that's close to both Yellowstone and Jackson Hole, but in an area that's a little less regimented than the park camps, check it out. But arrive very early.

Wyoming 28

LIZARD CREEK
Grand Teton National Park

Location: Northwest Wyoming in northern Grand Teton Park.

Access: From U.S. Highways 89/287/191 (Rockefeller Parkway) at a point 3 miles south of the north boundary of Grand Teton National Park and 23 miles north of Jackson Lake Junction, turn west onto a paved access road and go 0.2 mile; turn south (left) into the campground.

Facilities: 63 campsites, including several walk-in tent sites, in 2 loops; sites are medium to medium+ in size, with fair to good separation; parking pads are gravel, some are medium-length double-wide straight-ins, others are fairly long pull-throughs; some pads may require additional leveling; fireplaces; b-y-o firewood; water at several faucets; restrooms; paved driveways; gas and camper supplies, 6 miles north; limited supplies and services are available in Colter Bay Village, a few miles south.

Activities & Attractions: Trail to the lake; the view of the Tetons across the lake is phenomenal.

Natural Features: Located on Fonda Point at the north end of Jackson Lake in Jackson Hole; campground vegetation consists of tall conifers, grass and underbrush; some sites are situated on a hillside and others are on a bluff overlooking the lake; peaks of the Teton Range steadfastly stand in striking contrast to the lake and the valley plain; elevation 6800'.

Season, Fees & Phone: June to early-September; $8.00 for a site, $10.00 for the park entrance permit; 14 day limit; Grand Teton National Park Headquarters, Moose, (307) 543-2467.

Camp Notes: Lizard Creek has no boat launch or visitor center, but does it have a view! (A few people get a little queasy at the thought of spending the night among the reptiles here. Actually, most of the critters departed about the same time George Bush left the White House. Ed.)

Wyoming 29

COLTER BAY
Grand Teton National Park

Location: Northwest Wyoming in northern Grand Teton Park.

Access: From U.S. Highways 89/287/191 (Rockefeller Parkway) at a point 20 miles south of the north boundary of Grand Teton National Park and 6 miles north of Jackson Lake Junction, turn west at a well-signed intersection onto a paved access road; continue west for several hundred yards; turn north (right) into the campground. (Note that it's easy to confuse the public campground with private trailer village and tent village).

Facilities: 350 campsites in 15 loops; (a number of group sites are also available); sites vary considerably, from small, lightly forested hilltop sites to generous medium, fairly open, level sites; parking pads are gravel, mostly straight-ins of assorted sizes; many pads may require additional leveling; fireplaces; firewood is usually for sale, or b-y-o; water at several faucets; restrooms; paved driveways; holding tank disposal station; showers, gas and groceries are available in Colter Bay Village.

Activities & Attractions: Fantastic mountain scenery; museum and visitor center in the village; amphitheater for evening programs; boating; sailing; fishing; hiking.

Natural Features: Located on the middle east shore of Jackson Lake; vegetation and terrain varies from tall pines and lush, grassy slopes, to rocky hillsides dotted with evergreens; some tent sites are perched on a hill with a terrific view; the Teton Range rises stunningly from the lake's surface at 6700' to nearly 14,000'; campground elevation 6800'.

Season, Fees & Phone: May to October; $8.00 for a site; $10.00 for the park entrance permit, (valid for 7 days in Grand Teton and Yellowstone National Parks); 14 day limit; Grand Teton National Park Headquarters, Moose, (307) 543-2467.

Camp Notes: This spot is not only beautiful, but is also the hub of activity in Grand Teton National Park. With the wide variety of choices here, it's worth a few minutes to scout around for a campsite that best fills the bill.

Wyoming 30

SIGNAL MOUNTAIN
Grand Teton National Park

Location: Northwest Wyoming in central Grand Teton Park.

Access: From Teton Park Road at a point 2 miles south of Jackson Lake Junction and 30 miles north of the South (Moose) Entrance to Grand Teton NP, turn west into the campground.

Facilities: 80 campsites in 2 loops; sites are small+ to medium-sized, with nominal separation; parking pads are gravel, mostly short to medium-length straight-ins, plus a few longer pull-throughs; many pads may require additional leveling; medium to large areas for tents, may be sloped; fireplaces; b-y-o firewood; water at central faucets; restrooms; holding tank disposal station; paved driveways; gas and camper supplies nearby.

Activities & Attractions: Boating; fishing; hiking; amphitheater for ranger-naturalist programs; side trip on a paved, twisty, steep access road to the summit of Signal Mountain.

Natural Features: Located on a hillside overlooking the southeast shore of Jackson Lake in Jackson Hole; campground vegetation consists of some tall conifers, but mostly sparse grass, brush and young timber; Signal Mountain lies just behind the campground to the east; the Teton Range rises majestically from the lake's west shore; elevation 6800'.

Season, Fees & Phone: May to September; $8.00 for a site; $10.00 for the park entrance permit; 14 day limit; Grand Teton National Park Headquarters, Moose, (307) 543-2467.

Camp Notes: The 'Hole' in Jackson Hole is the term used by early trappers and fur traders for a deep valley surrounded by high mountains. Signal Mountain is an isolated mound that rises above the valley floor. There are excellent elevated vistas of the Tetons from its summit.

Wyoming 31

JENNY LAKE
Grand Teton National Park

Location: Northwest Wyoming in central Grand Teton Park.

Access: From Teton Park Road at South Jenny Lake Junction (8 miles north of Moose, 24 miles south of Jackson Lake Junction), turn west onto a paved access road and go west and north for 0.5 mile to the campground. **Alternate Access:** From North Jenny Lake Junction, a narrow, paved, one-way drive leads 6 miles along the east shore of the lake to the campground.

Facilities: 49 campsites in 2 loops; camping is limited to tents and small vehicles; sites are small to small+, with nominal to fair separation; parking pads are gravel, short to short+ straight-ins; some pads may need minor additional leveling; fireplaces; b-y-o firewood; water at several faucets; central restrooms supplemented by vault facilities; paved, narrow driveway; camper supplies are available at the camp store nearby.

Activities & Attractions: Small boats are permitted on the lake; fishing; a trail leads around the lake and up into Cascade Canyon; other, smaller lakes nearby.

Natural Features: Located within a short walk of Jenny Lake, a mountain gem nestled at the foot of the sharp, lofty peaks of the Teton Range; campground vegetation consists of medium-height conifers and light undergrowth; sites are situated in a glen near the east shore of the lake; elevation 6800'.

Season, Fees & Phone: June to September; $8.00 for a site, $10.00 for the park entrance permit; 7 day limit; Grand Teton National Park Headquarters, Moose, (307) 543-2467.

Camp Notes: Jenny Lake Campground draws a capacity crowd daily from early June to mid-September. Anytime from late September until the first lasting snowfall in late October is nearly perfect for camping. Even if you can only stay long enough for a glimpse of the lake or a hike around it, you'll be glad you stopped at Jenny Lake.

Wyoming 32

GROS VENTRE
Grand Teton National Park

Location: Northwest Wyoming in southeast Grand Teton Park.

Access: From U.S. Highways 89/191/26 (Rockefeller Parkway) at a point 8 miles south of Moose and 12 miles north of Jackson, turn east onto Gros Ventre Road (paved); travel northeast for 4.5 miles; turn south (right) and continue for 0.2 mile to the campground entrance.

Facilities: 408 campsites in 8 loops; (several small group sites are also available); most sites are medium to medium+ in size, generally level, with nominal to fair separation; parking pads are gravel, medium to long straight-ins or pull-throughs; tent spots are large, but a little rocky; fireplaces; b-y-o firewood; water at faucets throughout; restrooms; holding tank disposal station; paved driveways; camper supplies in Kelly, 2 miles east; complete supplies and services are available in Jackson.

Activities & Attractions: Fishing; amphitheater for ranger-naturalist programs; a number of roads lead into adjacent national forest lands.

Natural Features: Located on the ancient flood plain of the Gros Ventre River in Jackson Hole on the northern edge of the Gros Ventre Range of the Rocky Mountains; the campground is in a large grove of tall hardwoods, with a ground cover of some brush, sparse grass and stones; the Gros Ventre River flows by the campground and joins the Snake River just to the west; typically breezy; elevation 6600'.

Season, Fees & Phone: May to September; $8.00 for a site; $10.00 for the park entrance permit; 14 day limit; Grand Teton National Park Headquarters, Moose, (307) 543-2467.

Camp Notes: If you arrive in the park late on a typical midsummer day, you might find a spot here when the other camps are full. *Gros Ventre* is pronounced like "grow *vahnt*". It's the name early French mountain men gave to the local Indians. Literally translated it means 'Big Belly'.

Wyoming 33

ATHERTON CREEK
Bridger-Teton National Forest

Location: Northwest Wyoming east of Grand Teton Park.

Access: From U.S. Highways 89/191/26 (Rockefeller Parkway) at a point 12 miles north of Jackson and 8 miles south of Moose, turn east onto Gros Ventre Road (paved); travel northeast for 8.1 miles; at a well marked intersection, turn southeast (right) and drive easterly for 5.5 miles on a winding, paved road; turn south (right) into the campground.

Facilities: 20 campsites in 2 loops; sites are average or better in size, with minimal to nominal separation; parking pads are gravel, and some may need considerable additional leveling; sites nearer to the lake are level enough for tents; barbecue grills; b-y-o firewood is recommended; water at central faucets; vault facilities; steep, gravel driveways; camper supplies at a small store in Kelly, 7 miles west.

Activities & Attractions: Windsurfing; fishing; boating; self-guided Gros Ventre Slide Area nature walk; Grand Teton National Park is a few miles west.

Natural Features: Located in the Gros Ventre Range east of Jackson Hole; sites are situated on an open hillside overlooking Slide Lake; terrain is rather rocky, with only sage and a few small trees for very limited shelter; typically breezy; elev. 7000'.

Season, Fees & Phone: June to September; $7.00; 16 day limit; Jackson Ranger District (307) 733-4755.

Camp Notes: The drive up to the campground, along the Gros Ventre River, is very scenic. The area's dark green foliage contrasts sharply with the bright red soil of the bordering hills. Campsites are on a hillside just above the north shore of five-mile-long Slide Lake, which was formed when a 1925 landslide blocked the flow of the Gros Ventre River.

Wyoming 34

TRAIL CREEK
Targhee National Forest

Location: Western Wyoming west of Jackson.

Access: From Wyoming State Highway 22 at a point a few yards east of the Wyoming-Idaho border (5.6 miles east of Victor, Idaho, 18 miles west of Jackson, Wyoming), turn south into the campground. (To help you find your way from the Idaho side, it might be helpful to know that this highway is Idaho State Highway 31 on the west side of the state boundary.)

Facilities: 11 campsites; sites are small to medium-sized, with fair separation; parking pads are gravel, mostly level, long pull-throughs or straight-ins; some good tent spots in among the trees; leveled, framed-and-gravelled table pads; barbecue grills; firewood is available for gathering in the area; water at several faucets; vault facilities; gravel driveways; camper supplies in Victor; complete supplies and services are available in Jackson.

Activities & Attractions: Stream fishing for small trout; Grand Teton National Park is within an hour's drive to the east; superscenic drive along this highway, east or west.

Natural Features: Located in a stand of trees along Trail Creek, high in the Teton Range of the Rocky Mountains; campground vegetation consists of conifers and hardwoods with light underbrush; Teton Pass, at 8431', 7 miles east, offers some fantastic vistas of the southern end of the great valley to the east called Jackson Hole; elevation 6600'.

Season, Fees & Phone: May to October; $7.00; 16 day limit; Jackson Ranger District (307) 733-4755.

Camp Notes: Trail Creek Campground is situated in a beautiful mountaintop setting. The views along Highway 31 from the west are pleasant, as it winds through fertile Swan Valley and up the west slopes of the Teton Range. From the east, the highway leading to Trail Creek is quite steep--as much as a 10% grade. But the views--oh, the views--to the east, are spectacular. No, more than just spectacular. They are _____. (Fill in the blank.)

====

Wyoming
West
Please refer to the Wyoming map in the Appendix

Wyoming 35

STATION CREEK
Bridger-Teton National Forest

Location: Western Wyoming south of Jackson.

Access: From U.S. Highways 26/89 at milepost 128 +.6 (10 miles east of Alpine, 13 miles southwest of Hoback Junction), turn south onto a short, but steep, gravel access road and proceed 0.1 mile down into the campground.

Facilities: 15 campsites in 2 loops; sites are mostly medium-sized, with fair to good separation; parking pads are gravel, mostly medium-length, and level (though the sites are situated on a considerable slope); most tent spots are rather small; fireplaces; firewood is available for gathering in the area; water at faucets; vault facilities; gravel driveways with turnarounds at the east and west ends; camper supplies at Hoback Junction; complete supplies and services are available in Jackson, 24 miles northeast.

Activities & Attractions: Fishing; river rafting; Station Creek Study Enclosure is directly across the highway; the drive along Highway 26/89 through the Snake River Canyon is more than just pleasantly scenic.

Natural Features: Located on a bluff overlooking the Snake River; campground vegetation consists of tall conifers, fairly dense underbrush and tall grass; a timbered ridge rises from the south riverbank across from the campground; elevation 5800'.

Season, Fees & Phone: May to September; $7.00; 16 day limit; Jackson Ranger District (307) 733-4755.

Camp Notes: A rail fence separates many of the sites from the river's edge. It also adds a nice touch to the surroundings. Of the campgrounds in this stretch of the Snake River Canyon, Station Creek is one of the most popular.

Wyoming 36

EAST TABLE CREEK
Bridger-Teton National Forest

Location: Western Wyoming south of Jackson.

Access: From U.S. Highways 26/89 at milepost 130 +.1 (12 miles east of Alpine, 11 miles southwest of Hoback Junction), turn south and go 100 yards to the campground.

Facilities: 18 campsites; sites are medium to large, with fair to very good separation; parking pads are gravel, and vary from medium-length straight-ins to long pull-throughs; a few pads may require additional leveling; some good tent-pitching opportunities; fireplaces; firewood is available for gathering in the area; water at several faucets; vault facilities; gravel driveways; camper supplies at Hoback Junction; complete supplies and services are available in Jackson, 21 miles northeast.

Activities & Attractions: Fishing; river rafting; river access is 0.2 mile west of the campground entrance; superscenic drive through the Grand Canyon of the Snake River.

Natural Features: Located along the north bank of the Snake River in the Snake River Canyon; fairly dense vegetation in the campground consists of mostly tall timber, grass and light underbrush; elevation 5800'.

Season, Fees & Phone: May to September; $7.00; 10 day limit; Jackson Ranger District (307) 733-4755.

Camp Notes: The Snake River flows swiftly by this camp, and the canyon is a bit broader here than at Elbow Campground, a mile east. The canyon is bustling with rafters during the midsummer river-running season. (It might make you wish you had pontoons on the old pickup.)

Wyoming 37

ELBOW
Bridger-Teton National Forest

Location: Western Wyoming south of Jackson.

Access: From U.S. Highways 26/89 at milepost 131 +.2 (13.5 miles east of Alpine, 9.5 miles southwest of Hoback Junction), turn southeast into the campground.

Facilities: 17 campsites; (a group camp is also available); sites are average to large in size, and most are fairly well separated; parking pads are gravel, generally level, long pull-throughs; medium to large tent areas; fireplaces; firewood is available for gathering in the area; water at faucets; vault facilities; gravel driveways; camper supplies in Hoback Junction; complete supplies and services are available in Jackson, 22 miles northeast.

Activities & Attractions: Fishing; river rafting--the Snake River is accessible at this very popular 'put-in' point; scenic drive/bike/float through the Grand Canyon of the Snake River.

Natural Features: Located on the north bank of the Snake River in Snake River Canyon; campground vegetation consists of tall timber, grass and moderate underbrush; sites are situated along the riverbank, slightly below the highway level; high bluffs are visible across the river on the south bank; to the north, across the highway, is an open sage hillside; elevation 5800'.

Season, Fees & Phone: May to September; $7.00 for a single site, $12.00 for a double site; 10 day limit; Jackson Ranger District (307) 733-4755.

Camp Notes: Elbow Campground is located on the Snake River where the southbound serpentine stream sharply swings 90° to the west. Another smaller campground, Cabin Creek, is about 2.5 miles northeast. It has 10 forested sites and similar facilities.

Wyoming 38

HOBACK
Bridger-Teton National Forest

Location: Western Wyoming southeast of Jackson.

Access: From U.S. Highways 191/189 at a point 7.7 miles southeast of Hoback Junction and 13 miles northwest of Bondurant, turn south into the campground.

Facilities: 28 campsites in 2 loops; sites are average or better in size, with nominal to good separation; the south loop (across the river) has a bit more low-level vegetation for separation; parking pads are level and paved; some pads are straight-ins and some are pull-throughs spacious enough to accommodate larger vehicles; some nice, large, grassy tent sites, especially in the north loop; fireplaces or barbecue grills at each site; limited firewood is available for gathering in the vicinity; water at several faucets; vault facilities; paved driveways; minimal supplies at Hoback Junction; adequate supplies and services are available in Jackson.

Activities & Attractions: Fishing; self-guided nature trail near the southwest corner of the campground; amphitheater; Granite Hot Springs, about 15 miles east and north on a gravel road, has public swimming and picnicking facilities.

Natural Features: Located in the very green Hoback River Canyon; campground vegetation consists of tall conifers, a few hardwoods, light to moderate underbrush and a grassy forest floor; sites are on both sides of the river, linked by a narrow bridge; the river flows freely between tall, rocky ridges, with the peaks of the Gros Ventre Range rising to the north; elev. 6200'.

Season, Fees & Phone: May to October; $7.00; 10 day limit; Jackson Ranger District (307) 733-4755.

Camp Notes: Hoback Campground is a pleasant, green retreat. (That is, if the Grand Teton campgrounds are too busy for your preferences, you can retreat to this camp. Ed.) Another smaller campground, Kozy, is located six miles east. It has eight nice sites between the river and the highway, but no drinking water.

Wyoming 39

SWIFT CREEK
Bridger-Teton National Forest

Location: Far western Wyoming southwest of Jackson.

Access: From U.S. Highway 89 at milepost 86 (in midtown Afton, 70 miles southwest of Jackson), turn east onto Second Avenue South; proceed 0.8 mile to the end of the pavement; continue 0.7 mile further east on gravel; at a fork in the road turn south (right), cross a bridge, and turn east (left) into the campground (for a total of 1.5 miles from town).

Facilities: 11 campsites; sites are medium to large, with fairly good separation; parking pads are gravel, mostly level, short to medium-length pull-throughs or straight-ins; some nice, secluded spots for medium to large tents; barbecue grills; firewood is available for gathering in the area; water at faucets; vault facilities; gravel, rather narrow driveways; limited to adequate supplies and services are available in Afton.

Activities & Attractions: Stream fishing; creekside trail in the campground; hiking trails lead into the Salt River Range.

Natural Features: Located in a narrow forested canyon along Swift Creek, which flows westerly through Afton to join waters of the Salt River; campground vegetation consists mostly of tall grass and hardwoods, with some tall conifers; the area surrounding the campground is rather brushy; bordered by tree-dotted slopes to the north, timbered hillsides to the south; the peaks of the Salt River Range rise to the east; elevation 6300'.

Season, Fees & Phone: May to October; $6.00; 10 day limit; Greys River Ranger District, Afton, (307) 886-3166.

Camp Notes: Swift Creek is a pleasant, forested camp spot, conveniently close to Highway 89 and the settlement of Afton. This is a fairly remote part of Wyoming. You can be sure that you won't hear the Interstate traffic from here! (For that matter, what parts of Wyoming *aren't* fairly remote. Ed.)

ALLRED FLAT
Bridger-Teton National Forest

Location: Far western Wyoming south of Jackson.

Access: From U.S. Highway 89 near milepost 65 (12.5 miles southwest of Smoot, 9.5 miles east of the Wyoming-Idaho border), turn north onto a gravel access road and proceed 0.3 mile to the campground.

Facilities: 32 campsites; sites are medium to large, with fair separation; parking pads are gravel, mostly medium to long pull-throughs; some additional leveling may be required; tent spots are grassy and good-sized, but may also be a bit sloped; fireplaces; firewood is available for gathering; water at faucets and hand pumps; vault facilities; holding tank disposal station; gravel driveways; limited to adequate supplies and services are available in Afton, 20 miles east.

Activities & Attractions: Fishing on Salt Creek; foot trails lead off into the hills; pleasant views up and down the valley.

Natural Features: Located on a lightly forested slope along Little White Creek in the Gannett Hills; campground vegetation consists of aspens and lodgepole pines, with abundant tall grass in the more open meadow area to the east; Little White Creek flows south to join Salt Creek just across the highway; elevation 7100'.

Season, Fees & Phone: May to October; $7.00; 10 day limit; Greys River Ranger District, Afton, (307) 886-3166.

Camp Notes: Allred Flat is a really good stop along this main route. (Please keep us posted on the progress being made on the beaver dam.)

WARREN BRIDGE
Public Lands/BLM Recreation Site

Location: Western Wyoming southeast of Jackson.

Access: From U.S. Highways 189/191 at a point 24 miles northwest of Pinedale, 20 miles southeast of Bondurant (just south of the Green River bridge), turn west into the campground.

Facilities: 23 campsites; sites are medium sized, level, well spaced, but with virtually no visual separation; parking pads are gravel, long pull-throughs; large areas for tents, but they may be a bit rocky; fire rings, plus some barbecue grills; definitely b-y-o firewood; water at several faucets; vault facilities; holding tank disposal station; gravel driveways; limited to adequate supplies and services are available in Pinedale.

Activities & Attractions: River floating; fishing; easy access to the river from the campground and adjacent day use area; a number of mountain lakes in the Wind River Range are accessible from nearby forest roads.

Natural Features: Located along the bank of the Green River, west of the impressive Wind River Range and the Continental Divide; sites are situated on a large sage flat sheltered by a few, scattered, small trees; the headwaters of the Green River lie in the mountains to the north; tallest peak in the state, 13,804' Gannett Peak, is visible to the northeast; elevation 7500'.

Season, Fees & Phone: May to October; $5.00; 14 day limit; BLM Pinedale Office (307) 367-4358.

Camp Notes: There is a certain sense of vastness that can be felt only in places just like this one: out in the middle of an immense, high desert plain. Peaks that are snow capped nearly all year are visible in three directions. Another, smaller BLM campground with similar facilities, Upper Green, is nearby.

WIND RIVER
Boysen State Park

Location: West-central Wyoming south of Thermopolis.

Access: From U.S. Highway 20/Wyoming State Highway 789 at milepost 115 +.1 (15 miles north of Shoshoni, 18 miles south of Thermopolis, turn west onto a paved access road and proceed 0.2 mile down into Upper Wind River; or at milepost 116, turn west and go down into Lower Wind River.

Facilities: 88 campsites in 2 sections; sites are medium-sized, essentially level, fairly well spaced, with better visual separation in Upper Wind River sites; parking pads are medium to long straight-ins or pull-throughs; most sites have large grass/earth tent spots; fire rings or fireplaces; b-y-o firewood; water at several faucets; vault facilities; holding tank disposal station nearby; paved Upper driveway, gravel Lower driveway; limited+ supplies and services are available in Thermopolis.

Activities & Attractions: Playgrounds; public boat launch, 1 mile south, for boating and fishing access to Boysen Reservoir.

Natural Features: Located on a shelf above the Wind River in Wind River Canyon just below Boysen Reservoir Dam; vegetation consists of tall cottonwoods, some grass, bushes and low brush; sites are unshaded to lightly shaded/sheltered; the high, sheer rock canyon walls display several layers of strata dating back more than a half-billion years; elevation 4600'.

Season, Fees & Phone: Open all year, with limited services November to April; please see Appendix for standard Wyoming state park fees; park office (307) 876-2796.

Camp Notes: Compared to the state park's campgrounds in the dry, open country south of here, this unit is quite green, with a light to brisk breeze that rolls through the canyon much of the time. In early autumn, especially, it's a real treat to camp here. The 12-mile drive through Wind River Canyon is a time-traveling experience of sorts, and it is very, very impressive.

Wyoming 43

BRANNON & TAMARISK
Boysen State Park

Location: West-central Wyoming northeast of Riverton.

Access: From U.S. Highway 20/Wyoming State Highway 789 at milepost 113 +.4 (13 miles north of Shoshoni, 20 miles south of Thermopolis), turn southwest onto Brannon Road (paved) and proceed 0.3 mile to Brannon Campground; or continue past Brannon for another mile to Tamarisk Campground.

Facilities: *Brannon*: Approximately 20 campsites around the perimeter of an 'infield'; paved, parallel parking is provided in the loop driveway around the infield; large, grassy tent areas; (check the lawn-watering schedule and stay mobile); *Tamarisk*: Approximately 30 campsites; sites are medium-sized, with nominal separation; parking surfaces are gravel straight-ins/pull-offs; ample space for tents; **both camps**: ramadas (sun shelters) for a couple of sites; fire rings; b-y-o firewood; water at central faucets; vault facilities; holding tank disposal station nearby on the highway; gas and groceries in Shoshoni; limited+ supplies and services are available in Thermopolis.

Activities & Attractions: Boating; boat launch and dock; marina nearby; fishing; playgrounds.

Natural Features: Located along the northeast shore of Boysen Reservoir, near the head of Wind River Canyon; Brannon has a large, "infield" lawn; Tamarisk is on several small points of land, with 'landscaping' consisting of large hardwoods scattered along the shore, brush and rough grass; elevation 4800'.

Season, Fees & Phone: Open all year, subject to weather conditions, with limited services November to April; 14 day limit; please see Appendix for standard Wyoming state park fees; ark office (307) 876-2796.

Camp Notes: Numbers of campsites listed above are frugal figures which will give you an idea of the size of the areas and the campers they accommodate in normal times. Count on up to double those digits for summer holiday weekends. Chances are, these or the other camps along U.S. 20/Wyoming 789 (Wind River or Tough Creek) will suit the requirements of most campers. But if you really need to get out into the toolies, there are several roughcut camping areas on Boysen's west shore, from five to 15 miles up mostly gravel roads from U.S. 26/Wyoming 789 milepost 121 +.7. If you really *need* to, that is.

Wyoming 44

TOUGH CREEK
Boysen State Park

Location: West-central Wyoming northeast of Riverton.

Access: From U.S. Highway 20/Wyoming State Highway 789 at milepost 106 +.2 (6 miles north of Shoshoni, 26 miles south of Thermopolis), turn west onto a paved access road and proceed 1.2 miles to the campground.

Facilities: Approximately 30 camp/picnic sites; sites are medium to large, tolerably level, with fair to good separation; parking areas are gravel/dirt, spacious enough for most vehicles; ditto for tents; small ramadas (sun shelters) for a few sites; fire rings; b-y-o firewood; water at a hand pump; vault facilities; gravel driveways; gas and groceries+ in Shoshoni, limited+ supplies and services are available in Thermopolis.

Activities & Attractions: Fishing; small playground.

Natural Features: Located on a point of land on the middle-east shore of Boysen Reservoir; vegetation consists of a dozen medium-sized hardwoods along the shoreline, large brush and some stubby grass; bordered by dry low hills and bluffs, with a line of mountains to the north; elevation 4800'.

Season, Fees & Phone: Open all year, with limited services November to April; please see Appendix for standard Wyoming state park fees; park office (307) 876-2796.

Camp Notes: You can have your own little patch of beach here (when the lake level cooperates). The moderate number of sites are spread out over about a half square mile of rough lakefront property, so there's plenty of space between most campsites.

Wyoming 45

POPO AGIE & SAWMILL
Sinks Canyon State Park

Location: West-central Wyoming south of Lander.

Access: From U.S. Highway 287/Main Street in midtown Lander, turn south onto Fifth Street/Wyoming State Highway 131 and proceed 0.6 mile to a "T" intersection; turn west (right, onto Fremont Street) continuing on Highway 131 and travel west for 0.5 mile, then the road curves southerly; travel southwest on Highway 131 for another 5.5 miles to the park boundary; Sawmill Campground is just to the left inside the park; continue ahead for 2 miles to Popo Agie Campground (also on the left).

Facilities: *Popo Agie*: 28 camp/picnic sites, including 4 park 'n walk tent sites; sites are small to medium-sized, with nominal to fair separation; parking pads are gravel, mostly short to medium-length straight-ins; many pads may require additional leveling; tent areas tend to be smallish and a bit rocky; the park 'n walk sites are situated in nice spots just above the river; *Sawmill*: 4 camp/picnic sites adjacent to a small parking lot; ***both camps***: fire rings; limited firewood is available for gathering on national forest lands just south of the park, b-y-o is suggested; water at hand pumps; vault facilities; gravel driveways; adequate supplies and services are available in Lander.

Activities & Attractions: Short trail (0.1 mile) to the Sinks; hiking trails, into the mountains; self-guided nature trail; visitor center has nature exhibits and a film about the area; trout fishing (north and south of the park boundary).

Natural Features: Located along the Middle Fork of the Popo Agie River (pronounced "po-*po*-zsha") in a narrow canyon of sheer rock walls; Popo Agie vegetation is mostly grass and a few trees which provide very little to light shade; Sawmill sites are a little better shaded; all campsites are riverside or nearly riverside; the Wind River Range stretches for 100 miles from here toward the northwest; elevation 6000'.

Season, Fees & Phone: Principal season is mid-May to October, with limited availability and services in winter; 14 day limit; please see Appendix for standard Wyoming state park fees; park office (307) 332-6333.

Camp Notes: *Popo Agie* means "Beginning of the Waters", and refers to the canyon's geological phenomenon. The river makes a furious, roaring, headlong plunge into a mountainside cavern at the base of a cliff and just disappears. The madly foaming water travels through vertical clefts (the "Sinks") in the subterranean rocks, and reappears a half-mile downstream in a sparkling, tranquil pool (the "Rise") fully populated with trophy-size trout. (Lest you fishermen get too excited over the prospect of landing one of those beauties, it should be noted that the "No Fishing" shingle is conspicuously displayed.) This park is one of those neat little Wyoming surprises.

Wyoming 46

SINKS CANYON
Shoshone National Forest

Location: West-central Wyoming south of Lander.

Access: From U.S. Highway 287/Main Street in midtown Lander, turn south onto Fifth Street/Wyoming State Highway 131 and proceed 0.6 mile to a "T" intersection; turn west (right, onto Fremont Street) continuing on Highway 131 and travel west for 0.5 mile, then the road curves southerly; travel southwest on Highway 131 for another 5.5 miles to the park boundary; continue through the state park for 2 miles; at the end of the pavement just south of the state park boundary, turn southeast (left) into the campground.

Facilities: 11 campsites; sites are small to medium-sized, with fair separation; a pair of walk-in sites, on the east side of the river via a small wooden footbridge, are roomier and more secluded; parking pads are hard-surfaced, medium-length straight-ins; some pads may require additional leveling; small parking area for the walk-in sites at the south end of the campground; small to medium-sized tent areas; fire rings; a very limited quantity of firewood is available for gathering, b-y-o is suggested; water at several faucets; vault facilities; paved driveways; adequate supplies and services are available in Lander.

Activities & Attractions: Fishing; visitor center in the state park; a superscenic back road leads through the hills for 20 miles over to the South Pass area near Highway 28.

Natural Features: Located along the Middle Fork of the Popo Agie River on the north slope of the Wind River Range; all sites are right along the river, with only limited shade provided by a few small aspens and evergreens; bordered by a juniper-dotted sage slope; elevation 6000'.

Season, Fees & Phone: June to October; $7.00; 14 day limit; Washakie Ranger District, Lander, (307) 332-5460.

Camp Notes: Sinks Canyon is a nice little place, and this national forest campground is a nice little 'find'. The forest camp is a touch nicer, and is usually a bit less busy than, the nearby state park campgrounds. But it's worth the stop in any of the canyon camps.

Wyoming 47

ATLANTIC CITY
Public Lands/BLM Recreation Site

Location: Western Wyoming south of Lander.

Access: From Wyoming State Highway 28 at milepost 49 +.2 (30 miles south of Lander, 47 miles northeast of Farson, 1 mile south of the Atlantic City Mine and directly across from a highway maintenance yard), turn east at a sign for "Atlantic City"; drive east, then south for 1 mile on a gravel road; turn west (right) into the campground.

Facilities: 22 campsites; sites are medium-sized, with fairly good separation; parking pads are gravel, mostly medium to long straight-ins; some pads may require additional leveling; nice large, sheltered tent spots, but they may be a bit rocky; fire rings and barbecue grills; very little firewood is available in the vicinity, so b-y-o is suggested; water at several faucets; vault facilities; gravel driveways; camper supplies are available in Atlantic City, 1.6 miles south.

Activities & Attractions: The main attraction in the area is a pair of partially renovated ghost towns: Atlantic City and South Pass City were boom towns in the 1867-1868 gold rush; also nearby is the site of Fort Stambaugh; Beaver Creek, a few miles to the north, reportedly offers some very good fishing.

Natural Features: Located at the southern tip of the Wind River Range in historic South Pass; sites are situated in an aspen grove surrounded by miles of sage-covered hills to the east and mountains to the west; campground vegetation consists of young aspens, tall pines, sage and grass; elevation 7600'.

Season, Fees & Phone: June to October; $5.00; 14 day limit; BLM Lander Office (307) 332-7822.

Camp Notes: The setting for this campground is very remote and secluded. It's a really pleasant spot that's seldom occupied to capacity. Another BLM campground 0.2 mile north and east, Big Atlantic Gulch, has ten sites in a more open environment.

Wyoming 48

BUCKBOARD
Flaming Gorge National Recreation Area

Location: Southwest Wyoming south of Green River.

Access: From Wyoming State Highway 530 at milepost 24 +.6 (25 miles south of Green River, 23 miles north of Manila, Utah), turn east onto a paved road and proceed 1.3 miles to the pay station; turn south and go 0.1 mile to the campground.

Facilities: 68 campsites; sites are small to medium sized with minimal separation; parking pads are gravel, reasonably level, short, extra wide, straight-ins; medium to large, grassy tent areas; ramadas (arched wind/sun shelters) for table areas; water at central faucets; restrooms; holding tank disposal station; paved driveways; ranger station; camper supplies at a marina, 0.5 mile east; limited supplies in Manila; complete supplies and services are available in Green River.

Activities & Attractions: Boating; boat launch; fishing.

Natural Features: Located on a slightly sloping sage plain on the west shore of Flaming Gorge Reservoir; a minimal amount of natural shelter/shade is provided by small hardwoods; typically sunny, warm and very dry during the camping season; antelope are commonly seen; elevation 6100'.

Season, Fees & Phone: May to October; $7.00; 14 day limit; Flaming Gorge Ranger District, Manila UT, (801) 784-3445.

Camp Notes: This campground is also called "Buckboard Crossing" in some literature. Call it what you will, there's little question that its facilities and natural features make this spot the best of the Flaming Gorge camps in Wyoming. Most campsites have unrestricted, distant, sweeping views of Flaming Gorge.

Wyoming 49

HORSESHOE BEND
Bighorn Canyon National Recreation Area

Location: North-central Wyoming northeast of Lovell.

Access: From the junction of U.S. Highway 14A & Wyoming State Highway 37 (3 miles east of Lovell), travel north for 11 miles on Highway 37, then east on a paved access road for 1 mile to the campground.

Facilities: 128 campsites in 3 loops; sites are medium to large, with almost no visual separation; parking pads are hard-surfaced, level, short to medium-length straight-ins; small to medium-sized areas for tents; fire rings and barbecue grills; b-y-o firewood; water at central faucets; restrooms; holding tank disposal station at the nearby ranger station; paved loop roads; camper supplies at the marina, 1 mile south; limited+ supplies and services are available in Lovell.

Activities & Attractions: Excellent public boat launch and dock facilities; very good fishing; nature trail starts from the C Loop in the campground; campfire programs in summer; large Park Service visitor center, just east of Lovell.

Natural Features: Located on a treeless, sage-covered bluff overlooking Horseshoe Bend of Bighorn Canyon Reservoir; brilliant, multi-colored rock formations rise from the lake shore to the south and west; Bighorn Mountains lie to the east, Pryor Mountains are to the west; typically breezy; elevation 3900'.

Season, Fees & Phone: Open all year, with limited services September to May; $6.00; 14 day limit; Bighorn Canyon Visitor Center, Lovell, (307) 352-8749.

Camp Notes: The Bighorn Canyon area strongly resembles sections of northern Arizona or southern Utah. Although the campground is on a dry, windy hilltop, there are significant advantages to staying here: it's rarely filled to capacity, insects are usually not much of a problem, and you don't have to dig too deeply to come up with the fee.

Wyoming
East
Please refer to the Wyoming map in the Appendix

Wyoming 50

PORCUPINE
Bighorn National Forest

Location: North-central Wyoming west of Sheridan.

Access: From U.S. Highway 14A at milepost 36 (36 miles east of Lovell, 24 miles west of Burgess Junction), turn north onto a gravel access road and proceed 1.7 miles to the campground.

Facilities: 12 campsites; most sites are quite large, with good separation; parking pads are gravel, long and level; large, level tent areas; fire rings; firewood is available for gathering; water at central faucets; vault facilities; public holding tank disposal station one-half mile east of Burgess Junction on U.S. 14; gravel driveway; camper supplies at Burgess Junction; limited+ supplies and services are available in Lovell.

Activities & Attractions: 'Medicine Wheel', a unique archaeological discovery related to local Indian lore (access road is a half mile west of the campground turnoff); meadow walking; several forest roads and 4wd trails in the vicinity.

Natural Features: Located in a thin stand of conifers high in the Bighorn Mountains; the campground is carpeted with tall grass and wildflowers during midsummer; a rail fence completely surrounds the campground; adjacent to a large alpine meadow; count on cool or cold nights; elevation 8900'.

Season, Fees & Phone: June to September; $7.00; 14 day limit; Medicine Wheel Ranger District, Lovell, (307) 548-6541.

Camp Notes: This camp is in a classic, high mountain setting. It might be a good place for those who prefer a pleasant, low-key approach to camping. While there aren't a lot of formal attractions or activities here, just enjoying the terrific views of the high country will probably satisfy most campers.

Wyoming 51

BALD MOUNTAIN
Bighorn National Forest

Location: North-central Wyoming west of Sheridan.

Access: From U.S. Highway 14A at milepost 36 + .3 (36 miles east of Lovell, 23 miles west of Burgess Junction), turn south into the campground.

Facilities: 13 campsites, including a couple of double-sized units; most sites are fairly large and well separated; parking pads are gravel and level; large areas for tents; fireplaces; some firewood is available for gathering; water at several faucets; vault facilities; public holding tank disposal station on U.S. 14, a half mile east of Burgess Junction; gravel driveway, with large turnaround loop at the south end of the campground; camper supplies at Burgess Junction; limited+ supplies and services are available in Lovell.

Activities & Attractions: Access road to 'Medicine Wheel', a significant archaeological site associated with the local Indians, is a half mile west of the campground entrance on Highway 14A; several forest roads and 4wd trails in the area.

Natural Features: Located at the edge of a stand of timber on a large, high mountain plain, in the shadow of Bald Mountain; about half of the sites are well sheltered, others are out in the open; Crystal Creek flows through the campground; encircled by square miles of wildflowers in midsummer; elevation 9200'.

Season, Fees & Phone: June to September; $7.00; 14 day limit; Medicine Wheel Ranger District, Lovell, (307) 548-6541.

Camp Notes: Many of the campsites here provide grand sweeping views in most directions. The 'Medicine Wheel' (cited in the Attractions section) consists of an arrangement of large, flat stones in the shape of a spoked wheel about 30 feet in diameter on the surface of an alpine meadow. The origin and significance of the ancient pattern remains a mystery. Although some have loosely compared it to Stonehenge in England (a scientifically valid astronomical device), archaeologists generally believe Medicine Wheel was used in religious ceremonies.

Wyoming 52

PRUNE CREEK
Bighorn National Forest

Location: North-central Wyoming west of Sheridan.

Access: From U.S. Highway 14 at a point 4.3 miles east of Burgess Junction, 23 miles west of Dayton, and 64 miles east of Lovell), turn south into the campground.

Facilities: 21 campsites in 2 loops; most sites are medium-sized, with good separation; parking pads are gravel, medium-length and level; large, level tent spots; fire rings and barbecue grills; firewood is available for gathering; water at faucets; vault facilities; public disposal station, 4 miles west, on the north side of U.S. 14; gravel driveways; camper supplies at Burgess Junction; limited supplies and services are available in Dayton.

Activities & Attractions: Fishing; strolling along the water's edge is a simple, but apparently very popular, pastime here.

Natural Features: Located on a timbered flat at the confluence of the South Tongue River and Prune Creek in the Bighorn Mountains; campground vegetation consists of grass and wildflowers in a medium-dense conifer forest; a lush meadow lies south of the campground, across the river; surrounded by timbered ridges; elevation 7700'.

Season, Fees & Phone: June to September; $8.00; 14 day limit; Tongue River Ranger District, Sheridan, (307) 672-0751.

Camp Notes: For campers who prefer a riverfront setting, this spot provides one of the best opportunities for streamside camping in the Bighorn Mountains. Daytime weekend traffic can sometimes be bothersome, since the campground is close to the highway. Most of the time, though, it would probably be an excellent choice.

Wyoming 53

SIBLEY LAKE
Bighorn National Forest

Location: North-central Wyoming west of Sheridan.

Access: From U.S. Highway 14 at a point 5 miles east of Burgess Junction, 22 miles west of Dayton and 65 miles east of Lovell), turn south onto a gravel access road and proceed 0.3 mile to the campground.

Facilities: 10 campsites; most sites are small to medium in size, with reasonably level, medium-length, gravel/dirt parking pads; tent spots are medium-sized and fairly level; fire rings and barbecue grills in most sites; firewood is available for gathering; water at hand pumps near the campground entrance and at the lake; vault facilities; gravel/dirt driveways; public disposal station 5 miles west, on Highway 14; camper supplies at Burgess Junction; limited supplies and services are available in Dayton.

Activities & Attractions: Fishing; motorless boating; gravel boat launch; trail around the lake; day use area on the lake shore.

Natural Features: Located on a forested hilltop above Sibley Lake in the Bighorn Mountains, (although the lake isn't clearly visible from most of the campsites); surrounded by heavily timbered ridges; elevation 7900'.

Season, Fees & Phone: June to September; $8.00; 14 day limit; Tongue River Ranger District, Sheridan, (307) 672-0751.

Camp Notes: Admittedly, the campground here may not be highly notable for its facilities, but the location certainly is noteworthy. Sibley Lake itself, although small by some standards, is pleasantly picturesque; and it's one of the few easily accessible lakes in this region.

Wyoming 54

TIE FLUME
Bighorn National Forest

Location: North-central Wyoming west of Sheridan.

Access: From U.S. Highway 14 near milepost 42 (42 miles northeast of Greybull, 6 miles south of Burgess Junction), turn east onto a gravel road; proceed 2.6 miles to a fork; take the left fork for 0.1 mile to the campground.

Facilities: 25 campsites in 2 loops; most sites are quite spacious, level and reasonably well separated; parking pads are gravel, medium-length straight-ins; very good to excellent tent-pitching opportunities; fire rings and barbecue grills in most sites; firewood is available for gathering in the area; water at hand pumps; vault facilities; holding tank disposal station on U.S. 14, a half mile east of Burgess Junction; gravel driveways; camper supplies in Burgess Junction; nearest sources of limited+ to adequate supplies are Greybull, Dayton or Lovell, "a lotta miles from here".

Activities & Attractions: Fishing; foot trails meander through the trees and along the riverbank.

Natural Features: Located in a moderately dense conifer forest on the west bank of the South Tongue River in the Bighorn Mountains; a lush, open, riverside meadow is adjacent to the campground; a couple of rocky peaks, but mostly conifer-covered low hills, are visible from the campground; elevation 8400'.

Season, Fees & Phone: June to September; $7.00; 14 day limit; Tongue River Ranger District, Sheridan, (307) 672-0751.

Camp Notes: This is a winner. Tie Flume is one of the nicest of the easily accessible campgrounds in the Big Horn Mountains. It's just far enough off the main highway to provide convenient access coupled with peace and quiet. Another campground near milepost 42, Owen Creek, is located 0.2 mile off the west side of the highway, and has 7 sites along a small stream. You could also try Dead Swede (!) Campground, 2 miles south of Tie Flume.

SHELL CREEK & RANGER CREEK
Bighorn National Forest

Location: North-central Wyoming east of Greybull.

Access: From U.S. Highway 14 at milepost 31 +.3 (31 miles east of Greybull, 17 miles southwest of Burgess Junction), turn southeast onto Paint Rock Road (gravel) and proceed 1.7 miles, then turn southwest (right), and go 0.1 mile to Shell Creek; or continue for another mile to Ranger Creek. (Note that the turnoff onto Paint Rock Road is located in the midst of a series of sharp turns on the main highway and thus could easily be missed.)

Facilities: *Shell Creek*: 11 campsites; most sites are small to medium-sized, with fair separation; parking pads are gravel, level, but smallish, straight-ins or pull-throughs; tent spots are level and would accommodate at least medium-sized tents; several walk-in campsites; *Ranger Creek*: 11 campsites in 3 small groups; most sites are level, and fairly well separated, with gravel, small to medium-sized parking pads and tent spots; *both camps*: fireplaces; some firewood is available for gathering; water at faucets in Shell Creek; water at a hand pump in Ranger Creek; vault facilities; gravel driveways; camper supplies in Shell, 11 miles west, or at Burgess Junction; adequate supplies and services are available in Greybull.

Activities & Attractions: National forest interpretive center, interpretive trail and falls viewpoint in Shell Canyon, 5 miles southwest, near milepost 26 on U.S. 14; fishing for small trout on local streams; footbridges across the creeks; hiking trails.

Natural Features: Located on the banks of Shell Creek, at the upper end of Shell Canyon; shade/shelter in the campgrounds is provided by a mixture of conifers and hardwoods; Ranger Creek Campground is at the confluence of Shell Creek and Ranger Creek; many streamside sites in both camps; timbered ridges/bluffs to the west and south, sage-covered hillsides to the north and east; elevation 7600'.

Season, Fees & Phone: May to October; $7.00; 14 day limit; Paintrock Ranger District, Greybull, (307) 765-4435.

Camp Notes: The creekside setting within the walls of impressive Shell Canyon provides these simple camps with a certain distinction. Ranger Creek has a relatively small number of sites for its sizeable acreage. On weekends it can sometimes be busy with day trippers, but weekdays are typically quiet.

LEIGH CREEK
Bighorn National Forest

Location: North-central Wyoming southwest of Buffalo.

Access: From U.S. Highway 16 at milepost 34 (8 miles east of Ten Sleep, 57 miles southwest of Buffalo), go southeast onto Wyoming Secondary Route 435 for 0.9 mile to the campground.

Facilities: 11 campsites in 2 loops; most sites are rather small, with nominal separation; parking pads are short straight-ins, probably more suitable for pickups, vans, and smaller rv's; a few spots would be ok for tents; fireplaces; a limited amount of firewood is available for gathering in the area; water at a hand pump; vault facilities; very limited supplies and services in Ten Sleep; adequate supplies and services are available in Worland, 35 miles west.

Activities & Attractions: Primarily, the grand views of Ten Sleep Canyon, with its evergreen-studded, multi-colored, sheer vertical walls; reportedly good stream fishing; fish hatchery 0.3 mile east on Route 435.

Natural Features: Located in the heart of Tensleep Canyon along Tensleep Creek on the west slope of the Bighorn Mountains, in a grove of hardwoods mixed with some evergreens; Leigh Creek's confluence with Tensleep Creek is at this point; several sites are streamside; the area tends to be quite warm and sunny, but breezy, in summer; elevation 5400'.

Season, Fees & Phone: May to October; $7.00; 14 day limit; Tensleep Ranger District (307) 347-8291.

Camp Notes: Tensleep Canyon reminds many visitors of certain similar areas in the American Southwest: places like Oak Creek in Arizona and Zion in Utah. Another small national forest campground, Tensleep Creek, is a few tenths of a mile further east, has five sites, but no drinking water. Leigh Creek is the westernmost public campground on U.S. 16 in the Bighorns.

BOULDER PARK
Bighorn National Forest

Location: North-central Wyoming southwest of Buffalo.

Access: From U.S. Highway 16 at milepost 42 +.8 (17 miles east of Ten Sleep, 49 miles west of Buffalo), turn west onto a gravel access road and proceed 0.5 mile to the campground. (Note that the highway lies in a north-south line in this section.)

Facilities: 34 campsites in 2 loops; most sites are medium-sized, level and reasonably well separated; parking pads are gravel, and large enough for medium to long vehicles; fireplaces; firewood is available for gathering in the area; water at faucets; vault facilities; gravel driveways; public holding tank disposal station 10 miles east near milepost 53; camper supplies and showers may be available at a nearby lodge and in Ten Sleep.

Activities & Attractions: Sightseeing in spectacular Tensleep Canyon, just west of here; fishing.

Natural Features: Located along the moderately forested bank of Tensleep Creek in the Bighorn Mountains; 12 daily-fee sites are located on the east side of the campground on a high bank overlooking the creek; remainder of the sites are to the west, a short distance from the water's edge; elevation 8000'.

Season, Fees & Phone: June to September; $7.00 for 12 sites that are available on a daily fee basis, $90.00 for certain sites that are available on a monthly fee basis; contact the ranger station for additional information; 14/30 day limits; Tensleep Ranger District, Worland, (307) 347-8291.

Camp Notes: The dozen daily fee campsites are, in some ways, superior to the others in this campground. Although situated a bit closer to the main highway, they provide a somewhat nicer, streamside setting.)

SITTING BULL
Bighorn National Forest

Location: North-central Wyoming southwest of Buffalo.

Access: From U.S. Highway 16 near milepost 46 (20 miles east of Ten Sleep, 45 miles west of Buffalo), turn north onto a gravel access road and proceed 0.4 mile to the campground.

Facilities: 43 campsites; sites are medium-sized, level, with adequate separation; parking pads are gravel, mostly short to medium in length, though several pads are suitable for longer vehicles; most sites would accommodate tents quite nicely; fire rings; firewood is available for gathering; water at several faucets; vault facilities; public holding tank disposal station on Highway 16 near milepost 53; gravel driveways; camper supplies at a resort on the main highway near the campground turnoff; very limited supplies and services are available in Ten Sleep.

Activities & Attractions: Self-guided nature trail; fly fishing for trout is reportedly good on Lake Creek; fishing and limited boating on Meadowlark Lake; several 4wd roads in the area.

Natural Features: Located in a stand of moderately dense, tall conifers on the south edge of a large park (alpine meadow) in the Bighorn Mountains; low, semi-timbered ridges encircle the area; some views of distant peaks; Lake Creek flows just east of the camping area; Meadowlark Lake is 0.4 mile south; elev. 8600'.

Season, Fees & Phone: June to September; $7.00; 14 day limit; Tensleep Ranger District, Worland, (307) 347-8291.

Camp Notes: Many campsites here provide really striking views to the north out across the park. Since transient traffic tends to be less frequent here than in the campgrounds along the highway, Sitting Bull is usually a little quieter, even considering its relatively large capacity.

LAKEVIEW
Bighorn National Forest

Location: North-central Wyoming southwest of Buffalo.

Access: From U.S. Highway 16 near milepost 46 (20 miles east of Ten Sleep, 45 miles southwest of Buffalo), turn south-southwest into campground.

Facilities: 11 campsites; sites are generally of average size, with fair separation; parking pads are gravel, medium-length, mostly straight-ins, about half of which may require some additional leveling; some good tenting possibilities; fire rings or fireplaces; firewood is available for gathering in the vicinity; water at central faucets; vault facilities; gravel driveways; public disposal station 7 miles east near milepost 53; camper supplies at a nearby resort; very limited supplies and services are available in Ten Sleep.

Activities & Attractions: Tremendous scenery; fishing; boating; day use area along the lake shore.

Natural Features: Located on a small hilltop at the northeast corner of Meadowlark Lake; campground vegetation consists of moderately dense tall timber, grass and some low brush; surrounded by high ridges and peaks; elevation 8300'.

Season, Fees & Phone: June to September; $7.00; 14 day limit; Tensleep Ranger District, Worland, (307) 347-8291.

Camp Notes: The views of Meadowlark Lake and the surrounding mountains from several of the sites here are positively stunning. If Lake View is full when you arrive, a possible, close-by, alternative might be Bull Creek Campground, a half mile east, on the south side of the highway. Bull Creek has a half-dozen small sites, but no drinking water or fee.

Wyoming 60

LOST CABIN
Bighorn National Forest

Location: North-central Wyoming southwest of Buffalo.

Access: From U.S. Highway 16 at milepost 62 (30 miles southwest of Buffalo, 36 miles east of Ten Sleep), turn north onto a gravel road and proceed 0.2 mile to the campground.

Facilities: 20 campsites in a single large loop; all units are quite spacious and well separated; parking pads are gravel, long, level straight-ins or pull-throughs; large, level tent areas; barbecue grills; an ample amount of firewood is available for gathering; water at hand pumps; vault facilities; public holding tank disposal station 9 miles west, near Powder River Pass; gravel driveway; very limited supplies in Ten Sleep; adequate supplies and services are available in Buffalo.

Activities & Attractions: Just pleasant local surroundings, coupled with tremendous views of the heart of the Bighorn Mountains, east and west of here along Highway 16.

Natural Features: Located in the Bighorn Mountains on a knoll in a moderately dense forest of conifers mixed with some aspens and very little underbrush; the North Fork of Crazy Woman Creek, plus several lesser streams, are nearby; numerous varieties of wildflowers bloom in midsummer; Powder River Pass (9677') is 7 miles west; elevation 8200'.

Season, Fees & Phone: June to September; $7.00; 14 day limit; Buffalo Ranger District (307) 684-7981.

Camp Notes: This is really a huge campground for only 20 sites--one of the most spacious in this part of the country. Since it doesn't offer a lot of what many people consider to be 'attractions', it isn't overused. But it's probably one of the more accessible spots in the Bighorns in which to enjoy a quiet forest setting. The environment here seems to offer a good balance of sun and shelter, too.

Wyoming 61

SOUTH FORK
Bighorn National Forest

Location: North-central Wyoming southwest of Buffalo.

Access: From U.S. Highway 16 at milepost 75 + .5 (16 miles southwest of Buffalo, 49 miles east of Ten Sleep), turn east onto a gravel access road and continue for 0.1 mile to the campground. (Note that the highway follows a north-south line in this section.)

Facilities: 15 campsites, including several walk-ins, in 2 sections; sites are medium-sized, with fair to good separation; parking pads are gravel, essentially level, adequate for short to medium-length vehicles; excellent, level tent spaces on the entrance side of the campground; the walk-in sites can be reached via a footbridge across the creek at the far end of the primary camping area; barbecue grills; firewood is available for gathering; water at hand pumps; vault facilities; gravel driveway; camper supplies across the highway; adequate supplies and services are available in Buffalo.

Activities & Attractions: Fishing for small trout; spectacular viewpoints of the Bighorn Mountains near here.

Natural Features: Located on a moderately forested flat in a small, rocky canyon along the bank of the South Fork of Clear Creek in the Bighorn Mountains; the forest floor is thickly carpeted with conifer needles; deer are commonly seen in and around here; elevation 7800'.

Season, Fees & Phone: June to September; $7.00 for a standard site, $6.00 for a walk-in site; 14 day limit; Buffalo Ranger District (307) 684-7981.

Camp Notes: The majority of the campsites here are creekside, (although the water is actually 20 feet or so below the rim of the bank). A very small, streamside campground that's farther off the highway, Tie Hack (0.4 mile northeast of South Fork, then 1.7 gravel miles off the east side of the highway), is also available.

Wyoming 62

CIRCLE PARK
Bighorn National Forest

Location: North-central Wyoming southwest of Buffalo.

Access: From U.S. Highway 16 at milepost 76 +.5 (15 miles southwest of Buffalo, 50 miles east of Ten Sleep), turn west/northwest, and proceed 2.2 miles up a gravel road to the campground.

Facilities: 10 campsites; most sites are small to medium in size, with fairly good separation; parking pads are gravel, large enough for short to medium-length vehicles; a little additional leveling may be needed on some pads; good tent-pitching opportunities; barbecue grills and/or fire rings; ample firewood is available for gathering; water at a hand pump; vault facilities; gravel driveway; very limited supplies in Ten Sleep; limited to adequate supplies and services are available in Buffalo.

Activities & Attractions: Striking views of the Bighorns across the park; foot trail to Sherd Lake (2 miles).

Natural Features: Located at the base of a hill on the edge of a grove of conifers and aspens in an expansive sub-alpine park (meadow); Circle Park Creek runs along the south edge of the campground; easternmost peaks of the Bighorn Mountains are just west of here; elevation 7900'.

Season, Fees & Phone: June to September; $7.00; 14 day limit; Buffalo Ranger District (307) 684-7981.

Camp Notes: The access road passes through a grove of aspens and across the center of Circle Park. (Some campers prefer to jackcamp among the aspens.) Another nearby forest camp worth considering is Middle Fork, just off the north side of Highway 16, 1.2 miles northeast of the Circle Park access road. It's smaller and has a less open atmosphere than Circle Park. Middle Fork is the first forest campground you'll reach if you're approaching the Bighorns from Interstate Highways 25 & 90.

Wyoming 63

CONNOR BATTLEFIELD
Connor Battlefield State Historic Site

Location: North-central Wyoming northwest of Sheridan.

Access: From Interstate 90 Exit 9 for Ranchester (11 miles northwest of Sheridan, 9 miles southeast of the Wyoming-Montana border), travel west on U.S. Highway 14 for 0.8 mile into midtown Ranchester; turn south (left) onto Gillette Street and proceed 0.5 mile to the end of the pavement just past the south edge of town; turn east (left) onto a gravel park access road and go 0.2 mile to the camping area, along the loop driveway.

Facilities: 15 campsites; sites are small to medium-sized, level, with nominal separation; parking pads are gravel, medium-length straight-ins or long pull-throughs; plenty of space for tents; fire rings; b-y-o firewood; water at several faucets; vault facilities; gravel driveways; limited supplies and services in Ranchester.

Activities & Attractions: Small stone-and-mortar monument marks the battle site; large playground; suspension footbridge across the river; fishing; day use area.

Natural Features: Located on a large, grassy flat along the banks of the Tongue River; campsites are unshaded to moderately shaded; some sites are riverside; the Bighorn Mountains rise above 10,000' a dozen miles west of the park; elevation 3800'.

Season, Fees & Phone: Open all year, subject to weather conditions, with limited services October to May; you may camp up to a fortnight at no charge (subject to change); phone c/o Trail End State Historic Site, Sheridan, (307) 674-4589.

Camp Notes: On August 29, 1865, General Patrick Connor led over 200 troops in an attack on an Arapaho village here in what became known as the Battle of Tongue River. In truth, this small park is oriented more toward simple recreation than it is toward history, and that's quite all right. If you're traveling I-90 and need a convenient, nice camp spot, the place is certainly worth a good look. It's close enough to town that, if you run out of beans or whatever, a quick trip across the footbridge and down the street will get you to a vittle vendor without cranking up the Tin Lizzie. Good views of the Tongue River and of the beautiful Bighorn Mountains.

Wyoming 64

BELLE FOURCHE RIVER
Devils Tower National Monument

Location: Northeast corner of Wyoming north of Moorcroft.

Access: From Devils Tower Junction, travel north 5.9 miles on Wyoming State Highway 24 to its junction with State Highway 110; turn west (left) onto Highway 110 and proceed 1.3 miles to the visitor center; turn south-east (left) and go 0.3 mile to the campground. (Interstate 90 travelers can take Exit 153 if eastbound, or Exit 185 if westbound, to reach Devils Tower Junction.)

Facilities: 48 campsites in 2 loops; (several small group sites are also available); sites are medium to large, level, with minimal to nominal separation; parking pads are gravel, medium-length pull-throughs; large, grassy tent areas; barbecue grills; b-y-o firewood; water at several faucets; restrooms; paved driveways; camper supplies just outside the park entrance; limited+ supplies and services are available in Moorcroft and Sundance.

Activities & Attractions: Hiking trails, including one which encircles the Tower; climbing; limited fishing; visitor center; amphitheater for scheduled ranger-naturalist programs in season.

Natural Features: Located in a cottonwood grove on a large flat in a valley along the north-west bank of the Belle Fourche River; Devils Tower, a few hundred yards northwest, is visible through the branches of the mature hardwoods that shelter/shade most campsites; the Tower, a stone column that looms 867' above the river plain, is the core of an ancient volcano; elevation 3900'.

Season, Fees & Phone: Open all year, with limited services October to May; $8.00 for a site, plus $5.00 for the park entrance fee; 14 day limit; park headquarters (307) 967-7292.

Camp Notes: Camping here inspires a certain amount of awe and respect in both first-time and return visitors alike. This is probably one of the finest camping areas in Wyoming. Try to avoid the summer logjam of visitors, and instead, camp here in early spring or late fall. Unique!

Wyoming 65

KEYHOLE
Keyhole State Park

Location: Northeast Wyoming east of Moorcroft.

Access: From Interstate 90 Exit 165 for Pine Ridge Road (12 miles east of Moorcroft, 21 miles west of Sundance), travel north on Pine Ridge Road (paved) for 5.8 miles to the state park entrance; turn northwest (left) onto a good gravel road and proceed 1.2 miles to a fork; turn northeast (right) directly into the *Pronghorn* area; or take the left fork for 0.7 mile to *Pats Point*; or from the park entrance, continue ahead for another 0.6 mile, then swing west (left) into the *Homestead* area.

Facilities: *Pronghorn*: 25 campsites in 2 loops; sites are medium sized, with fair separation; parking pads are gravel, mostly short to medium-length straight-ins; adequate space for tents; water at several faucets; *Pats Point*: 15 campsites; sites are small+, with fair separation; parking surfaces are gravel, mostly medium to long pull-offs; medium to large areas for tents, including a few framed tent pads; ramadas (sun shelters) for a few sites; water at a hand pump; *Homestead*: 10 campsites; sites are large and well separated, with dirt/grass parking spaces and large, level areas for tents; *all areas*: fire rings or barbecue grills; b-y-o firewood is recommended; vault facilities; holding tank disposal station near the park entrance; gravel driveways; camper supplies at the marina and near the Interstate exit; limited+ supplies and services are available in Moorcroft and Sundance.

Activities & Attractions: Good fishing for walleye, northern pike, perch, smallmouth bass and catfish; boating; boat launch; designated swimming beach; playgrounds; amphitheater.

Natural Features: Located on rolling, moderately timbered hillsides near the east end of Keyhole Reservoir; Pronghorn and Homestead are above the shores of long, slender Cottonwood Bay; Pats Point is above the main body of the lake; sites in Pats Point and Homestead have light shade/shelter, Pronghorn sites are moderately shaded by large conifers; the reservoir, a sizable impoundment on the Belle Fourche River, is in a large basin ringed by low, evergreen-covered hills; elevation 4100'.

Season, Fees & Phone: Open all year, with limited services November to March; 14 day limit; please see Appendix for standard Wyoming state park fees; park office (307) 756-3596.

Camp Notes: If you're searching for an "extended season" camp, Keyhole might fill your needs. In early spring and late fall, the sunny skies and daytime highs can be very comfortable. (Bring some extra warmth for the chilly nights.) The evergreens help keep the "look" of winter from arriving too early in fall or lasting too long into spring. The flat-topped summit of eerie Devil's Tower can be seen rising above the hilltops in the north, and the Black Hills are visible in the distant east.

Wyoming 66

REUTER
Black Hills National Forest

Location: Northeast corner of Wyoming north of Sundance.

Access: From Interstate 90 Exit 185 (2 miles west of Sundance, 30 miles east of Moorcroft), travel northwest on U.S. Highway 14 for 1.1 miles to milepost 199 +.4; turn north (right) onto a paved access road and continue for 2.5 miles to the campground.

Facilities: 24 campsites in 2 loops; sites are medium to large, and fairly well separated; parking pads are gravel, short to medium-length, extra-wide, straight-ins; additional leveling probably will be needed in most sites; medium-sized tent areas; fire rings; firewood is available for gathering in the vicinity; water at several faucets; vault facilities; gravel driveways; limited+ supplies and services are available in Sundance.

Activities & Attractions: Some pleasant distant views from near the campground; Devils Tower National Monument, 26 miles northwest; Black Hills recreation areas, a dozen miles east.

Natural Features: Located on a gently rolling hillside amid medium-dense tall pines in the western foothills of the Bear Lodge Mountains; pine needle-carpeted forest floor; brilliant red-orange subsoil; elevation 5000'.

Season, Fees & Phone: Open all year, with limited services in winter; $6.00; 14 day limit; Bearlodge Ranger District, Sundance, (307) 283-1361.

Camp Notes: It may be true that this small, pleasant campground offers little in the way of outstanding facilities and attractions. However, it might serve very well as an attractive, less congested, peak-season alternative to camping at Devils Tower. Reuter is also a very handy spot for Interstate travel stopovers. All things considered, it's the most easily accessible national forest campground in northeast Wyoming.

Wyoming 67

RED HILLS
Seminoe State Park

Location: South-central Wyoming northeast of Rawlins.

Access: From Interstate 80 Exit 219 for West Sinclair (6 miles east of Rawlins, 17 miles west of Walcott), follow the signs along the loops and ramps of the interchange for 0.5 mile to the west edge of Sinclair and the intersection of Lincoln Avenue & 10th Street; head north on 10th Street for 0.2 mile to the north end of Sinclair, then the road bears northeast and becomes Carbon County Road 351; continue northeasterly on County Road 351 for 35 miles to the end of the pavement, then another mile on gravel; turn east (right) onto either of 2 gravel access roads and proceed 0.6 mile to the North or South Red Hills camp loops.

Facilities: 56 campsites in 2 sections; sites are small to large, with nominal separation; parking pads are short+ straight-ins or long pull-throughs; additional leveling probably will be needed in most sites; large tent spots, but they may be a bit sloped; some sites have ramadas (sun shelters); fireplaces or fire rings; b-y-o firewood; water at hand pumps; vault facilities; holding tank disposal station; gravel driveways; gas and camper supplies at the marina; gas and groceries+ in Sinclair; virtually complete supplies and services are available in Rawlins.

Activities & Attractions: Boating; boat launches and docks; marina; playgrounds; reportedly very good fishing for rainbow and brown trout, and walleye.

Natural Features: Located on sage-dotted, grassy hills and bluffs overlooking the northwest shore of Seminoe Reservoir, an impoundment on the North Platte River; vegetation consists mostly of sparse grass and low brush, plus some small, scattered junipers and pines; long, sandy beaches; Shirley Mountains lie to the east, Seminoe Mountains rise to the west, with extensive sand dunes shifting in between; typically breezy; elevation 6400'.

Season, Fees & Phone: Open all year, subject to weather and road conditions, with limited services in winter; 14 day limit; please see Appendix for standard Wyoming state park fees; park office (307) 328-0115.

Camp Notes: Seminoe's high-desert surroundings are made for anyone who likes colorful sweeping views, desolation, and silence interrupted only by the hum of an occasional motor boat or a sudden gust of wind through the sagebrush. The North Platte's famed "Miracle Mile", a stretch of blue ribbon trout water, is along the free-flowing segment of the river below the dam. "Seminoe" is an Americanized spelling of the French "Cemineaux", the name of an early French fur trapper.

Wyoming 68

SARATOGA LAKE
Saratoga City Park

Location: South-central Wyoming southeast of Rawlins.

Access: From Wyoming State Highway 130 at a point 19 miles south of Interstate 80 Exit 235 and 1 mile north of midtown Saratoga, turn east onto a well-signed, gravel access road; proceed south and east for 1 mile to the campground.

Facilities: Approximately 80 campsites, including 26 with electrical hookups; sites are small, with virtually no separation; parking pads are sandy pull-offs or whichever-way-you-cans; many pads may require additional leveling; some large, sandy tent spots; fire rings or barbecue grills; b-y-o firewood; vault facilities; water at several hand pumps; sandy driveways; resident manager; camper supplies at the park office/store; adequate supplies and services are available in Saratoga.

Activities & Attractions: Boating; fishing; swimming; Saratoga Hot Springs in town, is open to the public for a small charge; river floating on the North Platte.

Natural Features: Located in the wide, high and dry North Platte River Valley; campground vegetation is very scant, with only a few small trees, bushes and sparse grass growing in the sandy soil; most sites are situated along the shore of 2-mile-long Saratoga Lake; some sites are perched on top of a short bluff slightly above the shore; the Sierra Madre lies to the southwest, the peaks of the Medicine Bow Range rise the east; elevation. 6800'.

Season, Fees & Phone: Open all year, with limited services in winter; $7.00 for a standard site, $9.00 for a partial hookup site; park office (307) 573-1474.

Camp Notes: From all appearances, Saratoga Lake Campground is a desert camp. Its sunny and dry environment, and the reportedly therapeutic hot springs nearby, draw quite a few summer visitors.

Wyoming 69

ENCAMPMENT
Public Lands/BLM Recreation Site

Location: South-central Wyoming southeast of Rawlins.

Access: From the junction of Wyoming State Highways 230 & 70 (18 miles south of Saratoga, 27 miles northwest of the Wyoming-Colorado border), turn southwest onto Highway 70; travel 1 mile to the town of Encampment, then continue for 0.5 mile beyond; turn south (left) at a sign for "Encampment River Canyon and Trail"; proceed south for 2 miles on a steep and twisty, single-lane, gravel/dirt road to the campground.

Facilities: 8 campsites; sites are small to medium-sized and generally well separated; parking areas are gravel/sod, level, and not very well defined; some pads are straight-ins and some are however-you-like-its; several really nice, large, grassy, tent spots; fire rings and barbecue grills; some firewood is usually available for gathering in the area; no drinking water; vault facilities; gravel/earth driveways; limited supplies and services are available in Encampment.

Activities & Attractions: Stream fishing; trails into the Encampment River Wilderness; settlers museum, in the town of Encampment, has exceptionally fine exhibits; city park next to the museum has formal gardens, playground and a picnic area.

Natural Features: Located on the bank of the Encampment River, which flows down from the Sierra Madre past these sites to join waters of the North Platte River about 12 miles northeast of here; vegetation consists of mostly large cottonwoods and moderate underbrush over a grassy floor; elevation 7500'.

Season, Fees & Phone: Open all year, subject to weather; no fee (subject to change); 14 day limit; BLM Rawlins Office (307) 324-4841.

Camp Notes: If you're willing to venture off the beaten path, this place will offer you its rewards of beauty and serenity. The delightful stream and gentle breeze provide music which too few people are able to come this far to enjoy. Many miles southwest of Encampment on Highway 70 beyond the end of the pavement are three small camps in Medicine Bow National Forest. Bottle Creek, Haskins Creek, and Lost Creek are 7 to 18 miles from Encampment, high in the Sierra Madre. All reportedly have drinking water, vaults, fees, and midsummer availability. A call to the Hayden Ranger District in Encampment (307-327-5481) should draw information about their current status.

Wyoming 70

SOUTH BRUSH CREEK
Medicine Bow National Forest

Location: South-central Wyoming west of Laramie.

Access: From Wyoming State Highway 130 at a point 22 miles southeast of Saratoga, and 28 miles west of Centennial (0.5 mile east of the Medicine Bow National Forest western boundary, 0.5 mile west of the Brush Creek Work Station), turn north onto a gravel forest road; proceed for 0.2 mile to a fork; take the right fork easterly for 1.2 miles to the campground.

Facilities: 21 campsites in 2 loops; sites are average or better in size, with good to excellent separation; parking pads are gravel, mostly level, medium to long straight-ins; some really nice, grassy tent spots in the west loop; fire rings and barbecue grills; firewood is available for gathering in the area; water at a central hand pump; vault facilities; gravel driveways; camper supplies at a small store, 2 miles west; adequate supplies and services are available in Saratoga.

Activities & Attractions: Stream fishing (reportedly excellent); exploring the surrounding mountains via a network of trails.

Natural Features: Located on the west slope of the Medicine Bow Mountains; campground vegetation consists of fairly dense, tall conifers, some bushy hardwoods and a considerable amount of undergrowth; Brush Creek, a bubbling, free-flowing stream, rushes past many of the sites and down the slopes to join the waters of the North Platte River in the large valley to the west; elevation 7900'.

Season, Fees & Phone: May to September; $6.00; 14 day limit; Brush Creek Ranger District, Saratoga, (307) 326-5258.

Camp Notes: Sites at South Brush Creek are situated in a welcome, cool shady forest environment. It's hard to imagine that just 10 or so miles to the west is an immense, relatively dry, sage-covered valley.

Wyoming 71

RYAN PARK
Medicine Bow National Forest

Location: South-central Wyoming west of Laramie.

Access: From Wyoming State Highway 130 at a point 24 miles east of Saratoga, 3 miles east of the Medicine Bow National Forest boundary and 26 miles west of Centennial, turn south onto a gravel access road for 0.2 mile to the campground.

Facilities: 30 campsites in 2 loops; (a group loop is also available, by reservation); sites are medium to large, with fair to very good separation; parking pads are gravel, mostly level, medium to long straight-ins or pull-throughs; large, grassy tent spots; fire rings and barbecue grills; firewood is available for gathering in the area; water at faucets; vault facilities; gravel driveways; camper supplies at a small store 4 miles west; adequate supplies and services are available in Saratoga.

Activities & Attractions: Stream fishing; trails lead into the mountains and Savage Run Wilderness.

Natural Features: Located on the west slope of the Medicine Bow Mountains; sites in the middle loop border a large, grassy mountain meadow; sites in the east loop are more forested, with tall conifers, tall grass and considerable underbrush for fairly dense vegetation; the North Fork of Barrett Creek flows down past Ryan Park; elevation 8000'.

Season, Fees & Phone: May to October; $7.00; 14 day limit; Brush Creek Ranger District, Saratoga, (307) 326-5258.

Camp Notes: Ryan Park is a pleasant, high mountain campground with views of forested hills and lush meadows from many sites. The superscenic drive between Ryan Park and the settlement of Centennial crosses sub-alpine and alpine terrain, and it's one you'd be glad you took the time to take. Ryan Park was first a CCC camp in the 1930's, then the site of a different type of 'camp' in WW II. During the war, it was a minimum-security p.o.w. camp for captured German and Italian soldiers.

Wyoming 72

SILVER LAKE
Medicine Bow National Forest

Location: South-central Wyoming west of Laramie.

Access: From Wyoming State Highway 130 at a point 19 miles west of Centennial and 31 miles east of Saratoga, turn south onto a fairly steep, winding, gravel access road; proceed 0.3 mile to the campground.

Facilities: 14 campsites; sites are small to medium-sized, with fair to good separation; parking pads are gravel, short to medium-length straight-ins; many pads may require additional leveling; small tent spots, may be a bit sloped; barbecue grills and fire rings; some firewood is available for gathering in the area; water at a hand pump; vault facilities; narrow, rather steep, gravel driveways; camper supplies in Centennial; adequate supplies and services are available in Saratoga.

Activities & Attractions: Limited boating on Silver Lake; fishing on Silver Lake and nearby French Creek; foot trail down to Silver Lake; trail toward Savage Run Wilderness; superscenic drive across the Medicine Bow Mountains on Highway 130.

Natural Features: Located high in the Medicine Bow Mountains; campground vegetation consists of medium-height conifers, considerable underbrush and tall grass; Silver Lake is visible through the trees from some sites; Libby Flats alpine meadows lie to the east; elevation 10,400'.

Season, Fees & Phone: July to September; $7.00; 14 day limit; Brush Creek Ranger District, Saratoga, (307) 326-5258.

Camp Notes: Camping above 10,000' is an experience few have the opportunity to enjoy. You'll find patches of snow at least ten months of the year here. Another campground, Sugarloaf, a half-dozen miles northeast of Silver Lake, is even higher up and has an even shorter season.

Wyoming 73

BROOKLYN LAKE
Medicine Bow National Forest

Location: South-central Wyoming west of Laramie.

Access: From Wyoming State Highway 130 at a point 8.5 miles west of Centennial and 42 miles east of Saratoga, turn north onto an oiled gravel access road; proceed 1.8 miles (the road shortly becomes rough and narrow) to the campground.

Facilities: 16 campsites; sites are small to medium in size, with very little separation; parking pads are gravel, level, mostly medium-length straight-ins; some tent spots are spacious enough for large tents, but the terrain is very rocky; barbecue grills; b-y-o firewood is recommended; water at several faucets; vault facilities; gravel driveways; camper supplies in Centennial; complete supplies and services are available in Laramie.

Activities & Attractions: Fishing; limited boating; hiking; exceptional view across the lake.

Natural Features: Located in the Snowy Range of the Medicine Bow Mountains on a short bluff above a pair of classic alpine lakes; the campground is on the rocky north shore of Brooklyn Lake, at the foot of a sheer rock-faced cliff; across the lake is a forested flat; elevation 10,500'.

Season, Fees & Phone: July to September; $6.00; 14 day limit; Laramie Ranger District (307) 745-8971.

Camp Notes: Campers who are familiar with the area just about stand in line waiting for this place to open each year. The setting is really distinctive. With the melting of snow comes a thick yellow carpet of fawn lilies. Some campers say there's always at least a little snow here, year 'round.

Wyoming 74

NASH FORK
Medicine Bow National Forest

Location: South-central Wyoming west of Laramie.

Access: From Wyoming State Highway 130 at a point 8.5 miles west of Centennial and 42 miles east of Saratoga, turn north onto an oiled gravel access road; proceed 0.1 mile and turn west (left) into the campground.

Facilities: 27 campsites; sites are mostly large and well spaced; parking pads are gravel, medium to long straight-ins; some pads may require additional leveling; large, grassy, fairly level tent spots throughout; fireplaces and barbecue grills; firewood is available for gathering in the area; water at several faucets; vault facilities; gravel driveways; camper supplies in Centennial; complete supplies and services are available in Laramie.

Activities & Attractions: Fishing; hiking; Libby Flats Observation Site, 4 miles west; visitor center in Centennial; access to several nearby alpine lakes by foot or 4wd trails.

Natural Features: Located on the east slope of the Medicine Bow Range on a boulder-strewn gentle slope; Nash Fork of Libby Creek flows nearby; many alpine lakes are in the area; an incredibly green, alpine meadow here is surrounded by an open forest of tall conifers; patches of snow linger into midsummer; elevation 10,200'.

Season, Fees & Phone: July to September; $6.00; 14 day limit; Laramie Ranger District (307) 745-8971.

Camp Notes: This is a great little camp that is somewhat less likely to be snowbound than its neighbors, all of which are also above the 10,000' mark. If there's no available site at the local preferred campground at Brooklyn Lake, you might try Nash Fork, which you'll pass on the way up to Brooklyn Lake. Sites here may not have the great view available at Brooklyn Lake, but they're still nice, and the 0.1 mile trip off the highway is a little less bone-jarring.

Wyoming 75

LIBBY CREEK
Medicine Bow National Forest

Location: South-central Wyoming west of Laramie.

Access: From Wyoming State Highway 130 at a point 2 miles west of Centennial and 40 miles east of Saratoga, turn south onto Albany County Road 351 (just east of the Libby Creek bridge); proceed south, then turn west (right) into each of the 3 loops, Aspen, Pine, and Willow Flat (Willow Flat is the only loop that's an additional 0.5 mile from the main road); a fourth loop, Spruce, is accessible directly from Highway 130 from the west side of Libby Creek.

Facilities: 40 campsites in 4 loops; most sites are quite spacious and well separated; parking pads are gravel, mostly level, short to long straight-ins or pull-throughs; some good tent spaces; barbecue grills or fire rings; firewood is available for gathering in the area; water at hand pumps; vault facilities; holding tank disposal station near Centennial; gravel driveways; camper supplies in Centennial; complete supplies and services are available in Laramie.

Activities & Attractions: Fishing on Libby Creek and at nearby Barbour Lake; hiking; visitor center in Centennial.

Natural Features: Located along a refreshing mountain stream on the east slope of the Medicine Bow Mountains; campground vegetation consists of tall conifers, spreading willows, assorted hardwoods, and underbrush; Libby Creek flows east from here into the Laramie River; elevation 8600'.

Season, Fees & Phone: June to September; $7.00; 14 day limit; Laramie Ranger District (307) 745-8971.

Camp Notes: Because these four sections are spread out so much along Libby Creek, the sites are a lot more private than a 40-site campground might lead you to believe. You'll probably find just the right spot if you preview all loops before settling in. Libby Creek is at the eastern edge of a superscenic drive over the alpine and subalpine terrain of the Medicine Bow Mountains.

Wyoming 76

WOODS CREEK
Medicine Bow National Forest

Location: South-central Wyoming southwest of Laramie.

Access: From Wyoming State Highway 230 at a point 5.3 miles southwest of Woods Landing and 10 miles northeast of the Wyoming-Colorado border, turn west onto a gravel access road and proceed 0.1 mile to the campground.

Facilities: 9 campsites; sites are medium-sized, with fairly good to very good separation; parking pads are gravel, medium to long, mostly pull-throughs; some pads may require additional leveling; large tent spots on a floor of pine needles, but some may be a bit sloped; barbecue grills; firewood is available for gathering; water at a hand pump; vault facilities; gravel driveway; gas and camper supplies in Woods Landing; complete supplies and services are available in Laramie, 30 miles northeast.

Activities & Attractions: Hiking.

Natural Features: Located on a forested slope in the eastern foothills of the Medicine Bow Mountains; vegetation consists of medium-dense, very tall conifers, some sparse grass and a little underbrush; Woods Creek flows nearby; elevation 8900'.

Season, Fees & Phone: June to September; $7.00; 14 day limit; Laramie Ranger District (307) 745-8971.

Camp Notes: There's not a whole lot to do right at this campground, but it would make a good base of operations for local exploration. There are a number of small, remote camps in the nearby hills which offer fishing and boating. There's also a reservoir, Lake Hattie, about halfway to Laramie from here. Lake Hattie has dispersed camping around its treeless shore, and there's adequate boating and angling access. Then again, Woods Creek may be just the perfect place to simply appreciate the great outdoors, or to contemplate the next day's excursion.

Wyoming 77

TIE CITY
Medicine Bow National Forest

Location: Southeast Wyoming southeast of Laramie.

Access: From Interstate 80 Exit 323 for Happy Jack Road and the Lincoln Memorial (at the summit of Laramie Pass, 10 miles east of Laramie, 36 miles west of Cheyenne), travel northeast on Wyoming State Highway 210/Happy Jack Road for 1.2 miles; turn east (right) onto a campground access road and proceed 0.2 mile down into Upper Tie City, or 0.4 mile to Lower Tie City.

Facilities: 25 campsites, including 19 in the upper section and 6 in the lower section; sites are medium-sized, with fair to good separation; parking pads are gravel, short to medium-length, mostly straight-ins; many pads may require additional leveling; some good tent spots; fire rings or barbecue grills; firewood is available for gathering in the area; water at hand pumps; vault facilities; gravel driveways; complete supplies and services are available in Laramie.

Activities & Attractions: Hiking; Devil's Playground, with unique rock formations, picnicking, and rock climbing, is several miles southeast; Summit Rest Area, with a visitor information center and a large statue of Abraham Lincoln, at the junction of Happy Jack Road and I-80.

Natural Features: Located near the southern tip of the Laramie Mountains; sites are either on a forested hillside, a sage flat or along a creekbed; campground vegetation varies from tall conifers and a considerable amount of underbrush, to grassy, wildflower-covered slopes; Lodgepole Creek meanders past some of the campsites; elevation 8600'.

Season, Fees & Phone: May to October; $7.00; 14 day limit; Laramie Ranger District (307) 745-8971.

Camp Notes: Certainly, one of the campground's pluses is its three-minute access from one of the world's great transcontinental routes. Oddly, the freeway itself may be a reason to spend some time in this campground. Interstate 80 closely follows Old U.S. Highway 30, which for decades has been known as the Lincoln Highway. Thus the significance of the great likeness of the Great Emancipator at the rest area. Laramie Summit is the highest point on I-80.

Wyoming 78

YELLOW PINE
Medicine Bow National Forest

Location: Southeast Wyoming southeast of Laramie.

Access: From Interstate 80 Exit 323 for Happy Jack Road and the Lincoln Memorial (at the summit of Laramie Pass, 10 miles southeast of Laramie, 36 miles west of Cheyenne), travel northeast on Wyoming State Highway 210/Happy Jack Road for 1.2 miles; turn east (right) onto a campground access road and proceed 2 miles to the campground.

Facilities: 19 campsites; sites are medium-sized, with fair to good separation; parking pads are gravel, level, medium to long, mostly straight-ins; good, level tent sites; barbecue grills and fire rings; firewood is available for gathering in the area; water at several faucets; vault facilities; complete supplies and services are available in Laramie.

Activities & Attractions: Summit Rest Area, Visitor Center and Lincoln Memorial at the Interstate exit; nearby Devil's Playground has unusual rock formations, picnicking, hiking and rock climbing; fishing on nearby streams.

Natural Features: Located on a forested flat near the southern tip of the Laramie Mountains; campground vegetation consists of tall pines and a little underbrush on a forest floor of pine needles; South Fork of Lodgepole Creek flows nearby; elevation 8400'.

Season, Fees & Phone: May to October; $7.00; 14 day limit; Laramie Ranger District (307) 745-8971.

Camp Notes: Yellow Pine Campground is one of those relatively rare, convenient stops for Interstate travelers. The campground seems much farther than a mere 3 miles from the Interstate. If you had arrived by helicopter, you might think you were deep in the forest.

Wyoming 79

VEDAUWOO
Medicine Bow National Forest

Location: Southeast Wyoming southeast of Laramie.

Access: From Interstate 80 Exit 329 (16 miles southeast of Laramie, 30 miles west of Cheyenne), turn northeast onto Vedauwoo Road and proceed easterly for 1.2 miles; turn northerly (left) for 0.4 mile to the campground.

Facilities: 11 campsites; sites are mostly average-sized, with fairly good separation; parking pads are paved, level, medium-length straight-ins; most sites will easily accommodate a medium-sized tent, but the terrain is a bit rocky; fireplaces and barbecue grills; b-y-o firewood is recommended; water at hand pumps; vault facilities; paved driveway; complete supplies and services are available in Laramie.

Activities & Attractions: "Rocks of the Vedauwoo" self-guiding nature trail leads up to and around the unique rock formations; nearby wide vistas, north toward the Laramie Mountains and east toward the Great Plains; dozens of picnic sites.

Natural Features: Located on a forested flat just below a flat mountaintop in the Sherman Mountains; campground vegetation consists of tall conifers, hardwoods, and light underbrush on a grassy forest floor; huge, dome-shaped, granite boulders are scattered all over "Devil's Playground"; elevation 8200'.

Season, Fees & Phone: May to October; $7.00; 14 day limit; Laramie Ranger District (307) 745-8971.

Camp Notes: Between the campground and the trailhead is an enormous picnic area with over 60 extremely unusual sites tucked in among huge boulders, supposedly strewn by playful Indian spirits. The atmosphere here at Vedauwoo is truly unique!

Wyoming 80

GRANITE RESERVOIR
Curt Gowdy State Park

Location: Southeast Wyoming west of Cheyenne.

Access: From Wyoming State Highway 210/Happy Jack Road at milepost 24 (24 miles west of Interstate 25 Exit 10D in Cheyenne, 14 miles east of Interstate 80 Exit 323 east of Laramie), turn south onto the paved park access road and proceed 0.9 mile to the west tip of Granite Reservoir and a 3-way intersection; turn southeast (right) onto a gravel access road to a half-dozen south shore camp/picnic areas (all within 1.5 miles).

(Special Note: From the Cheyenne metro area, find your way to Interstate 25 Exit 10D, go to the west side of the freeway and onto Happy Jack Road/Highway 210, then west to the park; from Laramie, take Interstate 80 eastbound for 10 miles to Exit 323 for Happy Jack Road; from the north side of the freeway, travel north and east on Happy Jack Road/Highway 210 to the park.)

Facilities: Approximately 50 camp/picnic sites; (2 group camps are also available); sites are medium-sized, well-spaced, but with minimal visual separation; parking surfaces are gravel/grass/earth, mostly medium to long straight-ins or pull-offs; additional leveling will be required in many sites; large tent spots on sandy slopes; fire rings; b-y-o firewood is recommended; water at a hand pump near the southeast end of the lake; vault facilities; holding tank disposal station, 1 mile west on Highway 210; gravel/dirt driveways; nearest reliable sources of supplies and services (complete) are in Cheyenne and Laramie.

Activities & Attractions: Boating; boat launch; trout fishing; archery range; several miles of hiking trails.

Natural Features: Located in the foothills of the Laramie Mountains on the shore of Granite Reservoir; vegetation consists of prairie grass dotted with a few smaller trees; most sites are unsheltered or very lightly shaded/sheltered; elevation 6500'.

Season, Fees & Phone: Open all year, with limited services October to April; 14 day limit; please see Appendix for standard Wyoming state park fees; park office (307) 632-7946.

Camp Notes: Curt Gowdy State Park is considered to be one of the nicer water recreation retreats in southeast Wyoming. (Yes, it's *that* Curt Gowdy, a Wyoming native son, and the state's best-known sportscaster, television program host, outdoorsman, conservationist, and all-around good guy.)

Wyoming 81

CRYSTAL RESERVOIR
Curt Gowdy State Park

Location: Southeast Wyoming west of Cheyenne.

Access: From Wyoming State Highway 210/Happy Jack Road at milepost 24 (24 miles west of Interstate 25 Exit 10D in Cheyenne, 14 miles east of Interstate 80 Exit 323 east of Laramie), turn south onto a paved park access road and proceed 0.9 mile to the west tip of Granite Reservoir and a 3-way intersection; turn southeast (right) onto a gravel access road and travel 1.5 miles around the south shore of Granite Reservoir to the southeast shore near "Granite Point"; continue southeasterly on the gravel road (narrow, with steep sections) over the hill for another 1.5 miles to the northwest end of Crystal Reservoir and a 3-way intersection; hang a right (south) and continue to the camp areas (all within 1 mile of the northwest end of the lake).

(Special Note: From Cheyenne, you can make a "back door" approach to Crystal Reservoir and shave a few miles from the route; from State Highway 210/Happy Jack Road at a point 14 miles west of Cheyenne, take County Road 210, a gravel road that tends to be washboardy, for 6 miles to Crystal Reservoir.)

Facilities: Approximately 10 camp/picnic sites near the southeast end of the lake; sites are small+ to medium-sized, with nominal separation; parking surfaces are grass/earth, straight-ins or pull-offs; adequate space for large tents in most sites; fire rings; b-y-o firewood is recommended; water at a hand pump; vault facilities; holding tank disposal station at park headquarters; gravel/dirt driveways; nearest reliable sources of supplies and services (complete) are in Cheyenne and Laramie.

Activities & Attractions: Fishing for stocked trout; small playground; day use areas.

Natural Features: Located along the shore of Crystal Reservoir in a basin ringed by grass covered, evergreen-dotted slopes; sites are unsheltered or very lightly shaded/sheltered; elevation 6500'.

Season, Fees & Phone: Open all year, subject to weather and road conditions, with limited services October to April; 14 day limit; please see Appendix for standard Wyoming state park fees; park office (307) 632-7946.

Camp Notes: A big advantage to camping here or at the park's Granite Reservoir section is *elbow room*. Everybody isn't jammed into the same 200-site, two-acre campground. The sites may be primitive, but they're scattered.

Wyoming 82

ALCOVA LAKE
Natrona County Park

Location: Central Wyoming southwest of Casper.

Access: From Wyoming State Highway 220 at milepost 84 +.8 (32 miles southwest of Casper, 40 miles northeast of Muddy Gap Junction), turn south/southwest onto Lake Shore Drive/Natrona County Road 406 (paved), and proceed from 2.4 miles to 5.2 miles to the camping areas.

Facilities: Approximately 25 standard sites in 3 areas, plus 6 partial-hookup sites in the 'rv court'; standard sites vary from small to large, with fair to good separation; rv sites are small and closely spaced; most parking surfaces are sandy gravel, short to medium length straight-ins/pull-offs; additional leveling will be required in many sites; mostly sloped spaces for small to medium-sized tents; fire rings; b-y-o firewood; water at a central faucet; vault facilities; holding tank disposal station; gravel driveways; gas and groceries nearby and on the main highway.

Activities & Attractions: Boating; boat launch; fishing; designated swimming beach; small playground; day use areas.

Natural Features: Located in a large basin along the west shore of Alcova Lake, a reservoir on the North Platte River; camp spots receive very light to moderate shelter/shade from evergreens and large hardwoods; elevation 5500'.

Season, Fees & Phone: Principal season is May to September, but available at other times, subject to weather; $6.00 for a standard site, $9.00 for a hookup site; 14 day limit; Natrona County Parks Department, Casper, (307) 234-6821.

Camp Notes: All things considered, June is probably the best month to visit Alcova Lake. The greenery of late spring joins the basin's red rock and the lake's big, blue pool to produce a vividly hued environment. (The region around Casper is often the target of wisecracks and comments--mostly from the snobbish mountain dwellers of Colorado and Montana. But really folks, Alcova Lake and Casper Mountain Park (below) provide two good recreational options. And gas is usually cheap in Casper, too. Ed.)

Wyoming 83

CASPER MOUNTAIN
Natrona County Park

Location: Central Wyoming south of Casper.

Access: From Interstate 25 Exit 185 for East Casper-Evansville, travel south then west on Wyoming State Highway 258 for 5.6 miles; turn south (left) onto Casper Mountain Road/Wyoming State Highway 251; proceed south for 6 miles up a very steep and winding, paved highway to the campground. **Alternate Access:** From Interstate 25 Exit 188B for Poplar Street/State Highway 220, follow a less direct but a shorter (4.5 miles) route through west Casper via Routes 220 and 258 to the junction of Highway 258 & Casper Mountain Road and continue as above.

Facilities: 60 campsites in 3 loops, plus dispersed camping; sites are small to medium+ in size, with fair to very good separation; parking pads are gravel, mostly medium to medium+ straight-ins; many pads may require additional leveling; some large, grassy tent spots; fire rings; firewood is available for gathering in the area; water at several faucets; vault facilities; gravel driveways; complete supplies and services are available in Casper.

Activities & Attractions: Large day use area with kitchen shelters; playground; 4wd trails; snowmobiling; cross-country skiing.

Natural Features: Located high atop Casper Mountain with great views across the prairie in every direction--north to the Bighorn Mountains, west to the Rattlesnake Range, and south to the Laramie Mountains; vegetation consists of tall pines, aspens and grass; elevation 7000'.

Season, Fees & Phone: Open all year, subject to weather conditions, with limited services in winter; $6.00; 14 day limit; Natrona County Parks Department, Casper, (307) 234-6821.

Camp Notes: Views from this high point in Central Wyoming are phenomenal. Casper Mountain Park is within a few miles of a major community, but the sites seem to be much more remote than a mere half dozen miles suggests.

Wyoming 84

TWO MOON
Glendo State Park

Location: Eastern Wyoming southeast of Douglas.

Access: From Interstate 25 Exit 111 for Glendo (27 miles southeast of Douglas, 32 miles north of Wheatland), drive east on a local connecting road (A Street) for 0.3 mile to a 4-way intersection in the community of Glendo; turn south (right) onto Wyoming State Highway 319/Yellowstone Street and go 2 blocks; turn east (left) onto C Street, go 1 block, then turn south (right) onto Glendo Park Road and travel 1.5 miles to the park boundary; continue southeast for 1.8 miles to the campground.

Facilities: Approximately 80 campsites; sites are medium to very large, with good to excellent separation; parking pads are gravel, long straight-ins or pull-throughs; additional leveling will be needed on many pads; good tent spots in many sites; fire rings; b-y-o firewood is recommended; water at several faucets; vault facilities; holding tank disposal station; paved driveways; gas and camper supplies at the marina; gas and groceries in Glendo.

Activities & Attractions: Boating; several boat launches; fishing; playground; Twin Pine nature trail.

Natural Features: Located on a forested bluff overlooking the south shore of Glendo Reservoir, an impoundment on the North Platte River; medium to tall conifers, hardwoods and moderate underbrush provide campsite shade/shelter; bordered by hilly prairie; elevation 4700'.

Season, Fees & Phone: Open all year, with limited services October to April; 14 day limit; please see Appendix for standard Wyoming state park fees; park office (307) 735-4433.

Camp Notes: Two Moon Campground is named for the famous Cheyenne Chief Two Moon. In addition to the main camp, there are literally hundreds of camp/picnic sites in the various sections of the park, from beachside to bluff edge, sunny to sheltered.

Wyoming 85

GUERNSEY: EAST SHORE
Guernsey State Park

Location: Eastern Wyoming southeast of Douglas.

Access: From U.S. Highway 26 at milepost 14 +.4 (14 miles east of Interstate 25 Exit 92, 0.5 mile west of the town of Guernsey), turn north onto Wyoming State Highway 317 and proceed 0.9 mile to the park entrance; from the entrance, camp areas and mileages along Lakeshore Drive (the main, paved park road) are as follows: *Spotted Tail*, 1.6 miles; *Red Cloud*, 1.7 miles; Black *Canyon Point*, 2.6 miles; *Fish Canyon*, 3.3 miles, *Long Canyon*, 5.8 miles.

Facilities: *Fish Canyon*: 20 campsites; sites are small+ to medium-sized, with nominal to fair separation; parking pads are gravel, mostly long pull-throughs; some pads may require additional leveling; tent spots are large, grassy, but may be a bit rocky or sloped; fireplaces; b-y-o firewood is recommended; water at several faucets; vault facilities; ***Spotted Tail***, ***Red Cloud***, ***Black Canyon Point***, and ***Long Canyon***: 5 to 12 small campsites in each area, small to medium-sized parking spaces, small tent areas, assorted fire appliances, water at central faucets, vault facilities; small ramadas (sun shelters) at Spotted Tail, Red Cloud and Black Canyon Point; gravel driveways; limited+ supplies and services are available in Guernsey.

Activities & Attractions: Museum in a mid-1930's CCC building; interpretive and hiking trails; boating; boat launch; limited fishing for trout, on the river below the dam.

Natural Features: Located on coves and points along the east shore of Guernsey Reservoir (Spotted Tail, et. al.) in a large, high-walled canyon; most shoreline sites receive very light to light-medium shade from large hardwoods; located on grassy slopes dotted with small pines and junipers in a box canyon near the northeast corner of the reservoir (Fish Canyon); the lake is surrounded by high, grassy, evergreen-dotted hills; the reservoir is an impound on the North Platte River; elevation 4400'.

Season, Fees & Phone: Open all year, with limited services October to April; 14 day limit; please see Appendix for standard Wyoming state park fees; park office (307) 836-2334.

Camp Notes: Guernsey State Park preserves what are probably the finest remaining examples of CCC craftsmanship in the Rocky Mountain region. In addition to the man-made attractions, the views along the five-mile Lakeshore Drive are quite impressive: across the 'narrows' of the reservoir out to the walls of the canyon which loom hundreds of feet overhead.

Wyoming 86

GUERNSEY: WEST SHORE
Guernsey State Park

Location: Eastern Wyoming southeast of Douglas.

Access: From U.S. Highway 26 at milepost 14 +.4 (14 miles east of Interstate 25 Exit 92, 0.5 mile west of the town of Guernsey), turn north onto Wyoming State Highway 317 and proceed 0.9 mile to the park entrance; just beyond the entrance, swing north/northwest (left) onto Skyline Drive (gravel); proceed 0.4 mile, then turn east (right) into the *Skyline* area; or continue for 1.5 miles on Skyline Drive, then 0.6 mile northwest (left) on Sandy Beach Road to the *Sandy Beach* area.

Facilities: *Skyline*: 20 camp/picnic sites; sites are small, with nil separation; parking surfaces are gravel, short straight-ins; additional leveling may be required; small to medium-sized, grassy tent areas; ***Sandy Beach***: Approximately 40 camp/picnic sites; parking surfaces are sand/gravel, straight-ins/pull-offs of assorted sizes; adequate space for medium to large tents; ***both areas***: fire rings; b-y-o firewood is recommended; water at hand pumps; vault facilities; limited+ supplies and services are available in Guernsey.

Activities & Attractions: Boating; boat launch near Sandy Beach; 2-mile hiking trail; views from the 'Castle'.

Natural Features: Located in a small side canyon sparsely dotted with evergreens, well above the shore of Guernsey Reservoir (Skyline); located along the south/west shore of the lake in a stand of hardwoods (Sandy Beach); the lake is bordered by high hills and bluffs covered with grass and sage, topped by pines and junipers; elevation 4400' at Sandy Beach, 4600' at Skyline.

Season, Fees & Phone: Open all year, with limited services October to April; 14 day limit; please see Appendix for standard Wyoming state park fees; park office (307) 836-2334.

Camp Notes: Unless you *must* have waterfront property for your campsite, the tidy little Skyline area might be more to your liking than the often-congested Sandy Beach section. (Sandy Beach's lakeside advantage may be moot: the reservoir is subject to deep drawdown after early July each year.) The 'Castle' is a large, quarried rock shelter which stands imposingly on a point above a major bend in the river/reservoir. Fine views from here!

Wyoming 87

HAWK SPRINGS
Hawk Springs State Recreation Area

Location: Southeast Wyoming south of Torrington.

Access: From U.S. Highway 85 at milepost 67 +.4 (5 miles south of the settlement of Hawk Springs, 58 miles northeast of Cheyenne), turn east onto a dirt/gravel access road and proceed 3.5 miles east and north to the park entrance; swing east (right) past the boat launch parking lot for 0.1 mile to the camp area.

Facilities: 24 camp/picnic sites, plus some overflow areas; sites are small, with minimal to nominal separation; parking surfaces are gravel/sand, short to medium-length straight-ins or pull-offs; a bit of additional leveling may be needed in some sites; enough space for medium to large tents; fire rings; b-y-o firewood; water at central faucets; vault facilities; gravel driveway; gas and camper supplies in Hawk Springs; adequate+ supplies and services are available in Torrington.

Activities & Attractions: Boating; boat launch; fishing for largemouth and smallmouth bass, walleye, channel cat, yellow perch; ice fishing; designated swimming area.

Natural Features: Located along the west shore of Hawk Springs Reservoir; most of the several miles of sandy lake shore are lined with large hardwoods; campsites are lightly to moderately shaded from morning to midday; surrounded by prairie, agricultural land, and several massive buttes; elevation 4400'.

Season, Fees & Phone: Open all year, with limited services in winter; 14 day limit; please see Appendix for standard Wyoming state park fees; phone c/o Guernsey State Park.

Camp Notes: Hawk Springs may not be Yellowstone Park, but it's still a very popular spot throughout much of late spring and summer. Fishing is said to be good, although most of the success is achieved by boat fishermen. The lake water is used for irrigation, but summer drawdown is limited in order to maintain the quality of fishing and boating opportunities.

SPECIAL SECTION:

Jackcamping and Backpacking in the West's Parks and Forests

In addition to camping in established campgrounds, as do the majority of visitors, thousands of campers opt for simpler places to spend a night or a week or more in the West's magnificent parks and forests.

Jackcamping

"Jackcamping", "roadsiding", "dispersed camping", or "siwashing" are several of the assorted terms describing the simplest type of camp there is: just pulling a vehicle a few yards off the main drag, or heading up a gravel or dirt forest road to an out-of-the-way spot which looks good to you. Sometimes, especially when the "Campground Full" plank is hung out to dry in front of all the nearby public campgrounds, or there *aren't* any nearby public campgrounds, it might be the only way to travel.

From what we can determine "jackcamping" is an extension of the Medieval English slang word "jacke", meaning "common", "serviceable" or "ordinary". The explanations of "roadsiding" and "dispersed camping" are self-evident. "Siwashing" is an old term from the Southwest. It apparently refers to the practice of cowboys and other travelers making a late camp by just hunkering-down in an *arroyo* or 'dry wash'. After hobbling your horse, the saddle is propped-up against the *side* of the *wash*, (hence *si'wash* or *siwash*), forming a leather 'recliner' of sorts in which to pass the night out of the wind and cold. It may not be the most comfortable way to spend the night, but by two or three a.m. you get used to the smell of the saddle anyway.

As a general rule-of-thumb, jackcamping isn't allowed in local, state and national parks. In those areas, you'll have to stay in established campgrounds or sign-up for a backcountry site.

However, jackcamping is *usually* permitted anywhere on the millions of road-accessible acres of national forest and BLM-managed federal public lands, subject to a few exceptions. In some high-traffic areas it's not allowed, and roadside signs are *usually* posted telling you so. ("Camp Only in Designated Campgrounds" signs are becoming more common with each passing year.) In certain high fire risk zones or during the general fire season it may not be permitted. For the majority of areas in which jackcamping is legal, small campfires, suitably sized and contained, are ordinarily OK. All of the rules of good manners, trash-removal, and hygiene which apply to camping anywhere, regardless of location, are enforced. (Would *you* want to camp where someone else had left their "sign"?) For off-highway travel, the "Shovel, Axe and Bucket" rule is usually in effect (see below).

Since you don't want the law coming down on you for an unintentional impropriety, it's highly advisable to stop in or call a local Forest Service ranger station or BLM office to determine the status of jackcamping in your region of choice, plus any special requirements (spark arrestors, the length of the shovel needed under the "Shovel, Axe and Bucket" rule, campfires, stay limit, etc.) Local ranchers who have leased grazing rights on federal lands are sensitive about their livestock sharing the meadows and rangelands with campers. So it's probably best to jackcamp in "open" areas, thus avoiding leaseholder vs taxpayer rights confrontations altogether. (Legalities notwithstanding, the barrel of a 12-gauge or an '06 looks especially awesome when it's poked inside your tent at midnight.) Be sure to get the name of the individual in the local public office who provided the information "just in case".

If you're reasonably self-sufficient or self-contained, jackcamping can save you *beaucoups* bucks--perhaps hundreds of dollars--over a lifetime of camping. (We know.)

Backpacking

Take all of the open acres readily available to jackcampers, then multiply that figure by a factor of 100,000 (or thereabouts) and you'll have some idea of the wilderness and near-wilderness camping opportunities that are only accessible to backpackers (or horsepackers).

Backpackers usually invest a lot of time, and usually a lot of money, into their preferred camping method, and perhaps rightfully so (timewise, anyway).

Planning an overnight or week-long foot trip into the boondocks is half the work (and half the fun too!). Hours, days, even *weeks*, can be spent pouring over highway maps, topographic maps, public lands/BLM maps, and forest maps looking for likely places to pack into. (We know!)

Backpacking in Western National Forests

To be editorially above-board about this: Of all the possible federal and state recreation areas, your best opportunities for backpack camping are in the national forest wilderness, primitive, and wild areas. Prime backpacking areas in most state parks and many national park units are measured in acres or perhaps square miles; but the back country in the national forests is measured in tens and hundreds and thousands of square miles. Here's where planning really becomes fun.

Backpacking in Western National and State Parks

Finding a backpack campsite in the West's *parks* is relatively straightforward: much of the work has been done for you by the park people. Most state and many national parks which are large enough to provide opportunities for backcountry travel have established backcountry camps which are the *only* places to camp out in the toolies. Yes, that indeed restricts your overnight choices to a few small areas in many cases; but you can still enjoy walking through and looking at the rest of the back country.

Throughout this series, designated backpack campsites and other backpacking opportunities are occasionally mentioned in conjunction with nearby established campgrounds.

Backpacking in Rocky Mountain National Forests

Tens of millions of acres of incredibly beautiful backcountry can be explored in the Rockies, and you probably couldn't go wrong in selecting any national forest wilderness or primitive area. The very best places? The superlative *Bob Marshall* Wilderness in Montana and the equally stunning *Beartooth-Absaroka* Wilderness in Montana-Wyoming probably share First Place honors in the Northern Rockies. But be sure to consider smaller wilderness areas that get less attention, like the *Cloud Peak* Primitive Area in Wyoming's largely 'undiscovered' Bighorn Mountains; or the *Weminuche* Wilderness and the *Uncompahgre* Primitive Area in southwest Colorado.

Backpacking in Rocky Mountain National Parks

Throughout most of the Rocky Mountains, the opportunities for backcountry exploration have been maintained at a more liberal level than in most other regions in the West. Partly because of the winter conditions that begin in early September and often last well into late June, and the rugged geography, backpacking hasn't as yet exceeded its potential as it has elsewhere.

To many backpackers, national parks in the Rockies present the finest wilderness travel opportunities of all national parks in the 'Lower 48'. *Rocky Mountain* National Park and *Glacier* National Park each list a specific number of designated backcountry campsites (about 250 and 65 locations, respectively). Both *Yellowstone* and *Grand Teton* National Parks offer an unspecified "limited" number of suggested camp locations "throughout the parks". *Black Canyon of the Gunnison, Colorado*, and *Great Sand Dunes* National Monuments, also *Bighorn Canyon* National Recreation Area, all list small numbers of backpack sites. A permit is mandatory for backcountry camping in all the foregoing areas.

In some areas it is possible, or even necessary, to reserve a backcountry campsite. Backcountry reservation information and other 'regs' are highly subject to change. We therefore suggest that you use the *Phone* information in the text to contact your selected park's headquarters and ask for the "backcountry office" or "backcountry ranger" to initialize your trip planning. In virtually every case, they'll be able to provide detailed information and maps--at no charge, or at most a couple of bucks for first-rate maps. The majority of the backcountry people are enthusiastic boondockers themselves, and they'll generally provide sound, albeit conservative, suggestions. Let's face it: they don't want to have to bail anybody out of a tough spot by extracting them on foot, in a dusty green government-issue jeep, or a 'chopper'. (Try living *that one* down when you get home, dude!)

Flatwater Boat Camping in Rocky Mountain National Parks

Yellowstone, Grand Teton, and *Glacier* National Parks, *plus Curecanti* and *Bighorn Canyon* National Recreation Areas each provide specified boat-in camps along the shores of their lakes. Some of the most incredibly beautiful country in the West can be found in Yellowtone Lake's 'Arms' along its south shore. If you have a hand-propelled craft, the trips to Yellowstone's Shoshone Lake, Grand Teton's Leigh Lake, and to the backcountry camps on MacDonald, Bowman and Kintla Lakes in Glacier National Park will be trips of a lifetime. Bighorn Canyon also has several small, isolated boat camps. The same suggestion to ring the backcountry office for information applies to boat travel.

At the risk of demagoguery: We can vouch that it really pays to start planning months in advance for a backcountry trip. Besides, planning *is* half the fun.

Creative Camping

In their most elementary forms, outdoor recreation in general, and camping in particular, require very little in the way of extensive planning or highly specialized and sophisticated equipment. A stout knife, some matches, a few blankets, a free road map, a water jug, and a big sack of p.b. & j. sandwiches, all tossed onto the seat of an old beater pickup, will get you started on the way to a lifetime of outdoor adventures.

Idyllic and nostalgic as that scenario may seem, most of the individuals reading this *Double Eagle*™ Guide (and those *writing* it) probably desire (and deserve) at least a few granules of comfort sprinkled over their tent or around their rv.

There are enough books already on the market or in libraries which will provide you with plenty of advice on *how* to camp. One of the oldest and best is the *Fieldbook*, published by the Boy Scouts of America. Really. It is a widely accepted, profusely illustrated (not to mention comparatively inexpensive) outdoor reference which has few true rivals. It presents plenty of information on setting up camp, first aid, safety, woodlore, flora and fauna identification, weather, and a host of other items. Although recreational vehicle camping isn't specifically covered in detail, many of the general camping principles it does cover apply equally well to rv's.

So rather than re-invent the wheel, we've concentrated your hard-earned *dinero* into finding out *where* to camp. However, there are still a few items that aren't widely known which might be of interest to you, or which bear repeating, so we've included them in the following paragraphs.

Resourcefulness. When putting together your equipment, it's both challenging and a lot of fun to make the ordinary stuff you have around the house, especially in the kitchen, do double duty. Offer an "early retirement" to servicable utensils, pans, plastic cups, etc. to a "gear box".

Resource-fullness. Empty plastic peanut butter jars, pancake syrup and milk jugs, ketchup bottles, also aluminum pie plates and styrofoam trays, can be washed, re-labeled and used again. (The syrup jugs, with their handles and pop-up spouts, make terrific "canteens" for kids.) The lightweight, break-resistant plastic stuff is more practical on a camping trip than glass containers, anyway. *El Cheapo* plastic shopping bags, which have become *de rigueur* in supermarkets, can be saved and re-used to hold travel litter and campground trash. When they're full, tie them tightly closed using the "handles". In the words of a college-age camper from Holland while he was refilling a plastic, two-liter soft drink bottle at the single water faucet in a desert national park campground: "Why waste?".

Redundancy. Whether you're camping in a tent, pickup, van, boat, motorhome or fifth-wheel trailer, it pays to think and plan like a backpacker. Can you make-do with fewer changes of clothes for a short weekend trip? How about getting-by with half as much diet cola, and drink more cool, campground spring water instead? Do you really *need* that third curling iron? Real backpackers (like the guy who trimmed the margins off his maps) are relentless in their quest for the light load.

Water. No matter where you travel, *always* carry a couple of gallons of drinking water. Campground water sources may be out of order (e.g., someone broke the handle off the hydrant or the well went dry), and you probably won't want to fool around with boiling lake or stream water. (Because of the possibility of encountering the widespread "beaver fever" (*Giardia*) parasite and other diseases in lakes and streams, if treated or tested H$_2$O isn't available, boil the surface water for a full five minutes.)

(Reports from the field indicate that extremely tough health and environmental standards may force the closure of natural drinking water supplies from wells and springs in many campgrounds. The upside to this situation is that, if the camp itself remains open, chances are that no fees will be charged.)

Juice. If you're a tent or small vehicle camper who normally doesn't need electrical hookups, carry a hotplate, coffee pot, or hair dryer when traveling in regions where hookup campsites are available. The trend in public campground management is toward charging the full rate for a hookup site whether or not you have an rv, even though there are no standard sites available for you to occupy. In many popular state parks and Corps of Engineers recreation areas, hookup sites far outnumber standard sites. At least you'll have some use for the juice.

Fire. Charcoal lighter fluid makes a good "starter" for campfires, and is especially handy if the wood is damp. In a pinch, that spare bottle of motor oil in the trunk can be pressed into service for the same purpose. Let two ounces soak in for several minutes. Practice the same safety precautions you would use in lighting a home barbecue so you can keep your curly locks and eyebrows from being scorched by the flames. Obviously use extreme caution--and don't even *think* about using gasoline. A really handy option to using wood is to carry a couple of synthetic "fire logs". The sawdust-and-paraffin logs are made from byproducts of the lumber and petroleum industries and burn about three hours in the outdoors. The fire logs can also be used to start and maintain a regular campfire if the locally gathered firewood is wet.

Mosquitoes. The winged demons aren't usually mentioned in the text because you just have to *expect* them almost anywhere except perhaps in the dryest desert areas. Soggy times, like late spring and early summer, are the worst times. If you're one of us who's always the first to be strafed by the local mosquito squadron, keep plenty of anti-aircraft ammo on hand. The most versatile skin stuff is the spray-on variety. Spray it all over your clothes to keep the varmints from poking their proboscis through the seat of your jeans. A room spray comes in handy for blasting any bugs which might have infiltrated your tent or rv. Fortunately, in most areas the peak of the mosquito season lasts only a couple of weeks, and you can enjoy yourself the rest of the time. Autumn camping is great!

Rattlers. Anywhere you go in the Desert Southwest, expect to find rattlesnakes, so place your hands and feet and other vital parts accordingly. (While preparing the *Double Eagle*™ series, one of the publishers inadvertently poked her zoom lens to within a yard of a coiled rattler's snout. The photographer's anxieties were vocally, albeit shakily, expressed; the level of stress which the incident induced on the snake is unknown.)

Bumps in the night. When you retire for the night, put all your valuables, especially your cooler, inside your vehicle to protect them against campground burglars and bruins. While camping at Canyon Campground in Yellowstone National Park more than two decades ago, a pair of young brothers unwittingly left their stocked cooler out on the picnic table so they had more room to sleep inside their ancient station wagon. Sometime after midnight, they were awakened by a clatter in the darkness behind the wagon. After they had groggily dressed and crept out to investigate, the sleepy siblings discovered that a bear had broken into their impenetrable ice chest. Taking inventory, the dauntless duo determined that the brazen backwoods *bandito* had wolfed-down three pounds of baked chicken breasts, a meatloaf, one pound of pineapple cottage cheese, four quarters of margarine, and had chomped through two cans of *Coors*--presumably to wash it all down. The soft drinks were untouched. (We dined sumptuously on Spam and pork 'n beans for the rest of the trip. Ed.)

Horsepower. Your camping vehicle will lose about four percent of its power for each 1000' gain in altitude above sea level (unless it's turbocharged). Keep that in mind in relation to the "pack like a backpacker" item mentioned previously. You might also keep it in mind when you embark on a foot trip. The factory-original human machine loses about the same amount of efficiency at higher elevations.

Air. To estimate the temperature at a campground in the mountains while you're still down in the valley or on the plains, subtract about three degrees Fahrenheit for each 1000' difference in elevation between the valley and the campground. Use the same method to estimate nighttime lows in the mountains by using weather forecasts for valley cities.

Timing. Try staying an hour ahead of everyone else. While traveling in the Mountain Time Zone, keep your timepiece ticking on Central Time. That way you'll naturally set up camp an hour earlier, and likewise break camp an hour prior to other travelers. You might be amazed at how much that 60 minutes will do for campsite availability in the late afternoon, or for restrooms, showers, uncrowded roads and sightseeing in the morning.

Reptile repellant. Here's a sensitive subject. With the rise in crimes perpetrated against travelers and campers in the nation's parks and forests and on its highways and byways, it's become increasingly common for legitimate campers to pack a 'heater'--the type that's measured by caliber or gauge, not in volts and amps. To quote a respected Wyoming peace officer: "Half the pickups and campers in Wyoming and Montana have a .45 automatic under the seat or a 12-gauge pump behind the bunk". If personal safety is a concern to you, check all applicable laws, get competent instruction, practice a lot, and join the NRA.

Vaporhavens. Be skeptical when you scan highway and forest maps and see hundreds of little symbols which indicate the locations of alleged campsites; or when you glance through listings published by governmental agencies or promotional interests. A high percentage of those 'recreation areas' are as vaporous as the mist rising from a warm lake into chilled autumn air. Many, many of the listed spots are actually picnic areas, fishing access sites, and even highway rest stops; dozens of camps are ill-maintained remnants of their former greatness, located at the end of rocky jeep trails; many others no longer exist; still others *never* existed, but are merely a mapmaker's or planner's notion of where a campground *might* or *should* be. In summation: Make certain that a campground exists and what it offers before you embark on 20 miles of washboard gravel travel in the never-ending quest for your own personal Eden.

We hope the foregoing items, and information throughout this series, help you conserve your own valuable time, money, fuel and other irreplaceable resources. ***Good Camping !***

Appendix

State Maps

Colorado

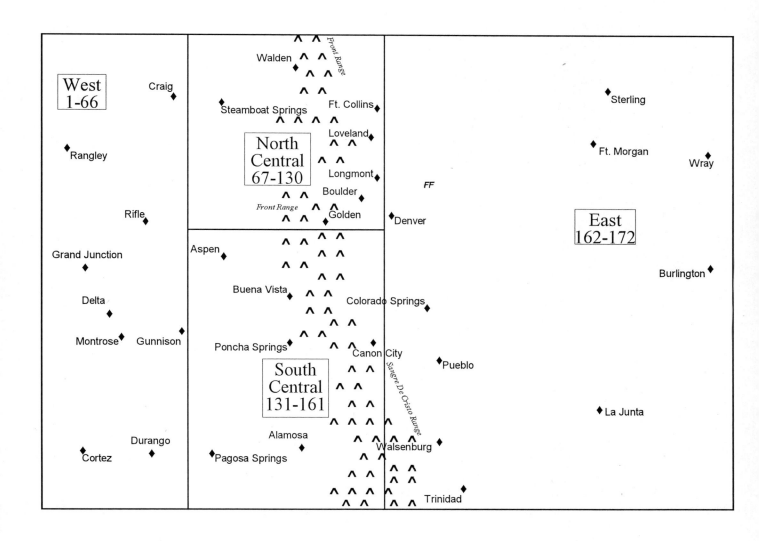

West
1-66

Craig

Rangley

Rifle

Grand Junction

Delta

Montrose   Gunnison

Durango

Cortez

Walden

Front Range

Steamboat Springs

Ft. Collins

Loveland

North
Central
67-130

Longmont

Boulder

Front Range

Golden

Aspen

Buena Vista

Poncha Springs

South
Central
131-161

Canon City

Sangre De Cristo Range

Alamosa

Pagosa Springs

Walsenburg

Trinidad

FF

Denver

Colorado Springs

Pueblo

Sterling

Ft. Morgan

Wray

East
162-172

Burlington

La Junta

Montana

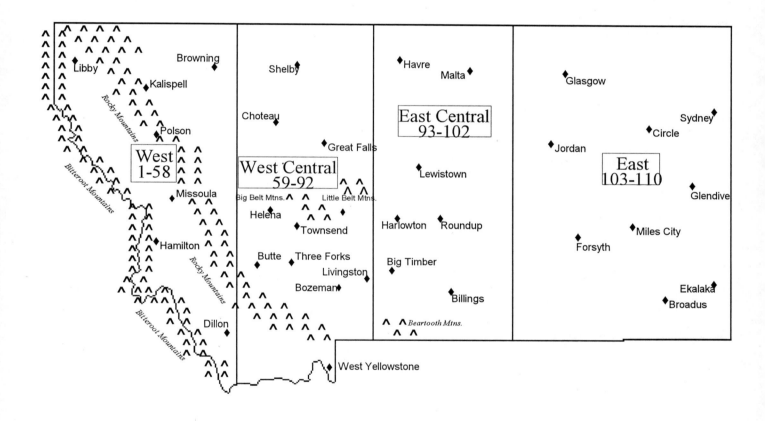

West 1-58

Libby
Browning
Kalispell
Polson
Missoula
Hamilton
Dillon

Rocky Mountains
Bitterroot Mountains

West Central 59-92

Shelby
Choteau
Great Falls
Big Belt Mtns.
Little Belt Mtns.
Helena
Townsend
Butte
Three Forks
Livingston
Bozeman
West Yellowstone
Beartooth Mtns.

East Central 93-102

Havre
Malta
Lewistown
Harlowton
Roundup
Big Timber
Billings

East 103-110

Glasgow
Sydney
Circle
Jordan
Glendive
Miles City
Forsyth
Ekalaka
Broadus

Wyoming

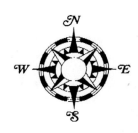

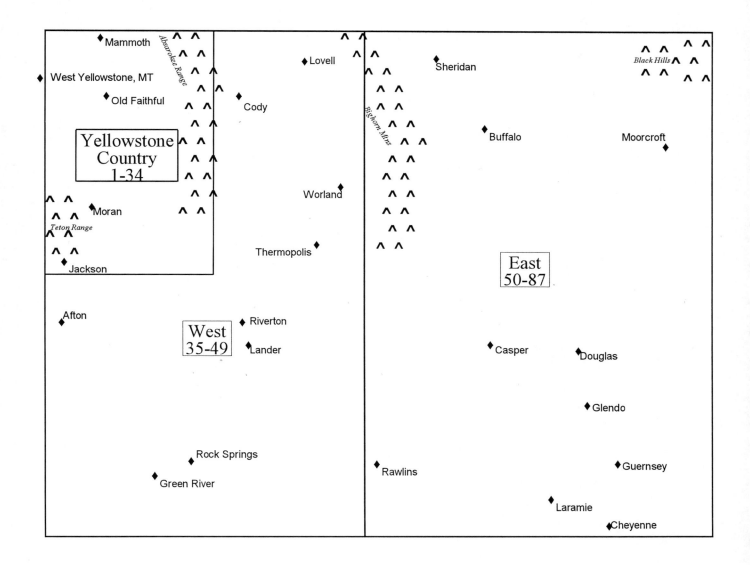

- ◆ Mammoth
- ◆ West Yellowstone, MT
- ◆ Old Faithful
- ◆ Lovell
- ◆ Cody

Absarokee Range

Yellowstone Country 1-34

- ◆ Moran
- *Teton Range*
- ◆ Jackson

- ◆ Worland
- ◆ Thermopolis

Bighorn Mtns

- ◆ Sheridan
- ◆ Buffalo
- ◆ Moorcroft

Black Hills

East 50-87

- Afton ◆

West 35-49

- ◆ Riverton
- ◆ Lander

- ◆ Casper
- ◆ Douglas
- ◆ Glendo

- Rock Springs ◆
- Green River ◆

- ◆ Rawlins
- ◆ Guernsey
- ◆ Laramie
- ◆ Cheyenne

ROCKY MOUNTAINS STANDARD STATE PARK FEES

Colorado

Daily park entry	$3.00
Primitive campsite (vaults)	$6.00
Standard/developed campsite (water, flush)	$7.00
Partial hookup campsite (water, electricity)	$10.00

Montana

Primitive campsite (no drinking water)	$7.00
Basic/semi-developed campsite (drinking water, vaults)	$8.00
Standard/developed campsite (water, flush)	$9.00

(Montana campground fee includes the park entry fee plus a state "acommodations tax".)

Wyoming

Campsite	$4.00
Daily Park entry fee for certain parks:	
Wyoming resident	$2.00
Non-resident	$3.00

It is recommended that you call your selected park a few days prior to arrival to determine the exact campsite fees you'll be charged.

Note: Annual park entry permits, offering substantial savings for frequent park users, are available in all states.

Please remember that all fees are subject to change without notice.

ROCKY MOUNTAINS CAMPSITE RESERVATIONS

Reservations may be made for certain individual and group campsites in national forests, national parks, and state parks in Colorado, Montana and Wyoming. As a general rule-of-thumb, reservations for midsummer weekends should be initiated at least several weeks in advance. Reservation fees are charged.

National Forest Reservations

The USDA Forest Service has established a reservation system which affects hundreds of national forest campgrounds nationwide. Continuous changes can be expected in such a large system as campgrounds with reservable sites are added or removed from the list. For additional information about campgrounds with reservable sites, and to make reservations, you may call (toll-free) the independent agent handling the reservation system.

800-280-CAMP   (800-280-2267)

Reservations can be made from 10 days to 120 days in advance. It is suggested that you take advantage of the full 120-day period for any medium-sized or large forest camp associated with a lake or sizeable stream, or near a national park, if you want to be assured of a campsite there on a summer holiday weekend.

National Park Reservations

For information about campsite availability and reservations at *Moraine Park* and *Glacier Basin Campgrounds* in *Rocky Mountain National Park* and *Bridge Bay Campground* in *Yellowstone National Park*, you may call (toll-free):

800-365-CAMP   (800-365-2267)

Reservations can be made from 10 days to 56 days in advance. To be reasonably assured of securing a site, it is suggested that you take advantage of the full 56-day advance period.

A fee of $6.00-$7.50 is charged for a campsite reservation. In addition to the $6.00 reservation charge, the standard campground user fees for all nights which are reserved also need to be paid at the time the reservation is made. (Reservations for consecutive nights at the same campground are covered under the same fee.) If you cancel, you lose the reservation fee, plus you're charged a cancellation fee. Any remainder is refunded. They'll take checks, money orders, VISA or MasterCard, (VISA/MC for telephone reservations).

Reservable campsites in national forest and national park campgrounds are assigned, but you can request an rv or a tent site; rv sites are generally a little larger and most will accommodate tents. When making a reservation, be prepared to tell the reservation agent about the major camping equipment you plan to use, (size and number of tents, type and length of rv, additional vehicles, boat trailers, etc.). Be generous in your estimate. In most cases, a national forest campground's *best sites* are also those which are *reservable*. Most of the national forest campgrounds which have reservable sites still can accommodate a limited number of drop-ins on a first-come, first-served basis.

State Park Reservations

Reservations for individual and group campsites in *Colorado state parks* may be obtained by calling the state parks office:

(800) 678-2267 (toll-free from outside Denver).
470-1144 (from within the Denver Metro area)

A non-refundable service fee of $6.75 is charged for a campsite reservation. (Paid by check, VISA or MC.)

Reservations for other campgrounds in the three states covered in this volume *may* be obtainable directly from the public agency responsible for the camping area, as indicated in the text.

For additional information about campsite reservations, availability, current conditions, or regulations about the use of campgrounds, we suggest that you directly contact the park or forest office in charge of your selected campground, using the *Phone* information in the text.

Please remember that all reservation information is subject to change without notice.

INDEX

Important Note:

In the following listing, the number to the right of the campground name refers to the Key Number in boldface in the upper left corner of each campground description in the text.

(E.G. **Colorado 30** is **Almont**. The number does *not* indicate the page number; page numbers are printed in the text only as secondary references.)

* A thumbnail description of a campground marked with an asterisk is found in the *Camp Notes* section of the principal numbered campground.

COLORADO

MONTANA

WYOMING

209

Other volumes in the *Camping* series:

The Double Eagle Guide to
CAMPING *in* WESTERN PARKS *and* FORESTS

__Volume I   Pacific Northwest   ISBN 0-929760-27-1
             Washington*Oregon*Idaho Hardcover 8 1/2x11 $18.95ˆ
             (Also in paper cover 6x9 (C) 1992 $12.95)

__Volume II Rocky Mountains   ISBN 0-929760-22-0
             Colorado*Montana*Wyoming Hardcover 8 1/2x11 $17.95ˆ

__Volume III Far West   ISBN 0-929760-23-9
             California*Nevada   Hardcover 8 1/2x11 $18.95ˆ

__Volume IV Desert Southwest   ISBN 0-929760-29-8
             Arizona*New Mexico*Utah Hardcover 8 1/2x11 $17.95ˆ
             (Also in paper cover 6x9 (C) 1992 $12.95)

__Volume V Northern Plains   ISBN 0-929760-25-5
              The Dakotas*Nebraska*Kansas Hardcover 8 1/2x11 $16.95ˆ

__Volume VI Southwest Plains   ISBN 0-929760-26-3
              Texas*Oklahoma Hardcover 8 1/2x11) $17.95ˆ

ˆˆˆ Softcover, spiral-bound editions are also available. Recommended for light-duty, personal use only.
    Subtract $3.00 from standard hardcover price and check here _____ for *Special Binding*.

Available exclusively from: *Double Eagle* camping guides are regularly updated.

Discovery Publishing

P.O. Box 50545   Billings, MT 59105   Phone 1-406-245-8292

Please add $3.00 for shipping the first volume, and $1.50 for each additional volume.
Same-day shipping for most orders.

Please include your check/money order, or complete the VISA/MasterCard
information in the indicated space below.

Name_____

Address_____

City_____ State_____ Zip_____

For credit card orders:

VISA/MC #_____ Exp.Date_____

Prices, shipping charges, and specifications subject to change.

Thank You Very Much For Your Order!

(A photocopy or other reproduction may be substituted for this original form.)